THE ENGLISH WATCH
1585-1970

*A unique alliance of art, design
and inventive genius*

Edward East. See Plate 19

THE ENGLISH WATCH
1585-1970

*A unique alliance of art, design
and inventive genius*

Terence Camerer Cuss

ANTIQUE COLLECTORS' CLUB

ISBN 978-1-85149-588-7

British Library Cataloguing-in-Publication Data
A catalogue record for this book is available from the British Library

Title-page: Robert Williamson. See Plate 42.

Printed in China
for the Antique Collectors' Club Ltd., Woodbridge, Suffolk

CONTENTS

Vulliamy. See Plate 201

FOREWORD

The publication of a new book on the subject of English watches would be a welcome event at any time – and the fact that this is the first ever study devoted exclusively to English watches from all periods makes the appearance of Terence Camerer Cuss's work even more of a pleasure for those of us who have always admired the artistry and unique inventiveness of these beguiling objects, and have sought in vain to find anything approaching a clearly-written and readily comprehensible survey.

Not only does this study incorporate enlightening information about the range of skills involved in the making of a watch – from the construction of the movements to the finish of the cases – but it makes this important subject both approachable and stimulating by describing with clarity and precision the evolution of English watchmaking and the ground-breaking inventions of our leading makers. These include such luminaries of the horological world as Thomas Tompion, Thomas Mudge and John Harrison. In parallel with technical developments in timekeeping, this survey also illuminates the flowering of the specialist crafts of embossing, chasing and enamelling watch cases during the eighteenth century. Choice examples from private and public collections, including a number of pieces of royal provenance, have been selected to illustrate these points.

The stimulus given to the clock- and watch-making trade by the active interest and patronage of the Royal Family is apparent at several periods, notably in the reign of King George III (whose handwritten instructions for taking apart and reassembling a watch movement are preserved in the Royal Archives). This interest is continued today through exhibitions and displays in The Queen's Gallery – frequently including examples from the Royal Collection illustrated in this book. Such exhibitions help stimulate and encourage interest not just in horology, but more widely in the applied arts of this country – a worthwhile aim to which this book will make a valuable contribution.

Sir Hugh Roberts
Director of the Royal Collection
St. James's Palace
July 2008

To my wife and family

INTRODUCTION

Few things are more significant to Man than time and its passing and so it is not surprising that timekeepers attract our attention. Until recently watches were made to be highly important personal possessions, and were decorated not only on the outside in the manner and style of the age, but also always on the inside.

Watchmaking spread to England from the Continent during the last quarter of the sixteenth century. By the end of the seventeenth the quality of English watches was such that they were in great demand, and they were sold throughout Europe. The reputation continued and was further enhanced during the eighteenth century by a series of pioneering inventions: it was in this period when the greatest contribution to the history of horology was made in England. Exports were now worldwide. The high standards were maintained and some watches of quite exceptional quality were produced in the nineteenth and early twentieth centuries. In addition to their well-deserved reputation, English watches had, almost from the beginning, a very distinctive character.

This book is designed to appeal to those fresh to the subject as well as those more familiar with it. The test of any book of this kind is that not only is it read, but referred to for information; it has been arranged with ease of reference in mind. I have divided the watches into six periods, each with a chapter and introduction. An outline of the period is followed by paragraphs on the trade in London and the provinces, on the watchmakers and on the case makers. Further separate sections are devoted to the style and decoration of the cases, the dials and hands and the mechanisms' characteristics and timekeeping. These are intended to be a guide to the reader as to what he should expect to find during the period in question.

The illustrations are in chronological order and have descriptions with relevant information. While some of the watches are important or significant, others have been chosen because they are good examples of their type. Sources and references for further reading are contained in the text, while the glossary has definitions of the terminology in common usage and some extended technical information.

When it came to making the book we – the publisher and I – faced a conundrum familiar to everyone who has reproduced images of small objects. If a watch is illustrated at its actual size on the page it appears, curiously, smaller than it does in the hand while an enlargement, which in some ways is more truthful and helps to show detail, can easily lead to confusion. This is especially so as the optimum size, the one with which one can feel most comfortable because it seems not to distort, varies from watch to watch. Our solution has been to repeat the image – actual size and enlarged – where it was felt appropriate. Generally speaking the movements have been shown enlarged.

Terence Camerer Cuss

July 2008

ACKNOWLEDGEMENTS

Most of all I would like to thank Sir Harry Djanogly CBE for his encouragement, sponsorship and help without which this book would not have been written. Diana Steel has once again undertaken the onerous task of publishing a book for me; I am grateful to her and her staff. I well remember how calm and decisive Diana was when, thirty years ago, she directed operations as I nervously balanced eight watches on a sheet of blue paper, this laid over a pile of books on my office desk, so that a photographer, I forget his name, could take a single shot for the front cover of my revised edition of one of my father's books.

I could not have begun without watches to illustrate. Three are shown from the Royal Collection with the gracious permission of Her Majesty The Queen. One is the famous lever watch by Thomas Mudge, another is by Henry Grendon and the third is by David Bouquet. I wish to thank Sir Harry Djanogly and a number of other private individuals who have very generously allowed me to include watches from their collections. Several institutions have also kindly given me permission and these are acknowledged below the plates.

I have been very fortunate in being able to rely on the formidable watchmaking skills of Toomas Rohulaan, his observations and notes on what he has found and his lucid explanations of mechanical niceties. Dr. Richard Edgcumbe, who has a special understanding of the work of the eighteenth century watch case chasers, has always been extremely generous with his encyclopedic knowledge. His book on the subject is one of the classics in horological literature. Another is Sir George White's on English lantern clocks to which I referred when I was writing the early period. Of course the watch and clock making trades were closely linked from the beginning and appear to have used some of the same sources for engraved designs. Anthony Randall's two works on chronometry and Brian Loomes's list of early makers are among many other books, articles and sources I could not have done without.

Over the last fifteen years or so Philip Priestley has carried out and published an enormous amount of research into watch case makers and has vastly increased our awareness and knowledge of their craft. Not only did he kindly agree to check and improve upon my entries to these, but he most generously went through my draft text and found typos (cast – not caste) and made some helpful comments.

I had a few most interesting hours with Nigel Rush comparing the designs for ornament in his library of architectural and other books with those on watches. Andrew Crisford has kindly both shared information and given his view on a number of topics. I would also like to thank the following who have helped me in various ways: David Thompson (British Museum), Dr. Richard Edgcumbe (V & A Museum), Jonathan Betts (Maritime Museum), George Dalgleish (National Museums of Scotland), Arnaud Tellier (Patek Philippe Museum), Pamela Wood (Nottingham Museum), Sir George White Bt (Clockmakers' Company Museum), Hubert Chesshyre (College of Arms), The Viscount Midleton, Roger Smith, Dr. Hans Boeckh, Jeremy Evans, John Griffiths, Simon Bull, Philip Whyte, Richard Stenning, Martin Matthews, Peter Linstead-Smith and Brandon Thomas. Finally I must apologise to anyone I have failed to mention – certainly I am most grateful to all those people with whom, over the years, I have shared a consuming interest in old watches and their makers.

Photographic Acknowledgements

The publisher and I have a strong preference for the results obtained with transparencies over those which can currently be achieved with digital photography. I owe a special thanks to Jeff Wilkinson who is now one of only a few professional photographers to use film and has the skill and experience required. He took all the photographs apart from those supplied by the Royal Collection Trust and a number of museums – these acknowledged below the plates – one or two privately and the following who also kindly supplied specific images:

Antiquorum S A.	Plates 22, 50 (part), 94 and 285
Bridgeman Library	Plates 11, 141 and 202, pages 98 and 254
Colin Crisford	Plate 112
Sotheby's, New York	Plate 64

Diagrams

The series of diagrams used in the glossary to illustrate the functions of the Emery lever escapement, the Arnold detent escapement and the Earnshaw detent escapement were drawn and supplied by David Penney and are his copyright.

Terence Camerer Cuss

July 2008

THES BE THE SONES OF TF RIGHT HONERABLES TERLLE OF LENOXE AD
TE LADY MARGAPETZ GRACE COVNTYES OF LENOXE AD ANGWYSE.

1563

CHARLLES STEWARDE   HENRY STEWARDE LORD DAR

Lord Darnley and his brother. Hans Eworth. Oil on wood, 25 x 15in. (64 x 38cm),
dated 1563. Lord Darnley (1545-1567), husband of Mary Queen of Scots and father
of James VI of Scotland (who became James I of England), would appear to be
wearing a circular watch with a key around his neck.

Chapter One

THE FIRST PERIOD

1590-1630

THE FIRST PERIOD

1585–1630

OUTLINE

Lord Darnley was left a watch by Mary Queen of Scots in the will she wrote in 1566 prior to giving birth to James I. There are archive documents from the 1570s which have watches recorded as gifts to Elizabeth I. None of these is extant, and it is not known whether they were made in England or imported. The first watches made in England to have survived date from the 1580s and resemble those being made in the Low Countries, France and, to a lesser extent, Germany, where watches had been made in very small numbers from the second quarter of the sixteenth century.

While a few late sixteenth century watchmakers had names which suggest they might well have been English most, although by no means all, were Protestant immigrants who came to England from France and Holland where they had been suffering from religious persecution. Those who settled typically married into the small communities already established by their fellow countrymen in and around the City of London. They employed specialist craftsmen who were available locally – founders, spring makers, gilders – and also fellow immigrants, especially chasers.

The decorative designs of the Italian Renaissance reached Britain during the second half of the sixteenth century largely through published prints of German, French, Dutch and Flemish artwork. Watchmakers, and the chasers they employed, used these as a source, and frequently two and more which were of very different character. A remarkable amalgam of arabesque, geometric patterns and floral, foliate and grotesque designs on the cases, dials and movements quite often gives the impression that these very early watches – that is, particularly those made prior to about 1605 – were not conceived as a whole, yet they have been. The influence of known designers at this period, and indeed later, is sometimes discernible but, except in a few instances, no more than that. Occasionally it would seem more than one chaser has been involved – no doubt it was cheaper to have a master chaser to engrave the covers and an apprentice or journeyman to do the repeat patterns and so on. Finally, and adding to their curious appearance, is the fact that an early English watch signed, for instance, by a Dutch immigrant, may well have German and French constructional overtones.

So, at first sight, and perhaps more than their Continental cousins, the constituent parts of the earliest English watches may appear to mismatch, indeed as if they might have been put together from a number of different watches during the intervening centuries – which, of course, could be true of some. Just about all have had some alterations early on and, again, most have had a degree of subsequent restoration. Many of the gilt-metal cases and dials have been re-gilded. Movements have been altered and updated, particularly the cocks and escapements and, again, often re-gilded. Unfortunately, hands have been replaced and front covers have been cut away or removed entirely. When a watch has lost much of the original gilding, it can look dull and perhaps a little sad, but not only can re-gilding hide changes, it can also introduce doubts where they might not otherwise exist. More than any other period, alterations to these very rare watches are to be expected.

The outbreaks of bubonic plague during the 1590s, followed by an especially large attack in 1603, had a devastating effect on the London watchmaking communities. The craft took most of the first twenty years of the new century to recover, during which time there were probably only a dozen or so makers active in England. Their chief inspiration came from France. By 1610 floral and scrolling foliate engraving was generally on a hatched ground. It was somewhat tighter in appearance than before, increasingly between about 1610 and 1615. The use of mythological subjects and the grotesque continued, but scenes from the Old and New Testament became popular from around 1615. Towards 1620 watches became generally somewhat smaller, but remained almost always oval, octagonal very occasionally, unless striking mechanisms were fitted, in which case they were mostly circular. Then, starting around 1625 to 1630, they were made substantially smaller, and it was about this time that octagonal and other shapes became quite common.

SOME EARLY MAKERS AND DATED WATCHES

Bartholomew Newsam is not only considered as one of the first watch and clockmakers working in England but also, possibly, the first Yorkshireman. Where he learnt his craft is not known, but he is recorded as having been in the Strand, London from 1568, and he probably lived there until his death in 1593. Three clocks survive, but no watch exists which can be ascribed to him with certainty. Brian Loomes, in his *The Early Clockmakers of Great Britain* (1981), records that three or four watches exist by a Randolph Bull, and that this maker was probably a French immigrant. A watch by him, which is in the British Museum, has the date 1590 (with a small dot each side of the one) engraved on the movement.

There are a number of other early watches with what are clearly intended to be dates engraved on the movements and, although it is very tempting to place these watches in order and make much of the one with the earliest, it is just too difficult to establish which, if any, are spurious. The dates are simple, without elaboration, or a prefix. An exception is a watch by the Dutch immigrant Gylis Van Gheelle which has Ao 1587. This watch was in the famous, although here and there problematic, collection formed by Percy Webster, which was sold at Sotheby's in 1954. Another, by the same maker, belonging to the Ashmolean Museum, has no prefix to 1589, and nor does a similar although rather better watch dated the same year in the British Museum (Plate 1).

Nicholas Vallin and Francis Nawe are two other well-known makers from the end of sixteenth century. David Ramsay is undoubtedly the most famous for the rest of the period up to 1630, followed, perhaps, by Cornelius Mellin and Robert Grinkin.

THE 'BOX' AND CASE

Some early records, one a 1591 court case, refer to watch cases as 'boxes', and their makers as 'boxmakers'. Manuscripts belonging to the Clockmakers' Company show that it used this terminology from its foundation, in 1631. A list of members of the trade and their skills working in the City of London was drawn up on 26 June 1662 giving the names of a number of box makers. When the box was given a protective outer it was called a case. This was generally leather or leather-covered and supplied by men who no doubt also made cases for any number of items. With the increasing use of metal in the case, the box and watch case making disciplines converged and, by the beginning of the eighteenth century, 'case makers' made both, and the term 'box' was used far less frequently. Today they are referred to as the 'inner case' and the 'outer case', the two together as 'pair-cases', and a watch having both as a 'pair-cased' watch. Neither case was given a maker's mark, or at least certainly no examples are recorded at this period, just a few signed by the engraver.

THE CASE AND ITS DECORATION

By definition watches are timekeepers small enough to wear or carry on the person, which meant they were worn, early on, as a neck pendant or were suspended from the waist band. Cases made were oval rather than circular: the oval is a more satisfactory shape as it has a lower centre of gravity. Their pendants were quite substantial for the same reason – so that the watch would hang better – but also so that it could be taken with ease from the small bag or purse in which it was sometimes carried. Complications of alarm and striking mechanisms were made for larger watches: these were generally circular but occasionally oval. Other shapes, such as octagonal (Plates 15 and 16) and cruciform (Plate 14), began to be popular from about 1625.

Whatever their shape cases were invariably formed, not cast. The edge of the case body – the band – was made with a flat or ribbed centre, and for striking watches it was pierced for sound emission. Initially the moulded edge was the norm (Plates 1-3), but it fell out of favour around 1610. The back and front covers were always convex to some degree; on circular watches with moulded bands they tended to be more so, and these cases appear cushion-shaped. All the surviving late sixteenth century English watches have gilt metal cases. This is also true of those from the first two decades of the seventeenth century, but from about 1615 there are an increasing number of watches with applied silver bands (Plates 7 and 8), some also with silver covers (Plate 10). Watches had become progressively smaller, but they remained fairly cumbersome until about 1625 or shortly after, when, presumably in response to the continuing demands of fashion, makers achieved a significant reduction in both their diameter and depth. If pendants were substantial, terminals would vary greatly in size and proportion to the rest of the case; occasionally, particularly during the first fifteen years or so, they were omitted entirely.

The chased and engraved decoration of the Renaissance was sourced from prints imported from the Continent. Up to about 1605-1610, when they fell out of favour, arabesques and geometric patterns were used in combination with plants, flowers, fruit, animals and human beings, often from more than one source and in some confusion. The plants, flowers, fruit, animals and human beings, sometimes in the manner of the grotesque, are, on occasions, clearly symbolic and, even though some may have more than one attribute, an overall theme is sometimes discernible. There was, of course, a great interest in plants for their medicinal properties – real or imagined - and indeed all things botanical, and there were a number of publications from the turn of the century onwards which would have been a source of inspiration. Early covers were typically engraved with related figures, such as Peace on one and Justice on the other, or representations of Life and Death, but occasionally armorial bearings were used (Plates 1 and 10).

Many cases were left plain, or nearly so, but, as the new century progressed, if they were engraved the overall decorative design became more controlled and the work somewhat tighter, generally on a hatched ground. Engraved scenes aside, scrolling foliage – often the stems and leaves of acanthus – inhabited by small animals, figures and heads, and flowers such as passion flowers, and fruit such as acorns and strawberries were standard fare until the end of the period. Between about 1615 and 1625 there was a fashion to have a band across the lower half of a cover scene denoting the subject: for instance, if from the Old or New Testament, the chapter, or, from Ovid's *Metamorphoses*, the book (Plate10).

THE DIAL AND HAND

The first dials had engraved Roman chapters and half-hour divisions, often radial decoration from the centre and, typically, continuous borders. Star half-hour divisions were the most popular from the start, but sometimes they were in the form of a V, an arrowhead, occasionally a T and, later, also heart-shaped. A ring of touch pins was common, one at each hour so that the time could be read in the dark (Plates 1, 2 and 3). Applied chapter rings – made separate to the dial and riveted – were fitted before, but increasingly from, 1615. They were invariably in silver so as to contrast with gilt dials (Plates 6 and 7).

Geometric and radial patterns had lost their popularity by 1605-1610; from then on dials had much the same treatment as engraved cases, although the work was done with at least as much care, or more so. The decoration was sometimes in the manner of the grotesque. Scenes aside, it consisted of scrolling foliage (often the stems and leaves of acanthus), flowers (mostly simple four and five leaf heads, marigolds and sunflowers, but also passion flowers), sometimes fruit (such as acorns and strawberries), but in any event inhabited by, for instance, small animals, the occasional figure (mostly putti, but also angel and cherub heads) and so on (Plates 7, 8 and 9). While this decorative style continued through to the end of the period, rural scenes, townscapes and scenes which sometimes related to the themes depicted on the cases all became increasingly popular in the 1620s. With these the foliate designs were restricted to the area outside the ring, typically with a figure or head above twelve and one or two small animals elsewhere.

The double-ended **hand** was likely to have been made of iron at the beginning, later steel. It was pinned to a square or riveted to a pipe, in both cases friction tight with the motion work so that the hand might be set. The head was either in the form of an arrow, especially early on, or followed one of a variety of floriate designs.

THE MECHANISM

The principal mechanical components of the watch were the same as its progenitor, the small portable clock: mainspring, fusee with a gut line, a short train of wheels, escape wheel, verge and balance. The dial feet were pinned to the bottom plate – or 'pillar plate' – and the pillars on this were pinned to the signed top plate which, in turn, had the balance cock and the maintaining power fixed to it.

Running time depended on the number of turns on the fusee, the number of wheels and their teeth, and the leaves on the pinions; in general it was little more than twelve hours and sixteen was unusual. Most trains had three wheels consisting of the fusee's great wheel, the second wheel and the contrate wheel. Their pinions generally had five leaves, the same as the escape wheel which had normally either seventeen or fifteen teeth. The fusee, mostly of eleven or twelve turns, had a four-pin driver mounted at the top end of it – on the dial side of the bottom plate – which turned an hour wheel of twenty-four or, sometimes, thirty-six teeth. So that the hand could be moved independently of the drive, the wheel was friction tight on and lightly riveted to either a post fixed to the hand's underside or the turned end of a square to which the hand was pinned. From the outset, a few watches had locking plate striking or alarm mechanisms (Plate 6), occasionally both (Plate 7), and once again the components were similar to those of a small portable clock.

Various forms of script, but occasionally block capitals, were used for the **signatures**. The surname was preceded by the Christian name which was frequently truncated, even to just the initial. Only a few makers followed their signature with a date (Plates 1 and 4), and early on not many with a place name, but Nawe did (Plate 2), and Henry Archer with 'at London' on a watch of about 1610 (Bonhams, New Bond St., November 2006), while Cornelius Mellin continued in French 'aux Blackfries' (Plate 5). Some makers, such as Ramsay (Plate 7), used 'Fecit' as a suffix. The engraved floral and foliate border became more formalized and somewhat narrower as the period progressed. The **cock** was pinned to the plate, its table generally taking a quite simple 'S' shape early on (Plates 1 and 2), and then becoming gradually more elaborate but retaining the 'S' within what was mostly floral and foliate decoration. With a few exceptions, such as that in Plate 2, the foot was pierced and engraved in a similar manner to the table, but considerably smaller. **Pillars** were baluster shaped (Plates 7, 8, 9 and 13) or, occasionally from about 1620, took the form known as 'early Egyptian' – divided or solid.

TIMEKEEPING

Whatever the proportions of the gearing, these watches needed to be wound every twelve hours or so. At the same time, it would have been necessary to check the position of the hand; this might well have needed correction by half an hour, probably often more. Some degree of regulation was achieved by either altering the mainspring set-up or adjusting the depth between the escape wheel and the verge pallets, but these methods were crude. Clearly watches were useful adjuncts to domestic and church clocks and sundials, but only over short periods. Although much less reliable than contemporary clocks, they would have been regarded as mechanical marvels and considered to be very significant possessions. To see and hear the eccentric waggle of the balance was surely entrancing, even as it is today. No doubt alarm watches would have proved useful: accuracy was unlikely to have been of paramount importance.

THE CLOCKMAKERS' COMPANY

The outbreak of the Thirty Years War in 1618 led to an influx of craftsmen of all kinds into England, particularly London, and the City Livery Companies had difficulty controlling the trades under their jurisdiction. Many of the refugees set up in business outside the City boundaries and, while they did not benefit from being a member of a guild, they avoided guild rules. A group of sixteen watch and clockmakers, quite a number of whom were members of the Blacksmiths' Company, were moved to form their own Company in an effort to restrict and control the competition. In 1620 and again in 1622 they appealed unsuccessfully to the Crown for a Charter of their own (PRO, *State Papers, Domestic Series*, 14 Vol.127).

Their petition is a clear indication that they felt their trade had enough identity to have its own Company. They were also disingenuous, however, and, with their complaint about unfair competition, they listed 'Straingers' who had long been established in and around the City. The rejection was probably advantageous; the trade expanded rapidly during the 1620s and London established itself as an important centre. By the time a Charter was eventually granted in 1631, the business was larger, more mature and inclusive, and the new Company was able to govern the quality of work, apprenticeship arrangements and so on.

Plate 1. Gylis Van Gheelle.
Gilt-metal case 48mm wide

The watch by Van Gheelle – a Dutch immigrant – is in the British Museum. The movement is signed and **dated 1589**. The oval **case** has Charity engraved on the front cover and Justice on the back where there is a winding shutter in the form of a shell. The armorial inside the cover is that of the Giffard family, St. James's Abbey, Northampton. The radial design on the **dial** is quite typical of the period: the cuneiforms align with the star half-hour marks on the chapter ring, and the leaves and stems with the Roman numerals. The double-ended hand has a floriate head. The border of flowers and foliage on the movement top plate is especially good; later they became more formalized and tighter. These borders continued to be popular on English work until about the 1640s, much less so on the Continent.

The blued steel ratchet wheel is missing from over the fusee square on the top plate of the **movement**, but the large click and bow-shaped spring appear to be original. The foot of the pinned-on balance cock is lyre-shaped and the table is in the shape of an elaborated 'S', the head of which is free to allow for a degree of final adjustment to the position of the balance. By the beginning of the seventeenth century the 'S' was fully incorporated into the decoration but, with many variations, it continued to be a common feature for more than fifty years. There are round baluster pillars, fusee and verge escapement.

Actual size.

Plate 2. Francis Nawe.

Gilt-metal case 54mm wide   late 16th century

The close knit watchmaking communities living in London, especially in Blackfriars, were devastated by outbreaks of bubonic plagues. They killed two of the most important makers of the period, Francis Nawe in 1593 and Nicholas Vallin in 1603. The illustrated watch by Nawe, who is thought to have been born in Brabant, Belgium, and to have moved to London about 1580, is owned by the Ashmolean Museum, Oxford. Since Nawe died in 1593, this must be one of the earliest surviving English watches. It was at one time in the Levy Collection, was in the Webster Collection and was bequeathed to the Museum by Eric Bullivant in 1974.

The engraving on the front cover of the **case** alludes to Life and is after Etienne Delaune, whose published designs were probably the single most popular source for both English and Continental watch case engravers. Delaune was also an engraver. Apparently of French extraction, he is recorded as having been born in Milan in 1518 and, after living in various cities throughout Europe, although not apparently England, is thought to have died in Strasbourg in 1583 or 1595. His influence continued for several decades into the sixteenth century. As the front cover engraving alludes to Life, so appropriately that on the watch back, with a canopy above an urn also surrounded by acanthus leaves and flowers, suggests Death. There is a shutter for covering the winding square in the form of a shell, and a most unusual arrangement in the centre, where a latch engages and locks the head of a post which in turn is fixed to the movement back plate. The dial cover is engraved inside with a decorative armorial surrounded by a palm-stem border.

The **dial** centre has a radial design indicating the hours and half-hours within a border of

swags and rosettes and outside the chapter ring, above and below, a border of palm stems. The flat blued steel arrow hand is typical of Flemish tradition, stout enough to be felt in the dark against the small raised touch pins on the inside edge of the chapter ring which has Roman numerals and star half-hour marks.

The **movement** has a similar border, a splendid signature 'Francois Nawe at Londen *[sic]*' within a ribbon and a simple 'S'-shaped balance cock with a baluster foot. The decoration around the hole or box for the verge is very particular. Unusually, rather than in the normal position on the back plate, he has put the mainspring set-up on the inside of the front. A Renaissance chamber clock by this maker, signed and dated 1588, is in the Victoria & Albert Museum.

ASHMOLEAN MUSEUM, UNIVERSITY OF OXFORD

Plate 3. Nicholas Vallin.
Gilt-metal case 67 x 42mm   circa 1600

Nicholas Vallin came to London from Brussels with his father, John, a native of Ryssell, Flanders, having in all probability previously worked in Spain. He married at Austin Friars Dutch Church in June 1590. The British Museum has a fine chamber clock by him dated 1598. He died of the plague in 1603.

The ribbed edge of the **case** body, the fixed pendant and bottom terminal are typical of the period. There is an allegorical figure of Peace engraved on the front cover and Justice on the back. The narrow chapter ring has touch pins, and the **dial** centre an hourglass on a table at which a seated cherub rests an elbow upon a skull – a solemn reminder that our lives pass with the hours. This engraving was probably adapted from an illustration in an *ars moriendi* block-book, books which were initially intended as teaching aids for the illiterate and poorly educated. Themes such as Life and Death, Peace and Justice were commonly used: they were reassuring to people who were living through a period of political upheaval and religious persecution, and who were constantly aware that they might die very swiftly of the plague.

The dial is fitted to the top of the case with a hinge, located in the aperture with four small lugs and secured to the **movement** with a tag and bayonet. There are baluster pillars, the top plate has a foliate border, and it has a ratchet, click and large bow-shaped spring on one side of the pinned-on cock and a small signature 'N vallin' – the 'v' is lower case – running parallel on the other side. The balance and verge are later. This watch was part of the Sandberg Collection, dispersed in 2001.

PRIVATE COLLECTION

Plate 4. Thomas Aspinwall.

Gilt-metal case 62 x 44mm

The plague that killed Vallin and his household in 1603 also had a devastating effect on the pubescent trade in London. But there was some continuity. One of the very first makers working outside the capital was Thomas Aspinwall (1577-1623) of Toxteth Park, near Liverpool, and Merseyside National Museums and Galleries have this watch by him signed 'Tho. Aspinwall' and **dated 1607**. It has a typical early oval **case** with a ribbed edge, not unlike the preceding watch by Vallin but without engraving. The bodies of these cases were not cast, but made from a strip cut to size, which was then formed, braised together and gilded with the rest of the case. The **dial** has a sunburst in the centre, palm-stem decoration above and below the chapters and the hand has a floriate head.

The palm-stem decoration is repeated on the border of the **movement**. The cock and balance are reproductions, and so is the ratchet wheel of the set-up, although not the bow and spring which are well made, as are the baluster pillars. The train is very unusual for the period, having four wheels rather than three, with pinion counts of eight instead of the normal five. There is a four-pin driver on the fusee, and the hour wheel has thirty-six teeth. These are features which, although more difficult and costly to make, could be expected to result in, if not a more accurate, at least a more reliable watch. The duration is sixteen hours.

Watchmaking became established in the area around Liverpool very early on, and it is clear that by the middle of the century it was supplying horological tools, as well as completed watches, far beyond the locality. It was to grow into a very important part of the trade in England (for the Aspinwalls and the early Liverpool trade see R.J. Griffiths, *Antiquarian Horology*, December 2002).

©WALKER ART GALLERY, NATIONAL MUSEUMS LIVERPOOL

Actual size.

Plate 5. Cornelius Mellin, Blackfriars.
Gilt-metal case 78 overall x 43mm

An early example of a watch by Cornelius Mellin with some similarities to the two previous watches, but made a little later, between about **1610** and **1615**. It is approximately the same large size – which, except for striking and alarm watches, was soon to become unfashionable. However, the edge of the case, rather than being ribbed, has a flat band in the centre, and the engraving is significantly different.

The **case** band is engraved with grotesque animal heads and fabulous birds within flowers and foliage, and this decoration is continued on the back. The pendant is decorated with acanthus leaves. Much of the front cover has been removed, probably within about twenty years of the watch being made, and replaced, as was frequently done, by a crystal glass held in by tags, so that the time can be read without the need to lift the cover. The **dial** centre has a townscape with a windmill and fortified gate while outside the chapters a winged angel head is amongst foliage and flowers, including acanthus. There is a very good double-ended steel hand with a floriate head.

The **movement** is signed 'C. Mellin aux Blackfries'. There is a pinned-on cock, a ratchet and click, tall vase-shaped baluster pillars, short train and gut fusee. It is not known when he began working, but by the time of the famous petitions of the London clockmakers to the King of 1620 and 1622, which were eventually to lead to the granting of the Clockmakers' Company Charter of 1631, Mellin was listed having not only four apprentices, but several other members of the craft as part of his household. He was one of the 'Straingers of ye Art dwelling in & about London' to which the petitioners objected.

hand. The remainder of the hand, which can be used for setting the alarm, is only friction tight. The two parts are illustrated in alignment, the intended position if the alarm is not required but, when the main portion of the hand is set against the Arabic figures engraved on the disc and the alarm train wound, the alarm will sound as the arrow head passes the twelve o'clock Roman numeral.

The **movement**, signed very simply 'George Smith', has an engraved border, a lyre-shaped foot to the cock, a ratchet and brass click set-up, blued steel alarm set-up, round baluster pillars, pierced and engraved alarm barrel and verge escapement. In his illustrated review of some of the watches in the Ashmolean Museum (*Antiquarian Horology*, September 2000), David Thompson records that George Smith, or Schmidt, came originally from Augsburg. PRIVATE COLLECTION

Plate 6. George Smith.
Gilt-metal case 55mm

George Smith and his two apprentices were, like Mellin, also 'Straingers'. This alarm watch, of about **1610–15**, was in the Time Museum, Rockford, Illinois, for some years until it was sold at Sotheby's in June 2002. The back of the **case** is quite plain except for a seeded rose at the centre; the flat band is extensively pierced and engraved with running foliage inhabited by dolphins. The fixed pendant, with acanthus leaf engraving, has a loose ring and there is a bottom terminal. Inside the applied silver chapter ring the **dial** revolves, and fixed to it is the arrow head of the double-ended

Plate 7. David Ramsay.
Gilt-metal and silver mounted case 43mm

This well-known clock-watch alarm by David Ramsay has never been fully illustrated. However, there is a photograph published in 1897 in a book devoted to the Evan Roberts Collection, and a line drawing, first used in the *Horological Journal* of July 1888, which appears in the earlier editions of F.J. Britten's *Old Clocks and Watches and their Makers.* Evan Roberts claimed the watch belonged to King James I, but gave no proof. Later, when it was offered

Actual size.

for sale by Christie's in 1953 as part of Robert Atkinson's excellent collection, the cataloguer simply referred to the entry in Britten. Britten says the watch was made **about 1615** and he is probably about right.

The bell inside the back of the **case** shows through very open pierced and engraved decoration consisting of stems and flowers. Within this a scroll terminates with a head, probably of a dolphin (in Renaissance allegory an attribute of Fortune).

The front cover has been reduced to a bezel which is now glazed, the fixed pendant is cruciform, and the terminal short but generous. The early use of silver for the band, which also has flowers and scrolls with dolphins' heads, emphasizes the quality and cost of the watch, and similarly the **dial's** applied silver chapter ring. The hours are indicated by a small bug mounted on a central revolving disc and this has a narrow Arabic figured alarm ring, flowers, foliage and a dog's head; when the appropriate hour is indicated by the double-ended hand the dog will sound the alarm! Above twelve a putto holds some blooms, at nine and three are baskets of fruit and flowers, at seven and five a pair of squirrels and by the movement catch at six, two strawberries.

Mounted on the **movement** top plate are blued steel stop-work for the alarm and striking mechanisms, a silver locking plate marked for each hour and a set-up ratchet with an elaborate brass click. This furniture partly obscures the signature, 'David Ramsay me Fecit'. According to the contemporary royal records Ramsay, who was probably active from the beginning of the century, was receiving payments from James I by 1613, and by 1619 had become an English citizen. It is thought that it was at the time of, or shortly before, his denization that he began signing his work '…Scotus me Fecit' or, at least on two occasions, '…Scottes me Fecit'. Later on, and probably by the time he became the first Master of the Clockmakers' Company in 1632, Ramsay dropped the reference to his origins.

PRIVATE COLLECTION

Plate 8. William Houllgatte, Ipswich.
Gilt-metal and silver mounted case 34 x 57mm overall

A bird and a salamander are amongst a profusion of flowers and foliage in the centre of the **dial**. The former represents the Soul which rises after Death and the latter, since it was considered unharmed by fire, represents Faith which is able to resist the Fires of Temptation. There is an angel's head above twelve and a wolf's near the case catch below six, these suggesting Heaven and Hell. The chapter ring, which has star half-hour divisions, is particularly narrow.

The silver **case** band has dolphin heads amongst scrolling acanthus stems and leaves engraved with the same grotesque overtones as the dial. The oval case has the slightly flattened appearance below the pendant and above the terminal and it

is relatively slender; these features are most typical of the period of this watch, around **1615**. The front is plain and the back has a simple winding shutter.

The top plate of the **movement** is signed 'W Houllgatte at Ipswich', the table of the pinned-on cock is rectangular, the mainspring set-up has an elaborate brass click and there are round baluster pillars. The blued steel hand is noteworthy: another watch by this maker in the Victoria & Albert Museum, the dial with a different scene but quite possibly by the same engraver has had, clearly, an identical floriate hand. The case has the same shape as well as a silver band. PRIVATE COLLECTION

Plate 9. William Nash.

Gilt-metal and silver mounted case 35mm wide

In his book *Henlein to Tompion*, which he published privately in 1938, Marryat correctly pointed out that this watch is a little later than the 1605 recorded for it in another publication: it is from around **1620**, but may be a little before. It is unusual for an English watch at this period to have the **dial** centre and chapter ring both of silver and to have touch pins. However, it is quite a common combination on contemporary German watches. The raised pins on the inside of each hour are so that the time can be ascertained by touch, a feature found more frequently on earlier watches. The dial centre has an engraved townscape with a huntsman in the foreground, a winged angel's head is above twelve within flowers and foliage, and the narrow silver band of the **case** has snails and squirrels, which also are amongst flowers and scrolling foliage.

The **movement**, which is signed simply William Nash, has baluster pillars, a steel ratchet and click, a pinned-on cock and a good engraved border of flowers and foliage inhabited by a hare at the base.

PRIVATE COLLECTION

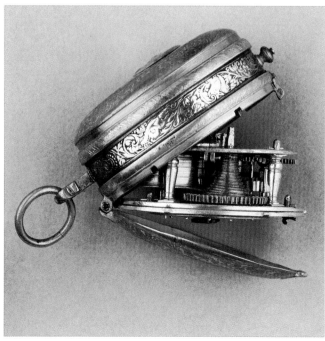

Plate 10. David Ramsay.
Silver and gilt-metal case 65mm long overall
Cover signed by Gérard de Heck, portrait of King James after
Simon de Passe

In the Victoria & Albert Museum, on permanent loan, is an oval watch signed 'David Ramsay Scotus me Fecit' which has scenes from the St. Luke's Testament engraved by Gérard de Heck on the **case** covers. Inside the front cover is a portrait of King James I after Simon de Passe and inside the back the Royal Coat of Arms. The King's monogram is on the silver band, while the **dial** has twin subsidiaries and four apertures. This watch is very similar; although there are many differences of detail, it is reasonable to assume that the two were made, possibly with others, more or less at the same time about **1618**, and to an order of the King. It is signed 'David Ramsay Scottes [as opposed to Scotus] me Fecit'. The scenes on the covers are taken from Ovid's *Metamorphoses*; below 'Metamorp> Livre 2' on the band of the front, a putto holds a tablet with the engraver's signature 'De Heck Scul', while the band of the back reads 'Metamorphose Livre 4'. Gérard de Heck, an outstanding engraver, is recorded as active between about 1608 and 1629.

The Royal Arms with the James's favourite motto, 'Beati Pacifici', is inside the front cover. Most interestingly, the portraits of the King on both watches have been taken from the same engraving by Simon de Passe, but modified, so that some elements of the original have been included on one but not on the other. Specifically, in the original the King holds a sceptre and he does in the red 'wax' filled engraving on this watch, but not in the Victoria & Albert Museum example. He also wears a feathered hat which the engraver used only for the watch in the Victoria & Albert Museum. The original engraving was used as one of the plates in 'Bazilologia', a series of engraved portraits of British monarchs first published in 1618 (Hugh Clayton, *Royal Faces*, page 30, HMSO, 1977). De Passe moved from Utrecht to England in 1615 or 1616 where he stayed until about 1624 (Hugh Tait, *The Art of the Goldsmith*, page 70, 1984). The portraits are framed with the inscription: 'Potentis Iacobus D.G. Magnae Britanniae Hibernia Galliae Rex Fidei Defensor'. Thus, it is probably safe to assume that the watch was made shortly before, or very soon after, 'Bazilologia' was first published, that is to say, in about 1618.

The silver band to the edge of the case is engraved and filled with red 'wax' rather than the normal black. It is commonly called 'wax' although, in reality, it is pitch. Chronos is supporting an hourglass on one side of the band and on the other Saint James the Greater is to be seen in a petasus hat holding his sword. Both figures are amongst flowers and foliage, including acanthus. The gilt metal pendant is in the form of addorsed reptiles. These are probably salamanders which, as they were considered unharmed by fire, were seen to represent Faith which was able to resist the Fires of Temptation. As a pendant they suggest resistance, longevity and strength.

The upper of the two narrow chapter rings has the days of the week indicated by the blued steel bug mounted on the revolving gilt metal centre, this being pierced and engraved with the months and the corresponding signs of the Zodiac. The centre of the lower hour ring also revolves indicating the time against a blued steel ground. There are four apertures in the dial plate: to the left the days of the week with the ruling planet, to the right the lunar date above the moon phase, and lower right the planet hour. The three hands are fixed to the dial plate; two, by the days of the week and planet hour, indicate the direction of the disc's rotation.

The **movement** swings out on the hinge from the front. There is an engraved border, a pinned-on cock in the form of an elaborated 'S' with a matching brass click for the steel ratchet set-up, a verge escapement, a fusee and a three wheel train. The elegant tapering pillars are early examples of a shape which, either divided, as these, or solid, is generally called 'early Egyptian'. Sold at Sotheby's, London, in March 1995 without provenance, this watch was sent for sale from the Continent. There is an old small French control mark adjacent to the Royal Arms. It is reasonable to assume that it was ordered by James or, very much less likely,

his son Charles, Prince of Wales. It could have been bought for their own use or to be given as a gift to another member of the family or, just possibly, close entourage. *Metamorphoses* are to a large extent tales of the love adventures of the gods with nymphs and the daughters of men: a suitable present for Frederick V (1596-1632), Elector Palatine and King of Bohemia, husband of James's daughter Elizabeth.

A third watch, very similar to those described above, signed 'David Ramsay, Scotus me Fecit', is in the National Museum of Scotland. The design of the movement is the same, and the dial configuration is a variation on the same arrangement. The silver covers of the oval case are engraved with scenes having horizontal bands telling us of the chapter in St. John's Gospel from which they come. Inside the front cover are the arms of Thomas Ker or Carr, who became the Earl of Somerset in 1613, while the back has an engraving of the King and Queen. It is quite possible this watch predates the two mentioned previously, partly because the scenes are not signed by de Heck, and also, if the watch was a gift from the King, the Earl of Somerset is known to have fallen out of favour in 1616.

THE DJANOGLY COLLECTION

Actual size.

Plate 11. David Ramsay.
Silver and gilt-metal case 45mm
Principal scene signed by Gérard de Heck

In the form of a hexagram, and dating from around
1625, this watch is supposed to have been found in
the 1790s, together with some apostle spoons, hidden
behind an arras at Gawdy Hall, Norfolk. It has the
same unusual form of signature as Plate 10 ('Scotus
me Fecit' is more common). It is part of the superb
collection of watches and clocks to be seen at the
Clockmakers' Company Museum at the Guildhall
Library. The principal scenes are concerned with the
birth of Christ and are beautifully engraved; the putto
above the dial holds a tablet signed 'de Heck Sculp'. It
has been suggested the shape of the case possibly
represents an heraldic mullet, or the Star of Creation
or, as Christ was of the house of David, the Star of
David. The movement follows the shape of the case;
it is a simple timepiece with no complications, and
stylistically little different from the previous watch.

Plate 12. Cornelius Mellin, Blackfriars.
Silver and gilt-metal case 58 x 36mm

Cornelius Mellin was one of the 'Straingers' who was objected to in the 1622 petition to King James for a clockmakers' charter. It was not so much because he was an immigrant – he had been in England for a number of years (Plate 5 is an earlier watch by him) – but because he did not belong to a guild (such as the Black-smiths' Company) and because he had too many apprentices. He had four, three of whom had very British names; clearly, not only was his business successful, he was training native watchmakers.

This watch, from the Sandberg Collection, is signed 'C. Mellin aux Blackfriers' and was made around **1625**. The oval shape continued to be popular, but watches were becoming smaller and somewhat slimmer. The pendants remained substantial but, generally, the terminals became shorter. Narrow silver chapter rings remained fashionable. The head of the hand is of a floriate design, and the half-hour divisions are heart-shaped marks. The plain silver front cover of the **case** and fixed back are gilt on their insides and, somewhat unusually, the cover closes on a bevel, rather than having the normal tongue and clasp. The **dial** centre has Cupid touching a figure, possibly Narcissus, with his arrow, and within the border of flowers and scrolling foliage a seated naked elderly man, suggesting Time. Two angel heads face each other either side of the movement catch. The silver band around the body of the case has putto reaching for fruit among small flowers and foliage.

The signed **movement** has a pinned-on cock with a matching brass click for the blued steel ratchet set-up wheel and bowed spring, but the top plate is without border engraving. There are baluster pillars, a short train and a gut fusee.

PRIVATE COLLECTION

Plate 13. Robert Grinkin.

Gilt-metal and silver mounted case 37mm wide

Robert Grinkin, both father and son, were members of the Blacksmiths' Company; indeed, Robert senior was the Master of that Company in 1609. He died in 1626. The signature on this watch reads 'Ro: Grinkin'. As it was made in **1625**, or shortly after, it is likely to be by the son. The **movement** is a very good example of the type and period: deep, with an engraved border, pinned cock, ratchet and click set-up, round baluster pillars, fusee with gut line and verge escapement. It is a common fallacy that the engraved border was an exclusively English custom; it is found on Continental watches, but just very much less frequently.

The gilt metal **case** has plain covers, the back fixed with a winding shutter, the front engraved with a foliate stem border inside. The band is silver and is decorated with flowers and acanthus stems and leaves. Inside the **dial's** applied silver chapter ring there is a townscape, outside a cherub's head is flanked by two dolphins at twelve, and within the foliage are birds and squirrels. It would seem the ring was probably replaced for reasons of clarity later in the century. Although, correctly for this period, there are no quarter divisions, it is particularly broad, the style of the half-hour is not what one would expect, and it is made champlevé with the chapters raised on a reduced ground.

Robert junior continued his association with the Blacksmiths' Company after he became a Free Brother of the Clockmakers in 1632. He was Master of the Clockmakers in 1648 and again in 1654. This watch was at one time in the Webster Collection. PRIVATE COLLECTION

Plate 14. John Willowe.
Silver and gilt-metal case 63 x 39mm

John Willowe was apprenticed in the Blacksmiths' Company to Robert Grinkin senior in 1609. He obtained his freedom in 1617 and, like Grinkin, he was one of the 1622 Petitioners of the Clockmakers to the King; he was also a witness to his former master's will. This watch (formerly in the Sandberg Collection) was made probably a few years before **1630** and before Willowe became a founder member of the Clockmakers' Company. He was one of the first three Wardens in 1631-2 and Master in 1635.

Both engraved silver covers of the gilt-metal **case** open from hinges below the elaborate fleur-de-lis pendant. The front has Christ on the Cross with the inscription INRI and the sun above. The surrounding facets show Instruments of the Passion and angels interspersed with floral scrolls. Angels are also on either side of the Virgin on the back cover, while the facets have

a cock and chalice within the engraving. The sacred monogram IHS is inscribed inside. The body of the case has a silver band with foliate decoration. The gilt chapter ring is applied to the silver **dial** mask which has, at the top, the head of Christ in a crown of thorns and drapery, suggesting the Holy Shroud and the Resurrection. At the bottom Christ stands between two soldiers; on the left is an angel and cross, and to the right an angel by a pillar against which Christ is scourged, scenes which together suggest spiritual strength and steadfastness.

The **movement**, which is signed 'Jo Willowe In Flee ste', follows the shape of the case. It is not fixed to the hinge in the normal way, but by the slightly unusual method of sprung bolts with catches in the dial plate. The pinned-on cock is in the form of an elaborate 'S'. There are round baluster pillars, a fusee and a verge escapement.

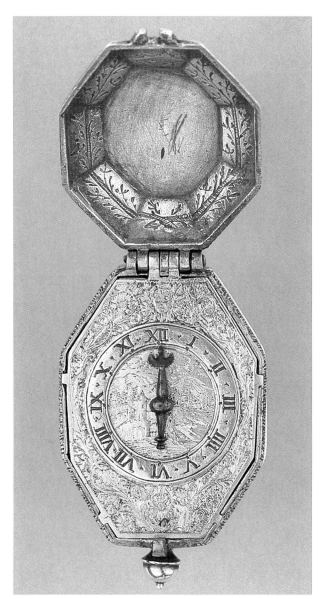

Plate 15. James Vautrollier.
Silver and gilt-metal case 24mm wide

Vautrollier was one of the 1622 petitioners for a Clockmakers' Company charter and he became an Assistant when the Charter was granted in 1631. This watch, measuring only about 24 millimetres across, was made around **1630**, about the time watchmakers were first able to produce watches of this size. It was in the Percy Webster Collection sold at Sotheby's in May 1954. The octagonal shape was popular during the 1620s and 1630s.

The centre of the **dial** is engraved with a landscape and there is an angel's head at the top of the floral and foliate decoration surrounding the applied silver chapter ring. There is a floriate style

Actual size.

hand. The central panel of the **case** silver dial cover has Chronos (Father Time) progressing across the sky holding his hourglass in front of an advancing crowd, one with a crutch – a solemn reminder that Time waits for no man. The surrounding panels are engraved in pairs and, within foliage, each with a dolphin accompanied by an owl, a hare and a bird: allegories of Wisdom, Salvation and the Soul. The darker side of the main theme is, appropriately, on the silver back cover: Pluto – more properly named Hades – is seen carrying off a reluctant Proserpine to his lower kingdom. The scenes are also linked because

Plate 15.

Chronos, the Greek personification of Time, was derived from Cronus; not only was Cronus, god of agriculture, the father of Hades, he was also the father of Demeter (Ceres, goddess of agriculture), who was closely associated in both myth and cult to her daughter Persephone (Proserpine). The surrounding panels are the same as those on the front and the silver band is engraved with foliage and recumbent nudes. Both covers are hinged.

The **movement** is signed 'Ja. Vautrollier Fecit', is wound via the back, and swings out of the gilt metal case from the front, the dial edge having location tags. The top plate is signed and it has a narrow engraved border. There is a pinned-on cock, a ratchet and click set-up, a verge escapement, a three wheel train, a fusee with a gut line and round baluster pillars.

PRIVATE COLLECTION

Plate 16. William Cory.
Silver and gilt-metal case 33mm wide   circa 1630

Although a somewhat larger watch, this is superficially very similar to the previous one by Vautrollier. It has a silver and gilt metal octagonal case of the same construction and a movement of similar design and appearance. However, the cherub head pendant is noteworthy and the engraved scenes are very different.

Henry Marryat formed an impressive and wide ranging collection and he included this watch in his book *Henlein to*

Tompion which he published privately in 1938. Having briefly described the movement, he continues with the case: 'The box is brass gilt inside with an engraved band of silver outside. The back and front covers are silver, richly engraved inside and outside, forming with the sideband 42 panels, comprising scenes and figures from the Bible. In two cases, chapter and verses are quoted, but being before the issue of the James I Bible, refer to the older book. The centre panel of the front cover illustrates David dancing before the Ark, and the corresponding back panel, Rahab lowering the spies from the window. The central panels inside the covers represent respectively, the Crucifixion and the Ascension.' Marryat goes on to identify the scene on the dial which, unusually, is of silver, as '...one representing Annon being killed by Absolom. A sword is being thrust though his back, whilst the guests at the feast raise their hands apparently in horror'.

PRIVATE COLLECTION

Plate 16.

Considered to be Edward East (1602-1696).
Unsigned, probably Thomas Flatman. Oil on copper
miniature 2¼in. (57mm) wide. From an inscription
on the reverse this would appear to be a presentation
portrait to Mr. East by Lady Chedworth.

Chapter Two

THE SECOND PERIOD

1630–1675

THE SECOND PERIOD
1630–1675

OUTLINE

Watchmaking was well established in England by 1630. The granting of the charter to the Clockmakers' Company in 1631 added to the overall confidence and the numbers of watchmakers increased. It was a luxury trade and initially a wide variety of styles and designs were produced. The practice of using prints imported from the Continent as sources for engraved work continued. The influence of known designers is sometimes discernible but, except in a few instances, no more than that. Generally, foliate decoration acted only as an adjunct to mythical and religious subjects and rural scenes during the first few years (Plates 17 and 18) but, increasingly, floral patterns, rather tight at first, but around 1640 more naturalistic and open, became dominant (Plates 25 and 31). The irrational market in tulip bulbs – tulipomania – collapsed in February 1637, but the flower's popularity was unabated and it soon became an important feature of decorative design (Plate 38).

In reaction to the religious and political upheavals of the time, fashion during the years immediately prior to the Civil War became markedly more sober. Watches began to be made from about 1635 onwards which were completely, or nearly completely, devoid of decoration or engraving (Plates 20, 21, 28 and 33). These, which much later became to be called 'Puritan' watches, were initially invariably oval. The inner case was silver with a simple ring pendant; the outer case was either silver and quite plain, or leather with modest pin decoration. The silver dials, too, were flat and, other than the Roman numerals, they had little or no decoration. However, some, particularly those of royalist persuasion, resisted the new fashion for a considerable time. Indeed, it seems a few would have little or nothing to do with it.

At the beginning watches were worn as neck pendants or suspended from the waist band, but they were consigned to a pocket as the period progressed. During the 1650s and 1660s the trend was for watches to be circular, larger and more manageable. As a result it was possible to make small but useful changes in the design of the movement and, along with a better finish, timekeeping improved.

The Civil War began in 1642 and lasted until 1647, after which the monarchy was abolished and, in 1649, the King executed. The effect on the trade was catastrophic throughout the country, made worse in London by an outbreak of plague in 1646, and not many watches were produced. After the Commonwealth government was established, demand came largely from the new rich and those who had profited from the war in one way or another. Recovery was slow through the 1650s and the disruption caused by the 1652-54 war with Holland added to the difficulties. Demand improved after the Restoration in 1660, only to collapse five years later with the Great Plague and, the following year, the Great Fire. The effects of the fire lasted several years, but the demand for watches was good and the number of watchmakers increased.

The influence of Continental floriate designs continued through the Commonwealth period. The arrangements became less formal, more free-flowing and, after the Restoration, the flowers were more open and voluptuous. However, the overall lay-out remained symmetrical and somewhat formalized repeat patterns were used, particularly in the pin-work of the outer case.

The majority of watches were considerably larger during the 1660s than they were in the 1630s and 1640s and around 1670 the relative depth was increased in order to accommodate significant mechanical improvements. Although the verge continued to be the only form of escapement, the four wheel train, better gear ratios and greater power meant that not only was the performance of the watch much improved, but it now ran for twenty-four hours or more. These advances were followed in 1675 by the introduction of the balance spring which, although it took some years to establish, had, by the early 1680s, brought about significant improvement in timekeeping and reliability. The seventeenth century scientific revolution, in embryo during the 1640s and 1650s, bore fruit in many fields including horology. This coincided with expanding trade, commerce and the increasing wealth of the nation.

SOME NOTABLE MAKERS, LONDON AND THE PROVINCES

Most London watchmakers lived grouped in a small number of locations. Perhaps the most important area was around Blackfriars, but also significant were Lothbury, Cornhill, the Royal Exchange and Fleet Street. While many premises were destroyed by the Great Fire, and there was some relocation to the north and west, there was a general return to the City as it was rebuilt.

The well-known makers at the beginning of, and indeed throughout, the period tend to be those who worked for a reasonable length of time, perhaps also becoming Master of the Clockmakers' Company, and their names are recognised because of the number – although it may well be no more than a dozen – of their watches which have survived. James Vautrollier, David Bouquet, Henry Grendon and Richard Masterson are typical and, later on, Benjamin Hill and Jeremy Gregory. Other makers, such as Nathaniel Barrow and Henry Jones, were active, but most of their work is from after 1675. However, Edward East (1602-1697) is an exception and his name dominates in much the same way as David Ramsay's did in the era to 1630. Not only was he remarkably long-lived for his time, he was also very successful and a significant amount of the best work of the period is signed by him. He must also have been an astute man politically because, although he was almost certainly a royalist and probably had Catholic leanings, he managed to be Master of the Clockmakers' Company both during the War (1645) and after it (1653). He became Clockmaker to Charles II immediately following the Restoration in November 1660.

It would appear that, in any event from the relatively few surviving watches, provincial makers followed the same fashions and trends as their London counterparts. There are clear indications that the provinces did not function in isolation. Some makers spent some of their working lives in London while others moved from one regional town to another. There was, of course, a tendency for the same family to have several members in the trade as well as successive generations. Brian Loomes in his *Early Clockmakers of Great Britain* (1981) lists no fewer than ten members of the Chamberlaine family working before 1700, three of these before 1650: John, father and son, in Bury St. Edmunds and Ipswich and Nathaniel in both London and Chelmsford. Nicholas Snow gained his freedom in Salisbury in 1629 and his brother, John, was there probably not long after. In his will Nicholas left his tools to his son, William, who, like his father and uncle, made both watches and clocks. William moved to Marlborough (*The Camerer Cuss Book of Antique Watches,* Antique Collectors' Club, 1976, and *English Lantern Clocks* by George White, Antique Collectors' Club, 1989).

There were other makers located in towns throughout the country, but the Aspinwalls, of Toxteth Park, near Liverpool, who made watches from the very beginning of the century, were the most notable. Thomas (see Plate 4), who lived until 1623 was succeeded by his son Samuel who was a reasonably wealthy man by the time he died in 1672. John Griffiths (*Antiquarian Horology,* December 2002) shows that the trade was firmly established in Toxteth by the middle of the century, and was supplying tools to watchmakers outside the area, as well as completed watches. By the late 1600s South West Lancashire was the most important centre for watchmakers and their specialist suppliers outside London.

THE 'BOX' AND CASE

Some early records, one a 1591 court case, refer to watch cases as 'boxes' and their makers as 'boxmakers'. Manuscripts belonging to the Clockmakers' Company show that it used this terminology from its foundation, in 1631. A list of members of the trade and their skills working in the City of London was drawn up on 26 June 1662 giving the names of a number of box makers. When the box was given a protective outer it was called a case. At the beginning it was generally leather or leather-covered and supplied by men who no doubt also made cases for any number of items. With the increasing use of metal in the case, the box and watch case making disciplines converged and, by the beginning of the eighteenth century 'case makers' made both, and the term 'box' was used far less frequently. Today they are referred to as the 'inner case' and the 'outer case', the two together as 'pair-cases', and the watch having both as a 'pair-cased' watch.

It would appear that few, if any, cases were marked by their makers, or hallmarked. The earliest mark so far recorded is on a gold case by Nathaniel Delander – the watch being by Robert Seignor – which cannot be any earlier really than 1675, and the earliest hallmark is for 1683 on a gold watch by Thomas Tompion. Philip Priestley explores the reasons why the case makers failed to conform to hallmarking laws and the Goldsmiths' Company practices in his excellent *Early Watch Case Makers of England* (NAWCC Inc., 2000).

THE CASE AND ITS DECORATION

A substantial reduction of the size of watches, both in width – often less than 30mm – and depth had been achieved shortly before 1630. They were made so that they could be suspended from the neck or waist band and, so as to hang well, were mostly oval or of a shape which had a low centre of gravity. They continued to be engraved with mythical and religious subjects during the first few years, but the small flowers within scrolling foliage, which generally had been adjuncts to the main scenes hitherto, became an increasingly important part of the overall decoration. The flowers and foliage began to be more naturalistic by 1640, or shortly before. By this date cases were increasingly left plain but, when they were engraved, it was very often with quite large and fleshy flowers, these formally arranged with their stems running south to north (Plate 22). Tulip flowers began to be a predominant feature of the design; this became more free-flowing in the 1650s, and the flowers more open and voluptuous during the 1660s (Plates 38 and 44). Engraved gilt-metal cases with rock crystal covers were popular between the mid-1630s and mid-1650s (Plates 17, 23 and 34), while a few enamel cased watches survive from the period 1640 to 1665 (Plates 24, 35 and 39). All watches were supplied with an outer case which was either leather covered, silver or silver-gilt. By 1640 many watches had rock crystal fitted to the front cover – with the advantage that the cover did not have to be lifted for the time to be read.

If the reduction in size meant watches had become less robust, it also meant they were small enough to wear with an outer case. In time the inner case – generally silver – was, typically, left plain without decoration, and had a winding shutter to cover the hole giving access to the winding square. Terminals were found to be an unnecessary adjunct although, initially, small ones were retained to make a good fit with the outer case. Increasingly, the outer cases too were made with the front cut to show the dial. Fashion during the years leading up to the Civil War of 1642 became increasingly sober; not only did this affect the watches' design, but in time they were worn less as pendants and were carried more modestly – and safely – in a pocket.

Cases were, in general, formed – the band, back and bezel being made from the strip and joined – but a few were cast from a single mould. Difficult shapes could be made by using the casting method and, of course, patterns and designs could be incorporated. Some cases were cast in the form of a tulip bud from around 1640

(Plate 32), and a few in other shapes (Plate 25), but mostly circular, up to about 1660. Cast **pendants** were made, typically with acanthus leaf decoration or, later, in the form of a tulip bud, but turned, round pendants were in general use after about 1650.

Once watches were consigned to a pocket, it was no doubt found that, not only was it easier to handle them if they were circular and a little larger but also, although they still ran for less than twenty-four hours, they were somewhat more reliable and better timekeepers. So their size increased progressively from about 1640. From having an outer case measuring, typically, 35mm across, by the 1660s it was invariably circular and generally in excess of 50mm. Watches became deeper towards the end of the period when, for a better performance and longer running time, the heights of the mainspring and fusee were increased.

Instead of rock crystal held in by tags, or a retaining ring (Plate 20), from about the middle of the century a domed glass, held in a groove of a split bezel, was fitted to the front of the inner case. Occasionally the outer cases were made of silver or, more rarely, silver-gilt, typically with a flat edge (Plates 20 and 23). However, most were of base metal with a rounded edge covered in leather and decorated with pins and having bezels matching the material – silver or gilt-metal – of the inner case (Plates 28 and 45). Gold, rather than gilt pins, were sometimes used.

Cases of gold and enamel are rare, as are plain gold cases up to 1675. A few large watches – coach watches – with striking and alarm mechanisms were made, particularly, it seems, in the late 1650s and 1660s (Plates 36 and 38). The band of the inner, invariably silver, case was pierced in order that the bell should be heard clearly. The outer cases, which measured up to about 100mm, were generally of leather-covered metal with pin-work decoration.

THE DIAL AND HAND

Until the late 1630s the dial was either engraved gilt brass with an applied silver chapter ring or, increasingly, engraved silver applied on a gilt brass surround. Initially the centres were generally engraved with mythical and religious subjects or rural scenes, with only the borders decorated with small, rather tight, scrolling foliage and flowers (Plates 17 and 18). At the end of the decade they had largely been superseded by densely packed flowers – typically, for instance, sunflowers, peonies, marigolds and anemones – and foliage. This work became more naturalistic and open while, from around 1640, designs with larger and fleshier flower heads appeared, at first quite formally arranged with the stems running south to north (Plates 22, 25, 31 and 32). By the 1660s the flowers had become still larger, more blowzy and were predominantly tulips, but also daffodils, and generally on a hatched ground (Plates 34, 36 and 38). One-piece silver dials were now standard, whether fully engraved or left plain with little or no decoration.

In the main, star **half-hour divisions** had been dropped by 1630, but the heart-shape pattern continued to be popular for the next decade and, when quarter-hour divisions were applied – as they were by about 1640 – the base of the heart was elongated into a stroke. This design sometimes has a short extension from the centre of the heart towards the edge of the dial and a further elaboration has what appears to be a pair of leaves below a flower head. Arrow heads – mostly pointing inwards, but sometimes outwards – were in frequent use throughout the period. The 'T' form seems to have fallen out of favour by 1650, while the fleur-de-lis was used very occasionally from the beginning.

After 1660 a few watches were given a date ring on the edge of the dial with a revolving pointer or 'bug' to indicate the relevant date (Plates 40, 42 and 43), while others had a central alarm disc (Plates 36 and 38) which could be set as required. Some bi-metal dials were made, the gilt-brass centre being overlaid with silver filigree (Plate 43).

Fully engraved dials were made for some years after the Restoration, but they were slowly superseded by champlevé dials on which any decoration was modest, rather stylised and restricted to the very centre (Plates 45, 46 and 47). Until the 1670s hands needed to be set with the finger, but from then on they were generally mounted on a square long enough so that it could be set with a key. Length became no longer necessary; indeed, if it were short not only was there less for the mechanism to drive, but the owner would not be so tempted to use his finger, loosen the hand, break it or cause damage to the dial. Thus, it was not just a change in fashion when, right at the end of the period, the chapters became noticeably longer, and the size of the inner ring, generally showing the hour, half-hour and quarter-hour divisions, was reduced towards the centre of the dial (Plates 45, 46 and 47). A few watches were made to show minutes and these were marked towards the edge of the dial (Plates 40, 41 and 42).

From about 1660, Continental makers occasionally fitted enamel dials to quite ordinary watches but, with very few exceptions, English watchmakers did not, only, it would seem, fitting them to a few special watches such as those with enamel cases.

Hands were double-ended and almost always of blued steel. Generally the head was either arrow-shaped, the point in the direction of the numerals, or in the form of a simple open flower head, with a short, frequently cross-ribbed, extension to indicate the time – often redolent of some classical images of the lotus flower – see, for example, the columns at the temple of Amun at Karnak, and the much illustrated neck ornament from a column at the temple of Apollo, Naukratis (James Curl, *Egyptian Revival*, George Allen & Unwin, 1982, page 16, figure 1c). During the 1650s and 1660s a few hands were shaped with turning at both ends and had no head. The majority were riveted to a pipe, some pinned to a square, these friction tight with the motion work. When, in the 1670s, the square was made long enough for the hand to be set with a key, there were clear advantages, mentioned above, if it were not so long, or indeed thick. On small watches these short hands were quite often headless. Moreover, with the exception of alarm watches, their tails were made proportionally very much shorter or omitted entirely. The tail had lost its primary function; it was no longer required to help in the manual setting of the hand.

THE MECHANISM

The basic mechanical design in 1630 was broadly the same as that established by the earliest watchmakers. There was a mainspring with a ratchet and click set-up, a gut line and fusee, a three wheel train, a steel two-arm balance and verge escapement – which was to be the only form of escapement for another hundred years. Initially, the preoccupation seems to have been with the making of the small size movements, fashionable from the very late 1620s. The diameter increased progressively from about 1640, there was some improvement in train counts, quality and finish and timekeeping improved somewhat. Certainly, the worm and wheel form of mainspring set-up (Plate 31), which slowly took the place of the ratchet and click (Plates 17 and 20) from about 1640, must have made for closer regulation. However, until the end of the 1660s the vast majority of watches still had three wheel trains and needed winding twice in twenty-four hours. The increase in size made it possible to add a fourth wheel to the movement train; it was now practical to raise the train count, and that of the fusee drive pinion, so the running time could now be twenty-six hours or more. A stronger mainspring was needed, so its height was increased, as was that of the fusee which required a more substantial gut line. Reliability and timekeeping improved further and watches ran for twenty-six hours, sometimes more. Finally, it was found difficult to fit gut line of adequate thickness securely to the fusee, and during the 1670s it was replaced by a chain (Plate 45). A few small striking and alarm watches are known. Those that strike and are of small or medium size are called 'clock-watches', while larger ones, in general, 'travelling' or 'coach' watches. It seems the majority were made in the 1660s. The locking plate for the striking mechanism and the stop-work for the alarm were invariably of blued steel and mounted on the top plate (Plates 36, 38 and 47).

Various forms of script were used for the **signature** on the top plate. The maker's name, preceded by his, often abbreviated, Christian name, was followed by the place name or, quite frequently, 'Fecit' – both only rarely. The thickening of each of the first letters in a signature was popular with many makers from about 1650 onwards. Slowly, but beginning shortly before 1640, rather than pinning the **cock** through a square in the neck – that is, between the foot and the table – on to a block in the top plate (Plates 17 and 20), watchmakers started to screw it on through the foot, this now having a steady pin into the plate (Plates 37 and 43). A few makers, however, initially retained the block while using the screw. Substantial necks continued to be incorporated in cock design, becoming gradually smaller only over time. At the beginning of the period the cock foot was generally short, becoming larger and frequently ovoid as watch sizes increased. The table was normally oval or nearly so. Both were pierced and, invariably, had foliate engraving while the table had an 'S' incorporated within the design frequently engraved to be a dolphin or serpent (a few very early watches had, of course, simple 'S' tables, a shape which could be easily adjusted to change the position of the verge and its end shake).

Around 1640 top plate border engraving, typical of many English, though not exclusively English, watches, gradually disappeared and the baluster, or vase-shaped, **pillar** (Plate 20) gave way to the 'early Egyptian' (Plate 43), which had been used occasionally, in either a divided or solid form, from about 1620. It was the most popular by far until the 1660s, when it was superseded by a number of floriate designs often referred to collectively as 'early tulip'. Typically, the body is delicately pierced-out with scroll-work and the outline is vase-shaped with a bell-shaped base (Plate 44). The classic tulip pillar – a narrow body with a distinctive waist to an open top – did not appear until the 1680s.

TIMEKEEPING

Although watches were clearly useful adjuncts to domestic and church clocks and sundials, their effectiveness was limited, particularly during the first part of the period. Not only was it necessary to wind them twice in every twenty-four hours, but the fashion for small watches in the 1630s and 1640s would have contributed to their unreliability. When they ran well they were within, maybe, ten minutes either way for each winding. The gradual increase in size, train counts and quality of finish would have made for a better performance, but it was from about the mid-1660s, when the wheel train was designed in such a way that the running time was in excess of twenty-four hours, that a significant step was made towards a practical watch. Timekeeping of five or so minutes between windings was probably achieved by the end of the period. The following anonymous humorous admonition from *Westminster Drollery*, dated 1671, might indicate that by this time watches were in everyday use. It is included by C.A.O. Fox in his 1947 privately printed *An Anthology of Clocks and Watches*.

On a Watch Lost In a Tavern

A watch lost in a tavern. That's a crime;
Then see how men by drinking lose their time.

Henceforth if you will keep your watch, this do –
Pocket your Watch and watch your pocket too.

THE CLOCKMAKERS' COMPANY

The Company gained its charter in 1631. Reference is made to the period building up to this event in the previous chapter. Samuel Atkins and William Overall in their *Some Account of the Worshipful Company of Clockmakers,* privately printed in 1881, give a good and detailed history, Brian Loomes in his *The Early Clockmakers of Great Britain* has a useful synopsis of the Company's organisation and George White in *English Lantern Clocks* covers some very interesting aspects of the Company's history and its vicissitudes during this period. A good number of makers who signed lantern clocks also signed watches.

Plate 17. Edward East.
Gilt-metal and rock crystal case 30mm wide

The Victoria & Albert Museum have an unusual gourd or marrow-shaped gilt metal watch of about **1635** which is signed on the top plate 'Edwardus East Londini'. The **case** back and front covers are of rock crystal which has been cut with naturalistic lobes. The **dial** centre is engraved with the Adoration, while outside the applied silver chapter ring there are buds and flower heads amongst foliate scrolls. Above twelve there is a female nude holding two attributes of Time, the scythe and hourglass, the scythe being the attribute of the Greek god of agriculture, Cronus, from which the figure of Father Time is derived. It is possible that the figure is intended as an allegorical figure of Truth, but otherwise the engraver may be demonstrating the transient nature of beauty, or simply engraving a nude and attaching the symbols of Time because he is engraving a watch dial. The link between Cronus and the form of the case may well be coincidental, and so too if the shape is intended to be a marrow's, but the marrow can suggest birth and the seeds of new life when it is associated with a scene of the Adoration.

The **movement**, which swings out on the case hinge from the front, follows the shape of the case. The pinned-on cock is pierced and engraved and the brass set-up click is decorated in a similar manner. There is a steel two-arm balance, verge, gut fusee, three-wheel train and round baluster pillars.

This is a relatively early watch for a man who became the most famous maker of his time. He lived between 1602 and 1697.

Actual size.

THE VICTORIA & ALBERT MUSEUM, LONDON

Plate 18. John Smeaton, York.

Gilt-metal and rock crystal case 52 x 30mm   circa 1640

Provincial watches from this period are, of course, rare. This octagonal gilt-metal and rock crystal cased watch, which is signed on the top plate 'John Smeaton in Yorke', was in the Sandberg Collection.

    The multi-faceted crystal on the back of the **case** is very deep so that, in order for the watch to hang well, the fixed pendant needs to be long. This arrangement, together with the overall style of the case (the pendant's acanthus leaf decoration in particular) and dial, suggests a date prior to 1640. Riveted to the **dial** is a narrow silver chapter ring which has half- but no quarter-hour markings. The head of the hand is of a floriate design. A rural scene is engraved in the centre, and amongst foliate scrolls the torso of a winged figure is above twelve. Below six, on either side of the movement catch, there is a pair of what are probably rabbits, suggesting fecundity but also wealth.

    Although the **movement** has clearly been made for the case and dial, it has elements which suggest the watch took some years to complete, possibly owing to the disruption to trade caused by the Civil War. It has a worm and wheel set-up, a screwed on cock, and early Egyptian pillars. John Smeaton would have been active prior to being granted his freedom of the city in 1646.   PRIVATE COLLECTION

Actual size.

Actual size.

Plate 19. Edward East.

Gilt-metal and rock crystal case 26.5 x 43mm

A remarkably small watch, made probably between **1635** and **1640**, of excellent quality where it seems nothing has been lost to miniaturization. The maximum width of the lobed gilt metal case is 26.5mm, and the length, without the loose ring but including the pendant and terminal, is only 43mm.

The **case** rock crystals, both back and front, are well cut and have a high degree of translucence. Radiating facets from small, slightly dished, centres suggest flower heads. The inner edges of the bezel and body have simple palm-leaf engraving. The **dial** has a townscape, which has a river and gnarled tree in the foreground; outside the applied silver chapter ring, which has quarter-hour markings, there is a profusion of flowers and fruit and a putto's head above twelve. The blued steel hand has a floriate – lotus – head, and the tail is elaborately turned.

The **movement** is signed in full, 'Edwardus East Londini'. The cock is pinned on, there is a ratchet and click set-up, a gut fusee, a three wheel train, verge, a two-arm balance and the pillars are turned balusters. PRIVATE COLLECTION

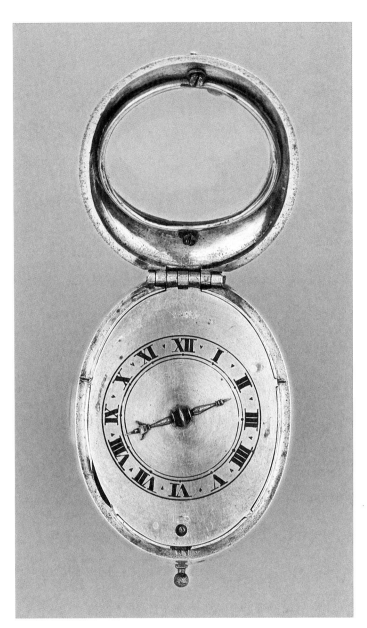

Plate 20. David Bouquet.

Silver cases 30 x 49mm excluding bow and outer case

Completely devoid of any decorative engraving on the silver dial and cases, this is a typical 'Puritan' watch – a name given to the style in the nineteenth century. It has a number of characteristics which suggest it is from the **mid-1630s**: the **dial** has no quarter-hour divisions, which were in common use by the end of the decade, the inner **case** has a short terminal, a feature which was soon dropped (it is of polished steel and locates in a hole in the silver outer) and the **movement's** ratchet and click and pinned-on cock are typical of the decade.

The rock crystal 'glass' is held on the underside of the cover by a brass rim secured by

Actual size.

two steel screws. The head of the hand is of a distinctive floriate design. The top plate is signed 'D Bouquet Londres', there are baluster pillars and a three-wheeled train. Bouquet, of French origin, was working in Blackfriars from before 1622. He seems to have generally signed both his lantern clocks and watches in French. Two of his sons and a grandson are recorded as following in the trade.

This watch was in the Webster Collection, is illustrated in the *Camerer Cuss Book of Antique Watches* and was shown at the tenth anniversary exhibition of the Antiquarian Horological Society.

PRIVATE COLLECTION

Plate 21. Edmund Bull.
Silver case 32 x 43mm excluding bow and leather-covered
outer case   circa 1635

A very similar 'Puritan' watch to that illustrated above by
David Bouquet and of about the same date, but with a
leather outer case. Subtle differences can be seen between
the designs of the floriate hands and the half-hour divisions.

The rock crystal lunette is also held in place by a screwed
brass ring on the underside of the cover, while the movement

has the same specification. The signature reads, rather
charmingly, 'Edmund Bull me Fecit'. A member of the
Blacksmiths' Company, Edmund Bull, together with his former
master, Robert Grinkin, was one of the 1622 Petitioners for a
Company of Clockmakers, but for some reason did not become
a member when the Company was founded in 1631.

PRIVATE COLLECTION

Opposite: Plate 22. John Midnall.
Silver cases 22.9 x 36.7mm

The charm of this tiny watch is revealed as it is removed from its
plain silver outer **case**. The engraving is all over the inner case
and matched on the dial. This type of floral engraving reached
Britain from the Continent around **1640**, about the date of the
watch. The flower heads are large and fleshy but, as can be seen
on the back, quite formally arranged around a central stem
running north to south. The layout on the **dial** of the watch by
Masterson illustrated in Plate 25 is not dissimilar. Later the trend
was for the blooms to be more voluptuous, looser and, after the
Commonwealth period, almost blowzy. The chapter ring has

features one would expect of the 1630s rather than 1640s:
heart-shaped half-hour and no quarter-hour divisions.

The **movement** has a ratchet and click set-up, pinned-on
cock and an engraved border around some two-thirds of the
top plate leaving space for the signature – 'John Midnall in
fleet street Fecit'. There are pierced-out early Egyptian pillars.

John Midnall was one of the first Assistants of the
Clockmakers' Company and a Warden in 1635. A watch by
him, said to have belonged to Oliver Cromwell, is in the
British Museum.

THE PATEK PHILIPPE MUSEUM, GENEVA

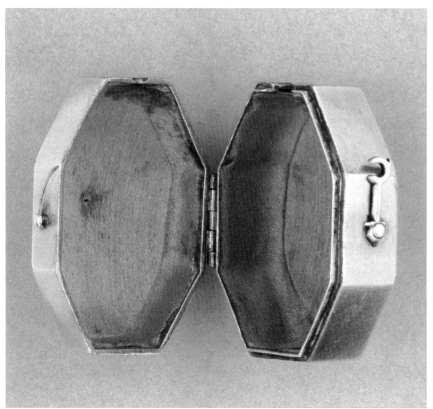

Actual size.

Plate 23. Gold, enamel and rock crystal case.

23 x 45mm excluding outer case   circa 1640

Not many enamel cased watches have survived and a proportionally large number of these have had the original mechanism removed and, as on this occasion, replaced by an especially made movement. The original octagonal dial plate has been retained and the oval movement, signed by the eighteenth century maker David Hubert, has been made to mimic, to some extent, the one of about 1640 which it has replaced. It is probable that all watches of this period – certainly those in rock crystal – would have had a protective outer case; this watch has one in silver gilt.

Some of the quality and technical diversity in the enamelling of the period is to be found on the dial and case, both of which are gold. The front cover and back are of rock crystal while the pendant and bezels are decorated in opaque white and turquoise enamel. The inside edge of the case and the underside of the cover have borders of translucent green enamel. Surrounding the gold chapter ring on a white ground are flower heads in blue, green and orange/brown opaque and translucent cloisonné and champlevé enamel, the dark spikes being painted on. The single open flower in the dial centre is executed in the same way. The blued steel double-ended floriate hand is typical of the period.   PRIVATE COLLECTION

Plate 24. William Partridge.

Gold and enamel case 29.5mm   circa 1640-45

Actual size.

Formerly in the Beyer Collection, this small gold and enamel watch signed 'William Partridge Fecit' is decorated in a similar manner – using a combination of cloisonné, champlevé and painting-on techniques – as the octagonal case also illustrated (Plate 23). Partridge joined the Clockmakers' Company as a Brother in 1640 having trained with someone who was not a member. The *Domestic Series* of the '*Calendar of State Papers*' records his appeal of May 1660 to Charles II in which he asked to be restored as Royal Clockmaker on the basis that he had served his father, had attended the King as clockmaker when at Oxford in 1645 and had fought for him during the war. His wife petitioned at the same time, claiming her husband had spent much time in France and Flanders improving himself in his trade when not under arms on the King's behalf or in prison. These entreaties were unsuccessful.

No other watch signed by William Partridge appears to be recorded; he is thought to have had some form of working relationship with Edward East. The design used for the enamel decoration, the lack of quarter-hour divisions, combined with what is known of the maker's career, suggest that this watch was probably made some time in the early 1640s. It has close similarities to contemporary French work of the Blois school, in particular the enamel case and the style of the movement cock.   PRIVATE COLLECTION

Plate 25. Richard Masterson.

Silver case 30 x 57mm   circa 1640-50

The **case** is cast in silver in the form of a scallop shell, the dial cover and back having identical decoration of polished ribs against a matt ground, but the back having a delightful shell-shaped winding shutter. The pendant, which is somewhat like a flower bud and is of a type often referred to as a tulip pendant, is balanced by a well-turned terminal.

The type of shading on the flower heads, which are larger and more varied than those found before about 1640, gives a good three-dimensional effect. Those heads in the **dial** centre are arranged vertically and emanate from stems above six o'clock in a quite formal manner, while the tight scrolls hark back to earlier work. The layout on case and dial of the watch by Midnall illustrated in Plate 22 is not dissimilar. The rondels at nine and three are to be found on the dial of a watch made in the

Commonwealth period by Thomas Alcock, also illustrated (Plate 31). The red numerals, half and quarter divisions make for an attractive contrast and the floriate – lotus – hand is blued steel.

'Richard Masterson Fecit' is in script across the top plate of the **movement** and there is a ratchet and click set-up, a pinned-on cock and early Egyptian pillars.

Masterson was a subscriber for the incorporation of the Clockmakers' Company. This watch was made between about the time he was Master in 1642 and his death in 1653. Of course, not many watches were made during the war years. It was in the Sandberg Collection. A similar one by the same maker, which may be a little earlier but is not in such superb condition, was at one time in the Nelthropp Collection and is now owned by the Clockmakers' Company. PRIVATE COLLECTION

Plate 26. William Judd.

Silver case 35mm

The Adoration of the Magi is on the front cover of the **case** and the Presentation to the Temple Elders is on the back. The scenes are surrounded by tight scrolling foliage and flowers and this is continued on the band. The silver **dial** has half- and quarter-hour divisions and the decoration in the centre echoes that on the case, the predominant scrolls being worked upwards to the left and right from six o'clock. The dial design, the shape and character of the case and the form of mainspring set-up – worm and wheel – suggest this watch was likely to have been made in the late **1640s** or early **1650s**. The short terminal at the base of the case would have helped locate the watch in a protective **outer**.

The top plate of the **movement** is signed 'William Judd, Fecit'. The cock is, unusually, of silver and there are early Egyptian pillars. It appears this maker is not recorded.

PRIVATE COLLECTION

Actual size.

Plate 27. Henry Grendon.
Silver-gilt and rock crystal case and leather outer case
28 x 38mm including pendant   circa 1640-50

This was given to the Royal Family in 1928 by a descendant of Jane Lane who, according to family tradition, received it as a gift from Charles II after he had stayed with her brother at Bentley Hall, Wolverhampton, for a few days, following his defeat at the Battle of Worcester in 1651.

Henry Grendon was working prior to his admission to the Clockmakers' Company as a Free Brother in 1640. He was made an Assistant in 1646, but there is no later record of him – probably because of the Civil War and its effects, particularly on those with royalist connections – and he is likely to have escaped abroad.

The silver gilt octagonal **case** has deep rock crystal covers and tulip style pendant. The sides are very nearly equal, making the watch proportionally shorter than earlier octagonal watches. There is an excellent outer decorated with pin-work. The **dial**, also silver gilt, is typical of the period a little after 1640 when, as can

Actual size.

be seen from the engraving in the centre, flowers were formally arranged, but were now larger, open and quite voluptuous. Shading was effected, not by cross-hatching, but only lengthways in the direction of the flowers' growth. The design of the floriate hand is echoed in the half-hour divisions on the outside of a quarter-hour ring.

The oval **movement**, signed 'Henry Grendon at ye Exchange Fecit', follows the shape of the dial plate. The thickening of the first letter of each word of the signature was a style popular with many makers over the next twenty years or so. There is a pinned-on cock and worm and wheel set-up.

Actual size.

Plate 28. Samuel Shelton.

Silver inner, leather-covered outer case 31 x 39mm including pendant

Shelton was heavily involved in the formation of the Clockmakers' Company, being Treasurer of the successful petition for a charter, one of the first three Wardens in 1631, and the Company's second Master in 1634.

He was Master again in 1638 and died ten years later. This charming little watch was probably made in the **early 1640s**, most likely before the Civil War was at its most disruptive and the outbreak of the plague in London in 1646. Traces of gilding are to be found on the silver **case** to match the pin-work on the outer. There is a ring pendant and bow, a

winding shutter, and the crystal is fixed from the underside of the cover with a screwed brass ring. The quarter-hour divisions are marked on the **dial** – typical of the period after 1640 – and there is a large, possibly anemone, flower head in the centre and another small head at the catch. The tail of the beautifully made floriate hand has cross-ribbing.

The **movement**, signed 'Sam Shelton, Fecit', has a florally engraved screwed-on cock and worm and wheel set-up. The early Egyptian pillars are engraved with drapery and are very pretty.

PRIVATE COLLECTION

Actual size.

Plate 29. Guliemus Godbed.

Gilt metal and rock crystal case 50mm overall   late 1640s

An octagonal gilt metal watch with rock crystal covers, the **dial** having a phase
of the moon aperture within a central astrolabic dial, the hours and quarters,
the age of moon and a separate outer date ring. The additional complexity has
made for a deep movement as well as **case** – this has a broad silver band
engraved with scrolling foliage and flower heads. There is a fixed foliate
pendant which is necessarily quite large, no terminal and a silver protective
outer.

The **movement**, which is signed 'Guliemus Godbed, Lombard Street,
Londini', has a screwed-on cock, worm and wheel set-up and early
Egyptian pillars. William Godbed is recorded as being apprenticed in
1638 and a Freeman of the Clockmakers' Company in 1646. Judging by
the overall style, in particular the engraving, this watch was completed
prior to 1650. It was in the Marryat Collection.   PRIVATE COLLECTION

Plate 30. Jeremy East.

Silver case and leather-covered outer 35mm   circa 1640

At one time this small silver watch was in the Marryat Collection. The signature, which reads 'Jeremia East Fecit', is more than likely to be that of Edward East's brother Jeremy – who sometimes signed himself 'Jeremie East Fecit' – and not Jeremiah East's, who is recorded as serving his apprenticeship between 1653 and 1661.

The **dial** centre has a townscape with a fisherman in the foreground, a scene commonly found on watches made in the early 1630s and before, but the engraving is more three-dimensional and employs techniques which were in common use only from about 1640. Moreover the quarter divisions – the numerals are filled red rather than black – suggest the watch should be dated 1640 or, indeed, a little later.

Actual size.

The **movement**, with round baluster pillars, a pinned-on silver cock and a ratchet and click set-up is redolent of the period before the Civil War. The inner **case** has a ring pendant and bow, and the glass (formerly crystal) is held in by a screwed brass ring. The outer is covered with leather and silver pin-work.   PRIVATE COLLECTION

Plate 31. Thomas Alcock.

Silver case 40mm   circa 1650

A watch from the very beginning of the Commonwealth period, made at the end of Alcock's working life when circular watches had become the norm and their average size was increasing.

The plain **case** has a small steel stud at the base to help secure the watch in an outer, and an old style (Julian) calendar is engraved on the inside of the cover. The **dial** has six different flower heads formally arranged, quarter-hour and long half-hour divisions and a band of rondels outside the chapter ring. There is a floriate hand.

'Tho. Alcock Fecit' is engraved in a semi-circle on the **movement** top plate. The pinned-on cock is well engraved with some of the same flowers as those found on the dial. There is a worm and wheel set-up and early Egyptian pillars.

PRIVATE COLLECTION

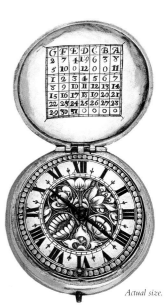

Actual size.

Actual size.

Plate 32. John Drake.
Silver case 41mm wide

Cast in the form of a tulip bud, the **case** halves to reveal the **dial** that is engraved with a variety of flowers on a strongly hatched ground and well-defined quarter- and half-hour divisions. The pendant is also in the form of a bud. The **movement**, which is signed 'John Drake in fleet street', has a screwed-on cock, a ratchet and click set-up, and baluster-shaped pillars. This watch was made probably in the **early 1650s**.

Tulips were – and are, of course – a well-loved flower. The price of tulip bulbs boomed in the 1630s only to implode at the end of the decade. Fortunes were made and lost. The centre of the 'tulipomania' market in England was at the Royal Exchange.

Drake would appear to have had a long career, having become a Freeman in the Blacksmiths' Company in 1605, a subscriber to the Clockmakers' in 1630 and active until after 1660. Also he seems to have been a little irascible for when, in 1654, he was forced to pay fifteen years of quarterage arrears, he referred to a Warden as a 'turd and a shitten fellow'. PRIVATE COLLECTION

Plate 33. Richard Crayle.   circa 1650

Silver case 34 x 42mm, leather-covered outer 37 x 48mm

A mid-century 'Puritan' watch, the leather-covered outer **case** decorated with gilt tooling, having the feel of a somewhat later date than those by David Bouquet and Edmund Bull (Plates 20 and 21). It is a little larger, and the **dial** has full quarter-hour divisions. The **movement** is of the same general specification: the cock is pinned-on, the set-up is a ratchet and click, and the pillars are vase-shaped balusters. It is signed 'Richard Crayle in Fleetstreet'.

Crayle was apparently never a member of the Clock-makers' Company, but was believed to have been a member of the Blacksmiths' by 1651. He is recorded as working in Fleet Street in 1662 and later, in 1676, 'at the Black Boy in the Strand near the Savoy'. This watch was in the Ruscitti Collection, sold by Antiquorum, Geneva in 2001. Another by this maker in the form of a tulip bud, and very similar to that in Plate 32 by John Drake, also of Fleet Street, was in the Time Museum, Illinois.   Private Collection

Plate 34. Edward East.

Gilt metal and rock crystal case 30 x 48mm   circa 1650

Pendant watches from the Commonwealth period are scarce because by the early 1650s watches were made to be worn in some form of pocket.

Rock crystals at both the front and back have radiating facets, which emanate from small, slightly dished, centres, matched by the edges of the gilt metal **case**. Shorter, subsidiary lobes are cut on the facets, giving the overall impression of flower heads much like, it has been suggested, the petalody of chrysanthemums. The pendant is slightly oval and quite plain, while the terminal is turned and of some length.

The flowers in the centre of the applied silver **dial**, among them daffodils and a variety of tulips, are seen from differing aspects and loosely arranged. The subtle and clever shading runs in the direction of growth of the stems, leaves and flowers, and gives a very good three-dimensional effect. Comparison can be made with the slightly earlier watches illustrated by Richard Masterson, Henry Grendon and John Drake (Plates 25, 27 and 32). There are quarter- and half-hour divisions and a good floriate hand. The exposed area of dial plate is engraved in the same manner with a similar variety of flowers.

The **movement** is signed 'Edward East Londini'. It has a pinned-on cock, worm and wheel set-up and engraved early divided Egyptian pillars.

PRIVATE COLLECTION

Actual size.

77

Actual size.

Plate 35. Edward East.

Gold and enamel case 30mm   circa 1650

Small gold and opaque and translucent polychrome enamel watch, the **case** and **dial** fully decorated with large flower heads and foliage, these arranged on a white ground so that the gold stems originate from six o'clock. Both cloisonné and champlevé enamelling techniques have been used. The gold chapter ring has quarter- and half-hour divisions, and the engraved gilt brass hand is quite typical of those found on mid-seventeenth century watches.

There is a plain silver outer protecting case, normal for the period. Signed 'Edward East Fecit', the **movement** has a worm and wheel set-up, a screwed-on cock and baluster pillars.

When the Time Museum purchased this watch from Christie's in June 1981 the catalogue stated: 'By descent through a family of title in Ireland. According to family tradition, given by Charles I on the scaffold at his execution to Bishop Juxon' and also noted an entry in a book of 1905 and an exhibition catalogue of

1943, each supporting the view that the watch had belonged to the King. As Cedric Jagger reports on pages 248 and 249 of his *Royal Clocks,* 'While this beautiful watch could certainly be described as of "royal" quality, there is sadly no proof whatever of such antecedents.' Moreover, the style of the watch suggests a few years after 1649. Family traditions, however, have often some truth to them and, maybe if it did not belong to the King, it might for instance have belonged to the Bishop who, for whatever reason, regarded it as some sort of memento.   PRIVATE COLLECTION

Plate 36. Edward East.
Silver inner and leather-covered outer case 95mm

A coach watch with hour striking and alarm, possibly from the late 1650s but more probably the early **1660s**, which demonstrates the variety and continuing importance of the work of Edward East.

The leather-covered outer **case** is decorated with floriate pin-work and two rows of 'portholes', one around the front bezel and the other the back, to allow for sound emission. The bell is housed in the back of the inner case, which is pierced and engraved with a continuous band of flowers – including daffodils and tulips – and foliage between two rows of palmettes.

The **dial** centre, which is engraved and has a profusion of large, closely ordered flowers, revolves with the hand head – pointer or 'bug' – on its perimeter indicating the time against the Roman numerals. The central hand is set against the Arabic numerals and, when the alarm spring is wound, the alarm will ring when it and the selected hour reach XII. When not required, the alarm hand can be aligned with the hour pointer creating in effect a complete hour hand.

On the top plate of the **movement** there are a pinned-on cock and balance, a worm and wheel set-up, a silver locking plate for the striking and stop-work for the striking and alarm trains, and little room is left for the signature, 'Edwardus East'. The Victoria & Albert Museum has a similar, possibly slightly later watch, with 'Londini' squeezed in. There are tulip pillars. PRIVATE COLLECTION

Plate 37. Richard Bowen.

Silver cases 58mm   circa 1660

The concentric astronomical, calendar and time indications from the edge of the exceptional **dial** are: months and number of days in the month, date, hours, age of moon, twice times twelve hours and, in the centre, an age of moon aperture within a fixed night sky.

The **movement** is particularly well finished. It has an attractive signature, 'Richard Bowen Londini Fecit', the screwed-on cock is decorated with flower heads and the worm and wheel set-up has fine steel-work. There are early Egyptian pillars.

The engraving on the outer **case** is a quite faithful, if somewhat naïve, copy of that by William Marshall (1617-1649) produced immediately after Charles I was executed in 1649 and used as a frontispiece of *Eikon Basilike* published the same year. Richard Bowen was free of his apprenticeship in 1657. It is most likely the engraving was done about the same time as the watch was made or soon after the Restoration of the monarchy in 1660 and before Bowen's premises were burnt down during the Great Fire in 1666.

Certainly the large flower heads framing the scene are commensurate with this period. On the back of the inner case a young man in doublet and hose listens to a figure in a heavenly cloud whose words are engraved within a ribbon – 'And what I sai to you, I sai to all, watch' – suggesting Charles II being encouraged by his father. One imagines this may have been some sort of rallying cry for royalists during the Civil War – they should watch, not lose heart, and be ready! In any event, double meanings in general and the guardedness that they afforded had, no doubt, been especially popular and continued to be so.

This was part of the extensive collection formed by Ralph Bernal which Christie's dispersed in March 1855 (lot 3920). The catalogue noted 'This watch is said to have been given by Charles I to Colonel Hammond, at Carisbrooke' – clearly a case of nineteenth century romanticism. *Eikon Basilike* proved very popular; it was reprinted many times and republished even in the eighteenth century.   PRIVATE COLLECTION

Actual size.

Plate 38. David Bouquet.
Silver case 120mm

A magnificent coach watch with striking and alarm mechanisms made between about **1660** and **1665**, the year of Bouquet's death. The **dial** is arranged the same way as the watch of about the same date by East also illustrated (Plate 36), the floriate pointer indicating the time while the alarm function is via the central hand. Along with the numerals, a wax or pitch fills the ground of the tightly packed flower heads in the dial centre.

The workmanship on the back of the **case** is outstanding and, at the time it was made, the overall imagery would have been perceived as extremely exotic. Six panels, each with a parrot amongst foliage and flowers, are divided by pillars with drapery, Ionic capitals and human heads.

The **movement** top plate, which measures approximately 103mm, is signed 'D Bouquet Londini'. The count wheel for the striking, the hammer head and the worm and wheel regulator disc are silver engraved and filled. The screwed-on cock is also of silver while the stop-work for the alarm and striking trains are of blued steel.

This watch in the Royal Collection is said to have been given to William IV by Countess Howe and that he was fond of using it.

Plate 39. David Bouquet

Gold and enamel case 46.5mm

A Huguenot, Bouquet was working in the trade before the foundation of the Clockmakers' Company which he joined in 1632. He was very successful, taking on a number of apprentices, including his son Solomon, and was active until 1665, or shortly before. He is known to have returned to France at least once during his working life and to have employed at least two journeymen from there.

The exterior of the gold **case** is decorated with exquisitely painted naturalistic flowers in relief enamel on a black enamel ground; the cover is also set with diamonds. The dial is painted with a couple within a landscape and on the inside of the case and cover there are further landscapes painted *en grisaille* on a blue ground. The **movement**, which has a well engraved screwed-on cock and worm and wheel set-up, is signed 'D Bouquet Londini'.

The style of the enamel work and techniques employed are of the Blois school and French. Some enamelling was carried out in England, but the case of this watch is of such sophistication that it was all but certainly made in France, rather than in England by a French immigrant. It is generally thought to have been made about 1650 and, because of its richness, for a very wealthy royalist, indeed a member of the Court. If it was made for a British client during the Interregnum it would have been delivered abroad but, as it is possible the watch is a little later than generally thought, it is also possible Bouquet may have supplied it soon after the Restoration in 1660.

Actual size.

Plate 40. Robert Whitwell.

Silver case 52mm

From about **1665**, this is an example of a watch showing minutes as well as hours. Clearly there was no particular technical difficulty in providing a minute hand, but the customer had to realise that no great accuracy could be expected of it and remember not to confuse it with an hour hand. Few minute hand watches survive from the period before the balance spring was introduced and established; this is a rare and early example. The centre of the **dial** rotates with a figure of Eros who indicates the hours. A gilt ring on the outside of the chapters turns and the pointer upon it shows the date on the exterior silver band. The figure, numerals and dial divisions are filled with red and black pitch or 'wax' for clarity.

The **movement** is signed 'Robert Whitwell Fecit'. It has an early four wheel train and thus runs for more than twenty-four hours on one winding. There is a worm and wheel set-up, a screwed on cock and early Egyptian pillars. The silver **case** has a split bezel, a reasonably early example of this method of glass retention.

Whitwell was apprenticed to Robert Grinkin in 1642. He lost his premises in the Great Fire of 1666 and was given ten shillings charity by the Clockmakers' Company for 'relief in his sickness' in 1673/74. He was dead by 1678. This watch was in the Charles Shapland Collection in 1894 and the Marryat Collection by 1929. It is described and illustrated in Britten, *Old Clocks and Watches and their Makers*, pages 180-181 of the Antique Collectors' Club reprint of the third edition.   PRIVATE COLLECTION

Actual size.

Plate 41. John Fitter.

Silver case 47mm

Actual size.

There are some broad similarities to the watch by Whitwell illustrated in Plate 40 and made about the same time –**1665** – but there is a **dial** for seconds mounted on the top plate. While the hand indicates the minutes, the hours are shown by Chronos – Father Time – engraved on the revolving central disc. The date can be read off the tabulated Julian calendar on the back of the silver **case**.

The owner could not expect any great accuracy from the minute hand and indeed he had to remember not to see it as an hour hand. The seconds would, of course, be good only for short durations. Another watch, also with seconds on the top plate of the movement, was offered by Christie's in Geneva in May 1995. By Isaac Pluvier, it had a gold case and painted enamel scenes, but the configuration of the dial and **movement** were not dissimilar. It, too, had a four wheel train (so running for more than twenty-four hours) with the seconds mounted on an extended arbor of the contrate wheel, a worm and wheel set-up, and a screwed-on silver cock with, unusually, an oval table and foot of near equal proportions. Pluvier's will, proved in January 1665/6, was the subject of an

article by John Stevens (AHS, Vol. IV, No.1, December 1962), and a list of his stock shows at least one watch which was designed for seconds.

The signature, 'John Fitter Battersea', is on either side of the seconds dial. Fitter or Fetter(s), who was probably trained by his father Nicholas, was known to the Clockmakers' Company and took apprentices through them, but he did not become a Free Brother until 1685. This well-known watch is shown in Britten's *Old Clocks and Watches and their Makers*, third edition with its outer case, very similar to the one on the following watch by Williamson, but it was unfortunately mislaid when the Bloch-Pimentel Collection was sold in Paris in 1961. It was in the Roskell and Camerer Cuss Collections and shown at the AHS 10th Anniversary Exhibition, 1964, and the Millennium 'Le Temps Vite' Exhibition, Paris, 2000.

PRIVATE COLLECTION

Plate 42. Robert Williamson.

Silver inner case, leather-covered outer 51mm

The **dial** has a central revolving disc with Father Time carrying his scythe low in one hand and pointing to the hours with the other. He is clearly in a hurry: engraved on a ribbon above his head is the missive 'I Stay For No Man'. The Greeks confused their word for 'time', *chronos*, with that of their name for their old god of agriculture, Cronus, who had a sickle for an attribute, and this in due course became the scythe of Father Time. His wings were added by Renaissance illustrators.

A small indicator mounted on a gilt ring shows the date. The inner **case**, with a split bezel for glass retention, is plain and the outer is leather-covered with silver pin-work. Signed 'Robert Williamson Royal Exchange', the **movement** has a screwed-on cock with a large oval foot, worm and wheel set-up and early Egyptian pillars. The escapement has been converted from the original verge to a lever and the fusee re-cut to take a chain in the nineteenth century.

Otherwise the entire watch, made about **1670** or possibly a year or two before, is in superb condition. At one time it belonged to Lord Harris of Belmont and subsequently Lord Sandberg who sold it at Antiquorum, Geneva in 2001.

PRIVATE COLLECTION

Actual size.

Plate 43. Daniel Fletcher.

Silver inner case, leather-covered outer 53mm

At one time owned by Cecil Clutton, this watch is illustrated in the well-known book *Watches* which he wrote with George Daniels. There is a pierced and engraved symmetric silver overlay integral with the chapter ring on top of the **dial** plate, and outside the chapter ring a gilt annular carries a bug, or pointer, indicating the date on the exterior silver band. The **movement**, which is signed 'Daniel Fletcher London', has a screwed-on cock, worm and wheel set-up and divided early Egyptian pillars with simple capitals. The silver inner **case** is plain and the leather-covered outer is decorated with restrained symmetric floriate pin-work.

When Daniel Fletcher senior died in 1653, his widow continued the business and their son, also Daniel, was bound as an apprentice by William Godbed on behalf of his mother in 1664. This watch dates from about **1665** to **1670**. One by Henry Harpur (free of the Clockmakers' Company in 1664), with a similar dial and configuration, was sold at Sotheby's, London in October 1998.   PRIVATE COLLECTION

Plate 44. Nathaniel Barrow

Silver inner case 54mm, later ray skin outer 60mm

An alarm and astronomical watch of about **1665** having a matted dial plate with off-set dials and sectors. The band of the **case** is beautifully decorated with flower heads, foliage and dogs' heads either side of the pendant, and pierced for sound emission. On the back is a pastoral scene with, in the foreground, Cupid and a gentleman with a seated lady holding a pen and, in the background, a shepherdess with her beau playing a flute – an allegory of love, literature and music, suggesting also that love is universal. The silver-mounted green dyed ray skin outer case was made for the watch in the eighteenth century.

Both **dial** centres have applied silver pierced out rosettes, a similar decoration to that on the watch by Fletcher illustrated in Plate 43. The upper consists of a central revolving disc with three concentric rings and a fourth outer ring which is fixed. The inner ring indicates the dates in each month on which the signs of the Zodiac commence according to the old style calendar, the signs being read on the ring next to those dates. Both are read, together with the months shown in the third ring, against the central hand which turns one twelfth

faster than the disc, so advancing one month in each revolution. A small steel pointer mounted on the disc indicates the date of the month on the fixed outer ring. The calendar is set annually when the two unused spaces between December and January are reached.

A pointer fixed to the revolving disc in the centre of the lower dial shows the hours and the alarm hand is set against the Arabic numerals. The left-hand sector has the days of the week in one window with their corresponding allegorical figures in the other. The right-hand sector consists of three windows; nearest the centre is the phase of the moon, above the time of moon rise and below its age.

'Nathaniel Barrow London' is engraved around the edge of the **movement** top plate on which there is a screwed-on cock, a worm and wheel set-up and alarm stop-work. The alarm barrel is pierced and engraved, and the pillars have a floriate pattern (sometimes called early tulip) with simple volute (Ionic) capitals.

Plate 45. Edward Bridgeman.

Silver inner case, leather-covered outer 51mm

This is a good example of the design that appeared around **1670**, but which may well date from later in the decade. Watches with four wheel trains, so running for more than twenty-four hours, were becoming increasingly common during the late 1660s. After a while these were fitted with short key-set hands and dials with interior divisions and large numerals. Clearly attractive to the owner as a new and distinctive design, it emphasized the quarter divisions – thus the watch's apparent timekeeping ability – and also made it less likely that he would catch the hand or damage the dial. He needed, of course, to use a key, but whether he did so every time is another matter!

The **dial** is an early one-piece champlevé dial with a foliate centre and the pinned-on hand is an early style of 'tulip'. The champlevé technique of cutting away metal to leave other portions standing, and then filling that cut away, in the case of dials, the numerals and divisions, with black or coloured 'wax' (actually a form of pitch) was, of course, in general use. Now, but for the numerals and divisions, the entire one-piece dial was cut away and, apart from some modest decoration, matted.

Signed 'Edwardus Bridgeman Londini', the **movement** is quite typical, with a worm and wheel set-up, screwed-on cock with an oval foot and table and floriate or 'early tulip' pillars; but it has an early fusee chain rather than a gut line.

The plain silver inner **case** has a split bezel and a ring pendant and bow. The leather-covered outer case is decorated with a circle of tulip flowers and foliage surrounded by bunches of grapes and vine stems.   PRIVATE COLLECTION

Plate 46. Richard Riccorde.

Silver inner case, leather-covered outer 42mm   circa 1670-75

This is similar in appearance to the watch by Bridgeman illustrated in Plate 45, but unusually small and so made with a very simple hand. The silver champlevé **dial** has a rosette in the centre, an interior division ring and large Roman numerals, while the inner **case** is plain and the leather-covered outer is decorated with floriate pin-work.

The **movement** is signed 'Richard Riccorde Londini'. There is a worm and wheel set-up, a pinned-on cock, early Egyptian pillars and the fusee has a gut line.

Riccorde, or Ricord and other spellings, was active from before the Civil War. His last apprentice was free of the Clockmakers' Company in 1675 when there is no further record of him. This watch was made about 1670 to 1675. PRIVATE COLLECTION

Actual size.

Plate 47. Edward East.
Silver-gilt inner case, leather-covered outer 62mm

A silver gilt clock-watch made by East during the **1670s**. The early one-piece champlevé **dial** has a rosette in the centre, large numerals and interior divisions. The tulip hand has a short tail.

Flowers and foliage decorate the pierced **case** band, and the back, through which the watch is wound, has similar chased and engraved decoration. This work can be compared with that on two clock-watches made some ten years earlier and previously illustrated, one also by East and another by Barrow (Plates 36 and 44) – it is noticeably less free-flowing and more formal with greater symmetry. The outer case has restrained pin-work.

The flowers and foliage on the screwed-on cock are also more formal and controlled. The **movement** is signed 'Edwardus East Londini' either side of the

Actual size.

striking train stop-work, there is a silver locking plate decorated with a large rosette in red and a worm and wheel set-up. The pillars are a variety of floriate or 'early tulip' design.

This watch was made in the period leading up to, or, possibly, during the time of, the introduction of the balance spring. It took a while for the trade to adopt the balance spring and watches with the same dial configuration as this, and without the spring, were made for a few years after 1675.

Thomas Tompion (1637–1713). Mezzotint by John Smith after Sir Godfrey Kneller.

Chapter Three

THE THIRD PERIOD

1675–1725

THE THIRD PERIOD

1675–1725

OUTLINE

There were three very good reasons why watchmaking in England became so successful and expanded so rapidly during this period: a series of inventions and developments; the vast increase in wealth of the nation with London established as the predominant trading city of Europe; the immigration of artists and craftsmen partly because of this, and partly also as a result of the Revocation of the Edict of Nantes.

The introduction of the balance spring made for a great improvement in both timekeeping and reliability and minutes could now be shown with some confidence. Indeed, it was not long before a variety of dial configurations were tried. The design of the movements and the methods of production and finish to the parts were further advanced. The invention of the repeating mechanism rendered some practical advantage and clearly a repeating watch would have been a 'must have' for those who could afford it. A way to pierce jewels was developed and occasionally jewelled bearings were fitted together with diamond endstones – perhaps of marginal benefit at the time, but significant when improvements on the verge escapement were invented later in the century.

The division of labour became increasingly sophisticated. Workshops specialised and parts were bought in. Movement frame and dial makers occasionally marked their work – the former most often on the underside of the top plate – but otherwise only case makers did so. Movements were supplied both unfinished and finished, and unsigned as well as signed, to order. Some evidence of this trade is well illustrated by a watchmaker's day-book discovered some years ago and subject to an article by Eric Bunt *(Antiquarian Horology,* March 1973). According to this day-book, which runs from 1704 to 1726, of the 160 watches and seventeen clocks sold by the maker in question – apparently Benjamin Gray of London – eighty-eight watches were supplied as motions and/or movements to other watchmakers. The remaining seventy-two consisted of thirty-eight gold and twenty-eight silver watches plus six noted as 'second-hand', and Gray records the names of the private individuals to whom he sold these completed watches. His purchases are not shown, but it is probable that he acquired movement parts and/or movements from third parties and, in all likelihood, south-west Lancashire – see 'London, Lancashire and the Provinces' below. Nevertheless, as many of the entries in the day-book are for, quite often, complex repairs, it appears that Gray was a working watchmaker. In 1741 his daughter married Justin Vulliamy, who became a partner, while he was made Watchmaker in Ordinary to George II the following year.

The influence of Continental decorative designs continued. The artists, designers and draughtsmen were largely of European, predominantly French, origin, as frequently were, in all probability, the chasers and engravers. However, the cases, dials and, of course, the movements of the English watch retained and continued to develop their very distinctive character. Significantly, both the silver and gold used for English cases was of better quality and of slightly thicker gauge, generally speaking, than that used on the Continent. A rich amalgam of the neo-classical and the grotesque, often echoing the Renaissance, and baroque and rococo designs produced a varied and enticing array of decoration on cases, dials and movements.

The reputation of the English watch increased immeasurably and many were sold abroad, such that, with varying degrees of success, copies were made on the Continent. Some Continental makers signed these imitations with their own names – Chapuis illustrates a few in his *La Montre Suisse* – while other watches were given made-up English names or the names of well-known makers which were often, deliberately or otherwise, misspelt. An excellent article by Sebastian Whitestone *(Antiquarian Horology, Winter 1993)* reports on his research into the early minute repeating watches made in Friedberg (adjacent to the city of Augsburg) and gives an outline of the industry there. He describes and illustrates a number of watches including one signed 'Marquch London' – suggesting, perhaps, Markwick. Daniel Quare's name was used quite frequently, typically without his forename and with an accent on the last letter. Although a few are really quite convincing, most fakes are reasonably obvious – they lack quality and have somewhat different proportions and decorative design detail.

The minutes of the Clockmakers' Company's Quarter Court meeting of July 1704 state that both the Master and Mr. Quare received letters from a Patrick Caddell in Amsterdam which reported the existence of false signatures. Although a committee was set up, it appears nothing was done, and probably nothing really could be. An Act of Parliament of 1695 had required all English watches to be engraved with the maker's name and place of abode, but it was up to the Clockmakers' Company to apply its rules, maintain its jurisdiction, and ensure its members employed craftsmen working in England. Of course, watches and watch movements could be had from abroad more cheaply. There are some, particularly around 1710, whose cases, dials and movements – although not necessarily all three – have strong Swiss and French overtones; they are often signed by recorded immigrant makers and the quality of the dials can be rather ordinary. The cases, generally silver, can be somewhat deep, bulbous and thin and, while some have identifiable English marks, others are unmarked or have marks which have not been identified. One must hasten to add, however, that this does not mean all unmarked cases or those with unidentified marks fall into this category, but only a group some years either side of 1710.

SOME NOTABLE MAKERS, LONDON, LANCASHIRE AND THE PROVINCES

Thomas Tompion, of course, has been always a name to conjure with and the reputation is certainly deserved. For innumerable reasons Tompion (1639-1713) was the foremost clockmaker of his day and his close involvement with the introduction of the balance spring for watches establishes his credentials in this field as well. Once established, his reputation carried him forward. His workshop was extremely well organised and, being one of the first to adopt a sequence of numbers for the purposes of identification, he introduced what can only be described as batch production. His watches are always of high quality and sometimes the highest, but they cannot be put above those sold by many of his contemporaries.

Some are deservedly famous, as much for their clocks as for their watches. Tompion's immediate contemporaries in the early part of the period, Daniel Quare, Joseph Windmills, Henry Jones and John and Joseph Knibb, for instance, belong to this category, although the last two in particular signed very few watches. But there are other well-known makers and the work of some are illustrated in this chapter. Of course, some famous makers, such as Quare, were active from the beginning of the period, while others were not but continued into the next, for instance George Graham and Daniel Delander. Both these men worked for Tompion and they too would have relied on the complex network of trade suppliers.

A small number of towns in south-west Lancashire – Liverpool, Toxteth Park and Prescot among them – were a significant source of supply for the London trade, and no doubt other areas of the country, not only of watchmaking tools, but of both finished and unfinished movements. A notebook of one supplier, a Richard Wright of Cronton, survives in the Preston Public Record Office; Alan Smith wrote a full summary of it for *Antiquarian Horology* (December 1985). The earliest entry is for 1713 and the last 1756. Alan Smith establishes that Wright, although he is entered in parish church records as a watchmaker, acted as a middleman and agent. He took orders and arranged delivery via carriers to some of the best London names. In the main he supplied them with completed movements but, perhaps surprisingly, the notebook also shows that on occasions they sent him incomplete watches from London for him 'to finish'. The men on the bench he employed were probably reliant on him, or other similar agents, and were unlikely to be in a position to market their own work.

By the beginning of the eighteenth century quite a number of towns had watchmakers, but signed provincial watches from this period are not common and, in general, those which survive resemble the watches being sold in London, and the cases quite often have a London case maker's mark. It is clear, however, that a few provincial watchmakers made, to a greater or lesser extent, a contribution to the finished article they sold – at least finishing to a degree, and casing-up.

THE CASE MAKERS, THEIR MARKS AND HALLMARKS

Although case makers, or 'box' makers as they were called at the beginning of the period, belonged to a well-established specialist trade, they failed to conform to practices laid down by the Goldsmiths' Company, mark their work, or submit it for hallmarking as required by law. Most belonged to the Clockmakers' Company, but their craft came under the Goldsmiths' jurisdiction. Philip Priestley explores the various reasons for the failure to conform in his excellent *Early Watch Case Makers of England* (NAWCC Inc., 2000).

However, some controls and perhaps, it would seem, the threat of them soon began to take effect. The earliest maker's mark so far recorded is on a gold case made probably a little after 1675 by Nathaniel Delander for a watch by Robert Seignor, and the earliest recorded full set of maker's mark and hallmark is for 1683-4 on a gold case by the same maker, the watch by Thomas Tompion. The hallmark date letter was changed annually on 29 May.

The Goldsmiths' Company started a 'copper plate' in 1682 which contains the marks of goldsmiths, including case makers – although not identifying them as such – working between 1682 and 1697. Priestley has managed to correlate these marks with the names of known makers and give a clear attribution to the majority. Most makers now marked their work assiduously, but initially they submitted gold cases for hallmarking only occasionally and silver cases almost never. Priestley's survey of 112 gold and 275 silver cases made between 1631 and 1720 shows 54% of the first were hallmarked and just 2.2% of the second. The earliest full set of silver marks recorded is a Britannia style mark for 1698-9 by Richard Blundell on a watch by Joseph Banks, Nottingham.

The Goldsmiths' Company also possess their first Register of Small Workers' Marks covering the period from 1697 to 1739. Several of the entries are annotated 'case maker', others 'small worker', but many are without any description of trade. Some case makers, and Richard Blundell is an example, were noted as small workers. Whereas this description covered categories other than case making, it also allowed for case makers who might have made other small articles. Case makers' marks are found very occasionally on dials (Plates 52 and 74).

Before 1675 the majority of outer cases had been of base metal covered in some form of leather with only the bezels and decorative pin-work of precious metal. From around 1680 the majority were either of gold or silver, while the leather-covered case was made only occasionally. In very many instances, as Priestley demonstrates, both silver and gold watches have different makers' marks on the inner and outer case – both of which are perfectly correct for the watch – in spite of the fact that the makers were able to supply both. Some of the background to why this was so is suggested in previous chapters. Not before the second quarter of the century does one consistently find the same mark on both cases. Skin-covered outer cases – and those covered with shell, which were quite popular until a little after 1700 – were not marked.

THE CASE AND ITS DECORATION

The inner case was left plain, with a few exceptions, unless the watch had a striking, repeating or alarm mechanism, when it was pierced out for sound emission and engraved. The stirrup **bow** and **pendant** supplanted the loose ring and pendant quite rapidly from a year or two before 1700. It was quite simple to start with, longer for repeaters, but in time the waist and length of the joints increased a little.

Initially the outer case hinge – strictly speaking 'joint' – was modest, but during the 1690s some makers made it so that it was much more pronounced and, for strength, squared the end joints. Square end joints can be seen on cases made up to about 1720 but, increasingly from the early years of the century, almost equally bold hinges were made on which the end joints were shaped and moulded. The corners of some square end joints have been reduced subsequently with much the same effect. Some makers favoured a chamfer, often quite deep, for the inner edge of the front bezel. These reached their most extreme when, typically, they were combined with square hinges around 1710. It was about this time that watches were, on average, somewhat broader and deeper than they had been hitherto; they were much the same size – again on average – at the end of the period as they were at the beginning.

Up to about 1680 the majority of outer cases were **skin-covered** and, although far fewer were made, they continued to be quite popular. For some people the term shagreen refers only to those dyed green, while for others it includes those dyed black as well – indeed, any other colour but not leather – that is to say not horse or donkey skin. Again, for others it is a broad generic term which can be used to refer to any skin. All in all a good reason for trying to apply a closer description! It is clear that dyeing shark and ray skin (with its large enamel caps and bold mosaic pattern) green became fashionable for watch cases – mostly gilt-metal ones – particularly around 1710.

Tortoiseshell, more accurately the belly of a hawksbill turtle, was a popular covering between about 1680 and a little after 1700. The shell is invariably under-painted red during this period. There is always some pin-work – pins are needed to hold the shell in place – but sometimes also most attractive inlay, generally in silver and sometimes having engraved figures, birds and so forth.

The case decorative designs were, from the beginning of the period, an increasingly rich amalgam of neo-classical and grotesque, often echoing the Renaissance, and baroque ornament. The influence of the classical styles was continuous, while the grotesque was generally, but not always, limited as far as the cases are concerned to a mask at the base of the inner from the 1690s.

The scene on the back of Plate 71 has been made from a cast. Very few English **embossed and chased** outer cases from the late seventeenth century are known. One of the earliest is in the British Museum: it has no hallmark but belongs to Daniel Quare number 0233 which has an inner case hallmarked for 1692-3. A small group survives from the period up to 1715 and the John Halsted (Plate 86) has an excellent example. It has a central reserve, as do those on slightly later watches seen in Plates 92-95. Scenes from, typically, classical mythology, the New and Old Testament (Plate 96) were embossed on the back from, it would seem, shortly before 1718.

The cases were embossed with punches from the inside and then chased from the outside. The process of embossing hardened the metal, so that it needed to be annealed frequently in order to remain malleable. The impurities which appeared on the surface of the metal after annealing were cleaned off in an acid solution. This solution was also used after the final chasing and the wonderful lustre to the gold found on some cases in the very best condition – for instance Plates 86 and 103 – is the result. It seems that at first the chasers did not sign watch cases and their work remains anonymous. There are a couple of cases hallmarked for 1719-20 known which are signed within the embossing by Ishmael Parbury, and these may be the earliest to survive. Not many cases were signed during the 1720s. Richard Edgcumbe in his superb study, *The Art of the Gold Chaser in Eighteenth Century London* (Oxford 2000), discusses the techniques used, the progression in designs and styles, and records much information about the men who employed them.

The word 'repoussé' is often used to describe this type of decoration.

THE DIAL AND HANDS

English watches made prior to 1720 with original enamel dials are extremely rare; many champlevé dials were replaced with enamel ones, particularly during the second half of the century. The dials were made in gold, silver or silver-gilt to suit the watch. The centres had a simple rosette until the mid-1680s when the makers began to sign their work within an embossed **cartouche**. Generally speaking, the name was on one cartouche above the centre and the place name in another below. These were surrounded by scrollwork, drapery, shells and masks reflecting the neo-classical, baroque and grotesque designs of the period. Some makers, such as Tompion, used the same design repeatedly (Plates 64-65, 70 and 78). The majority of cartouches were slightly convex, but as the period progressed many were flat (Graham, Plate 87) and also curved and radial (Quare, Plate 90).

The minute band had Arabic figures at every five minutes from the beginning. **Half-hour** divisions were retained. They were mostly diamond shaped throughout the period, but variations on the fleur-de-lis were quite popular, particularly, but not exclusively, it seems, with makers of Continental origin and from around 1700 onwards.

The majority of **six-hour** dials (Plate 60) – these are really quite rare – were made between about 1680 and 1700. A number of variations to the two-handed watch dial were produced, mostly between about 1690 and 1710. The most common to survive is the **'sun and moon'** (Plate 61) and, less common, the **'wandering hour'** (Plate 75). Single-handed watches made between 1685 and 1710, other than those with alarm, are scarce, while there seem to be only a couple of **digital** watches (Plate 84) extant.

The tulip **hour hand**, with its many subtle variations (Plates 57, 63, 66 and 70 are examples), in general gave way to the ubiquitous 'beetle' slowly from shortly before 1700, but a few makers continued to employ it, Daniel Quare (Plate 81) in particular. 'Beetle' as a term is too well established to be challenged, but it poorly describes what was intended, clearly, to be a floriate design. Again there were many subtle variations, but Plates 64, 74 and 86 have early examples with a pronounced baluster shape to the stem which often has a cross-rib at its base. Plates 91 and 93 are a little later. The pattern continued to evolve. Although they are sometimes to be seen fitted to watches of this period as replacements, 'beetle' hands made later in the century are very different. Occasionally other, generally more complex, designs were used (Plates 73 and 95) which have no generic description.

As with the hour hand, the **minute hand** was invariably made of steel and blued. So many have been lost, broken and replaced that it is impossible to have a clear view as to precisely what patterns were followed prior to the 1690s, but the two shapes seen most frequently are a very simple slight taper with the sides chamfered and a single tapering baluster with a single cross-rib adjacent to the collet. For watches with standard dials, one should expect, from about the early 1690s onwards, a double baluster 'poker', tapering first from a cross-rib to the quarter-hour ring, and then again from a second rib to over the minute band. At the beginning the balusters could be quite voluptuous, but as the new century progressed they tended to be less bulbous from the rib and to have a more even taper.

THE MECHANISM

Four-wheel trains were now standard and the escapement used throughout this period was the verge. Robert Hooke wrote that he taught Thomas Tompion 'the way of the single pallet for watches' on 15 October 1676 and in 1695 Tompion took out a patent, in conjunction with William Houghton and the Reverend Edward Barlow, which describes a new form of escapement with 'teeth made like tenterhooks'. A movement signed by Tompion, now in the Science Museum, seems to be the only surviving example of a project which was clearly never developed.

The circumstances surrounding the introduction of the **balance spring** has resulted in more research, discussion, conjecture and contentious argument than any other. At the time Clutton and Daniels wrote their *Watches* (revised 1979) they covered the subject very adequately as did David Landes in his *Revolution in Time* (1983), but subsequent research, reassessment of known manuscripts and the discovery of new ones has modified a complex and incomplete story. The basic fact remains, of course: the Dutch scientist Christiaan Huygens claimed the idea of the use of a spring to control the oscillations of a watch balance in 1675, while Robert Hooke counter-claimed, saying that it was his prior invention.

Following her biography of Robert Hooke, Lisa Jardine undertook some collaborative research for the 2006 Roy Porter lecture. In it she gave a resumé of the efforts to design a sea-going clock during the 1660s and up to 1675. It was the search for a way to determine longitude at sea by means of a timekeeper which, although unsuccessful at the time, resulted eventually in a great improvement being made to the domestic watch. A version of the lecture was published by *Antiquarian Horology* in September 2006 in which the author demonstrates why, as she states, there is no doubt that Hooke's idea of using springs as isochronous regulators in place of pendula was transmitted to Huygens by both Sir Robert Moray – who was collaborating with Huygens on sea-clocks – and Henry Oldenburg. She also reports on the discovery in 1991 of a draft patent by Hooke which can be dated no later than 1668.

In 1675 Huygens and Hooke both employed men to produce a watch with a balance spring, both trying to gain commercial privilege in England. Various forms of spring and methods of attachment were tried. Huygens had certainly delivered one watch by mid-1675 and possibly, by the end of the year, another with modified springing. Hooke had Thomas Tompion make a watch at the beginning of 1675 which he presented to Charles II; this passed back and forth between the parties being altered, corrected and so on for at least eighteen months. A period of gestation followed when probably quite a few systems were tried. Certainly Hooke worked towards a greater understanding of the behaviour of springs and he also tried, unsuccessfully, to have the King support him. In the end the philosophy discouraging the granting of patents and privilege in the matter of science, promoted vigorously by the Royal Society, prevailed.

Intriguingly, the style and shape of both the cases of Plate 48 – the outer bearing the King's coronet and cipher – in combination with the dial, suggest that they belonged to a balance spring watch made during the second half of the 1670s or, at the latest, the first couple of years of the 1680s. Unfortunately, the movement has been replaced. No balance spring watch or watch movement has survived which can be dated any earlier than about 1678-1680. Two watches are known with straight-line springs, one by Henry Jones, the other unsigned and now in the Patek Philippe Museum, which could well be from this period, but it is impossible to be sure. The spring is fixed, together with a worm adjustment, above an oval cock, and acts on the balance below in much the same way as a pendulum suspension. However, two forms of spring emerged, one with a 'Barrow' regulator (Plates 50 and 51), the other a 'Tompion' regulator (Plates 52-54), so called, although it is not known for sure who invented them. It is sometimes thought that the 'Barrow' regulator was the first of these but there is certainly no proof. Quite a number of makers took it up, but after just a few years it was dropped in favour of the Tompion form. There were about one and a half turns to the spring initially, but these were soon increased.

The Reverend Edward Barlow, having invented a rack-striking system for clocks, had Tompion apply the same idea as a watch **repeating mechanism** in about 1685 and applied for Letters Patent. However, Daniel Quare had been experimenting with a similar system; the Clockmakers' Company supported him and petitioned James II in Council on 2 March 1687. Barlow's application was refused and, after a trial of two watches, the King favoured Quare's design as it required just one action to sound the hours and quarters whereas Barlow's required two.

The watch made by Barlow does not seemed to have survived, but Quare's, or one thought to be identical to it, number 611, is in the Ashmolean Museum, Oxford. Francis Wadsworth starts his four-part review of the main repeating mechanisms, both English and Continental *(Antiquarian Horology,* September 1965 to June 1966), by comparing the function of this watch in detail with an early un-numbered repeater by Tompion. The systems continued to differ as they were refined. Quare's type became dominant until Mathew Stogden's form was introduced in the early 1720s.

Repeating watches were no doubt immediately desirable, but surviving examples made prior to 1700 are scarce. The vast majority struck the hours and quarters to the nearest quarter, but a few half-quarter and five-minute repeaters had appeared before the end of the period (Plate 94). Dumb-pieces were fitted quite early on, while a few dumb repeaters – striking small blocks inside the case rather than a bell – appeared a little while before 1720.

Dust rings (Plates 73 and 85) and bayonet fitting dust caps (Plate 74) were being fitted to repeating watches during the first decade, while thereafter the bayonet gave way to a sliding catch (Plate 95).

On 1 May 1704 Peter (Pierre) and Jacob Debaufre took out patent 371 jointly with Nicholas Facio de Duillier for the **piercing of jewels** (Plate 77). These men were Protestants who had come to London following the Revocation of Nantes. Although the patent was initially granted, it was withdrawn following strong opposition from the Clockmakers' Company who cited a watch by Ignatius Huggerford as proof of prior use. The claim was false and the watch in question, with its purely decorative unpierced stone, is now in the Company's collection.

The watch in Plate 77 is a very early, possibly the earliest surviving, watch with a pierced jewel. The top plate, which simply reads DEBAUFRE LONDON, has IAM – for James – under the adjacent stop work. The balance staff pivots are jewelled with rubies top and bottom, each jewel having a deep blind hole and a brass setting. The top jewel has a separate steel end-piece screwed to the cock, the bottom held in by a wedge.

Thomas Tompion began fitting pierced ruby bearings with diamond endstones about 1708-9. Very few other makers seem to have taken the idea up early on, but Daniel Delander did and there are a number of surviving watches of his which have their original jewelling. Plate 89 is an example. The jewelling at each end of the balance staff consists of two plates of rubies, the inner pierced through and chamfered for the pivot. As with those on Tompion's watches, there is no decent oil sink and there would have been problems with oil retention.

Quite a large number of watches have been jewelled after they were made when, invariably, diamond endstones were used (Plate 74). Often the cock has been cut away and the steel setting, rather than being screwed to a ring on the inside of the cock decoration, is screwed to the decoration itself. Holes in the brass are left un-gilded. Ruby endstones have also been replaced with diamond ones.

The **signatures** were invariably in script at the beginning of the period, while block letters, used occasionally during the first decade, became increasingly popular for all or at least part of them – most often the place name. Gothic script seems to have been fashionable around 1710 (Plate 86).

A pre-balance spring watch by Robert Seignor made probably a little after 1675 would appear to be the **earliest numbered** watch recorded; the gold case has Nathaniel Delander's first mark and the number 3. Tompion started his first series of numbers in about 1682 and, with a few exceptions, most makers numbered their movements and sometimes the cases by the end of the decade.

Immediately the balance spring was introduced the **cock** table increased in size and the foot retreated towards the edge of the plate. The neck between the table and foot broadened, as did the foot itself, and by the early 1690s it followed the edge of the plate with a continuous border. So-called wings on either side of the table adjacent to the neck, always to be found on cocks of this period, were modest at first, became longer and more elaborate and then smaller again from about 1715. The tables were pierced and engraved with a wide variety of swags, scrolls and foliage, often with rosettes and scallop shells and inhabited by animals – birds, squirrels, serpent heads and so on – and putti with, mostly by the neck, and from about 1685, angel and classical, mainly female, heads and grotesque masks.

The **pillars** shown in Plate 49 follow just one of a number of floriate designs used during the period immediately prior to the introduction of the balance spring. Plate 52 shows an early tulip and Plate 65 the style of tulip pillar which dominated the 1685-1700 period. It is not untypical of repeating and striking watches to have two styles of pillar. Where space is limited a round baluster pillar or, generally later on, a cylindrical pillar is used. The repeating watch by Tompion (Plate 78) has five pillars, two round balusters and three of the late Egyptian style. Another view of the Egyptian style, popular between 1700 and 1715, can be seen in Plate 87. The watch by Quare (Plate 81) has a form of pillar which has been called a 'crested Egyptian'. Certainly it has the dot and dash piercing down the centre which is characteristic of Egyptian pillars, but the convex outline is typical of the later tulip style. The pierced foliate gallery – cresting – adds something to the confusion. Square baluster pillars were used occasionally after about 1710.

TIMEKEEPING

Cecil Clutton delivered an amusing paper to the Antiquarian Horological Society in December 1954, in which he reported that he had been wearing a waistcoat throughout the previous summer – as well as winter – in order to make in-wear tests at various temperatures on a number of his watches. Two were from this period. One, a watch of about 1695, varied in January as much as three and a half minutes per day, with an average gain of two and a half minutes, but it improved in the summer, when the maximum variation was one and three quarter minutes and average gain was only half a minute.

Referring to the other, a watch by Andrew Dunlop of about 1710, he said: 'It had accompanied me as a pilot on many R.A.F. flights during the War, and I like to think of it as having been the oldest watch on active service'. He had observed its rate closely in wear in 1940, and that 'during a fortnight it was never more than half a minute away from Big Ben'.

By about 1700-1710 watches were probably expected to keep time to within about one minute per day, but not at a particularly constant rate.

Plate 48. Royal coronet and cipher.
Gold inner case: unidentified mark in shaped cameo (see illustration); outer 53mm: no marks   circa 1675-80

The cushion-shaped inner **case** has a similar style and character to those made for late pre-balance spring watches in the latter half of the 1670s, but the bezel is especially deep and the split hinge proud. The outer has the royal coronet and cipher, Charles Rex conjoined and reversed, in particularly fine gold pin-work. The exquisite **dial**, with the provision of hour and minute divisions, is enamelled on gold with a translucent royal blue centre.

Unfortunately, the movement has been replaced but, bearing in mind the dial layout and that there would have been a minute hand, it would have had, all but certainly, some form of balance spring. The style of the inner case, as has already been mentioned, is consistent with the second half of the 1670s. If
it was made in the first few years of the 1680s it would

represent a late use of the style, unlikely for a royal watch. There is no question that the cases and dial belong to a royal watch – their quality and character preclude an alternative. It is tempting to speculate as to whether the original movement might just possibly have been the one Thomas Tompion is known to have made for the King (see page 107).

It is quite possible that the original **movement** was not a success but, in any event, there is every indication that the replacement, signed and numbered 'Mathieu Des hais London 79' and made shortly after 1700, has been especially fitted. It is of the very highest quality and, indeed, reminiscent of some of Tompion's output at this time, and arguably better concerning the balance spring, which is fixed in square holes at each end with square tapered pins. The

number is punched, much in the manner of Tompion, on the underside of both the cock and top plate, and scratched on the dial plate. The barrel is scratched with three names recognisable as London outworkers of the period – Good, Blundell and Rogers. The Egyptian pillars have a concave outline with a pierced foliate capital, gallery or 'crest'. A watch with a movement of similar quality by the same maker is illustrated in Plate 66.

The **history** is really most interesting. Conclusive evidence is lacking, but what is known makes perfect sense. In précis, the watch was certainly found just a few years ago wrapped, together with some mourning rings, in newspaper dated 1822 in a house which had belonged to the same extended family since the sixteenth century. By a process of deduction it was very clear the rings belonged to Richard

Benyon de Beauvoir, one of whose forebears married a Mary Tyssen, widow of one Paulet Wrighte. On the eighteenth century watch paper is written 'Dr. Wright £- 4s 6d'. Mary Tyssen was the daughter of Francis Tyssen of Sacklewell (1690-1717) and Rachel, daughter of Richard de Beauvoir – whose name Benyon assumed the same year as the wrapping paper. Richard de Beauvoir provided not only the Coronation rings for James II and Mary but also designed her Coronation Crown. The Tyssen and de Beauvoir families were goldsmiths and bankers; the royal family often turned to these when it was in need of money. The watch could have been sold to either the Tyssens or the de Beauvoirs, maybe after the king died in 1685.

PRIVATE COLLECTION

111

Plate 49. Richard Ditchfield, London.

Silver inner case: indistinct mark; outer 50mm: no marks

A watch without a balance spring, all but certainly made after the balance spring was introduced in 1675 and before it was universally adopted, that is prior to the **very early 1680s**.

The inner **case** is plain, the back of the tortoiseshell – more properly turtle-shell – covered outer case is inlaid with an engraved silver tulip surrounded by a wreath of stylised foliage and pin-work. The **dial**, typical of the 1670s, has large numerals, an interior ring of quarter- and half-hour divisions, small central rosette and a tulip hand.

Ditchfield was apprenticed through the Clothworkers' Company, only becoming a Free Brother of the Clockmakers' in 1677/78. He is recorded as an engraver which might explain the flourishing signature on the **movement**, 'R. Ditchfield London', and the excellent piercing and engraving to the oval foot and table of the cock, the elaborate floriate pillars and the foot of the fusee stop work. There is a fusee chain, the arbors of the four wheel train have baluster turning and the rim of the two-arm balance is also turned. PRIVATE COLLECTION

Plate 50. Henry Jones, London.

Silver inner case: no marks; outer 60mm: no marks

A remarkable feature of this watch, made about **1678–1680**, is that the minute hand lengthens and contracts as it progresses around the oval minute ring. No other examples, English or Continental, survive from this period and only a handful is known from any period. This watch is also a very early example of one fitted with a balance spring. It was the attendant accuracy of the spring which really allowed the

minute hand to be a practical possibility, although pre-balance spring watches did have them - see Plates 40 and 41.

The champlevé **dial** has a rosette in the centre, a short tulip hour hand and a ring for the quarter-hour divisions. Note the early use of diamond half-hour marks between the hour chapters. The Arabic five-minute figures are within the minute ring.

The **movement** has an exceptionally early balance spring of

only one and a half turns, and a rare 'Barrow' regulator consisting of a worm along which curb pins can be moved against a scale, so adjusting the effective length of the straight outer end of the spring. This form of regulation, attributed to Nathaniel Barrow, soon gave way to that attributed to Thomas Tompion where the curb pins are mounted on a semicircular rack moved by a pinion below a simple, generally silver, figure plate.

The top plate is signed 'Henricus Jones London'. The table

and foot of the large cock are extensively pierced out and engraved with foliate decoration. It is noticeable how much bigger the balance is compared with those previously fitted to pre-balance spring watches and it has three arms rather than two. The mainspring set-up is between the plates, the fusee has a chain and the tulip pillars have volute (Ionic) capitals.

The superb pin-work on the outer **case** suggests scrolling stems with small flowers.   THE PATEK PHILIPPE MUSEUM, GENEVA

Plate 51. Christopher Maynard, London.

Silver cases, inner: indistinct mark; outer 47mm: later

The **movement** has a 'Barrow' regulator, one of the first systems for regulating the balance spring. It was not used much beyond the first few years of the **1680s**. Not many survive but, when they do, they are signed by a fair number of makers, as if the system was widely taken up but soon superseded by the rack and wheel method attributed to Tompion.

The top plate is signed 'Christo Maynard London'. The open piercing and floriate engraving on the cock is typical of the period; indeed it is not unlike the watch by Tompion number 286 of 1682 (Plate 53). Although smaller than the previous watch by Jones, the configuration of the movement is similar. However, the **dial** layout is for hours only, with a single hand and inner quarter divisions. For a balance spring watch to have a single hand is unusual but not unique at this period or, indeed, later. The customer had the benefits of the improved timekeeping that the balance spring brought without the confusion of the extra hand.

Both **cases** are plain; the inner has an indistinct maker's mark while the outer is a later replacement.

PRIVATE COLLECTION

Opposite: Plate 52. Jonathan Puller, London.

Gold cases: inner mark indistinct, possibly JH conjoined incuse (John Harbert); outer 48mm: no marks

Most of Courtenay Ilbert's quite remarkable collection is in the British Museum but a few watches were inherited by his nephew Michael Inchbald who sold them at Sotheby's in October 1963. The catalogue refers to the superb condition of the gold outer **case** and draws attention to the raised flower heads between the wire filigree and floral patterns. It also notes that this watch, which was made between about **1682** and **1685**, was exhibited at the Heritage Exhibition in 1952 (no. 277) and ten years later at the International Art Treasures Exhibition (no. 402).

The gold champlevé **dial** has raised radial foliate decoration in the centre, diamond half-hour divisions between the hour numerals but, most unusually for the period, no quarter divisions. Very rarely found is a dial maker's mark on the underside; here it is WB (possibly William Bertram). The minute ring, with outside Arabic five-minute figures, is standard. The

Actual size.

hour hand is an early example of a style found just occasionally up to about 1715.

Signed 'Jonathan Puller London', the **movement** has characteristics generally associated with the few years before 1685: the shape of the cock and its very open piercing, a short spring for the three-arm balance, and a small regulator plate with only a modest number of divisions located adjacent to the case hinge. The somewhat unusual 'early tulip' pillars are of a particularly open and attractive design. PRIVATE COLLECTION

115

Plate 53. Thomas Tompion, London, no. 286.
Gold cases 54mm: both WI incuse (William Jaques),
hallmarked 1717-8   movement circa 1682

The early **movement** has a coded number of two dots either side of 86 (.86.) which, according to Jeremy Evans' research *(Antiquarian Horology,* June 1984), should be decoded 286. Evans in his book *(Antiquarian Horology* monograph 2006*)* also lists all the known numbers against hallmark dates and case makers' marks, so that the approximate year of 1682 for this movement can be established: it is one of the earliest fitted with a balance spring. Very few gold, and no silver, cases were hallmarked at this time.

The style of the cock table and neck can be compared with those on other Tompions of the period as well as those on the watch by Maynard illustrated in Plate 51. The regulator is an early example of the type attributed to Tompion, the silver figure plate having simple divisions. There are tulip pillars and the mainspring set-up is between the plates. The 'London' part of the signature, 'Tho. Tompion London', is partly obscured by the cock. The figure 19 prefixes the original number (the 1 partly beneath the cock foot); it is over the gilding, clearly later and suggests the watch might well have been brought back and resold – a serial number 1986 corresponds to circa 1695. There is no prefix to the original number .86. on the plate under the dial.

Cecil Clutton owned and included this watch in his *Collectors Collection* (AHS 1974), before the numbering system was understood, and for him the dial, hands and the cases added to the conundrum. Early on, and in accordance with the prevailing fashion, Tompion **dial** centres had a simple rosette, but he was one of the first to sign his dials – for instance number 713 of 1685-87 which has similar, though not identical, cartouches above and below the centre. Shortly before the end of the century Tompion adopted just one form of dial centre, that in which the upper cartouche is flanked by two putti holding garlands of flowers (Plate 64). Thus the dial could have been fitted when the watch was re-numbered, as it seems possible, around 1695. The hour hand is of an early beetle pattern and the minute a typical poker.

The outer **case** has a square hinge, a chamfer to the inner edge of the bezel and a narrow neck for a short pendant: the current pendant is waisted to fit the neck and, together with the bow, is a mid-eighteenth century replacement. It is just possible the cases were made soon after the square hinge first appeared in the 1690s – the narrow neck in the outer in particular suggests the original pendant was short and early. The maker, William Jaques, made a few for Tompion at this time but not, it seems, later (nor for George Graham who succeeded Tompion in 1713). There is a monogram on the back of the outer. PRIVATE COLLECTION

Plate 54. John Knibb, Oxford, no 56.
Silver inner case: SB incuse (Samuel Bowtell), outer 53mm: no marks

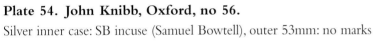

John Knibb, famous as a clockmaker, was responsible for very few watches and this must be one of his earliest. He was apprenticed to his elder brother Joseph in about 1664, active on his own behalf from about 1675, and twice mayor of Oxford. This watch was made in the early **1680s**.

The silver champlevé **dial**, with foliate decoration in the centre, has a tulip hour hand and a poker minute. The top plate of the **movement** is signed in fine script 'John Knibb att Oxon', the cock foot is of an early form without a border, there is a block at the neck and the table has a bird of paradise within a symmetric foliate design. The early balance spring has a silver regulator disc with simple divisions I to III adjacent to the case hinge, and there are tulip pillars.

The inner **case** maker, Samuel Bowtell, became free of the Clockmakers' Company in 1681 and his mark is on Goldsmiths' Company registration plate of 1682. The case is numbered 56; there is a ring pendant and bow, split bezel for glass retention and a winding cover. The tortoiseshell (more accurately – at least generally – the belly shell of a hawksbill turtle), with its features heightened by under painting and glued and fixed with silver pins to the outer in the normal way, is inlaid with silver stems, leaves, rondels and engraved silver flowers, birds – possibly doves – and, in the centre, possibly vine leaves.

Pasted inside the outer case is a rare paper table, headed December XXXI, showing the saints' days, the dates for the four states of the moon and the equation of time for the month.

PRIVATE COLLECTION

Plate 55. Daniel Quare, London, 568.
Silver case 48mm: ND conjoined coronet above in cameo
(Nathaniel Delander)

An alarm watch of about **1685**, the hours indicated by the
pointer fixed to the revolving centre of the **dial** and the alarm set
by the hand against the Arabic numerals. It is typical of alarm
watches of this period that there is no provision to show minutes.

The top plate of the **movement**, signed and numbered 'Daniel
Quare London', has the mainspring set-up as well the regulator plate.
The cock is pierced and engraved with foliate scrolls and there is no
border to the foot. The fixed alarm barrel, also pierced and engraved,
has a short train and a hammer to strike the bell mounted inside the
case. There are three tulip and two vase-shaped pillars.

The **case** band is pierced with scrolling foliage. The back, through
which the watch is wound, has similar quite tight symmetrically
arranged decoration on a matt ground, an eagle upon a pedestal in the
centre, a vase of flowers above, and the heads of an angel and two
dolphins below. This design would have been taken from a
contemporary Renaissance-inspired published source; the back of the
watch signed 'Markwick' (Plate 56) is not dissimilar. The original
outer case may well have been of silver decorated turtleshell; a much
later one was fitted to this watch when it was illustrated by Marryat in
the book of his collection *Henlein to Tompion*. PRIVATE COLLECTION

Plate 56. James Markwick, London.

Silver inner case: WF incuse (probably William Finch) numbered 3; outer 54mm: no marks

Of about **1685** or a year or two after, this watch is shown with the alarm hand aligned with the hour arrow-head pointer mounted on the revolving centre of the **dial**, the position it can be moved to when the alarm function is not in use. The hand can be moved away from the pointer, set against the Arabic circle, and the alarm will be set off, provided the spring is wound, when it points to the Roman twelve.

The band of the inner **case** is pierced and engraved with small flowers and foliage inhabited by birds. This decoration is continued upon a matt ground on the back where there is a vase in the centre, a basket of flowers above and an angel head below. It would have been taken from a contemporary Renaissance-inspired design. The back of the watch by Daniel Quare 568 (Plate 55) is not dissimilar. The tortoiseshell (more accurately – at least generally – the belly shell of a hawksbill turtle) outer case has superb silver inlay work, the back with four engraved birds between four large flower heads and, in the centre, Cupid with his bow and quiver. A row of large silver-lined open rondels are around both the front edge and the bezel for sound emission.

The signature on the **movement**, 'Markwick London', is not prefixed by a Christian name. Markwick had a son, also James, who became free of the Clockmakers' Company by patrimony in 1692. The cock, which has a small borderless foot, is pierced and engraved with foliate decoration, and the alarm barrel is similarly treated. There are tulip pillars. PRIVATE COLLECTION

Plate 57. John Wills, London.

Silver inner case: indistinct mark; outer 51mm: no marks

Generally speaking **dials** were beginning to be signed between **1685** and **1690**. The centre is unusually large, the cartouche particularly good, the matting and overall quality excellent. The tulip hand is finely cut.

The inner case is plain, the tortoiseshell – more properly turtleshell – outer is inlaid on the back with a single piece of pierced silver engraved with an allegorical subject. The young woman in the centre holding a small dog may suggest faithfulness and thus fidelity. She has an eagle on either side – guarding her perhaps – and below a winged angel/cherub head.

The movement is signed 'John Wills London'. It has an early balance spring, large silver regulator plate, a cock which has no border to the foot and good tulip pillars.

This watch is illustrated in *The Country Life Book of Watches,* 1967, by T.P. Camerer Cuss.

PRIVATE COLLECTION

Plate 58. Henry Jones, London.
Gold cases 50mm: inner ID incuse (James Delander), hallmarked 1690-1; outer WI coronet above incuse (John Wightman), hallmarked 1699-1700

The gold inner **case**, pendant and bow are original, while the outer, which is hallmarked nine years later and bears a monogram, is a contemporary replacement.

The excellent gold champlevé **dial**, with a simple spiral of leaves in the centre, has a tulip hour hand and a tapered poker minute. Tapered minute hands, straight sided, without turning and more or less triangular in section are quite unusual, although often poor reproductions are to be found.

The **movement** is signed 'Henry Jones London'. The cock, with a large table with foliate decoration and no border to the foot, is typical of the early 1690s. The use of a serpent to indicate the figure on the regulator scale with its tongue is very common, but it has, nevertheless, a certain charm. There are tulip pillars.

Jones was Master of the Clockmakers' Company in 1691, about the time this watch was made.

PRIVATE COLLECTION

Actual size.

Plate 59. Richard Baker, London.

Gilt metal case 52mm: no marks

By the early 1690s a limited number of well-finished and decidedly compact clock-watch mechanisms were made, amply demonstrated by this example which was at one time in the Marryat Collection. While clock-watches continued to be produced in small numbers, from the beginning of the eighteenth century the newly invented repeating watch proved immensely popular. Of course, the clock-watch served a somewhat different function, that is, to remind the owner of the time automatically, whereas the repeater, so long as he thought to operate it, told him the time instantaneously. Richard Baker died in 1700, but his widow carried on his business at least until 1710.

The **movement**, signed 'Richard Baker London', has a silver regulation disc and locking plate, a cock with a small borderless foot, tulip pillars, pierced and engraved striking barrel and a blued steel gate. The balance arms are so shaped as to allow for the going train winding square to extend through the cock.

The gold **dial** has a tulip hour and a poker minute hand. The centre has a crown at the top and a lion and unicorn at the sides taken from the royal arms. The crown is of the form used by William and Mary rather than by Queen Anne, suggesting the date of the dial conforms with that of the movement, but implying a very early date for the flat semi-circular signature cartouches. Watch dials from the last dozen or so years of the seventeenth century displaying the royal arms are to be found, but the majority were made after the Act of Union of 1707 which united the English and Scottish Parliaments.

The leather covered gilt metal single **case** cannot really be dated any earlier than about 1710. The bell is housed in the back in which there are winding shutters for both trains and the body; the bezel and inner bezel have open rondels for sound emission. The pendant and bow are from the period 1790-1810.

PRIVATE COLLECTION

122

**Plate 60. C W P Invt, possibly Charles Goode,
London and William Parsons.**

Silver case 51mm: RB in cameo (probably Richard Blundell)

Formerly in the Hornby and Atwood Collections, this watch, made between **1690** and **1695**, belongs to a very small group which have a number of most unusual features.

The hand rotates every six hours indicating the minutes on the outer band and the hours against the Roman figures in the centre. The movement is wound through the **dial** which has a full calendar below twelve, seconds above six and, in raised relief, engraved trophies of war.

The single **case** has a spring-loaded bezel hinged below the pendant to allow for easy access to the dial. The inner bezel is engraved 'Richard Dashwood of Dereham Grange in Norfolk', while the back has three oval bosses with intaglio armorials and the cipher 'RD' in the centre.

A lever in the inner bezel acts on the contrate wheel to start and stop the **movement**, allowing the watch to be used as a seconds timer. The front bezel needs to be open for the lever to be operated. The oval bosses on the case would ensure a good grip. The top plate is engraved 'CWP Invt', and the foot of the large and beautifully decorated cock, which has an angel head at the neck, follows the edge but it has no border. There are excellent tulip pillars.

An article by Paul Tuck (*Antiquarian Horology*, Winter 1988), a letter from Jeremy Evans (Summer 1989) and Paul Tuck's response (Autumn 1989) give a good background to

measuring the pulse from the maker Samuel Watson (Denis Gibbs, *Medical History*, Vol. XV No. 2, April 1971 and, edited with Philip Wilson, Floyer's *Advice to a Young Physician*, pages 20 and 21, William Sessions, 2007). It is unclear what form these watches took, but, in whatever form, one imagines the doctor would have found it easier to use two hands to operate the watch and an assistant to indicate the patient's pulse.
PRIVATE COLLECTION

Actual size.

this watch and another similar one in the La-Chaux de-Fonds Museum. A third, signed Charles Goode, written up by C.F.C. Beeson (*Antiquarian Horology*, June 1966), is referred to, and there is a fourth one illustrated by Henry Marryat in his *Henlein to Tompion*. William Parsons is known to have commissioned two globes from the instrument-maker Thomas Tuttell. It seems probable that Parsons was drawn to horology through his interest in navigation, commissioned Goode to make watches to his own plan and had him use a cipher: Parsons published *A Book of Cyphers* in 1703.

By the end of the seventeenth century the medical profession were well aware of the importance of the pulse, and indeed Sir John Floyer (1649-1734) in the first volume of his *The Physician's Pulse Watch* of 1707 wrote: 'And I must express my gratitude to an unknown benefactor who sent me a pulse-watch, which runs out but one second short of my minute glass'. Floyer is known to have ordered another watch to assist in

indicates the minutes on the Arabic ring.

The **movement** top plate is signed 'Jos Windmills London' and the number 183 is beneath the foot of the cock which, although quite small, has a border. The large table is tightly pierced and engraved with a good symmetric foliate design and it has modest 'streamers' by the neck. There are tulip pillars.

The inner **case**, which has a ring pendant and bow and winding shutter, is punch-numbered adjacent to the maker's mark. The outer, punch-numbered on the silver rim of the back, is overlaid with what is commonly called tortoiseshell – more accurately, turtleshell – and decorated with stylised foliate pin-work.

Made in about **1695**, or shortly before, this watch is illustrated in Philip Priestley's book on early case makers and by J.A Neale in his book on Joseph and Thomas Windmills (AHS, 1999). Four other 'Sun and Moon' watches signed by Joseph Windmills are known.　　PRIVATE COLLECTION

Plate 61. Joseph Windmills, London, no. 183.
Silver inner case: I.I coronet above in cameo (Jonathan Jones), outer 52mm: no marks

The blued steel sector above the elaborate signed **dial** cartouche rotates: as the gilt sun sets to the right the polished steel moon rises from the left, each in turn pointing to the Roman hour numerals. The central hand

Actual size.

Plate 62. William Bertram, London.
Silver cases 59mm: both WB incuse (probably William Bertram), inner: no. 555

An unusually large watch of about **1700** signed by William Bertram, who became free of the Clockmakers' Company in 1684, having been apprenticed to the case maker Samuel Bowtell in 1677. The mark, WB, to be seen on the Goldsmiths' Company copper plate of 1682, and on both the **cases**, is probably his. He registered a Britannia mark, BE in a cameo, with the Goldsmiths' Company during April 1697.

The champlevé **dial** is typical of the period and of high quality. It is signed in the centre on two cartouches; there are trefoil half-hour divisions, a tulip hour hand and an elaborate poker minute.

The **movement** is interesting. The escape wheel has a normal six leaf pinion but, exceptionally, the train has one more wheel than is normal; all have a high tooth count and their pinions have twelve leaves. This arrangement was not intended to produce a longer running time but, theoretically at least, to result in a better transmission of power and a more reliable watch. The top plate is signed but not numbered. There are tulip pillars, except that, for reasons of space, the one adjacent to the contrate wheel is a narrow turned baluster. The neck of the cock has a grotesque male head and the table a bird above some fruit.

A Clockmakers' Company minute of 1708 records that William Bertram – also Bartram – was excused Stewardship as he was 'at present busy on the Queen's business'. Clearly he was an interesting man about whom little is known. PRIVATE COLLECTION

Plate 63. Peter Garon, London, no. 481.
Silver cases 72mm: both AR conjoined in cameo (Adam Roumieu)

The exceptionally large movement of this watch, made about **1700**, possibly shortly before, runs for some eight days. The outer case is decorated with exquisite engraving in the baroque style, reviving classical designs and interpretations of it made during the Renaissance, sometimes with elements of the grotesque. The design was no doubt adapted from a contemporary source; there were a number of, particularly French, artists active in England at this time.

Very few eight day English watches exist from this period; there is another signed by Richard Street and possibly one or two others. The **movement** is well engraved with the full signature 'Peter Garon London' together with the number. The unusual cock has a half-figure on the foot holding a basket of fruit upon her head – personifying Summer – while the table, which has two bird-head 'streamers' at the base, is engraved with two dolphins and a bird with outstretched wings. Two of the pillars are in the tulip style and two are round balusters in

order to allow room for the large barrel and fusee. There is a long wheel train and a remote cannon pinion.

The back of the outer **case** is covered with a complex design consisting of scrolls, swags and acanthus leaves within which are grotesque masks, a pair of exotic birds and two putti, these last on either side of a central reserve containing a scene of Orpheus charming the animals with his music (Ovid, *Metamorphoses*, 10: 86-105). Putti are also associated with Erato, muse of lyric and love poetry. The narrow band is decorated with grapes and vine leaves, the bezel with acanthus and four cherub heads. The plain inner case has an oval ring pendant.

A cherub is below the signature in the centre of the champlevé **dial** and a date aperture is at three. There is an elegant tulip hour hand and well-proportioned minute hand which has been made slender in order to keep drag on the motion work to a minimum.   PRIVATE COLLECTION

Actual size.

Plate 64. Thomas Tompion, London, no.144.
Gold inner case: WS incuse (William Sherwood senior),
hallmarked 1697-8; outer 53mm: no marks

Not only is this a really quite special early repeating watch by Tompion, it is also in excellent condition. It was in the Chester Beatty Collection which was auctioned in June 1968, then in the collection formed by Seth Atwood and later sold by Sotheby's, New York, in June 2002 (their photographs are gratefully acknowledged).

The gold champlevé **dial** is signed within two cartouches, the upper with putti holding garlands of flowers. The poker minute hand is a marvellous example of the early style, a good rib preceding a strong hip with a pronounced taper and a second, equally strong, from half way. The elaborate hour hand, not unlike those found on clocks of the period, is of a floriate design which has been given the unfortunate generalised description 'early beetle'. The term 'beetle', too well established to be challenged, is used to describe an over-broad category of hour hands made up to the end of the eighteenth century.

In order that it would be difficult to tamper with the signed and numbered **movement**, it is secured in the inner case by secret latches which are released through pin holes. Regulation can be achieved without opening the case, the index being within an aperture in the case back. Some of the complexity of the repeating mechanism can be gleaned from the photographs. For a general discussion on repeating mechanisms the reader is referred to the beginning of the chapter, while a detailed description of the function of early Tompion quarter repeating work, written by Francis Wadsworth, was published on pages 460 and 461 of the Spring 1999 edition of *Antiquarian Horology*. The cock, which is numbered on the underside, has a broad bordered foot, tight foliate decoration and a small shell at the neck. There are tulip pillars.

The inner **case**, pierced and engraved with scrolling foliage inhabited by birds, has the number and a landscape by the pendant. The number is also beneath the bell adjacent to the hallmark. The simplicity of the early repeat pendant and bow are noteworthy. The outer case is decorated gold pin-work and has gold lunettes – 'portholes' – for sound emission.

PRIVATE COLLECTION

131

Plate 65. Thomas Tompion, London, no. 2628.
Silver cases 55mm: both IB coronet above incuse (John Banbury)

A plain silver timepiece but well up to Tompion's standards, this watch was made in about **1698**.

The design of the **dial**, the cartouches – the upper having putti holding garlands of flowers – and signature are identical to those on the repeating watch 144, hallmarked for 1697 (Plate 64). There is a tulip hour and poker minute hand.

The **movement** is engraved with a typical signature: 'Tho. Tompion London'. The number is on the edge of the plate and is repeated beneath the balance cock and on the front plate. The cock and the large three-arm balance are also typical of Tompion's work at this period. There are tulip pillars.

The watch number is on the inner **case**. It is good to see an original early stirrup bow and pendant; so often these have been replaced because of wear or damage, or because it was thought a ring pendant and bow was more appropriate. The outer case has a square hinge – they could be more pronounced a little later – and the bezel has an inner chamfer typical of the period.

PRIVATE COLLECTION

Actual size.

Actual size.

Plate 66. Mathew Des hais, London, no. 254 and 57.
Silver cases 55mm: inner GN incuse (George Nau), no. 254;
outer BI incuse (probably Benjamin Jeffes)

Very little is known about Des hais, but his early work is of exceptional quality. In some respects it has a close resemblance to Tompion's. This watch was made within a year or two of **1700**.

The champlevé **dial** has a splendid grotesque head in the upper cartouche looking over the maker's signature. The aperture on the left shows the date while the one on the right has a fixed radiant sun. Sight of the movement confirms that this arrangement is entirely original – it is simply to achieve a balanced design. There are excellent hands: a tulip hour and a minute – all but identical to those on Tompion's work at this period – with two bulbous parts, the first closing on the quarter-hour divisions and the second reaching to the minutes.

The **movement** number 254 follows after the signature 'Mathew Des hais London' and is partly obscured by the regulator plate. Near the edge of the top plate adjacent to the signature and the attractively turned end of one of the tulip pillars is the number 57, while 54 is scratched on the underside of the cock. This is beautifully engraved with a particularly amusing grotesque mask at the neck and, on the table, an angel's head, two squirrels and a bird amongst scrolls of acanthus leaves. A special feature of this watch and another by Des hais – number 79 (Plate 48) – is that both ends of the balance spring are secured not by the normal circular pin and hole, but the superior method of square tapered pins in square holes. The heads of the tulip

pillars above the top plate have decorative turning.

The inner **case** by George Nau is numbered 254 with individual punches. Philip Priestley *(Early Watch Case Makers of England,* NAWCC, 2000) records just three other cases with his mark; two have movements by Tompion and one by Henry Jones. Nau was probably dead by 1698, but it is possible that his widow might have used his mark. If the incuse case mark BI on the outer indeed belongs to Benjamin Jeffes, it may be significant that he was not free of his apprenticeship to John Willoughby until 1702.

A fascinating day-book, which came to light in 1967, was subject to an excellent analysis by E.F. Bunt *(Antiquarian Horology,* March 1973*)*. It seems to have belonged to Benjamin Gray (1676-1764) and covers the years 1704-1726. More than half the sales listed are to trade customers and consist of movements, mostly repeaters, without cases. Well-known makers are featured, including Quare, Windmills, Garon, Massy, Watson and Dunlop. His best customer was Des hais (sometimes spelt Dehais, at others Dehay) who purchased no less than thirty-eight movements, most of them between 1704 and 1710. PRIVATE COLLECTION

Plate 67. Peter Garon, London.

Silver inner case: no marks; outer 58mm: no marks

Garon completed his seven years apprenticeship to Richard Baker in 1694, but when he applied to the Clockmakers' Company for his freedom it refused on the basis that he was an alien. However the Lord Mayor granted him the freedom of the City.

Made around **1700**, this 'mock pendulum' watch has a partly skeletonised cock: if the owner opens up his watch he can admire the action of the balance and spring. The balance and cock table had become larger during the 1690s and the foot had become narrower in consequence, but also significantly broader.

The deep **movement**, which is signed simply 'Garon London', has tulip pillars. The cock table is made so that just under half reveals a 'mock pendulum' and a balance spring of approximately three turns; a circular brass insert in one arm of the balance swings as the balance oscillates. On the other part of the table are two birds of paradise amongst foliage and scrolls engraved on a hatched ground.

The champlevé **dial**, typical of the period, has the signature above the centre and a date aperture below. There are tulip hands.

The plain inner **case** has a split bezel for glass retention and a ring pendant and bow. The outer is tortoiseshell – more accurately turtleshell – covered and decorated with pin-work, the foliate scrolls in silver and small flowers in gold. These cases ceased to be quite so fashionable after the turn of the century.

PRIVATE COLLECTION

Plate 68. Fromanteel & Clarke, London.
Silver-gilt cases 58mm: both IB coronet above (probably
John Banbury)

A clock-watch, from shortly after **1700**, which was part of
the Edward Hornby Collection sold by Sotheby's in
December 1978. There were clearly still those who had a
preference for a striking, as opposed to a repeating, watch
– it did, of course, mean that there was no need for an
insomniac to have to find his watch in the dark and then
to wrestle with the repeating plunger!

The champlevé is signed in two cartouches,
Fromanteel above and Clarke below, and there are steel
dial beetle and poker hands.

The **movement** is signed in block letters which were

now being used by several makers, including Tompion and
Banger. It is not numbered. The locking plate for the
striking is in the usual place next to the signature. In
order to allow clearance, a simple cylindrical pillar has
been used by the pierced striking barrel and mechanism,
but otherwise there are plain Egyptian pillars.

Both **cases** are pierced and engraved in a similar
manner with swags, foliage and flowers and a number of
birds. The inner has a stirrup pendant and bow, while the
square hinge on the outer is modest and mostly flush with
the case. PRIVATE COLLECTION

Plate 69. William Sinclare, London no. 78.

Silver cases 54mm: inner W and S (separate punches), numbered 78; outer: TW shaped cameo, rays above (unidentified)

The maker of this watch, which was probably made within a couple of years after **1700**, may well be the Irishman with a very similar name who is recorded as being active between 1698 and 1741: there is a watch signed 'William Sinclaire Dublin' numbered 224.

The **dial** has a mock pendulum within an aperture below the offset chapter ring. The balance is mounted between the bottom plate and the dial and, when it oscillates, one of its arms has the appearance of a pendulum. The square in the centre of the calibrated segment on the left is for regulation, while that on the right locks the movement to the case. There is a tulip hour hand and poker minute.

Having the balance and cock on the other side of the **movement** allows for special treatment of the top plate. This is signed and numbered and flanked within a finely engraved cartouche by two half figures of winged nymphs. The pillars are most unusual, being round balusters with circular foliate capitals.

The plain inner **case**, which has a good early stirrup pendant and bow, is marked W and S with single, well separated, punches. These are, of course, the watchmaker's initials, but it is very unclear whether or not he made this case. The end joints of the plain outer case have a modest chamfer.

Actual size.

PRIVATE COLLECTION

138

Plate 70. Tompion and Banger, London, no. 3842.

Silver cases 55mm: both WS coronet above (William Sherwood senior)

Thomas Tompion signed watches jointly with Edward Banger from 1700 or 1701 for about seven years; this quite typical example was made in **1704** or 1705. It can be compared with Tompion number 2628 (Plate 65), with which there are differences not only in the decorative detail, signature and pillar style, but also size; there was a fashion for larger watches.

There is a typical champlevé **dial** and signature flanked by putti holding garlands of flowers. The tulip hour hand is a late example. The **movement** is signed 'T Tompion, E Banger London' in block letters together with the number which is repeated on the underside of the cock. The cock table has swags and foliage, a fabulous bird, a mask at the neck and a pair of particularly large 'wings' typical of the period on the lower edge of the rim. There are Egyptian pillars.

The inner **case** is marked and numbered. It has a good early stirrup pendant and bow, a square hinge with a split bezel for glass retention and a winding shutter. The outer case also has the maker's mark while the watch number is on the inner edge of the back bezel.   PRIVATE COLLECTION

Plate 71. James Banks, Nottingham.

Silver cases 52mm: inner T.P in rectangular cameo with device above; outer: no marks

One of four watches known by Banks, each varying somewhat from one another but to approximately the same specification. This example was probably made about **1705**.

The differential **dial** has a single hand which indicates the minutes on the outer ring and the hours on the central disc which, so that the current hour is always under the hand, revolves one twelfth slower at each rotation. The signature is within an embossed and chased band decorated with trophies of war. Bands with the same decoration are to be found on a few watches of this type signed by other makers.

The top plate of the **movement** is covered with pierced and engraved decoration and the signature 'J Banks Nottingh'm' is on an oval reserve on the cock table. The 'crested Egyptian' pillars have concave outlines below pierced foliate galleries.

The other three watches of this type by Banks have **cases** made by Richard Blundell – or have the RB mark which is probably his – and of these one has the earliest silver hallmark on a watch so far recorded: London 1698 together with the Britannia mark (see Priestley, *Early Watch Case Makers of England,* NAWCC, 2000, page 6). Very few cases bearing Blundell's mark are recorded after 1702; for the inner case of this watch Banks employed, another, unidentified, maker. As with the 1698 hallmarked watch, much of the back of the outer has a scene which appears to have been cast, rather than embossed; there is no maker's mark. The allegorical scene of the triumph of love has above it 'Amoris tela omnium querela'. Cupid, with a pair of doves beside him, drives the chariot pulled by compliant lions. A seated maiden holds a heart and her beau, his hands in fetters, is consumed with love. The hinge has shaped end joints.

THE DJANOGLY COLLECTION

Actual size.

Plate 72. John Carte, London.

Silver case 45mm: RB in cameo (probably Richard Blundell)

Made probably around **1705**, the signed **dial** is registered so that both the hours and minutes can be read off a single tulip hand. It has been suggested that these – a few others exist – were made for owners who were used to single-handed pre-balance spring watches and were confused by two hands. But two hands had been the norm for some twenty years and this arrangement is related to the prevailing fashion to present time in a variety of ways. Of course, about a hundred years later the famous Paris watchmaker, A.-L. Breguet, made a series of very popular single handed watches.

The signed **movement** is, in general, typical of the period. The foliate pierced and engraved cock has animal-head 'streamers' by the neck but the pillars, although they are solid (pierced out only in the centre with a simple dot and dash in the Egyptian style), have a waist to the tapered outline – quite as the tulip shape. The single **case** is plain; the outer case is lacking.

John Carte started his working life in Coventry, as indeed his illustrious contemporary Samuel Watson did, and was in London by 1695. Jeremy Evans in his book on Thomas Tompion (*Antiquarian Horology*, monograph 2006) quotes from a manuscript in the Bodleian Library, where Carte praises Tompion and his work soon after his death in 1713. Only a few watches signed by Carte are known; he may well have worked within the trade as a supplier or journeyman. This watch is in Henry Marryat's book illustrating some of the watches in his collection. PRIVATE COLLECTION

Opposite: Plate 73. Daniel Quare, London, no. 237.

Silver cases 55mm: inner WI incuse (William Jaques), outer: AR conjoined in cameo (Adam Roumieu)

Quare is known to have had two series of numbers, one of which is thought to have been reserved for repeaters, but it is not clear whether he used it for them from the beginning. Very few of his watches are in hallmarked cases and consequently the serial numbers can act only as a general guide for establishing dates. However, this watch was probably made in about **1705**, possibly a little before.

The **dial** has, most unusually for a repeating watch, a square and scale for front regulation. The hands are eccentric, complex and beautifully made.

A dust ring round the edge of the **movement** is held with

screws into the top plate which is signed 'D: Quare London' in simple script and numbered. The cock table, decorated with acanthus leaves, has a small head wearing a headdress at the neck and well-defined streamers from the edge. The end-piece for the repeating mechanism is also engraved.

The band of the inner **case** is pierced and engraved with acanthus, 'C' scrolls and strap decoration with a grotesque mask at the base. The outer is decorated with open rondels and the hinge has shaped end-joints. The eighteenth century cut steel chatelaine attached to the watch has a later brass key between a seal and a hinged crank key. PRIVATE COLLECTION

dumb repeating facility where, fixed to the inner case at five o'clock, there is a push at the end of a pipe which extends significantly beyond the bezel of the outer. Delander was one of the very first makers (from about 1712) to use pierced rubies and ruby or diamond endstones for his balance staff pivots. Quite a number of watches, this one included, have had jewels fitted after they were made. One would expect a small collet to be incorporated in the original cock design when a jewel was intended and the holes to be gilded. The signature and number are on the band between the bottom and dial plate. There are Egyptian pillars.

The band of the inner **case** is beautifully pierced and engraved with particularly tight scrolls of foliage inhabited by fabulous birds and dolphins. Beneath the pendant there is a river scene with church in the foreground and at the base a grotesque mask. The brass stem of the dumb-piece extends through the outer which is decorated with open rondels.

For many years this watch belonged to David Landes, professor of both History and Economics at Harvard, and it is illustrated in his very excellent book *Revolution in Time* (Harvard, 1983).

PRIVATE COLLECTION

Plate 74. Daniel Delander, London, no. 52.
Silver cases 58mm: both WI incuse (William Jaques)

Delander was one of Tompion's journeymen, but also he was certainly in business on his own account for a few years prior to 1713 when Tompion died. He did not produce many watches, particularly early on, but they all seem to have been to a very high standard. This can be dated between about **1705** and **1710**.

The **dial** cartouche is distinctive, with a shell above the signature and a grotesque mask below. Most unusually, the underside of the dial has a maker's mark: 'William Jaques' Britannia mark Ia incuse. There is an early beetle hour hand and a good poker minute of the period.

The **movement**, which has Tompion's chain and hinged quarter rack type of repeating, has two particularly noteworthy features: an early bayonet-type dust cap and a possibly unique arrangement for

Plate 75. David Lestourgeon, London no. 1331.
Silver cases 57mm: inner PW in rectangular cameo
(unidentified), outer: no marks

Watches with wandering hour dials are quite rare. This can be
dated reasonably accurately in so far as the royal arms on the
balance cock follow those adopted by Queen Anne after the Act
of Union of **1707**. It was in the Kalish Collection sold at
Sotheby's in July 1964.

The minutes are marked in a semicircle across the top of the
dial. Between these and the four quarter divisions near the centre
is an engraved gilt band which rotates and carries with it the hour
showing in a circular aperture. This rises – as the sun – and
travels right indicating the hours and quarters and disappears to be
replaced by the next hour. In the lower part of the dial Chronos
is drawing Helios's – Phoebus (Radiant) Apollo's – chariot.

The **movement** is numbered and signed 'L'eturgeon
London' in a type of curvaceous script common at this period.
The use of the Queen's new armorial on the cock
demonstrated the sense of national identity and the promise of
collective prosperity. It would have been popular with
Hanoverians, less so with Jacobites. There are Egyptian pillars.

The inner **case** has a rather curious pendant. The ring is
certainly later. The outer case hinge is resolutely square.

PRIVATE COLLECTION

Actual size.

Plate 76. Henry Massy, London.
Gold cases 56mm: outer IB or TB coronet above (John Banbury or Thomas Beseley)

Henry Massy, or Massey, came from a watchmaking family – his father Nicholas was a French Protestant immigrant. This watch was made about **1710**, possibly a little before.

The gold **dial** is signed and there are fleur-de-lis half-hour divisions. The ends of the petals of the tulip hour hand are well defined; in fact this design is not so far removed from the so-called beetle hand, where the lower petal on each side is brought round in a full circle to close on the stem.

The **movement's** quarter repeating mechanism follows, in general terms, the design established by Daniel Quare. The top plate is signed, but not numbered, and the cock has a grotesque mask at the neck. The three-arm balance is of brass and the round baluster pillars are arranged to allow room for the complex mechanism between the plates.

The body of the inner **case** is pierced and engraved with foliate scrolls, straps and birds. The flat top of the pendant has a grotesque mask. The original bow was replaced later in the century. The cases Massy seems to have favoured at this period had a simple loop bow of a rope-twist design. The outer case, decorated with open rondels, has a square hinge with exaggerated end joints and contains a watch paper on which the full Lord's Prayer has been minutely written.

PRIVATE COLLECTION

Actual size.

Plate 77. James Debaufre, London.
Silver inner case: no marks; outer 104mm: no marks

The signature on the **movement** of this large striking, repeating and alarm coach-watch, which really cannot be dated closer to a few years prior to **1710**, simply reads 'DEBAUFRE LONDON' while, engraved in the same manner, but concealed below the adjacent alarm stop-work, is 'IAM'.

The balance is jewelled with rubies top and bottom, each jewel having a deep blind hole and a brass setting with the ends closed at the edges. The top jewel has a separate blued steel end-piece screwed to the cock, the bottom held in place by a wedge. The fact that the jewels are not pierced through would seem to suggest that this is an early, prototypical arrangement. On 1 May 1704 Peter (Pierre) and Jacob Debaufre took out patent 371 jointly with Nicholas Facio de Duillier for the piercing of jewels. As

Protestants, these men had settled in London after the Revocation of Nantes. The patent was initially granted, attracted opposition from the Clockmakers' Company (*see various sources but also David Landes, Revolution in Time,* Harvard, 1983, pages136-140), and then withdrawn. The Company was not only following the generally accepted principles of the day, that restriction would only hinder scientific innovation but also, since the patent could not be enforced abroad, its own members would be at a serious disadvantage. As it was, although jewel piercing was a highly important development for horology, it was difficult and expensive and was taken up only slowly in England and hardly at all on the Continent.

So what of the abbreviated Christian name under the alarm stop-work? James (Jacques) was born, apparently, in 1691. He is recorded as apprenticed to

Roger Nicholls in 1708 and free in 1713 (even though Nicholls was almost certainly dead by 1708). Nicholls (or his name) may have been used as a nominee – a fairly common practice – but, in any event, James was no doubt working with his family when this watch was made.

The verge potence is riveted to the top plate and, rather in the seventeenth century manner, the rivet is engraved. Also, five leaf pinions have been used in various parts of the movement. There are square baluster pillars, a fusee for the going train and stop-work for both the hour striking and alarm going barrels on the top plate. A strike/silent lever is in the bezel and repeating is via a pull cord.

Winding for going and striking is through the **dial** in which there is also a female square for setting the alarm against the tail of the hour hand. The alarm is wound through the back of the inner **case**; this is most beautifully pierced and engraved and there is an excellent grotesque mask at the base. The leather outer has open rondels in silver, the back with fine pin-work of swags and drops and, in the centre, a complex floriate rosette. Interestingly, as is quite often found with cases of this size, the hinge is significantly less than ninety degrees to the pendant. This is possibly to ensure that the front bezel will tend to remain closed even if the catch is inadvertently sprung when the watch is vertical.

This watch was in the Van Steenwegen and Van Cauwenburgh Collections. No other watches by the Debaufres with pierced jewelling are recorded to have survived from this period. Daniel Delander made a number of watches with both pierced and partly pierced jewels about the same time (number 386 is illustrated in Plate 89).   PRIVATE COLLECTION

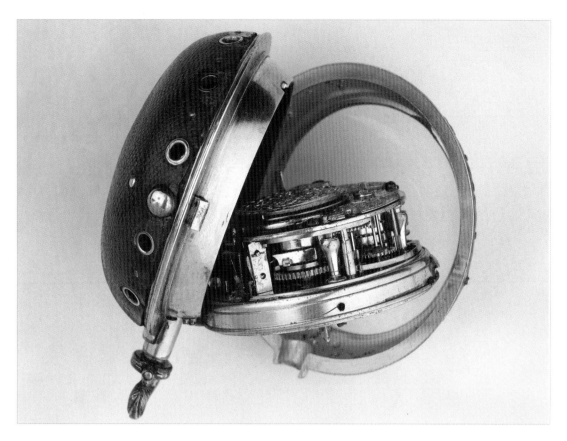

Plate 78. Thomas Tompion, London, no. 328.

Gilt metal single case 53mm: no marks

While the vast majority of English watches were given pair-cases, some makers had begun, by **1709-1711** when this was made, to fit, occasionally, a single case. Obviously without an outer case, access to the winding square via a simple shutter is somewhat easier. They could be cheaper to produce and, given the same size of movement, the watch could be somewhat smaller than it would be in pair-cases.

The gilt metal **case** is covered with green dyed sharkskin. This is a quarter repeating watch, so the inner second bezel is decorated with open rondels in a manner typical of the period. The back has a winding shutter.

The gold champlevé **dial** is typical, the signature flanked by putti holding garlands of flowers. Because Tompion has had the **movement** top plate made slightly smaller than is usual, his signature is on one line rather than two and the number, rather than following it in the normal way, precedes it beneath the banking piece. Tompion was one of the first makers to fit diamond endstones and another repeating watch, which has the earlier number 307 and cases hallmarked for 1708/9, has original pierced ruby bearings with a diamond endstone. This watch does not have one, maybe to save the expense, but certainly the cock, which is numbered on the underside, is thinner and less likely to be fouled by the bell fixing screw. Rather than being screwed, the dial is attached to the front plate with a 'secret' catch. There is a dust ring, two baluster pillars and three Egyptian. PRIVATE COLLECTION

Actual size.

151

Plate 79. Richard Williamson, London.

Silver cases 60mm: both WI coronet above (John Wightman)

Sun and moon dials continued to be popular during the early years of the century. This watch was made about **1710** when there was a fashion for somewhat larger and deeper watches than hitherto.

The sun and moon move across the semicircular aperture in the **dial** indicating the hours, while the central hand indicates the minutes. The signature, 'Williamson, Fecit', is flanked by birds within foliate scrolls on the cartouche below.

The deep **movement** is quite typical of English watches of the period, although the cylindrical pillars, which have ribbed capitals, are somewhat unusual. No place or number follows the signature. The **case** maker's mark is that of John Wightman, a London maker who was free of his apprenticeship to Jonathan Jones a couple of years before he registered his mark in 1697. The stirrup pendant and bow are unremarkable, but the hinge is particularly prominent and has strong chamfers to the end joints. PRIVATE COLLECTION

Actual size.

Plate 80. Fromanteel & Clarke, London.

Silver cases 58mm: both ID coronet above (James, possibly John, Delander)

The **dial** signature is within the most unusual pierced, chased and engraved silver centre which has a date aperture showing through the gilt ground. The design has a grotesque head below twelve o'clock, apparently about to swallow a bird, and a feeding squirrel at three, within foliate decoration. The half-hour divisions are seen on other watches by this partnership which was active from about 1700. This watch was made around **1710**, possibly shortly before.

The large **movement**, typical of the period, is signed but not numbered. The large balance cock has exotic birds within foliage and flowers and there are Egyptian pillars. The outer **case** is characteristic of the type: the hinge is square and prominent and the inner edge of the front bezel has a deep chamfer.

PRIVATE COLLECTION

Actual size.

153

Plate 81. Daniel Quare, London, no. 3762.

Silver cases 50mm: inner WI incuse (William Jaques), outer: WG incuse (probably William Ginn)

Made in about **1710**, this is a good example of the series of large watches by Quare which have particularly deep movements with large balances and which are wound, set and regulated from the front. It would seem that they may well have been made in response to the well-established French fashion for watches with a similar configuration but without front regulation, the so called 'oignon'.

The **dial** signature has lion and unicorn supporters borrowed from the royal arms, a popular form of decoration at this period. The Act of Union, uniting the English and Scottish Parliaments, was passed in 1707. Quare continued, quite often, to fit tulip hands long after most of his contemporaries. The minute hand is stepped to clear the winding square. A female square for adjusting the regulator is immediately above the blued steel figure plate.

Actual size.

The **movement** is signed 'Dan Quare London' and numbered. The impressively large cock is decorated with foliage, birds and dolphin heads and a female mask at the neck. Of course no regulation figure plate is present, this being in the dial. There are crested Egyptian pillars.

The watch number is in the inner **case** which has a stirrup pendant and a bow with modest foliate decoration. The back of the outer is engraved with a complex monogram. PRIVATE COLLECTION

Plate 82. John Brockhurst, London.

Silver single case 52mm: no marks

The signature on the **dial** is gilt on a blued steel ground, while the simplified royal arms was a popular motif for some years following the 1707 Act of Union. The **movement** is quite typical of the period around **1710-1712**, having a cock with foliate decoration inhabited by birds and dolphin heads, and plain Egyptian pillars.

The single **case** is also typical of the type where both the hinge end joints and the inner edge of the front bezel have modest mouldings. The stirrup bow has a well-defined waist – it is quite an early example of the style. The case maker's mark may well have been lost originally when the good recessed winding shutter was fitted. PRIVATE COLLECTION

Actual size.

Plate 83. De Charmes, London. Silver-gilt cases 58mm: inner ML, coronet above (unidentified); outer: no marks

Simon De Charmes and David, probably his son, were Frenchmen who joined the Clockmakers' Company as Free Brothers in 1691. Although their watches are in the English style, they tend to have strong Continental overtones and this watch, probably of about **1710**, is no exception. Generally the signatures are either prefixed by 'Simon' or the Christian name is omitted.

The **dial** is signed 'De Charmes London' below the off-set chapter ring and mock pendulum aperture. A front regulation square and index is to the right of the aperture, while a disc on one arm of the balance beneath the dial mimics the action of a pendulum. Birds and a small mask within foliate decoration occupy the space to the sides and below the chapter ring.

The **movement** is deeper than normal because of the half-length portrait of the lady in period costume, painted in enamel on copper, mounted on the top plate. At first sight the contrate wheel appears upside down, but this is because the balance is between the bottom – or 'pillar plate' – and dial plate. There are Egyptian pillars. Another very similar watch by De Charmes is known (Jonathan Snellenburg's catalogue, April 1997) which has a nearly identical portrait thought to be of the Duchesse de Fontanges (1660-1681), mistress of Louis XIV. The lady has very much the same dress and hair style, the significant difference

being that the hair has a ribbon omitted in the present portrait, tied on the left-hand side. It is said that the Duchesse – who was considered a great beauty – tied the ribbon in her hair after she lost her hat whilst riding and that, thereafter, the ladies of the Court wore their hair up tied with a *fontange*, this fashion spreading to England. Both **cases** are plain and in silver gilt.

Plate 84. Maurice Smith, London, no. 492.

Silver inner case: no marks; outer: 55mm: no marks

Two similar watches are signed by John Bushman; one is in the Victoria & Albert Museum and the other was at one time in the Time Museum, Rockford, Illinois. This one was in the Sandberg Collection and would seem to be from the same **1710–1715** period.

The silver **dial** is decorated in the baroque manner, the foliage inhabited by dolphin heads and birds with overtones of the grotesque. Two blued steel shutters covering apertures for the hours above and the minutes below open when the pendant is depressed and shut when it is released, the numerals being on rotating rings beneath the dial. The time is set by a central square.

The **movement** is signed in full, 'Maurice Smith, Royal Exchange, London', and numbered. The foot and table of the cock are pierced and engraved and there is a grotesque mask at the neck. A serpent's tongue indicates the divisions on the silver regulator disc. There are square baluster pillars.

The plain inner **case** is silver-gilt, the outer gilt-metal covered in rayskin dyed green.   Private Collection

Actual size.

foliate scrolls and a shell in the centre. A serpent's head on the index plate points to the regulator scale. There are round baluster pillars and the design of the repeating mechanism is similar to Daniel Quare's. The dust ring around the edge of the movement is engraved with shells and foliate scrolls.

The place of the maker's mark in the inner **case** has been taken by the bell stand. The band is beautifully pierced and engraved with inhabited foliage and there is a splendid grotesque mask at the base. The long lopped bow is a form which is found occasionally during this period, while the square hinge and open rondels on the outer case are typical. PRIVATE COLLECTION

Plate 85. Francis Gregg, London.
Gold cases 54mm: inner no mark; outer: AR conjoined in cameo (Adam Roumieu), both cases hallmarked 1711-2

This high quality gold pair-cased quarter repeating watch is signed by a very respectable maker and it is typical of the period. The decorative designs owe much to those of the Renaissance revival.

The **dial** has signature cartouches with robust 'C' scrolls and quatrefoil half-hour divisions. The **movement** is fully signed but un-numbered. The cock table has female and dolphin heads amongst the

Plate 86. John Halsted, London.
Gold cases 58mm: inner EE rectangular cameo (possibly Edward East II), hallmarked 1712-3; outer: no marks

Sarah Churchill, Duchess of Marlborough, wrote in her will '…I give to Mrs. Ann Pattinson my striking watch which formerly belonged to her mistress my Lady Sunderland…'. Lady Sunderland was the Duchess of Marlborough's (and, of course, the famous Duke's) second daughter, Ann, who died in April 1716.

The back of the **inner case** is plain with a rosette in the centre and a garland around the winding aperture. Somewhat poorly engraved between them is the letter A while left of the rosette is S and to the right is C. The monogram in the centre of the outer case consists of A with SC and SC reversed, so clearly this must surely be the quarter repeating watch mentioned in the will which belonged to Ann Spencer Churchill, Duchess of Sunderland.

It is equally clear that the provenance given in the sale of the Bernal Collection at Christie's in April 1855 (lot 3878), that the watch was presented by Queen Anne to Sarah Churchill, is only partly correct but understandable, given that six of the twelve busts on the back of the **outer case** are an identical crowned portrait which certainly could be Queen Anne.

If this is accepted, then who might be the young woman in profile? Engraved on the inner case band below six o'clock is the bust of a young woman beneath a canopy (which suggests high rank), flanked by a lion and unicorn. By 1712 Queen Anne was expected to die but had not named her successor. The Protestant communion, of which the Marlboroughs were a prominent part, supported the Hanoverian cause. The future George I had no wife, while that of his son, the ever popular Caroline Ansbach – later Queen Caroline – had already been in England for ten years and it is very likely that she is the subject of the portraits. This is an excellent and early example of embossed – and chased – work with the repeated use of a series of single punches.

The lower part of the signed **dial** cartouche has a cherub's head. The design of the early beetle hour hand is noteworthy; there is a good poker minute hand and distinctive half-hour divisions. The high quality **movement**, which is signed in Gothic script, and is unnumbered, has round baluster pillars and is typical of the period.   THE DJANOGLY COLLECTION

Plate 87. George Graham, London, no 4580.

Gold cases 55mm: inner WS incuse (William Sherwood senior) rubbed hallmark 1713-4 or 1714-5; outer: IW incuse (probably John Willoughby), no hallmark

As Tompion's partner and successor, Graham continued the watch numbering series when the former died in 1713. This appears to be the earliest complete and hallmarked timepiece signed by Graham alone; there is a repeating watch hallmarked 1713 recorded. Graham continued the established standards of quality and, indeed, as can be seen here, he employed a quite excellent engraver.

The **dial** is signed and there is a date aperture and beetle and poker hands. Graham seems to have favoured dials with unusually long, slender half-hour divisions.

The numbered **movement** is signed 'Geo. Graham London'. The cock has 'C' scroll and free-flowing foliate decoration, a classical female head at the neck and a rosette in the centre. There are elegant plain Egyptian pillars.

The inner **case** has the number, maker's mark and a hallmark which is somewhat rubbed. William Sherwood made cases for Tompion from the late 1690s and continued to work for Graham.

Actual size.

PRIVATE COLLECTION

163

Plate 88. David Lestourgeon, London, no. 1709.

Silver single case 55mm: IW incuse (probably John Willoughby)

This is an early dumb half-quarter repeating watch made, probably, around **1715**.

The **movement** has rack and pinion repeating with two hammers. The quarter rack has an extension so that a single blow can be struck for the half-quarters, that is when seven and a half minutes or more has passed since the previous quarter. Rather than striking a bell, the hammers hit blocks fixed inside the case – not so melodious, but quieter. For total discretion, the hammers can be held away from the blocks and at the same time pulse of the repeating can be felt, using the 'dumb-piece', a small push in the case bezel. The top plate is signed in full, 'David Lestourgen', with the number. The neck of the cock is engraved with a female head, while the table has foliate and scrollwork inhabited by bird, maybe eagle, heads. There are round baluster pillars.

The **dial** is unusual in so far as the centre is unsigned and quite plain. The silver **case** is covered with leather and decorated with modest pin-work. It has an integral silver winding shutter, the extended steel arm of which hides the first part of the maker's mark.

Actual size.

PRIVATE COLLECTION

The deep **movement**, which is signed in full in block letters, has a large, beautifully engraved cock. This is unusually thick and tapered towards the end of the table below which is a blued steel frame carrying the regulator and silver index. The jewel holes for the balance staff consist of two plates of rubies at each end, the inner pierced and chamfered for the pivots. Note that the polished steel setting for the upper jewelling is screwed to a brass ring incorporated in the cock design: a ring that is often absent from watches which have had jewelling added at a later date. The bottom plate is stamped with the frame maker's mark A (possibly for Allatt or Anderson). There are crested Egyptian pillars.

The **dial** is signed in a typical cartouche of the period and there are beetle and poker hands. A maker's mark on the single **case** may be obscured by a pivoted steel arm operated by a lever near the case catch which carries a gold winding shutter. The ring pendant and bow is a stylistic throw-back. A later watch, number 567, with much the same pendant and bow is in the Victoria & Albert Museum. It is wound through the dial and it has the maker's mark WI – presumably William Jaques. PRIVATE COLLECTION

Plate 89. Daniel Delander, London, no. 386.
Gold single case 52mm: no marks

It appears Delander watches are always made to an exceptional standard; the movement of this watch is superbly engraved and the finish is quite exquisite. He was one of the first makers to fit jewelled bearings to his balance staffs. This watch was made about **1715**.

Actual size.

foot is un-pierced but similarly engraved. There is an early three-arm brass balance and round baluster pillars. The repeating barrel is decorated with vertical hatching.

The high quality inner **case** is typical of the work of the maker, William Jaques. His mark is struck three times – not an infrequent occurrence around this time – adjacent to the number. The number is also repeated below the pendant on the body of the case which is excellently pierced and engraved with inhabited foliage. The outer is decorated with variegated open rondels.

PRIVATE COLLECTION

Plate 90. Daniel Quare, London, no. 769.

Gold cases 55mm: inner WI incuse (William Jaques), outer IL incuse (possibly John Lowe or Laing, more likely John Lee)

Few, if any, of Quare's later repeating watches are hallmarked but, from the invaluable list of makers published by G.H. Baillie in which he records Quare's serial numbers (there were two series, one for repeaters and another for timepieces), one can deduce that this watch was made around **1715**.

The **dial** is signed on ribbon cartouches above and below the centre. The hands are excellent: the minute is of the early poker form, the first waist being coincident with the half-hour divisions; the hour is in the tulip style which Quare continued to use long after his contemporaries had adopted 'beetle' forms.

The **movement** has a signed dust cap and the top plate is signed and numbered 'Dan. Quare London 769'. The cock table, which has a diamond endstone, is pierced and foliate engraved with a shell at the neck, while the

Plate 91. John Wright, London.
Gold cases 50mm: both IB coronet above (John Banbury) and hallmarked 1717-8

The coat of arms on the back of the outer **case** belongs to the Earls of Oxford and Mortimer. The widow of the second Earl sold the Harlian Collection of manuscripts to the British Library in 1753.

The gold champlevé **dial** is signed and there is a good pair of beetle and poker hands. The high quality **movement** is signed but not numbered. It has square baluster pillars, and, unusually, quite early ruby bearings and end-caps for the balance. PRIVATE COLLECTION

Plate 92. Richard Vick, London, no. 625.
Gold cases 52mm: both IP six point star above incuse, struck three times in each (unidentified)

The style of the embossed and chased decoration on the outer case was fashionable by **1720**: the square hinge joints in particular suggest that the watch might well have been made shortly before.

There is a good but very simple **dial** signature, blued steel beetle and poker hands, the latter with unusual turning near the centre square. The dust cap is signed and the quarter repeating **movement** is also signed 'Rich. Vick London', along with the number. The cock has a pierced and engraved table, a mask at the neck and a foot which is engraved but not pierced. There is a three-arm brass balance, the pillars are cylindrical and the repeating barrel is engraved.

The pierced body of the inner **case** has foliate engraving inhabited by birds and dolphins and there is a mask at the base. The stirrup bow is a simple loop with foliate sides. The back of the outer has unusually complex embossed and chased decoration around the central reserve, a four part symmetric scroll cartouche with half-round indents for four bust medallions which alternate with pierced, chased and engraved panels. The front bezel, in which there is a repeating dumb-piece, has similar panels and floriate cartouche. It is just possible the embossing is an example of Augustin Heckel's early work. Certainly Vick employed him – a signed case, sharing one or two of the same design elements, is illustrated in Plate 104.

PRIVATE COLLECTION

Plate 93. Daniel Quare & Stephen Horseman, London, no. 991.

Gold cases 49mm: inner SL.IL incuse (Sarah Jaques and John Lee), outer: AR conjoined in outline cameo (almost certainly Adam Roumieu the younger)

The combination of the signature, movement number and case marks indicate a date for this watch of between **1719** and **1724**, and probably nearer the former. It has an interesting provenance.

The **dial** is signed 'D. Quare & S. Horseman London' and there are beetle and poker hands. The dust cap and **movement** are signed 'Quare and Horseman', the top plate is numbered, and the cock table, decorated with symmetric foliate scrolls and a shell at the neck, has a diamond endstone. The balance is of brass – some watches, particularly repeaters, were fitted with brass balances, rather than steel, from about this period. There are round baluster pillars.

The inner **case** has the number beneath the bell together with the maker's mark which is struck three times. The band is pierced and engraved with flowers and foliage inhabited by birds and dolphin heads and, at the base, there is a youth's head, probably Phoebus Apollo. The number is repeated below the pendant. A plain central reserve on the back of the outer is surrounded by embossed shells, flowers, grapes and scrolls. Outside the modest four-part simple scroll cartouche, there are four portrait busts alternating with four pierced chased panels. One of the busts might possibly be of Homer. The front bezel has four floral medallions between pierced panels.

The **provenance** of this watch is interesting. It was lent to the Hartlebury Museum, Worcestershire, during the 1970s by Richard Bevan, Rector of Abberley, and it was recorded as inherited by his great-great-grandfather, also Richard, from his uncle, the well-known Quaker apothecary Silvanus Bevan F.R.S. (1691-1765). A family tradition is that it was given to Silvanus by Quare on the occasion of his marriage to Quare's daughter, Elizabeth, in 1715; this cannot be true, however, as the watch was not made by this date. Sadly, Elizabeth died in 1718, but it is difficult to believe Silvanus would have carried a watch other than one by Quare so that it is still very likely that family tradition is correct and that this watch belonged to him. The wedding was a significant affair and important members of society attended, including the Duchess of Marlborough (see Jagger, *Royal Clocks*, among other sources).

PRIVATE COLLECTION

Plate 94. Andrew Dunlop, London.

Gold cases 48.2mm: both IW incuse (John Willoughby), inner (and possibly outer) hallmarked 1720-1

This must be one of the very earliest English five minute repeating watches.

The **movement** is signed but not numbered. Much of the five minute repeating mechanism can be seen mounted on the underside of the pillar plate. There is a diamond endstone, verge escapement and round baluster pillars.

The outer **case** has very good embossed and chased decoration and the gold champlevé **dial**, signed simply Dunlop with a shell motif below, is typical of the period.

Cecil Clutton told an informal meeting of the Antiquarian Horological Society in November 1954 that a five minute repeating watch by Dunlop accompanied him as a pilot on many flights during World War II. He said he liked to think of it as having been the oldest watch on active service! PRIVATE COLLECTION

Actual size.

Plate 95. Thomas Cartwright, London.
Gold cases 54mm: both JB Gothic – struck three times –
(possibly John Birdwhistle)

The design of the chased and embossed outer case suggests the **1720-1725** period.

Following the signature on the unnumbered quarter repeating **movement** is 'Principi Horologs' and on the silver dust cap 'the Prince's Watchmaker'. Cartwright became the Royal watchmaker on George II's accession in 1727. He took over, according to PRO sources recorded by Cedric Jagger in *Royal Clocks* (Robert Hale, 1983), from Richard Vick. Otherwise the movement is typical of the period and there is a three-arm brass balance.

The **dial** has a crown in the centre of the signed cartouche. The hour hand is unusually elaborate, the minute a 'double baluster', the first waist indicating the half-hour divisions.

The inner **case** is pierced and engraved with inhabited foliage and flowers, and the stirrup bow with 'C' shaped ends. Four scrolls,

each indented to allow room for framed portrait busts, form a circular cartouche on the back of the outer case. This is the most common form of cartouche employed for embossed and chased cases during the first quarter of the eighteenth century. On the inside is a repeated floriate punch within matting, and a polished central reserve while, on the outside, the four portrait medallions are interspersed with pierced, chased and engraved flowers and foliage. The possible sources for the portrait busts are extensive and, although they are likely to be of classical figures, they have not been identified. The shell to be seen at the scroll ends was a popular embossed motif on cases in the early eighteenth century – sometimes more than one punch was used on the same case. The floriate punch is subtly different from the one used on the watch by Quare and Horseman numbered 991 (Plate 93).

PRIVATE COLLECTION

173

Plate 96. Charles Clay, London.
Gold cases 48mm: inner hallmarked 1724-5; outer: no
traceable marks

Both the repeating mechanism, which is an early example of the Stogden type, and the decoration to the outer case are of interest.

Not many embossed and chased outer **cases** with a scene in the centre of the back as early as this example survive, and those which have scenes from the New Testament – this has Christ and the lame beggar – are rare. Figures in panels, representing the Four Seasons with pierced foliate decoration between, lie outside the symmetric cartouche. The front bezel has similar treatment with floriate panels. This is fine work and one wonders who is responsible. The piercing and engraving around the band of the inner case, with its amusing amalgam of grotesque birds, beasts and flowers, is particularly delightful.

The gold champlevé **dial** is signed 'Clay' on a single cartouche below twelve, the hour hand is in a floriate design and there is a poker minute hand. In order to leave room for the repeating mechanism, however, it is constructed and fitted in a most unusual way. First, it has been made in one piece – normally the centres of

champlevé dials are made separately and those dials that are not are, in general, reproduction. Secondly, it has only one foot, rather than the normal three, and this is simply to locate it in the snap-fitting dial ring, which in turn is bayonet-fitted to the movement.

The **movement** has a quarter repeating mechanism, a very early example of the type which is generally accredited to Mathew Stogden. Both it and the dust cap are signed 'C. Clay London' but neither is numbered. The cock has a grotesque mask at the neck and the verge has ruby bearings and diamond endstones top and bottom. Both the barrel and bell have 'Clay' scratched upon them. The cylindrical pillars have a baluster foot.

Charles Clay moved to London from Stockton, Yorkshire. In 1716 he petitioned the King for a patent in respect of a repeating device and the Attorney General reported in his favour. He might well have been successful, but for the Clockmakers' Company's strong support of Daniel Quare who demonstrated he had priority with a watch which answered the same end.

PRIVATE COLLECTION

Plate 97. William Scafe, London, no. 165.

Gold cases 50mm: both HR conjoined incuse (Henry Rawlins) and hallmarked 1724-5

Scafe, a Yorkshireman, joined the Clockmakers' Company by redemption in 1721 and became Master in 1749.

The **dial**, signed in a cartouche 'W. Scafe', has London in a rectangle below. The beetle and poker hands are typical of this date. The silver furniture on the **movement** top plate is good and unusual; the index is of blued steel inlaid with gold and there is an excellent classical bust in profile. To enrich the overall appearance, a highly polished end-cap set with a particularly small ruby endstone has been used. There are crested Egyptian pillars. The design of the **cases**, pendant and bow are quite typical of the period.

PRIVATE COLLECTION

Actual size.

Thomas Mudge (1715-1794). From an engraving by Luigi Schiavonetti after a portrait by Nathaniel Dance. The Trustees of the Clockmakers' Company Museum

Chapter Four

THE FOURTH PERIOD

1725–1775

Chapter Four

THE FOURTH PERIOD
1725-1775

OUTLINE

The population of England increased from about 5.3 million to some 6.4 million people between 1721 and 1771. There was political stability. Between 1720 and 1770 exports doubled in value and agricultural and industrial production rose by 60 per cent (R. Porter, *English Society in the Eighteenth Century* 1982; P. Mathias, *The Transformation of England in the Eighteenth Century, Essays in …,* 1979): overall wealth increased significantly. By 1725 watches were quite practical, and probably considered reliable enough for the general requirements of the age. Increasing numbers were being produced and by 1775 ownership had broadened considerably.

Judging from the overall condition of those which survive, many were used occasionally rather than on a daily basis, with the plain, simple and silver cased watches often appearing to have had the harder life. Occasionally inner cases are found to have greater wear than the (often decorated) outer, suggesting that the former have been worn by themselves and the latter put on one side. Watches are also known which have been supplied with an alternative outer – a 'day case' – these being, typically, of gilt-metal and leather. Very high standards were maintained and watches continued to be highly prized. Some, those decorated with chasing or enamelling, were made primarily as objects of vertu and were generally consigned to the display cabinet. But this is not to deny their usefulness; indeed, as commerce and travel increased, so did their importance.

Moreover, even if the population as a whole was satisfied, mariners could not be. The story of John Harrison's success in his struggle to find a way to make a timepiece good enough to meet the Board of Longitude's requirements to help establish longitude at sea is well known. His work and inventions, those of his contemporaries – Thomas Mudge in particular – and the standards of craftsmanship they set were of immediate and long lasting benefit.

The inter-relationship between London and the associated industry in Lancashire outlined in Chapters 2 and 3 continued. The established reputation of English watches was maintained and was enhanced by immigrant craftsmen, particularly chasers and engravers. The decorative designs, mostly of Continental origin, were developed and frequently adapted. Asymmetric forms began to be applied from 1738 to 1740, while rococo slowly gave way to neo-classicism during the 1760s.

Copies, signed with both real and imagined British names, continued to be made on the Continent. One suspects that some, especially, although not exclusively, those with English cases, may well have been ordered by British vendors, particularly former immigrants with European connections. Of course there are instances where the origin may be unclear but, generally speaking, even setting aside variations in technical detail, the style and quality are just not the same. Although probably not the country of origin, Holland featured quite strongly in this trade, so much so there is a collective name 'Dutch Forgery' given to a large group of pathetic imitations. They are signed with names such as Rivers, Wilders, Sampson and Tarts, sometimes preceded by an initial and followed by 'London'. They have verge escapements, frequently bridge cocks. The pair-cases, mostly silver but occasionally gold, are always in a thin gauge, and the outer very often has a poorly produced classical scene in relief. Typically, the dials, whether metal or enamel, will have arcaded minute bands. Importantly, however, these watches should not be confused with those, generally from South West Lancashire, which also have enamel dials with arcaded minute bands.

SOME NOTABLE MAKERS, LONDON, LANCASHIRE AND THE PROVINCES

George Graham, the worthy successor to Tompion, introduced the cylinder escapement in 1726 (Plate 98) and used no other up to the time of his death in 1751. Assisted of course by apprentices, journeymen and so on, he made approximately 400 repeating watches and a little over 1,500 timepieces (Jeremy Evans, *Thomas Tompion*, AHS monograph 4). One of his apprentices was Thomas Mudge who, although he did not succeed him in business, was in many respects his successor, arguably the foremost maker of his day. Mudge is generally considered to be the first man to make a watch with a perpetual calendar (Plate 129) and also is thought to have made the first thoroughly English minute repeater (Plate 137). He made some marine timepieces with escapements having constant force devices but, above all, he was the inventor of the lever escapement – the first watch fitted with this is illustrated in Plate 140. There are many sources concerning Mudge and his work and these include Charles Allix, *Antiquarian Horology* Summer 1981, George Daniels and Richard Good, *Antiquarian Horology* December 1981 and *Pioneers of Precision Timekeeping*, AHS monograph 3. Although he began signing a few watches soon after his apprenticeship, for many years he was content to supply watches to other members of the trade. One of these was the firm Ellicott which probably sold more high quality watches than any of its contemporaries, more than 6,000 between 1725 and 1775 (David Thompson, *Antiquarian Horology*, Summer, Autumn 1997). There were other men who, like Mudge, worked within the trade and signed little, such as the formidable Larcum Kendall (Plate 143), or nothing at all, and John Harrison (about whom so much has been written) who spent much of his working life on just five machines – 'H5' is shown in Plate 141. Watches representing the work of many of the better known makers are included in this chapter.

Lancashire's contribution to the watches sold by the London trade was touched on in Chapter 2 and a little more detail was given in Chapter 3, both in 'Outline' and 'Lancashire and Provinces'. There is little doubt the inter-relationship continued, with Lancashire being an important supplier of tools, partly finished and probably some finished movements but few, if any, completed watches; it seems that only a handful of case makers were active in the Liverpool area during this period. Provincial makers also sourced from the Lancashire trade. The pubescent industries in Coventry and Birmingham came into their own during the next period.

THE CASE MAKERS, THEIR MARKS AND HALLMARKS

A simple analysis of the watches in this chapter, and which is likely to be reasonably typical of the period, shows that about three-quarters of the cases have makers' marks in one or both cases. For the reason given below, however, less than half of the marks can be positively identified. Fewer than half of the watches have a hallmarked case, four of these being without a maker's mark. As regards embossed outer cases, when the inner has a maker's mark often traces of one also can be found, together with any hallmark, on the reverse of the embossing.

The Goldsmiths' Company's Register of Small Workers' Marks is all important in the process of case maker identification. The Register for the period 1697-1739 is extant, but the one covering 1739-1759 is missing, possibly lost in a fire at the House of Commons where it was on loan for the 1773 review of English Assay Offices. Attempts to fill this gap (with help of a Clockmakers' Company 1747 quarterage list and the Goldsmiths' Company register of broken plate (1762-1772) have been reasonably successful, but there are a sizeable number of marks which cannot be identified, where identification is refutable, or where there is more than one possible user. The initials of a maker known to have been working during the 1739-1759 period may be coincident with a recorded mark but, of course, there must be a degree of uncertainty even when there is only one apparent match. The repercussions are felt into the 1770s as, even after a maker registered a new mark, there is no knowing if, or when, he took it into his head to use his old one. Philip Priestley used some of his on-going research for *Watch Case Makers of England 1720-1920*, NAWCC 1994, and included his further work on this period in appendices in his later book, *Watch Case Makers of England 1631-1720*, NAWCC 2000, and in an article for *Antiquarian Horology* in December 1999. *London Goldsmiths 1697-1837* by Arthur Grimwade (Faber and Faber, 1976) remains another useful reference.

THE CASE AND ITS DECORATION

With the exception of small variations, the **pendant** styles of repeaters and timepieces remained much the same throughout the period. Many, whether the case was of gold or silver, had a small rosette – in the head (Plate 104). In general the **stirrup bows** had a greater waist and more decoration after about 1740, becoming plainer again around 1765-70. There was a tendency for the bow joints to be a little more robust as the period progressed and sometimes very slightly longer towards the close. Very few single cases were made until the 1770s.

Leather, ray and shark **skin** cases were made, but mostly either as a third protective outer or as a 'day case'. The former were frequently to preserve an embossed or enamelled case; the latter, which can be decorated with pin-work, was supplied so that the embossed or enamelled case could be put on one side. **Tortoiseshell**, more accurately the belly of the hawksbill turtle, was used very infrequently, although its appearance was imitated by under-painting horn, this mostly on the outer cases of inexpensive watches from around 1760 onwards. Tortoiseshell was commonly employed during the last quarter of the century on watches made for export to Turkey and Arabic speaking countries.

Symmetric classical, baroque and grotesque designs, the latter mostly limited to the base of the inner case of repeating watches, continued to be used but rococo and asymmetric designs were fashionable from 1738-40. The new style was adopted quite rapidly but, of course, elements, including some symmetry, persisted. The engravers and chasers were mostly first or second generation immigrants familiar with original, invariably Continental, design sources which they happily adapted, sometimes radically. The **embossed and chased** watch case achieved a popularity and status not matched on the Continent. They were falling out of favour by the time the classical style and symmetric designs came back into favour during the 1760s and it was then that enamel work attracted the attention of the wealthy public. The *Art of the Gold Chaser* by Richard Edgcumbe (Oxford, 2000) is a wonderful study of the art form and the artists but, in addition, is a very useful reference for the watchmakers and their serial numbers, hallmark dates and the makers of the cases the chasers worked on.

THE DIAL AND HANDS

Enamel dials became increasingly popular and were probably in the majority by about 1740. They were not often signed. The lay-out was the same as metal ones, Roman hour numerals, minute marking between two rings and Arabic five-minute figures. There is always, until the1770s at least, a ring on the inside of the chapters in the position occupied by the quarter-hour band of champlevé dials (Plate 98).

The ring and chapters tended progressively to be slightly further from the centre; Plate 103 can be compared, for instance, with Plate 128 and Plate 155. The very best dials were enamelled on gold rather than copper. Arcaded minute rings are most often associated with so-called 'Dutch Forgeries' (see 'Outline'). A surprising number of watches from this period – and earlier – have been updated with later dials.

The ubiquitous **beetle and poker** hands, with many subtle variations, reigned supreme throughout the period. 'Beetle', a term too well established to be challenged, poorly describes what was clearly a floriate design probably based on the lily. Slowly, starting in about 1770, the very tip became oblanceolate (Plate 146) and not trefoil, reminiscent perhaps of a palmette leaf and maybe in response to the return of classicism. This shape became the norm for beetle hands and it is sometimes found as a replacement on earlier watches. Arrow heads began to appear, at first only on small watches, about the same time (Plate 149). Most makers fitted poker hands with two cross ribs, the second coincident with the ring inside the chapters mentioned above. But there are exceptions; Ellicott dispensed with the second rib at least by about 1760.

Finally a small number of watches have gold 'Louis' hands which, despite the name given to them and their popularity on the Continent, are redolent of many eighteenth century English clock hands.

THE MECHANISM

With but a few exceptions, the basic components and lay-out remained much the same throughout the period, makers having the choice of just two **escapements**, the verge and the cylinder. George Graham developed the cylinder escapement in 1726 and used no other from then on. It was gradually taken up by his contemporaries and by the mid-1750s most of the best London makers fitted it more or less exclusively. Although possibly somewhat better from a timekeeping point of view, particularly when the cylinder was made of ruby, as it was occasionally towards the end of the period, it was not as robust as the verge and was inclined to need more frequent attention. It was some years before Thomas Mudge's invention, the lever escapement (Plate 140), was developed, but Harrison's sophisticated and vast improvement on the verge (Plate 141) was not: in effect its maritime use was soon superseded by the detent escapement. **Repeating** mechanisms were generally according to the design attributed to Mathew Stogden which had been introduced in the early 1720s (see previous chapter but also Plate 137 for minute repeating).

Dust caps were fitted to most good quality watches and they are generally signed. Similarly, the majority of good watches, especially those with cylinder escapements, had diamond endstones and jewelled holes for the balance arbor. **Signatures** were commonly in script. As would be expected, the decoration of the cock and index plate followed broadly the same style changes as the case, but lagged somewhat, and the response to neo-classicism after 1765 was muted with designs continuing to be asymmetric. Both the square baluster and cylindrical **pillar** were used until the mid-1750s, after which the cylindrical pillar became the dominant form.

TIMEKEEPING

Cecil Clutton's paper to the Antiquarian Horological Society in December 1954 about his in-wear tests was quoted in the previous chapter. These tests on a number of watches from different periods were made throughout the year so that the effect of temperature variations could be assessed.

One of the watches, a verge of about 1710, was, over a fortnight, 'never more than half a minute away from Big Ben'. Perhaps we should regard this as a remarkable performance, but it has to be an indication of what could be achieved in the eighteenth century with a new watch. Having given his reasons for believing that the timekeeping of verge watches probably did not improve, and indeed may have been not so good later in the century, he then tested a number with cylinder escapements. The best performance was from a freshly overhauled Mudge and Dutton of 1762: a maximum variation over a fortnight of one and a quarter minutes. It seems he did not try a ruby cylinder from later in the period. In point of fact he had introduced his results for the cylinder by saying that he was 'unable to understand why it had got such a good reputation for I have never had an English 18th century steel cylinder which was much better than a good verge'. Possibly his bias was expressed in the results, but the take-up of the cylinder would undoubtedly have been quicker if it had been demonstrably superior to the verge.

It is difficult not to conclude that watches were considered quite reliable enough so long, of course, as they were performing as they should – unless, that is, you were at sea trying to find longitude!

Plate 98. George Graham, London, no. 5227.
Gold single case 49mm: WS incuse (William Sherwood, possibly junior), hallmarked 1727-8

Graham ceased using the verge escapement immediately after he had developed the cylinder escapement in 1726. He did not attempt to protect his idea in a formal way, but initially, as here, perhaps demonstrated priority by giving the dust cap a secret catch.

The **movement** needs to be removed from the case in order that the secret catch can be released via a pin-hole in the edge of the cap. To give his new escapement the best advantage, Graham fitted a diamond endstone to the bottom of the balance staff as well as the top. The escape wheel is brass and the cylinder steel. The index plate and cock foot are engraved; it appears Graham ceased to pierce these out when he adopted his new escapement. There are Egyptian pillars.

While the **dial** signature and beetle hour hand may be typical, the minute hand is stepped to clear the winding square – as can be seen in the edge-on illustration.   PRIVATE COLLECTION   *Actual size.*

Actual size.

Plate 99. G. Burgis, London, no. 2079.
Gold single case 28mm: WI incuse (William Jaques junior),
hallmarked 1730-1

This extremely small watch is a good miniaturisation of the
normal sized watches of the period and is much more
sophisticated than those made a century earlier.

The **movement**, which has cylindrical pillars, a fusee and a
verge escapement, is signed G. Burgis, London. F.J. Britten in
Old Clocks and Watches and their Makers, third edition, records
the signature George Burgis on a longcase clock of 1720-40.

The **dial**, which is also signed, and the beetle and poker
hands are typical of the period. William Jaques junior adopted
his deceased father's **case** punch mark in 1725.

Opposite: Plate 100. Simon De Charmes, London.
Gold cases 50mm: inner IL in cameo (John Lee), outer SG
fish above (Stephen Goujon); embossed and chased outer
signed by John Valentine Haidt (1700-1780)

Simon De Charmes, a Free Brother of the Clockmakers'
Company in 1691, is thought to have been active up to around
the time this watch was made, that is about 1730.

The signature, 'J.V. Haidt', on the embossed and chased
outer **case** is on the step below the scavenging dog. The scene
of the Four Seasons has Phoebus Apollo as the Sun; Flora with
an infant, Spring; Ceres, Summer; Bacchus, Autumn; and
Saturn, Winter. Four subsidiary scenes outside the symmetric
cartouche alternate with pierced foliate scrolls containing shells

and dolphin heads. Haidt, the son of an Augsburg goldsmith, married in London in 1725 and worked there until 1740. It appears G.M. Moser worked for Haidt in the early 1730s and shared a drawing school with him (see Edgcumbe, *Art of the Gold Chaser*). The inner case is pierced and engraved with inhabited foliage and has a mask at six.

The good quality half-quarter repeating **movement** is signed, has a verge escapement and a silver dust cap which is also signed. There is a white enamel **dial** with beetle and poker hands.

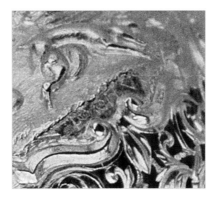

PRIVATE COLLECTION

Plate 101. Henry Thornton, London, no. 1261.

Gold cases 48mm: inner indistinct Gothic JB (unidentified)

Actual size.

Henry Thornton, a liveryman of the Clockmakers' Company between 1699 and 1732, specialized in the Russian market. This watch, in the Russian taste, is from about 1730. Three clocks and two watches are included in a 1908 inventory by E. Alfred James of the Czar's collection. The description of one of the watches is 'Repeating watch in heavy gold cases, gem-set and repoussé case'.

Embossed and chased – repoussé – decoration surrounds the silver-set diamonds and garnets of the outer **case** back which has pierced panels for sound emission and a diamond-set push-piece. Diamond-set silver settings on the front bezel also allow for sound emission. The inner case is pierced and engraved with dolphins, flowers and foliage and there is a rural village scene engraved by the pendant neck.

There are elaborate 'C' scrolls on either side of the signature on the gold champlevé **dial** which has blued steel

beetle and poker hands. The signed and numbered dust cap and **movement** – which has a verge escapement and round baluster pillars – are typical of the period. PRIVATE COLLECTION

Actual size.

Plate 102. George Graham, London, no. 5775.
Silver cases 52mm: both IW star above (John Ward), inner numbered

Only a limited number of watches with centre seconds were being produced in the first half of the eighteenth century and Graham appears to have made most of them. The serial number 5775 suggests circa 1737. The **dial** is un-cluttered by a signature and, while the steel hour and minute hand have been blued in the normal way, for contrast the counterpoised seconds hand has been left polished.

The dust cap is signed, as is the **movement** which is also numbered. The balance cock has a large diamond endstone, a pierced and engraved table, with a mildly grotesque male mask at the neck and a solid foot. There are square baluster pillars and the escapement has a steel cylinder and brass wheel. A start/stop whip mounted between the plates, operated by a lever protruding from below the bezel of the inner case, acts on the outer circumference of the cylinder.

The understated character of the dial and **cases** is maintained by the stirrup bow which is completely plain; just the top of the pendant is allowed to be decorated with a rosette in relief. PRIVATE COLLECTION

189

Plate 103. David Hubert, London, no. 2581.
Gold cases 50mm: both AR or AP conjoined in cameo (possibly Adam Roumieu junior), inner hallmarked 1737-8; embossed and chased outer signed FFF, probably François Fourestier Fecit

Cybele, a personification of Earth, is seen seated with two lions on the back of the **outer case**. The cartouche surrounding the scene is interesting. Cartouches were symmetric up to 1738-1740, while soon thereafter a degree of asymmetry is generally present: the elaborate scroll-work east and west are the same but the scrolls north and south are not. Richard Edgcumbe in his *Art of the Gold Chaser* suggests that the splendid masks, north and south, look back to Jean Berain (1638-1711). He also points out that the attribution to François Fourestier would associate a Huguenot decorator with a notable Huguenot watchmaker: David Hubert was naturalized in 1709.

There is an excellent enamel **dial**. The extra turning on the minute hand was fashionable at this date. The signed and numbered **movement** has a verge escapement and is typical of the period. PRIVATE COLLECTION

Plate 104. Richard Vick, London, no. 557.
Gold cases 51mm: inner case with indistinct maker's mark, hallmarked 1738-9; embossed and chased outer with initials AH for Augustin Heckel (circa 1690-1770)

The *commedia dell'arte* scene on the back of the **outer case** is of Harlequin surprising two lovers while Pierrot looks on. Outside the symmetric cartouche, between swags of flowers, are four heads of, presumably, the players with Harlequin below the pendant. Richard Edgcumbe illustrates this watch in his *Art of the Gold Chaser* and says the scene appears to be a conflation of two compositions of J.-A. Watteau (1684-1721).

The gold champlevé **dial** has a date aperture and beetle and poker hands. The **movement**, which is signed and numbered, has a silver cock and a verge escapement. PRIVATE COLLECTION

Plate 105. John Ellicott, London (un-numbered).
Silver cases 65.5mm (middle case): WK incuse coronet above (possibly William King), no hallmarks; third case: sharkskin and silver pin-work; embossed and chased middle case signed Manly F for Henry Manly (1698-circa 1773)

Although the movement is un-numbered, the case not hallmarked and the maker's mark problematic (see below), this watch must come from the late 1730s, or close to 1740 not only because of the style and symmetric decoration of the movement but, more importantly, Manly's use of symmetric cartouches and the manner of his decoration.

Few English embossed and chased **silver cases** were made either of such quality (nearly all being generally rather ordinary at best) or as large. Dr. Richard Edgcumbe has confirmed that it is the largest recorded case signed by Manly and the only one in silver. He has identified the scene as the Abduction of Europa (Jupiter is seen disguised as a bull by the seashore) which, taking substantial changes made by Manly into account, he suggests is from an engraving by Michel Dorigny (1617-1655) after Simon Vouet (1590-1649). He has kindly identified the work to be '…within a symmetrical cartouche composed of C scrolls. Outside the cartouche on the back, inside symmetrical reserves of scrollwork, four figures representing the Four Seasons: NE, Summer, a woman holding a sickle; SE, Autumn, a huntress holding a bow and a deer; SW, Winter, a winged male figure, blowing his hands; NW, Spring, a woman holding a flower. The figures can reasonably be identified as Ceres, Diana, Chronos (Father Time) and Flora. The corresponding reserves on the bezel are chased and embossed with the Four Elements: NE, Earth, a hare; SE, Fire, a phoenix; SW, Air, a bird; NW, Water, a fish.'

The case maker's mark does not appear to be registered prior to the period 1739-1758 for which the Goldsmiths' register of small workers is missing. A very similar mark is recorded for William King in 1761 and Arthur Grimwade – *London Goldsmiths* – tentatively suggests a man of this name who initially belonged to another livery company.

The inner case is pierced and engraved and there is an excellent grotesque mask at the base. The **dial** has a central alarm disc which is set by a female square at eight o'clock. A silver dust cap is signed John Ellicott, Royal Exchange, London and the **movement** is also signed but not numbered. It has a diamond endstone, verge escapement, cylindrical pillars and, unusually, an alarm mechanism.

PRIVATE COLLECTION

Plate 106. John Hodges, London, no. 1022.

Silver single case 38mm: EG star (or daisy) above (Edward Gibbons)

This is an unusually small watch of about 1740, although possibly a year or two earlier. John Hodges was in Clements Lane in 1729 and in Exchange Alley nine years later.

The signed champlevé **dial** and elaborate steel hands are of excellent quality, as is the **movement**. The index plate and cock, which has a fine grotesque mask at the neck, are fully pierced and engraved. There are square baluster pillars and a verge escapement.

The **case** by Edward Gibbons, who registered his mark in 1736, has a winding shutter flush with the back.   PRIVATE COLLECTION

Actual size.

Plate 107. Nathaniel Delander, London, no. 285.

Silver single case 47mm: no maker's mark, hallmarked 1740-41

Signed simply 'Delander', this watch was sold by Nathaniel, Daniel's son and successor.

The **dial** has winding squares for the going and alarm trains, and a female square to adjust the alarm setting. The **case** maker's mark was no doubt lost when the alarm bell stand was fitted. Both the bezel and inner bezel are pierced and engraved for sound emission. The back is engraved with the arms of James Helsby of Helsby, Cheshire, his motto 'en Dieu est mon esperance' and 'James Helsby. Gent' below. Around the perimeter there are four pierced foliate panels separated by three engraved masks and a shell adjacent to the push-piece.

The signed and numbered **movement** has an engraved cock foot with a pierced table and a diamond endstone. There is a verge escapement and cylindrical pillars.   PRIVATE COLLECTION

Plate 108. Joseph Martineau Senior, London, no. 1483.

Gold and bloodstone mounted single case 47mm: no marks

Martineau is one of those makers whose name is familiar but about whom very little is known. If he made his watches with his numbers in chronological order, and the few hallmarked watches were used as a reference, then a date of about 1740 is suggested. However, they may not be a reliable guide. This type of watch, which is often difficult to date, is more common in the 1760s.

Unlike many, mostly somewhat later, **cases** of this type, the body is complete with a gold dome beneath the bloodstone. This is slightly flattened in towards the centre and is recessed and held in place by a floriate engraved gold cartouche. The front bezel has six panels of bloodstone. Later watches of this type have backs which are frequently made up of panels, often of agate, where no solid backing is required. However, when they do consist of a single piece of stone they are often simply pinned around a back bezel.

The good quality **movement**, which has a verge escapement, is numbered and signed 'Joseph Martineau Snr. London'. It is wound through the **dial** which has, typically for the period, an arcaded signature.

PRIVATE COLLECTION

Actual size.

196

Plate 109. Godfrie Poy, London, no. 307.
Gold cases 50mm: inner, incuse mark either JG (possibly James Gray), or TG (possibly Thomas Goore), third protective glazed, gilt and skin-covered case; embossed and chased outer signed 'Manly f' for Henry Manly (1698-circa 1773)

Poy, recorded 1718-1750, sold some fine watches and clocks. This example is from around 1745.

The **outer case** has Alexander crowning Roxana. This scene, and one where the king is offering the crown to his wife, was popular with Manly and his contemporaries. Outside one of his complex asymmetric cartouches surrounding the scene are four asymmetric subsidiary panels between pierced foliate decoration. The inner case is engraved and also pierced for sound emission.

The signed and numbered **movement** has a verge escapement, diamond endstone and cylindrical pillars. The enamel **dial**, which is also signed, has blued steel beetle and poker hands.

Plate 110. Christopher Jennymore, London.

Gold cases and chatelaine 180mm: inner IW star above incuse (John Ward), hallmarked 1746-7; chatelaine, WH coronet above (probably William Hudson), hallmarked 1747-8

Most chatelaines are of gilt metal, and not so many gold ones remain together with the watch for which they were originally intended.

Apollo, within a strong asymmetric cartouche, is seen on the back of the **outer case** pouring a heap of dust into Cumaean Sibyl's hand as he attempted seduce her with the promise to prolong her life by as many years as there were grains. When she refused him, he kept his promise but denied her perpetual youth, and she lived many centuries as a wizened old crone.

On the **chatelaine** clip Apollo holds a rudder. Above him a putto holds a laurel crown, laurel crowns being the victor's award at the Pythian festivals at Delphi held in Apollo's honour. Sibyl acted as the god's priestess at Delphi. The subsidiary links would seem to allude to Apollo's triumphs. Two contemporary scent bottles are suspended from the catches.

The signed **movement** has a verge escapement and square baluster pillars. There is a white enamel **dial** and beetle and poker hands.   PRIVATE COLLECTION

Plate 111. Embossed and chased case back.

Gold case back 42mm: SG scroll above (Stephen Goujon), embossed and chased outer signed 'G M Moser f' for George Michael Moser (1706-1783)

This, the back portion of a watch case from about 1745-1750 fitted with a brooch pin, is an excellent example of Moser's work. It is in superb condition.

The scene is of Apollo and the Four Seasons. It is cleverly arranged, full of interest, but not overcrowded. In *The Art of the Gold Chaser* Richard Edgcumbe records two embossed cases and one enamel case with this scene by Moser, all three of a later date. He says the source of the figure of Apollo appears to be from the *Tombeau de Charles Sackville, Comte de Dorset,* engraved by Michel Guillaume Aubert after an illustration by François Boucher for a 1741 publication by E. MacSwiny.

PRIVATE COLLECTION

Plate 112. John Ellicott, London, no. 2700.

Gold cases 68mm: no marks

There is a small difference, varying throughout the year, between the length of a solar day – that shown on a sundial – and mean time. The variation, irregular in amount and direction, is due in part to the Earth's eccentric path around the sun and in part to the inclination of the Earth's axis, the two factors sometimes acting in concert and sometimes in opposition. While the greatest difference is on 23 November, when the solar day is sixteen minutes shorter than mean time, there are only four days when the two are within just a few seconds.

Ellicott 2700 is one of five known English watches which have two minute hands – one for showing solar time, the other mean, the difference between them being the equation of time. It was in the Marryat Collection and is illustrated by Clutton and Daniels in *Watches*. A very similar, apparently un-numbered watch was in the Webster Collection sold by Sotheby's in May 1954 and was well illustrated by Antiquorum when it was resold by them exactly forty years later. David Thompson, in his two part article which includes an analysis of the Ellicott numbering sequence (*Antiquarian Horology*, Summer, Autumn 1997), dates these watches about 1747. He illustrates the third, un-numbered and in a later case, which is in the British Museum. The fourth, number 5060, has no second dial on the back and has a later case; from the number it is from about 1762. The fifth, a rather simpler affair signed by Richard Gregg and numbered 591 and hallmarked 1758, is in the Patek Philippe Museum.

The **dial** is illustrated showing the radial annual calendar approaching the 23 November maximum equation of time variation. Zodiac signs for each month are on an inner ring. The **movement**, which has a cylinder escapement, brass escape wheel, maintaining power and cylindrical pillars, has complex wheel trains and an equation of time sun and planet mechanism with a kidney cam which is set on and revolves with a year calendar wheel.

A biography published in the *Universal Magazine* in July 1795 makes plain that for much of his life Thomas Mudge was quite content to make watches for other makers. Two recently discovered letters of 1752 and 1757 (Anthony Turner and Andrew Crisford, *Antiquarian Horology*, Winter 1977) substantiate that Ellicott sold an equation watch to King Ferdinand VI of Spain, that the king heard that Ellicott, unable to attend to a problem with it, had given the watch to Mudge, and that thereafter the king began commissioning Mudge direct. It seems clear Mudge supplied all the equation watches signed by Ellicott. Also, from other evidence, it is more than likely that Mudge continued to supply the trade after his reputation was established in the public domain and continued to do so, it seems, throughout the 1750s – for instance, probably with Gregg 591 referred to above and the Andrew Dickie 2292 illustrated in Plate 122. Of course, he would have to have had the support of a small group of specialist craftsmen.

PRIVATE COLLECTION

Plate 113. John Ellicott, London, no. 2835.

Gold cases 49mm: inner JB script incuse (possibly John Bayley or John Beesley), hallmarked 1748-9, numbered 2835; embossed and chased outer signed 'Manly fec' (Henry Manly 1698-circa 1773)

Ellicott probably commissioned more chased and embossed cases than anyone else, and Manly and Moser together account for most of the signed cases which have survived.

The scene on the **outer case**, which is in superb condition, is of Atalanta and Meleager setting out on the Calydonian boar hunt. It is within an asymmetric cartouche surrounded by four subsidiary cartouches containing flowers and the front bezel has similar flowers with shells and scrollwork. The signed and numbered **movement** has a cylinder escapement and is typical of Ellicott's work at this period. There is an enamel **dial** and gold beetle and poker hands.

This watch, which was in the Chester Beatty Collection sold at Sotheby's in December 1962, is illustrated and described by Richard Edgcumbe in *The Art of the Gold Chaser*. He says the scene is derived from an engraving by Bernard Picart, after François Chauveau, and that Manly's version is indebted to a design to be seen in the collection of 152 drawings by Augustin Heckel held in the Victoria & Albert Museum.

PRIVATE COLLECTION

Actual size.

Plate 114. Thomas Gardener, London, no. 2043.

Gold and enamel cases 56mm: inner DA incuse (probably Daniel Aveline), hallmarked 1748, numbered 2043, outer counter enamel – no mark; embossing initialled G B for Guillaume Bouvier; third gilt, shagreen with gold pin-work protective case

Except for the gold and enamel decoration on the back of the **middle case**, everything about this watch is thoroughly English. The embossed scene of the Toilet of Venus is in silhouette against an opaque blue enamel ground and within a symmetric border of white enamel. The initials 'GB' are embossed at the base of the scene and either side of the ruby-set push-piece. Guillaume Bouvier is recorded as working in Paris and possibly Switzerland, and his work appears on Continental watches. Did he work for a while in England, or did the case go there and back across the Channel?

The signed and numbered **movement**, typical of the period, has a verge escapement. The decoration on the cock table – there is no diamond endstone - is symmetric, that on the foot in part asymmetric. There is a high quality enamel **dial** and good beetle and poker hands.

PRIVATE COLLECTION

Plate 115. George Graham, London, no. 6498.
Silver cases 49mm: inner script IW incuse star above (John Ward), hallmarked 1750–1; outer no marks

Although he had been fitting enamel **dials** for some time, it would seem some of Graham's customers had a preference for metal – in this case silver – dials. It is a typical example which shows how the maker was able to maintain his simple but elegant style right to the end of his life. Many have been subsequently replaced with enamel dials which look and are horribly out of period. There are blued steel beetle and poker hands.

The signed and numbered **movement** has a signed dust cover (scratched-numbered on the inside), a pierced and engraved cock table, diamond endstone, a cylinder escapement, brass escape wheel and square baluster pillars.

The **cases** are quite plain with just a rosette in the head of the pendant and foliate decoration on the sides of the stirrup bow. The inner is scratched-numbered.

PRIVATE COLLECTION

Plate 116. William Webster, London, no. 2245.
Gold cases 50mm with chatelaine 180mm (7⅛ in.): inner Gothic HR incuse (probably Henry Rawlins), hallmarked 1751-2; embossed and chased outer signed 'Moser f' for G.M. Moser; contemporary gilt metal chatelaine, WH for William Hunt with gold embossed plaques

Two episodes are combined into a single scene on the back of the **outer case**. Odysseus on the far right is almost naked, as he was when Nausicaa saw him the first time and, centre right, he is as he appeared before her on one knee at her father's court. The cartouche is symmetric except immediately below the pendant and at the base where there is a bat with outstretched wings supporting the step at the bottom of the scene. Moser's signature as usual is on the step. The snake, which he was fond of winding around the push-piece, is present. Hercules, club in hand, is on the **chatelaine** clip. William Hunt was a goldsmith and chatelaine maker who is known to have worked in association with Moser. It is quite possible the original owner purchased the watch and chatelaine at the same time.

The white enamel **dial** has an arcaded signature, 'Webster, London', and beetle and poker hands. The signed and numbered **movement**, typical of the period, has a verge escapement and square baluster pillars.

PRIVATE COLLECTION

Plate 117. Thomas Hally, London, no. 1497.

Silver cases 100mm: both AM star between incuse (possibly Andrew Moreton)

The engraving on this quarter repeating coach watch is quite exceptional. The arms are those of John Carmichael (1701-1767), the third Earl of Hyndford, a successful Scottish diplomat who was George II's special envoy to both Russia and Prussia and Ambassador in Vienna between 1752 and 1764. He was made a Privy Councillor in 1750.

The **movement** and dust cap are both signed and numbered, the dust cap being also engraved with what could well be the date, 1753. The grotesque piercing and engraving on the cock table, which has a diamond endstone, is symmetric, while that on the foot is asymmetric. There are cylindrical pillars and a cylinder escapement.

The mask shown at the base of the **inner case** is especially noteworthy. The bow is of a similar design to the un-marked case of the equation watch Ellicott 2700 (Plate 112). There is a very high quality **dial** and an excellent pair of blued steel beetle and poker hands. PRIVATE COLLECTION

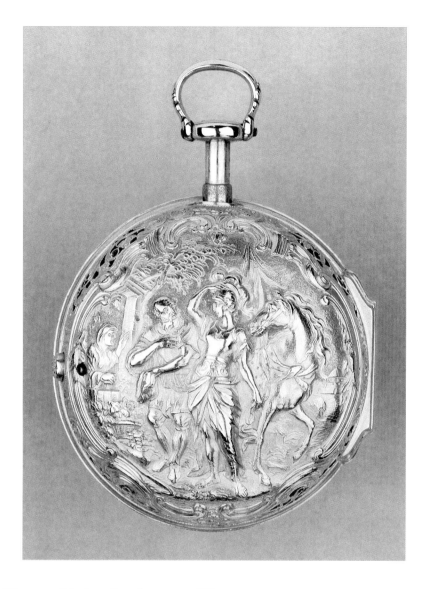

Plate 118. Thomas Mudge, London, no. 279.
Gold cases 48mm: both TC in rectangular cameo (possibly Thomas Colley or Thomas Carpenter senior), inner hallmarked 1755-6; embossed and chased outer signed G.M. Moser F.

The scene on the **outer case** of Erminia dismounted from her horse talking to a shepherd with his wife to the left is from an episode in the romantic epic poem of the first crusade by Tasso. Erminia, daughter of the Saracen king, was in love with the Christian knight Tancred and, in her search for him, she disguised herself in armour. This armour had belonged to the female warrior Clorinda whom, in turn, Tancred himself had loved but had tragically and accidentally killed in battle. The old shepherd whom Erminia came across extolled the virtues of his peaceful existence in contrast to the war which she, in her armour, seemed to typify. Moser used the surrounding rococo cartouche, which is symmetric west and east, asymmetric north to south, quite frequently. This case is discussed and illustrated, together with Moser's extant design for the scene in line and wash and a preparatory sketch, by Richard Edgcumbe in his *Art of the Gold Chaser*.

The signed and numbered **movement** has a quarter repeating mechanism and so the inner case is pierced and engraved for sound emission. It is of high quality with a cylinder escapement and typical of Mudge's work at this period. The **dial** is also typical, being enamelled on gold, and there are gold beetle and poker hands.

PRIVATE COLLECTION

Plate 119. Graham Successor, London, no. 976.

Silver cases 50mm: both TC in rectangular cameo (possibly Thomas Colley or Thomas Carpenter senior)

When George Graham died in 1751 his business was continued by two of his workmen, Samuel Barkley and Thomas Colley. Barkley died in 1753 leaving Colley to continue alone until he was joined about ten years later by a new partner, John Priest. The watches were initially signed 'Graham Succrs.', then, for a while 'Graham Succr.', as in the case of this watch which can be dated about 1755.

The cock table of the signed and numbered quarter repeating **movement** is pierced and engraved and has a diamond endstone. The cylinder escapement has a steel escape wheel. Both **cases** are pierced and engraved, the plain pendant and bow continuing a style favoured by Graham. The **dial** is enamelled on gold and there are blued steel beetle and poker hands.   PRIVATE COLLECTION

Plate 120. Ellicott, London, no. 4313.

Gold cases 50mm: both JB script incuse (possibly John Bayley or John Beesley), inner hallmarked 1756-7; embossed and chased outer signed 'Manly fct' for Henry Manly (1698-circa 1773)

The **outer case**, depicting the Continence of Scipio, is in exceptionally fine condition. Scipio is seen returning his prize of war, a beautiful maiden, unharmed to her fiancé. Outside the asymmetric cartouche, characteristic of Manly's work at this period, the case is decorated with flowers between scrolls and shellwork. A different version of the scene is on a watch by James Grantham (Plate 126).

The **movement**, which has a verge escapement, is signed Ellicott LONDON 4313. This style of signature replaced 'Jno. Ellicott London' when John Ellicott junior's son Edward joined the business in 1756. The **dial** is enamelled on gold and there are elaborately pierced gold hands.

This watch is illustrated by Richard Edgcumbe in his *Art of the Gold Chaser*.   PRIVATE COLLECTION

Actual size.

Plate 121. Andrew Dickie, Edinburgh, no. 2045.
Gold cases 50mm: no maker's marks, inner hallmarked 1756-7, embossed, chased and enamelled outer attributable to George Michael Moser (1706-1783)

The **outer case** painting in enamel of Alexander the Great crowning his queen Roxana follows one of the two versions of this scene G.M. Moser employed. An amoretto holds Alexander's sword, his companion, Haephestion raises a torch aloft while an attendant arranges Roxana's hair. The painting can be attributed to Moser on stylistic grounds and the surrounding embossed cartouche is a type he used frequently from the 1740s to the end of the 1760s. Moser was fond of winding a snake around the push-piece and this can be seen in the illustrations. He appears to have begun working in enamel between about 1753 and 1755, so this is an early example. The inner case is pierced and engraved.

The high quality half-quarter repeating **movement** is signed and numbered. It has a pierced and engraved cock, diamond endstone and cylinder escapement. Whereas Andrew Dickie of Edinburgh generally did not number his movements, Andrew Dickie of London, who may well have been his son (and who had a son Andrew) did. It may well be a coincidence, but the number 2045 fits with the latter's known sequence, and so maybe this watch was supplied by Dickie of London. There is an enamel **dial** and blued steel beetle and poker hands.

This watch was in the Atkinson, Nyburg and Burton Collections. THE DJANOGLY COLLECTION

Plate 122. Andrew Dickie, London, no. 2292.

Gold case 51mm: no marks

The number of this double **dialled** watch suggests that it was probably made in the late 1750s. The front dial has conventional hours and minutes and the days of the week, the back a radial annual calendar arranged in a five-turn spiral and a rotating blue enamel centre carrying beneath it a calendar hand which expands and contracts as it indicates the days in the year. The centre, which is used to set the hand, has, on its perimeter, the name Dickie and the equation of time settings for the 10th and 25th day of each month: the difference between the varying lengths of the solar day as recorded by a sundial through the year and the mean time day as measured by a watch.

Actual size.

The **movement**, with a cylinder escapement and cylindrical pillars, is signed and numbered on the top plate. It is sandwiched between separate plates for the going and calendar mechanisms. The cock is of blued steel and, to save room, the diamond endstone is flat and its fixing screws are on the underside. The sophisticated calendar mechanism is beautifully made and consists of twenty or so separate parts. Curiously, a spring on the primary calendar plate is shaped as a lizard or salamander. The extent of expansion of the two-part calendar hand is governed by a spiral groove in a secondary plate below. In this runs a stud fixed to the underside of the spring-loaded outer part of the

hand. The stud is raised once it reaches the inner end of the groove (31 December) and is automatically relocated at the outer end, the hand expanding instantaneously to indicate 1 January on the dial.

The watch is wound and regulated via the time of day dial. The balance, with its spring and regulator, are on the opposite side of the movement, and the regulator square has been taken, remarkably, straight through the barrel arbor. Both dials are, as only the best eighteenth century dials, enamelled on gold. The **case** is stylistically correct but later.

There is one other watch known with a radial annual calendar from this period and this is in the British Museum. It too is double dialled, but it is unsigned and slightly larger, and the calendar hand does not expand but is fixed, the dial centre being taken up with a revolving moon and moon phase.

It has long been suggested that the watch in the British Museum was made by Thomas Mudge. Although this watch is signed by Andrew Dickie, it has even more of the ingenious character and flavour of Mudge's work. For much of his life Mudge was quite content to make watches for other makers (see the last paragraph of Plate 112, Ellicott 2700).

Andrew Dickie was one of the five professional watchmakers on a committee of eleven appointed by Act of Parliament – it came into being on 31 March 1763 – to examine John Harrison's H4 timepiece (Alexander Cumming, who according to his will was one of his executors, Thomas Mudge, William Frodsham and James Green were the others). It is likely he was the son of Andrew Dickie, Edinburgh. PRIVATE COLLECTION

Plate 123. John Raymond, London, no. 3390.
Gold cases 50mm: inner IW incuse (possibly John Watkins or John Wright), hallmarked 1762

The embossed and chased **outer case** has a scene of Orpheus and Eurydice surrounded by an asymmetric cartouche. Cerberus, the three-headed dog, is in the foreground.

There is an enamel **dial** and beetle and poker hands. The **movement**, which has a verge escapement, is signed and numbered. There are other watches signed by Raymond whom Arthur Grimwade (*London Goldsmiths*, Faber and Faber, 1976) records as free of the Goldsmiths' Company in 1743. The 1739-59 Register is missing, but it appears Raymond registered his first mark in 1762, his second in 1768. PRIVATE COLLECTION

Plate 124. Isaac Alexander, Birmingham, no. 3398.
Gold cases 50mm: inner IW incuse (possibly John Watkins or John Wright), hallmarked London 1757-8

The embossed and chased scene on the **outer case** is of the Death of Dido from Virgil's *Aeneid* and follows closely an engraving by Michel Dorigny (1617-1655) of 1643 made after a painting of about 1640 by his father-in-law, Simon Vouet (1590-1649). The painting is in the museum at Dole, France, and a print of the engraving belongs to the Metropolitan Museum, New York. As is always the case, of course, when printed the engraved image is reversed, and this is how the scene was executed by the watch case chaser more than a hundred years after the engraving was made. The embossing and chasing is of high quality, but it is unsigned. The rococo cartouche might put one in mind of the work of Henry Manly. Plate 125 has a related scene.

The **movement**, which is signed and numbered, has a verge escapement and square baluster pillars. The white enamel **dial** and blued steel beetle and poker hands are also typical of the period. PRIVATE COLLECTION

Plate 125. George Graham, London, no. 795.

Gold cases 47mm: inner IW script star above incuse (John Ward), hallmarked 1739-40

Of about 1760, the embossed and chased **outer case** is later than the rest of the watch. The scene is of Aeneas departing from Dido. His ship is behind him on the left, to his right the seated Dido reaches out towards him and above, resting on the central pillar, Cupid reads what was fore-ordained by Jupiter, that in her love-torn grief Dido would kill herself. The outer case of the watch by Isaac Alexander illustrated in Plate 124 shows the Death of Dido from an engraving by Michel Dorigny after Simon Vouet; it is possible this case is taken from other work by the same artists. The high rococo cartouche extends with scrolls and shell patterns to the bezel at the bottom of the case. Pierced panels allow for the sound of the watch repeating. This decorative style bears comparison with that on the inner case of some twenty years earlier. The watch number is beneath the bell and below the pendant.

The **movement** is typical of Graham's work. It is signed and numbered and the dust cap is signed. There is a plain steel balance, brass escape wheel, cylinder escapement and cylindrical pillars. The enamel **dial** has blued steel beetle and poker hands.

PRIVATE COLLECTION

Plate 126. James Grantham, London, no. 3835.
Gold cases 48mm: inner IW incuse (possibly John Watkins or John Wright),
hallmarked 1761-2

The embossed and chased **outer case** of the Continence of Scipio is in very
high relief, and apparently from a single sheet of metal. The quality and
condition is unusually good for high relief work. Note how the cartouche
allows room for the figure of Scipio to the right. Scipio is seen returning his
prize of war, a beautiful maiden, unharmed to her fiancé. She is standing and
fettered in this version of the scene, but kneeling in that used by Manly on
Ellicott 4313 (Plate 120).

    Both the **movement**, which has a verge escapement, and the white
enamel **dial**, which has beetle and poker hands, are typical of the period.

PRIVATE COLLECTION

Plate 127. Francis Perigal, London, no. 13818.

Gold, agate, stone-set and enamel cases 42mm: inner SG fish above incuse (Stephen Goujon)

Stephen Goujon, who became Master of the Clockmakers' Company in 1760, registered the maker's mark on the inner case in 1720. This watch, of about 1760 or shortly after, comes from near the end of his working life. Francis Perigal, Master in 1756, was succeeded by his son, also Francis.

The **outer case** is of agate overlaid with embossed flowers and scrolls with diamonds in silver settings, and emeralds, rubies and a sapphire in gold settings. The panel in the centre of the back has diamonds and emeralds arranged as a posy of flowers surrounded by ruby-set scrolls and there are similar subsidiary panels. The bezels are diamond-set, the front also agate-mounted and overlaid with further rubies, emeralds and diamonds. The pendant and bow is diamond-set and the inner case is pierced, chased and engraved. The back is decorated with blue and orange flowers and green foliage of *basse-taille* enamel (see Glossary).

The signed and numbered quarter repeating is quite small and slim and has a dust ring. The pierced cock table has asymmetric **movement** decoration and a diamond endstone. There are cylindrical pillars and a nineteenth century lever escapement. The **dial** is white enamel and the beetle and poker hands blued steel.

PRIVATE COLLECTION

Actual size.

217

Plate 128. Ellicott, London, no. 5141.

Gold cases 48mm: both HT incuse (probably Henry Cleaver Taylor, possibly Henry Teague), inner hallmarked 1762-3 and numbered; embossed and chased outer signed 'Manly fe' for Henry Manly (1698-circa 1773)

The Judgement of Hercules after a painting by Paolo Matteis, now in the Ashmolean Museum, is on the back of the **outer case**. Hercules is seen making his choice between Virtue and Vice, the latter reclining into the surrounding asymmetric cartouche to his right. It was in the 1984 Victoria & Albert Rococo exhibition and discussed in the catalogue, and is also illustrated, together with a detail of Manly's signature, by Richard Edgcumbe in his *Art of the Gold Chaser*.

The **dial** and hands are typical of those used by Ellicott at this time. Note the characteristic minute hand with a continuous taper, lacking the more normal cross-rib at the end. Signed 'Ellicott LONDON', the movement is also characteristic of Ellicott's work at this period. It has one of the two forms of Ellicott's distinctive pillars: a single fluted column flanked by pierced foliate scrolls (the other is where the column is of two flutes diverging towards the top plate). The cock has asymmetric foliate decoration.

PRIVATE COLLECTION

Plate 129. Thomas Mudge, London, no. 525.

Silver case 50mm: mid-nineteen century replacement

Mudge is generally considered the first to make a watch with a perpetual calendar and this, of about 1762, is the earliest by number to survive. The second earliest, and indeed the only other one, is number 574 in the British Museum, which has its original 1764 hallmarked case. In the December 1981 issue of *Antiquarian Horology*, George Daniels illustrates the top plate and under-dial work of 525 and Richard Good discusses 574 – they are visually and mechanically very similar – using sixteen photographs and line drawings.

A fixed pointer on the **dial** above twelve indicates the date shown on the silver date ring which revolves taking into account the long and short months. Below twelve there is a circular aperture with the phases of the moon and a female reset square. The silver sector at nine indicates the months (February is within an auxiliary aperture and is illustrated showing the leap year) while the sector at three indicates the days of the week.

The dust cap and **movement** are signed and numbered. The cock foot is engraved; it has a mask at the neck and the table has a diamond endstone within pieced asymmetric scrolls. As number 574, there is a ruby cylinder escapement – Mudge was probably the first to use a ruby shell – and square baluster pillars.

This watch was in the David Landes Collection.

Actual size.

PRIVATE COLLECTION

Plate 130. Ellicott, London, no. 5152.
Gold cases 48mm: inner HT incuse (probably Henry Cleaver Taylor, possibly Henry Teague), hallmarked 1763-4 and numbered

Three or four other watches with the same design on the chased **outer case** are known. When this example, part of the S.E. Prestige Collection, was sold at Sotheby's in April 1968, it was suggested that the central rosette and radiating foliage was reminiscent of a chrysanthemum. The inner case is plain, there is a normal rosette in the head of the pendant, and the simple stirrup bow was a form popular with Ellicott at this period.

The **dial**, hands and **movement** – which has a cylinder escapement – are typical of those used by Ellicott.

PRIVATE COLLECTION

Opposite: Plate 131. William Deards, London, no. 531.
Gold cases 49mm: inner DA coronet above incuse struck three times (probably Daniel Aveline): enamelled outer no marks

From the early 1760s, this high quality gold and enamel chatelaine watch, which is in exquisite condition, is signed by someone who appears not to be a member of the Clockmakers' Company. However, Arthur Grimwade has a biographical note in his book on London Goldsmiths' marks of two makers of this name, presumably father, who died in 1761, and son who continued working into the 1770s. They were recorded as goldsmiths and toymen, a toyman being a vendor of luxury goods including watches with embossed and decorated cases.

The **outer case** and chatelaine, which is constructed with gold plaques on gilt-metal, are decorated with roses of pink enamel painted on a white and *basse-taille* enamel (see

Glossary) foliage on a ground of bright-cut line-work. The back, which has a diamond-set push-piece, has four pierced and chased panels for sound emission – this is a repeating watch – and the enamel extends to the front bezel. The pierced and chased inner case is engraved with a mask within rococo scrolls below six and a basket of flowers on the back.

Both the dust cap and the quarter repeating **movement** are signed and numbered. The cock table has dolphin heads within scrolls and a diamond endstone. There is a brass balance, verge escapement and cylindrical pillars. The enamel **dial** has elaborate gold hands. This watch was in the Kenneth Snowman, Wartski Collection. PRIVATE COLLECTION

Plate 132. Stefano Thorogood, London, no. 1627.
Gold cases 48mm: both R.P eagle head above in shaped cameo (Richard
Payne), hallmarked 1763-4

Exceptionally – for an English watch – the back and the front bezel of the
outer case are covered entirely by *basse-taille* enamel (see Glossary) of four
colours: that is red for the tied ribbon and some of the flowers, clear showing
gold for other flowers, green for the foliage and blue for the ground. Because
different metal oxides are used for each colour, the enamel powders will fuse
into their glass-like states at different temperatures, requiring several firings, the
colours with the highest melting point first. This is an extremely
difficult procedure. Most unusually, the inner case has no bezel
but a flange to secure it in the outer and the glass is fitted to
the outer.

'Thorogood London' is in an arc above and below
the centre of the enamel **dial** which has a pair of
fine, elaborate, sometimes called 'Louis', gold hands.
Both the dust cap and **movement** are signed and
numbered. The cock table is particularly well
pierced and engraved and it has a diamond
endstone. There are cylindrical pillars and a verge
escapement.   PRIVATE COLLECTION

Actual size.

222

Plate 133. William Garrett, London, no. 219.

Case 132mm high: glass and gold cage-work

Scent bottles incorporating watches were one of the luxury items made around this time. This example is from about the mid-1760s.

The emerald green faceted glass is overlaid with embossed rococo gold cage-work of scrolls, floral swags and foliage. A bird rests on a vase of fruit (suggesting abundance) above the dial and garnet-set bezel while, on the reverse, an offering in front of a classical pillar occupies the same position above a compass and garnet bezel. The base of the bottle is set with diamonds and opens to form a patch box and mirror. At the top of the bottle is a ring of diamonds and a garnet-set stopper.

Both watch and compass **dials** are enamel. The **movement**, which is wound through the dial, is signed and numbered. The cock is engraved with a bird in flight; there are cylindrical pillars and a verge escapement.

PRIVATE COLLECTION

Actual size.

Plate 134. Charles Burges, London, no. 210.

Gold cases 47mm: inner hallmarked 1765-6; enamelled outer no marks

The back of the **outer case** has a fine *en grisaille* enamel of Hector's farewell to Andromache on a dark chocolate ground. The neo-classical border of alternate white enamel 'pearls' and gold foliate garlands on a blue ground matches the hallmark for date, but it is early and it is possible the painting was finished a year or two later – not an unreasonable delay which must have occurred quite frequently. The bezels, back and front, have similar borders of white 'pearls' and gold scrolling foliage. Hector is seen setting off for the Trojan War leaving behind his wife and infant son Astyanax.

The signed **movement** has a verge escapement and square baluster pillars, while the slightly later white enamel **dial** has elaborate 'Louis' gold hands.

This watch was in the Atkinson Collection sold at Christie's in October 1953. PRIVATE COLLECTION

Actual size.

Plate 135. Alexander Cumming, London.

Gilt-metal case 80mm high

The mainspring of this very small eight day quarter striking table clock is dated 1765. Of course, this is not, strictly speaking a watch, but it has much of the character of one.

The **movement** has two trains between three plates, the going above the striking, the bottom being signed below the bell which fits around it. Both fusees are wound through the base and bell. The verge escapement has block pallets with white sapphire linings, and the highly polished steel balance is visible within a dial aperture. Regulation is via a square adjacent to the front bezel hinge which turns an endless screw. There is no compensation.

The high quality **dial**, made further attractive by the oscillating balance, has an excellent pair of beetle and poker hands. The glazed **case** is engraved with continuous bands of flowers and foliage in the neo–classical manner.

Alexander Cumming FRS (1732-1814) was born in Edinburgh. A highly respected maker, he was a member of the committee appointed by an Act of Parliament – it came into being on 31 March 1763 – to examine John Harrison's fourth timepiece. He published *The Elements of Clock and Watch Work* in 1766.

PRIVATE COLLECTION

Plate 136. Andrew Dickie, London, no. 3086.
Gold and enamel cases 45mm: no marks

From Dickie's numbering sequence this quarter repeating watch was made around 1765.

The back of the **outer case**, with a tied ribbon of blue flowers in blue *basse-taille* enamel on a radial engine-turned ground, has blue enamel and bright-cut gold borders between two bands of piercing for sound emission. The bezels have blue ovals filled with black.

The inner case also has elements of the neo-classical revival, the body with pierced scroll decoration inhabited by dolphin heads, the back a pair of doves on a pedestal.

The signed and numbered quarter repeating **movement** has a cock table with a grotesque mask, scrolls and a diamond endstone and a cylinder escapement. The enamel **dial** has gold beetle and poker hands.

PRIVATE COLLECTION

Plate 137. Thomas Mudge, London, no. 681.
Cases 52mm: gold inner P.M pellet between incuse (probably Peter Mounier), no hallmark; outer gold, gilt-metal and leather

Mudge seems to have been the first to have made a minute repeating watch which can be considered thoroughly English. Only four signed by him survive of which this, of about 1766, is the fourth. Another, generally considered by him, is signed by Ellicott (number 2844 and not 2744 as sometimes noted) and this repeats, as the present watch. Unlike the other three which strike the hours, quarters and minutes in the conventional manner, after the hours a double blow to the nearest ten minutes is struck and then the minutes.

The back of the **outer case** has the monogram and coronet of Graf von Schulenberg. It is very possible that

Actual size.

Schulenberg was introduced to Mudge by his important patron Count von Bruhl. The inner case is pierced, decorated with scrollwork and engraved with a mask at the base and a rosette in the centre of the back.

The enamel **dial** has elaborate gold hands and the

movement is signed by Mudge and numbered. The dust cap is engraved 'Thos. Mudge Willm. Dutton', reflecting the fact that William Dutton became a liveryman of the Clockmakers' Company in 1766 and from this date was beginning to sign work jointly with his partner. The false plate is engraved with scrolling foliage on a hatched ground and the bridge cock – so rarely seen on English watches and Mudge used it only occasionally – has pierced foliate scrolls and a diamond endstone. There is a steel balance, cylinder escapement with a brass wheel and cylindrical pillars. The repeating mechanism is based on Mathew Stogden's design. For an illustrated description of Ellicott 2844 referred to above see Arndt Simon, *Antiquarian Horology*, Autumn 1991. Private Collection

Plate 138. Augustin Heckhel, Wein, no. 711
Single gold case 58mm: PM incuse (Peter Mounier), embossed, chased and enamelled, the enamel signed 'GMMF' for George Michael Moser (1706-1783) Fecit

The utterly charming polychrome enamel on the back of the **case**, probably of about 1767, is of George (born 1762) and Frederick (born 1763), the two eldest sons of George III, taken from two separate portraits by Zoffany both painted, it is considered, about 1765. Richard Edgcumbe (*Art of the Gold Chaser*) gives detailed discussion of this watch. He illustrates another watch with not dissimilar neo-classical gold decoration of the Duchess of Marlborough and her daughter which, according to a bill from G.M. Moser, can be dated to March 1767. He points out that Moser nevertheless continued for a time to use rococo cartouches. A dog, it would seem the same dog, appears in one of the portraits. Note the *en grisaille* painting on the stand supporting the vase of flowers.

The large **movement** is of Continental origin and is signed 'Augustin Heckhel No 711 in Wein'. Edgcumbe suggests that, bearing in mind the work was a personal commission (he cites an 1808 record to this effect), Queen Charlotte may have brought it with her (in another case) when she came from Germany.

Plate 139. William Auckland, London, no. 758.
Gilt-metal and porcelain cases 53mm: no marks

Watches with painted porcelain **cases** were popular during the third quarter of the century. This quite typical example, from around 1770, of two lovers in an Arcadian setting with a classical ruin has the Italianate serenity of the landscape painter Richard Wilson (1715-1782). Outside the symmetric yellow four-part, slightly raised cartouche there is a white stipple border. The front bezel has scrolls similar to the cartouche with polychrome flowers between.

The signed and numbered **movement** has asymmetric scrolls on the cock, a verge escapement and square baluster pillars. The enamel dial has beetle and poker hands.   PRIVATE COLLECTION

Plate 140. Thomas Mudge, London.

Gold cases 61mm: both P.M incuse (Peter Mounier) and hallmarked 1769 70

While Mudge is thought to have begun developing the idea of a detached lever escapement in about 1754 it seems he did not pursue it with any degree of urgency. If arguably not the first, this is certainly the most famous watch with the escapement. It was acquired by George III – how is not recorded – soon after it was made. Mudge refers to it in a letter to his patron Count von Bruhl in 1776 as 'Her Majesty's' watch. The King seems to have given it to Queen Charlotte who is said to have complemented Mudge upon the performance of 'her watch'.

In the same letter Mudge explains that, for the reasons the Count would understand, he did not have time to make another but that '…as to the honour of the invention, I must confess I am not at all solicitous about it: whoever would rob me of it does me honour'. Mudge would have been amazed to

know that, with some further development, his lever escapement would have been used for countless millions of timekeepers and that it would still be used in mechanical watches over two hundred years later.

The **cases**, **dial** and hands are typical of the period, although the minute hand has a head similar to the hour hand and the centre seconds hand is an early feature. The **movement** is signed but un-numbered. There is a large four-arm balance bridge, large balance with two springs, complex micrometer regulator, bimetallic compensation and, of course, Mudge's lever escapement.

The watch rests on a contemporary plinth which has been especially made or adapted to fit. Richard Good contributed a full and detailed description of this watch to *Pioneers of Precision Timekeeping* published by the Antiquarian Horological Society in the 1960s.

Actual size.

Plate 141. John Harrison & Son, London, no. 2.
Silver cases 130mm: both HT incuse (probably Henry Cleaver Taylor, possibly Henry Teague),
hallmarked 1768-9

Harrison's first three attempts to make a marine timepiece and win the prize offered by Parliament were clocks. He received some ex gratia grants for these, but it was only after the successful trials of his fourth (H4, as it is now called), a large watch, were complete and various conditions met, that he received about half the £20,000 prize. He received much of the balance after George III took an interest and organised his own tests of this, the fifth timepiece (H5). It has much the same configuration as H4, and Harrison numbered it 2: he also had it engraved with the year of completion, 1770. It never went to sea.

Much has been written about Harrison, his career and machines, and a full bibliography of these and manuscript sources by William Andrewes can be found in *Antiquarian Horology* June 2006. Richard Good's illustrated analysis of this watch, part of *Pioneers of Precision Timekeeping* (AHS monograph 3),

which should be read in combination with Anthony Randall's article (*Antiquarian Horology*, Summer 1989), has some historical and much technical information.

The quality, finish and everything about the **movement** is, of course quite wonderful. The balance and spring are both steel and the compensation takes the form of two bimetallic strips, although one, an auxiliary, is now disconnected. The escapement is Harrison's final version of his sophisticated form of the verge with diamond pallets. A remontoire acts on the contrate wheel eight times every minute. Because the train moves forwards in steps, the remontoire is required to drive the seconds hand. As the remontoire is not self-starting, a stop mechanism is incorporated to prevent the watch running down completely. There is maintaining power.

The style of the **dial** is common to those of the period. So are the hands, the seconds hand lying underneath the minute but over the hour. However, the hand-set is particular: a gold star, friction tight on the minute hand boss, protrudes though a hole in a fixed second, inner, glass, the outer glass and bezel being hinged in the normal way.

Plate 142. James Barton, London, no.1420.
Gold cases with third fish-skin outer 57mm: inner TL star above incuse (Thomas Layton), hallmarked 1771-2, chased outer with portrait enamel attributable to George Michael Moser (1706-1783)

The **outer case** *en grisaille* portrait on a chocolate ground is of John Harrison after James Tassie (1735-99). By the case catch and hinge is a globe, each with navigational and other instruments associated with Harrison's achievements and including the gridiron pendulum which he invented. These and, at the pendant, Phoebus (Radiant) Apollo and below his lyre interrupt a border of continuous scrolls and rosettes, typical of Moser's work at this period (see also Plate 138).

James Barton was married to Harrison's daughter Elizabeth. The **movement**, which is well finished, has an asymmetric decorated cock and diamond endstone, a verge escapement and cylindrical pillars. Both it and the dust cap are signed and numbered. The **dial** and hands are exemplary.

This watch was illustrated by G.H. Baillie in his *Watches* (Methuen, 1921), and Humphrey Quill in *John Harrison, the Man who found Longitude* (John Baker, 1966). It was in the Webster Collection sale (Sotheby's 1954). It was also illustrated in an article on the portraits of Harrison by Andrew King in *Antiquarian Horology*, June 2006. THE DJANOGLY COLLECTION

Actual size.

Plate 143. Larcum Kendall, London.

Silver cases 130mm: both PM incuse (Peter Mounier), hallmarked 1771-2

This, the second of the timepieces which Kendall made for the Board of Longitude, was with Captain William Bligh on his famous voyage on HMS *Bounty*, 1787-9. Known as K2, it was kept by the mutineers when they turned Bligh and the eighteen loyal members of his crew adrift in the ship's twenty-two foot launch. Some eighteen years later it was purchased by a Mayhew Folger, captain of an American whaler who put ashore for drinking water at the remote Pacific island of Pitcairn, from John Adams (alias Alexander Smith), the sole surviving mutineer. It was then stolen from Folger in Valparaiso, sold to a Spanish muleteer and, in 1840, sold by the muleteer's family to Captain Thomas Herbert R.N.

Now safe in the National Maritime Museum, the story of K2's journey home is almost as remarkable as Captain Bligh's 4,000 miles to Timor, East Indies, in an open boat! Until it stopped twelve days into the journey, Bligh had use of an ordinary pocket watch, signed 'Richard Vernon 3197', which the ship's gunner had managed to retain. Alas this was stolen from an exhibition held during World War II.

In his contribution to *Pioneers of Precision Timekeeping* (AHS monograph 3), Peter Amis gives a fuller account of K2's history together with an illustrated description of the mechanism. The exact copy (K1) of Harrison's fourth timepiece (H4), which Kendall had been commissioned by the Board of Longitude to make and which went with Captain Cook on his second and third journeys, had cost £500. He was then persuaded to make a simpler version 'leaving out any unnecessary complication' for £200.

The principal changes to the **movement** were that he left out the remontoire and many of the embellishments, used a different arrangement for the mainspring barrel and fitted a spiral compensation curb (the tool for making this was subsequently purchased from Kendall's estate and used by Vulliamy). Although quite adequate, the performance was not as good as K1, largely probably because of the omission of the train remontoire. Not only does the enamel **dial** lay-out, with plain hands, provide clarity, the friction inherent in the motion work of a normal dial and hands is avoided.

THE NATIONAL MARITIME MUSEUM

Plate 144. James Cox, London.
Gold, gilt and striated agate: base 70mm, height closed 150mm

An octagonal lamp-cum-watch made for the eastern market around 1770. The **case** has panels of red agate with white striations held in a frame overlaid with rococo ornament decorated with flowers and fruit. The base has a catch to a mirrored compartment and a push which releases the spring-loaded candle lamp in a delightful if somewhat alarming manner. The glazed lamp has a semi-circular silver reflector at the back and hinged gold cover, consisting of three tiers of open-work, decorated, as is the base and upper band, in the neo-classical manner.

The signed **dial** and the regulator subsidiary above have ruby-set bezels and the beetle and poker hands are gold. Note that for this small dial the line drawn inside the Roman numerals, traditional up to this period, has been omitted and there are dots rather than strokes for the minute markings (see also Plate 146). The **movement**, which has a cylinder escapement, is shaped so that the balance is below the regulator dial.

Plate 145. John Kentish Junior, London, no. 1033.

Gold and enamel single case 57mm: HT incuse (probably Henry Cleaver Taylor, possibly Henry Teague)

Number 1073 (Plate 146) is hallmarked for 1770-1 which would suggest circa 1770 for this watch. It is interesting that the unusual cases, both of which have spring-loaded winding shutters, should have different makers' marks.

The **case** winding shutter is in the border to the oval *en grisaille* medallion and is operated by a lever adjacent to the hinge. Surrounding the medallion, which is painted *en grisaille* with symbols of everlasting love and fidelity on a pink ground, are crossed palm fronds and a tied ribbon in imperial blue *basse-taille* enamel within engine turning. There are foliate borders of blue and white enamel interrupted by further foliate decoration at the quarters and the front bezel has similar enamelling.

The high quality **movement** is unusual. It has a ruby cylinder escapement, sun and planet maintaining power. A stop lever, which acts directly on the amplitude controlling pin on the balance staff, is operated from the edge of the case. This allows the watch to be set to less than a second or used as a simple stopwatch. There is a diamond endstone and square baluster pillars. The **dial** is very similar to that belonging to number 1073 (Plate 146) and is signed, as the movement, in the same manner: 'John Kentish Junr., London'. There is a small eccentric chapter ring immediately below the pendant and a stop/start lever for the centre seconds hand at five o'clock.   PRIVATE COLLECTION

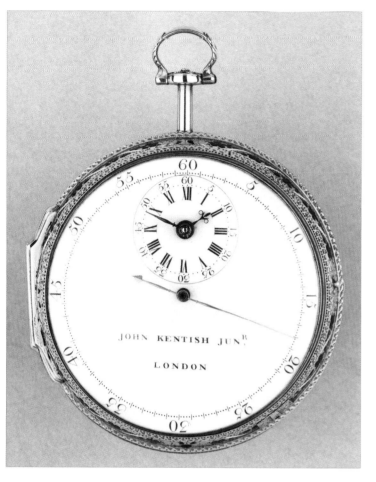

Plate 146. John Kentish Junior, London. no.1073.

Gold and enamel single case 57mm: RP incuse (probably Richard Palmer), a 2 above this mark, hallmarked 1770-1

The crest painted in enamel on the back of the **case** belonged to Evelyn Pierrepont (1711-1773), second Duke of Richmond-upon-Hull. He was installed as a Knight of the Garter in 1741 so the crest has the garter and motto with the royal crown above. The painting is on an oval light grey ground surrounded by borders of blue and white champlevé enamel and crossed palm fronds and a tied ribbon in *basse-taille* enamel within engine turning. The style and decoration of the case are very similar to Kentish 1033 (Plate 145); a winding shutter in the border of the central oval opens via a catch by the hinge.

The **movement** is also very similar. The cock, which has a diamond endstone, and the particularly elaborate regulator plate are well decorated. There is a ruby cylinder escapement, sun and planet maintaining power and square baluster pillars. A stop lever, which acts directly on the amplitude

Actual size.

controlling pin on the balance staff, is operated from the edge of the case. This allows the watch to be set to the second – indeed less – or used as a simple stopwatch. The fully signed **dial** is marked for fifth seconds on the annular ring and there is an eccentric for hours and minutes.

The Duke, whose seat was Holme Pierrepont, Nottinghamshire, served with distinction in the Army – raising his own 'Kingston's Light Horse' – and became a general in 1772. He was Lord Lieutenant of Nottinghamshire and Steward of Sherwood Forest 1763-5. He 'married' the bigamous Elizabeth Chudleigh, the notorious 'Duchess of Kingston' who, in the late 1770s appears to have been instrumental in introducing James Cox to business in St. Petersburg (Yuna Zek and Roger Smith, *Antiquarian Horology*, June 2005).

This watch was in the Chester Beatty Collection sold by Sotheby's, London, in December 1962.

PRIVATE COLLECTION

Plate 147. Ellicott, London, no. 6528.

Gold cases 50mm: inner PG fish above incuse (Peter Goujon), and numbered, enamel outer: no marks; enamel signed twice 'Moser' and 'Moser F' for George Michael Moser (1706-1783)

Using the known hallmarked watches by Ellicott as a guide (David Thompson, *Antiquarian Horology* Autumn 1997), this watch was made in 1770, maybe a year or so later.

The scene on the **outer case**, painted *en grisaille* on a maroon ground, has been researched by Richard Edgcumbe. It is related to a 1693 engraving entitled *'Nuptiales choreae'* (Borghese Dancers) by P.S. Bartoli, adapted by G.M. Moser into a delightful scene of maidens celebrating a wedding. It is not too fanciful to suppose that this watch may well have been a wedding gift to a lucky eighteenth century bride.

Edgcumbe points out that the vigour with which the figures move in Moser's composition results from his having spent the previous forty years chasing and painting in a baroque and rococo style, rather than following the more restrained rules of neo-classicism. The double signature, one in the normal place at the base below the 'step', the other just to the left on the edge of it, suggests the supposition that Moser was using his own (maybe signed) drawing as the source for his own enamel – a little affectation, but quite understandable.

The scene is surrounded by a ring of diamonds, blue *basse-taille* and white champlevé enamel. The push piece is diamond-set. The inner case, which is numbered inside and also below the pendant, is pierced and engraved in a typical Ellicott style with a fabulous bird by the winding square.

The half-quarter repeating **movement** and the enamel **dial** are also typical of Ellicott's style. The cylinder escapement has a steel wheel and there are cylindrical pillars.

Plate 148. Conyers Dunlop, London, no 3659.
Cases 45mm excluding gilt–metal and rayskin outer: enamel inner A&D coronet
above star below incuse (unidentified)

This can be dated very close to 1770; another watch by this maker,
number 3640, has a case hallmarked for 1770-1.

The polychrome enamel flowers on the back of the **case** are raised
in relief over the striking imperial blue *basse-taille* enamel. The
asymmetric character is further enhanced by the foliate design within
the enamel. The engine turning between the enamel has bright
cut flowers, foliage and rococo scrolls and, towards the bezel,
piercing for sound emission. The front and inner bezel are
decorated en suite.

The quarter repeating **movement**, which is wound
through the enamel **dial** at twelve, and dust cap are both
signed and numbered. There is a diamond endstone, cylinder
escapement and cylindrical pillars.   Private Collection

Actual size.

241

Plate 149. James Cox, London, nos. 621 and 628.
Gold and enamel cases 34 and 35mm: both PM incuse (Peter Mounier)

These watches were made around 1770 for the eastern market where there was a demand for matched pairs. They are identical except that one is a subtle miniaturisation of the other. The movements are eight numbers apart and it is safe to assume that these were made as part of two small batches of each size. There are a number of theories as to why they may have been deliberately paired in this way – one is said to be an acknowledgement of the belief that for Man to be in harmony with Nature he should, like her, never make any two things precisely the same.

The silhouettes of Asiatic war elephants on the back of the **cases** are in *basse-taille* enamel. Their mammoth-like hairiness, the turreted howdahs they carry and the ground on which they stand are chased and engraved in

Actual size.

detail below the enamel. The surrounding radial engine turning is beneath a clear glaze and the foliate borders and the bezels have translucent blue enamel. The bezels, bows, pendants and push-pieces are set with rubies. The inner cases are pierced, chased and engraved with asymmetric decoration with masks at the base.

Although the **dials** are most unusual, being painted with a continuous rural scene, they are found on other watches by Cox. The arrow head on the hour hand is another feature which is quite characteristic of his watches. The cocks of the signed and numbered quarter repeating **movements** are decorated with asymmetric scrolls and flowers and there are verge escapements and cylindrical pillars.

These watches were in the Swartz and Sandberg (Antiquorum, Geneva, April 2001) Collections.

Plate 150. James Upjohn, London, no. 5783.
Gold and enamel single case 43mm: DA incuse (Daniel Aveline) hallmarked 1771-2

James, the best known member of an Exeter family of makers, is thought to have had his movements made, or at least finished, in Exeter. The Upjohns exported, particularly to the Dutch market.

The amphora on the back of the **case** is decorated with champlevé enamel, while the imperial blue ground, tied ribbon (symbolising harmony) and crossed palm fronds (for victory but also peace) are in *basse-taille* enamel. The watch is wound clockwise through the **dial** and there is a very good pair of gold 'Louis' hands. In contrast to the strong symmetry of the neo-classical case decoration, the **movement** cock and figure plate have asymmetric intertwining foliage and flowers. There is a signed dust cap, verge escapement and cylindrical pillars. PRIVATE COLLECTION

Plate 151. Thomas Grignion, Covent Garden, London, no. 1686.

Gold cases 48 x 180mm: inner no marks, enamelled outer HT incuse (probably Henry Cleaver Taylor, possibly Henry Teague)

The neo-classical enamel decoration is very similar to the watch by James Upjohn illustrated in Plate 150 and hallmarked 1771-2. It might be a year or so earlier as another watch by Grignion with a slightly lower number, 1643, is recorded with a case hallmark for 1765-6.

The back of the outer **case** and matching gold mounted chatelaine are decorated with amphora, palm fronds, flowers and tied ribbons in imperial blue and white *basse-taille* and champlevé enamel. Suspended from the chatelaine is the original

crank key; the other three items, a snuff bottle, vinaigrette and a scent flask, are simply associated. The inner case is decorated with pierced scrolling foliage inhabited by dolphin heads and a grotesque mask at the base.

The quarter repeating **movement** and silver dust cap are signed and numbered with the address. The cock has a diamond endstone, the cylinder escapement has a steel escape wheel and there are cylindrical pillars. The white enamel **dial** is typical of the period and the beetle and poker hands are of blued steel.

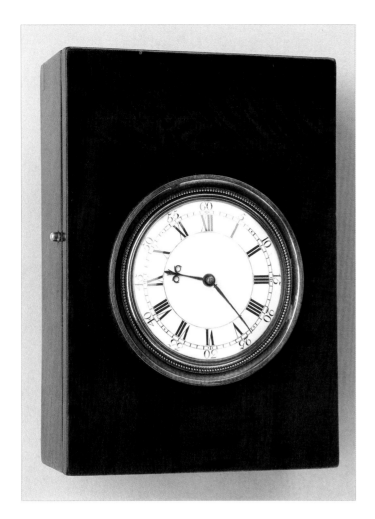

Plate 152. Justin Vulliamy, London, no. cmn.
Silver cases 78mm: inner no marks, outer PM incuse (Peter Mounier), mahogany box

Vulliamy continued to employ letter code numbering after his father-in-law and partner Benjamin Gray died in 1764. This striking and half-quarter repeating coach watch, which typifies his distinctive style, is from the early 1770s. A brass strut fitted to the bottom enables the owner to set the mahogany box towards upright and use the watch as a small clock: ideal when, as a house guest, he needs to know when to go down for dinner!

The bezels of the outer **case** are pierced and decorated with foliate scrolls while the body of the inner, which has a good mask at the base, has similar work inhabited by dolphin heads. The pendant is plunged to actuate the repeating and there is a strike/silent lever for the striking at two and a dumb-piece at three. There is an excellent **dial** and fine pair of hands. Within the minute ring are double dots at the quarters and a single dot marking the half-quarters. The **movement**, which is fully signed, has two hammers for repeating and a third for striking, a cylinder escapement, diamond endstone, steel balance and cylindrical pillars. The cock and figure plate are fully pierced, the decoration being similar to the case. Typical of Vulliamy's work, a snake is engraved within the figure plate, the tongue indicating the regulator setting.

Plate 153. James Cox, London, no. 5680.

Gold cases 40mm: no marks

Made for the Oriental market during the period after 1770 and before Cox's over-extended business ran into serious financial difficulties in 1775.

The **case** back and front bezel are set with rubies, emeralds and pearls, while the central panel has a pheasant and pagoda in *basse-taille* enamel. To the Chinese the pheasant was a symbol of beauty and good fortune, and was one of the twelve elements on the imperial robes. A secret catch allows the panel to be lifted to reveal the painted enamel erotic scene. The inner case is pierced and foliate engraved.

The **dial** has a central zone of white enamel with Roman chapters surrounded by a continuous rural polychrome enamel border similar to those shown on Plate 149. The blued steel hands have poker style bodies with arrow heads, a form favoured by Cox. The signed and numbered quarter repeating **movement**, which has a verge escapement, is also typical. There is a contemporary silver-gilt, enamel and pearl-set matching neck chain.   PRIVATE COLLECTION

Plate 154. William Hughes, London.
Silver and gilt-metal case: no marks. 270mm long

William Hughes, recorded from 1766, was made an honorary freeman of the Clockmakers'
Company in 1781. He concentrated on export markets, particularly those in the Far East. This
fan is probably from about 1775.

The watch **case** in the pivot has a silver bezel set with pastes and silver-set pastes decorate the
gilt-metal guard sticks with birds alternately with glazed ovals of *basse-taille* enamel birds and
flowers. The ivory sticks are carved with Oriental figures. The paper leaf is painted with a scene
from the *Aeneid* in which Venus is asking Vulcan to make a set of armour for her son Aeneas. The
reverse has a painting of two ladies dressed in period.

The miniature **movement** is signed, has a verge escapement and is wound through the Roman
figured white enamel **dial**. PRIVATE COLLECTION

Plate 155 Gold and enamel watch case

Gold outer case 53.7mm: no marks

Enamel plaque signed on the reverse by Henry Spicer (1742/3-1804), miniaturist and painter in enamel

> ARABELLA HAMLYN
> 1774
> H. Spicer. Pinx.

Actual size.

Plate 156. George Philip Strigel, London, no. BBLD.
Gold single case 47 x 183mm: I.R incuse (James Richards), enamel signed Moser F for George Michael Moser (1706-1783)

The superb neo-classical enamels on the diamond-set watch and chatelaine were painted by G.M. Moser about 1775. The scene on the watch **case**, *Amor leonem domans*, is after an engraving by Bernard Picart which in turn derives from a cameo by the sixteenth century artist Alessando Cessati. It is also on a coloured gold box signed 'G M Moser f 1774' in the Gilbert Collection. The medallion of Medusa on the chatelaine clip seems certain to have been taken by Moser from the same source, a 1724 publication by Philippe de Stosch, *Gemmae antiquae caelatae* (no. LXV). A fuller illustrated description of the enamels and their sources are in Richard Edgcumbe's *Art of the Gold Chaser* from where the above information has been taken.

The enamel **dial** has gold diamond-set hands and the square for winding the **movement** is immediately below twelve o'clock. Strigel has signed the dust cap, abbreviated his forenames on the top plate where his signature is followed by his number code. There is a diamond endstone, cylinder escapement and cylindrical pillars. Strigel (1718-1798) was well connected and supplied a pair of Chelsea porcelain clocks to Queen Charlotte.

The Phillips London auction catalogue of September 1984 states that they were auctioning this watch 'By order of the beneficiary of the late Madam Maria Callas'.

PRIVATE COLLECTION

Plate 157. William Allam, London, no. 1451.

Single gold case 46mm: PM incuse (Peter Mounier); enamel signed AT for Augustin Toussaint

A watch with a similar movement by Allam, number 1416, has a case by the same maker hallmarked for 1772-3, and the same scene signed by Toussaint is on the chatelaine hook of a watch by Josiah Emery (number 660), the case of which (the scene on this is also signed) is hallmarked for 1774-5. The present watch can be dated to about 1775.

The back of the **case** has an oval scene of a woman sacrificing at an altar, painted *en grisaille* with the initials AT below the step. The frame of blue *basse-taille* and white champlevé enamel is surrounded by gold foliate scrolls on a green *basse-taille* ground. Shells and ovals are at the quarters and the same blue and white colours are used to decorate the bezels. There is a diamond-set push piece. Toussaint was apprenticed to G.M. Moser in 1768; Moser chased and embossed the same scene on a case hallmarked for 1770-1 (Richard Edgcumbe, *Art of the Gold Chaser*, figure 105).

The enamel **dial** has gold beetle and poker hands and the winding square is below twelve.

The dust cap is signed and the **movement** is signed and numbered. As number 1416 mentioned above, it has an early ruby cylinder escapement with a brass wheel. The cock has a diamond endstone, a grotesque mask at the neck and is decorated with foliate scrolls similar to those on the case. The quarter repeating mechanism sounds on steel blocks fixed to the inside of the case.

This watch was in the Chester Beatty Collection, Sotheby's, June 1963, lot 246.

Actual size.

251

Plate 158. Ellicott, London, no. 7063.
Gold cases 48mm: both TL star above incuse (Thomas Layton), hallmarked 1775-6

The back of the outer **case** has the crest and motto, *Nil veritur veritas*, of Napier, Ballikinrain, Dumbartonshire surrounded by flower heads enclosed within cross palm fronds and surmounted by a partly embossed eagle.

The **dial** is an excellent example of where, although the basic design remained unaltered, there was a trend from about 1775 towards slightly smaller numerals, particularly the Arabic minutes. The ring on the inside of the Roman chapters remained, although it had been dropped on a few small dials (Plate 146). The hands are typical of those used by the firm. The minute hand has only one cross-rib: unlike some other makers, the firm did not employ a second – one over the dial ring referred to above – from the early 1760s or before, at least not in general. They continued to have a well-defined trefoil tip on the beetle hour hand.

The cock of the signed and numbered **movement** has entwined foliate decoration and a diamond endstone. There is a cylinder escapement and cylindrical pillars.

PRIVATE COLLECTION

Actual size.

252

Benjamin Vulliamy (1747–1811). Unsigned oil on canvas

Chapter Five

THE FIFTH PERIOD

1775–1825

Chapter Five

THE FIFTH PERIOD

1775–1825

OUTLINE

We are so used to having easy access to accurate Mean Time; it is difficult to imagine how it was otherwise. The majority in most communities in the eighteenth century depended on the church or public clock in their locality. It was of no consequence to them that the timekeeping varied from one to another. This inconsistency would have been irritating to the traveller, especially for those fortunate enough to own a watch, but otherwise it was of little importance.

For mariners the matter was entirely different. If John Harrison made the first timekeepers consistently accurate enough for finding their longitude at sea, in practice the process was transformed by John Arnold and Thomas Earnshaw who began to fit their detent escapements to both watches and box chronometers in significant numbers from the 1780s onwards (for instance Plates 168, 174 and 179). Watches with these escapements were not only very good timekeepers but, most importantly, once set to time – at a major port – they could be relied upon to perform at a constant known rate which could be allowed for during the voyage. They continued to be an important and very successful part of the English watchmaking industry.

Also very important was the introduction of the lever escapement, first realized by Thomas Mudge in the 1770s (Plate 140). Josiah Emery (Plate 178) and others made an extremely limited number of high quality lever watches in the initial phase of the development between 1782 and about 1805. The second phase, initiated by Edward Massey with his 1812 patent, began tentatively and was not truly under way until the early 1820s.

Two important developments began at the end of the period and prototypical examples are shown in Plate 234 (keyless winding) and Plate 240 (chronograph).

Leonard Weiss in his book *Watch-making in England 1760-1820* (Robert Hale, 1982) covers many aspects of the trade during this period. He gives some statistics for both the number of workmen involved and the number of watches produced, while going into some detail about the tools used and the methods of production. London remained at the hub, with much of the productive work being carried out in and around Clerkenwell. Weiss records that in 1798 it was estimated there were about 7,000 engaged in the trade in Clerkenwell and a further 1,000 just north of the City in the parish of St. Luke's Without Cripplegate. The vendors of the finished article were, of course, generally located in the City itself, the Strand and further west.

Of the 120,000 watches finished in Clerkenwell each year in the period immediately before 1797 (when a tax on watches and clocks badly affected the trade) approximately 70,000 – more than half – were exported.

In 1796 more than 191,000 gold and silver watch cases were marked at Goldsmiths' Hall, while the total for 1798 was less than 130,000. Although the figure recovered for a while, a decline set in: just over 100,000 watch cases received the 1816 London hallmark. Liverpool makers continued to supply incomplete watches to the London trade but also, as well, used London cases early on for watches they completed and sold on their own account, in particular Litherland (see Plate 192, hallmarked 1795-6), or used locally made cases – fluctuating around 1,500 per annum in the 1790s – hallmarked in Chester (see Ridgway and Priestley, *Chester Gold and Silver Marks 1570-1962*, Antique Collectors' Club, 2004). Watches which were completed in Coventry and Birmingham were hallmarked in Birmingham. Weiss has a table of the annual weight of silver watch cases hallmarked there between 1796 and 1817: taking each to weigh about one and a half troy ounces, production ranged between about 7,000 in 1796 to 38,000 in 1810 and 17,000 in 1817. Although statistics are not available, as with the Clerkenwell trade, one may assume a large proportion of these watches were exported.

In broad terms, the watch trade in London held the high ground and shared the middle ground with south-west Lancashire and Liverpool, while Coventry and Birmingham concentrated on the cheaper end of the market. Towards the end of the period the French and Swiss watchmakers were making inroads into the British markets, both home and abroad, and overall English output slowed, apart, that is, from the more specialized area of pocket, marine and survey chronometers, which was largely unaffected by foreign competition.

Neo-classical designs were, in general, used for both movements and cases. Enamelled, embossed and chased cases had fallen out of favour by the 1790s, after which cases were mostly left plain or engine-turned – that is unless they were made for the Eastern markets. The Far Eastern trade, dominated by James Cox until the 1780s, was satisfied by William Ilbury, John Ilbery, the brothers Bovet and others who supplied many gold and enamel watches up to the 1850s. The enamelling, the backs with scenes or, from about 1815, often flowers, is generally of Swiss origin; so too are the cases (a few have false London hallmarks, quite often for 1814). These watches are outside the scope of this book.

SOME NOTABLE MAKERS, LONDON, LANCASHIRE AND THE PROVINCES

As in previous periods, there are makers whose work may be of the first rank, but for one reason or another – maybe because their output was limited – they are not particularly well known. The firm of Ellicott faded towards 1800, while the Vulliamys strengthened their position with, undoubtedly, more wealthy clients than any other.

They sold only few chronometer watches and concentrated on high quality pocket watches, frequently with duplex escapements. Both the Brockbank and Barraud businesses engaged in both markets, as did the much smaller firm of John Grant.

The remarkable George Margetts fairly described himself as 'a maker of astronomical Clocks and Watches and other Apparatus used in the Science of Astronomy and the Art of Navigation' but, as they all did, he bought in elements of his work from the trade. He used detent escapements according to both John Arnold's and Thomas Earnshaw's designs, two makers who made important contributions to English horology. Robert Pennington must be included in any list: he was one of the makers engaged by Thomas Mudge junior to make timekeepers to his father's design who made some excellent chronometers and who made a significant contribution to the development of the compensated balance. The names of Josiah Emery and Richard Pendleton will always be famous for a small series of early lever watches. Finally, James Ferguson Cole who, from about 1821, produced a wide variety but only a limited number of watches, has always caught the imagination.

Some idea of the output of the main watchmaking areas – London, south-west Lancashire, Birmingham and Coventry – to be found in *Watch-making in England 1760-1820* (Leonard Weiss, Robert Hale, 1982) – is given in the 'Outline' above. This book, quoting from many contemporary sources, paints a fascinating picture of the inter-relationship between them and the suppliers outside these areas. Not surprisingly, steel and some rollers came from Sheffield and brass could be had from Birmingham but, perhaps more surprisingly, watch glasses from Bristol or Newcastle-upon-Tyne.

The complex trade of tools, materials, completed components and part finished or finished movements continued. Watch vendors from all over the country could buy movements finished or unfinished, and with or without cases. While London vendors were still by far the most numerous, by 1825 Liverpool had some well-established retail names with its own makers, Roskell for example, beginning to sell a considerable number of watches. While Liverpool makers veered towards the quality end of the market, their watches increasingly with rack lever and, after 1820, lever escapements, Birmingham and Coventry watches found their way to more rural vendors. These had customers who were happy to own a silver watch in pair-cases, some having dials with painted scenes.

THE CASE MAKERS, THEIR MARKS AND HALLMARKS

Unlike the previous period, the vast majority of cases have the maker's mark and hallmark. Of the exceptions, some are of the best quality. Enamelled cases may have no marks or just the maker's. A few marks are impossible to identify or identify with any certainty, particularly those at the beginning of the period following the loss of the Goldsmiths' Register of Small Workers' Marks covering 1739-1759. This is because there were makers who continued to use marks which they had registered before 1759 for some time after 1775. Some, if not all, of the best makers are represented in this chapter. On page 72 of his book referred to above, Leonard Weiss has a long quotation of 1806 from a German traveller, P.A. Nemmich, part of which continues '…Cases are best made in London, and are sent to Coventry and Derby and even Lancashire…' (for an example see the watches by Litherland, Plate 192, and Waight, Plate 228). London lost this trade, however, as the regional case makers became more effective.

Philip Priestley's *Watch Case Makers of England 1720-1920* (NAWCC, 1994), with additional information in the companion volume published subsequently (*Early Watch Case Makers of England 1631-1720*, NAWCC, 2000), is an invaluable book of reference for London, Birmingham and Chester marks. Further research produced a good deal more information on watch case makers who registered at the Chester Assay Office, and this he published with Maurice Ridgway (*Chester Gold & Silver Marks 1570-1962*, Antique Collectors' Club, 2004).

THE CASE AND ITS DECORATION

Both pair and single cased watches were made throughout this period. The **hunter** (Plate 210) and half-hunter (Plate 222) styles appeared very shortly before 1800. Some cases were engraved in the neo-classical manner in the early part of the period (Plate 181). They were no longer embossed, but there was some excellent **chasing** (Plate 175) and, up to about 1800, this can be found combined with **engine-turning** (Plates 183 and 201). Thereafter cases were engine-turned or left plain, the case body – band – sometimes with ribbing. Cast decoration, typically shells, flowers and foliage, to the band, and often the pendant and bow, was popular with Liverpool makers from about 1820 (Plate 236).

Plates 160 and 170 have **enamel** paintings signed by William Craft, while Plates 163, 165, 171 and 176 are good unsigned examples executed during the period to about 1785. Thereafter, and in any event by about 1800, enamels with painted scenes and, typically, flowers (so excluding some plain translucent coloured enamels) sold by British vendors were, with a few exceptions, of Swiss origin (see Outline).

Watches made for the Turkish and nearer eastern markets invariably had a second or, more often, third outer case generally covered in **tortoiseshell** (more accurately the belly of the hawksbill turtle) either reddish brown or, more rarely, stained green on the underside (Plate 176). Plate 199 has a third outer case covered in green-dyed **rayskin**, while Plate 190 has this simulated with under-painted **horn**. Plate 185 has horn under-painted with a scene.

At the beginning of the period timepieces in general had a long stemmed **pendant**, circular in section, little different from those of repeaters, and this remained in fashion after the 'Regency' pendant, oval in section, appeared in the mid-1790s.

Movements continued to be deep, and thus the cases thick, and it was helpful if the pendant was of some length so that the watch could be removed from the pocket with ease. The stirrup **bows** were long and had modest joints up to the late 1770s (Plate 162), when, although the stirrup shape continued for a while, some slightly flatter bows appeared. Whatever the shape of the bow, however, their joints were made noticeably stronger from the late 1770s and during the 1780s (Plate 174); by the 1790s the fashion for positively long joints and the classic D-shaped bow had evolved (Plates 184, 192 and 213). This bow style is found not only on the circular-section pendant, but also on the Regency pendant (Plate 196).

The Regency pendant had D-shaped bows fitted even after 1820 (Plate 232) but most frequently bows with oval 'knuckle' joints (Plate 222). Initially Regency pendants were fitted to single cases as well as pair-cases, but after about 1825 only to some provincial pair-cased verge watches (Plate 231). The long flat-topped pendant with a circular section stem ceased to be fashionable shortly before 1810 when the pendant with a round, or a nearly round, head was introduced. These have knuckle jointed bows (Plate 223) or 'joint-less' bows, the ends of which are closed within the pendant head and screwed together (Plates 228 and 240).

THE DIAL AND HANDS

The classic **dial** design, complete with five minute Arabic figures, full minute track and an annular ring inside the Roman chapters, persisted, even occasionally after 1800 (and on 'Turkish' market watches for very much longer), but by this time the vast majority of dials no longer had the annular ring, and the five minute figures, though quite often retained, had been reduced in size. So called 'regulator dials', with an annular minute zone and subsidiaries for hours and seconds, were fitted by some of the best London makers, mostly before 1800, and especially to watches with early lever escapements (Plate 178). Watches giving astronomical information or indicating both mean and sidereal time are exceptionally rare; the dials shown in Plates 172 and 198 are unique to George Margetts.

Just about every dial made between 1775 and about 1810 was of white enamel, but there are of course many subtle variations in the colour and glazing. Some appear quite granular, others smooth. Plate 208 shows a very good example of the dials John Roger Arnold employed: it is slightly off-white and, when viewed edge on, the strong glaze becomes iridescent, this over a granular surface – lovely. A few gold dials, typically with engine-turned centres and numerals on a contrasting ground, either engraved and filled or, much more frequently, of raised polished gold, were fitted by London makers after about 1810 (Plates 226 and 235). They became popular with Liverpool makers, especially after about 1820 when frequently they were given vari-coloured gold decoration (Plate 236).

Arabic hour chapters, both radial (Plates 192 and 195) and vertical (Plates 215, 216 and 225), in a variety of styles were reasonably popular – but only that – from the 1790s. In place of the hour numerals Plate 231 has a radiant sun for twelve, a crescent moon for six and the name James Lymen on either side. The dial centre is painted after, loosely, a well-known picturesque subject in a naive manner. Other examples of this rather charming genre can be found on Plates 216 and 225.

A few makers, typically Vulliamy, continued to fit late beetle and poker **hands** (Plate 201) and continued to do so even after 1800, while Barraud revived the beetle, using a straight minute, between about 1815 and 1820 (Plates 230 and 235). However, by 1780 the majority of makers had begun to fit other styles – spade (Plate 168), heart-shaped (Plate 205) and arrow (Plate 184) with variations such as in Plates 192 and 193). Skeletonised cusped diamonds (Plate 174) appeared quite early on. The firm of Vulliamy adopted a style of skeletonised heart – on both the hour and minute – a couple of years after 1800 and used it frequently and for many years (Plate 214). Unlike their Continental counterparts, English makers were far less enthusiastic about the moon hands and used them sparingly (Plate 239). Plate 219 might just be considered a variation while Plate 207 is more probably a skeletonised spade.

THE MECHANISM

The **verge** escapement (see Glossary) was employed throughout the period and beyond, indeed as late as the 1870s. It was more robust and cheaper to make even if it was not such a good timekeeper as the alternatives. The **cylinder** escapement (see Glossary), a somewhat better performer, particularly if the cylinder was well made and of ruby, was used only occasionally from about 1785 but, since it could be made to fit a slim watch, it had something of a renaissance between about 1820 and 1835. The **duplex** (see Glossary), introduced in England following Thomas Tyrer's patent of 1782, proved a very successful escapement. It was found to have greater accuracy than the verge or cylinder and was fitted to many high quality watches by London makers. One of its greatest exponents was Justin Vulliamy, for example Plate 175 in a case hallmarked 1784-5, and his successors continued to use it regularly throughout the period (Plate 238). It did not perform quite so well as the detent escapement (see below) and was not considered for chronometers, although, for instance, Pennington, a chronometer maker, fitted it together with a compensation balance in Plate 224. Much more common during the heyday of the duplex escapement in English watches, that is up to 1820, was a plain balance, with a compensation curb (by Vulliamy in particular) or without. The escape wheel needed to be made very precisely and with any wear performance was badly affected; nevertheless the duplex escapement continued to be used after the end of the period and it had a revival in the 1850s and 1860s.

The introduction of the pivoted **detent** by Arnold in the 1770s (Plate 168) followed by the spring detent, his 1781-2 (Plates 169 and 179) and Earnshaw's version patented 1783 (Plate 174), soon transformed time measurement at sea. Not only were watches with these escapements very good timekeepers, most importantly they could be relied upon to perform at a constant known rate. During the first few years both makers made small improvements. The principal difference between the designs is that Arnold's is arranged so that the detent was in tension, while Earnshaw's was in compression (see Glossary). Both systems were very effective, but Arnold's escape wheel teeth suffered from greater wear and it was Earnshaw's final design which in the end proved superior. James Petto devised a form of detent – the so-called cross detent – which combined Arnold's in-tension detent and Earnshaw's impulse, but his detent had high inertia and oil was found to be necessary between the detent and passing spring (Plate 217). The oil available at the time soon thickened and became gummy. The spring detent was hardly ever made in England after the early 1780s – the watch by Sleightholm (Plate 193) is unusual in this respect.

A great deal of historical record and technical background concerning the detent escapement can be found in Anthony Randall's two books, *Watches in the British Museum V1* (The British Museum, 1990) and *The Time Museum Catalogue of Chronometers* (The Time Museum, 1991). Vaudrey Mercer's book *John Arnold & Son* (AHS, 1972) is excellent, and the subject is further covered in *Watches* by Clutton and Daniels (third edition, Sotheby's, 1979).

Josiah Emery was encouraged by Count von Bruhl, a long-time patron of Thomas Mudge, to make watches with **lever** escapements (see Glossary) based on Mudge's design. Plate 178 is a good example of some twenty-three of these watches which, in various states, have survived. Jonathan Betts' series of four articles on Emery's levers and their 'derivatives' (Pendleton, Plate 197) in *Antiquarian Horology* (Spring-Winter 1996) is comprehensive and informative. A few of Emery's contemporaries also experimented with the escapement although, judging by the number of watches to survive, none of them made many. Eight by John Grant are known (Plates 182 and 204), but otherwise just one or two each – for examples see Plates 188 (Perigal), 197 (Pendleton), 198 (Margetts) and 207 (Recordon).

Just two exist signed by John Leroux. The case of one of these, belonging to the Clockmakers' Company, is hallmarked for 1786-7; the other, a slightly later movement without a case, is in the British Museum. These watches are especially important in so far as they are the first known watches with, as Jonathan Betts puts it, the 'intelligent' use of **draw** (AHS, Autumn 1996), this designed to prevent the lever from moving after locking with the escape wheel and interfering with the free oscillation of the balance. The angle between the locking surfaces of the lever pallets and the escape wheel teeth are such that the pallets tend to be drawn to the centre of the wheel and the lever drawn towards the banking.

Although they would have been aware of the problem of mis-locking, no other maker appears to have employed draw until just before 1820, attempting to minimize the effect in other ways. Whereas Emery's lever was of a rather heavy construction, the straight-line lever in George Margetts' more advanced watch number 1128 (Plate 198) is poised and light, and the separate safety roller has been made very small so that, when the watch receives a jolt and the guard pin touches the roller, the effect on the oscillating balance is kept to a minimum. The fact remains there are disadvantages to draw – the need for greater impulse and an increase in friction. Importantly, the oil available at the time soon thickened and became gummy and, as the pallets needed to be oiled, incorporating draw would have exacerbated the problem. Even though a better overall configuration for the escapement had been arrived at by about 1800, it was still not ideal; it was expensive to make and the detent had proved to be more reliable and a better performer.

Edward Massey did not include draw in his patented design of 1814 (Plate 228), but employed it from about 1820 or shortly before (there is a degree of overlap between those watches with and without draw). Massey brought the lever escapement to practical and economic use (see Glossary). George Savage is credited with a variant to the Massey form during the same period – the 'Savage two-pin' lever escapement – the principal characteristics being that there are two pins rather than one on the roller, these acting for both unlocking and receiving impulse from a further pin mounted on the lever, this pin also acting as a guard pin.

In addition to the articles by Jonathan Betts, both books mentioned above by Anthony Randall and that of Clutton and Daniels have further historical and technical information on the lever escapement.

Few **spiral springs** on English watches were given terminal curves during this period: the watch by Recordon of 1802-3 (Plate 207) has an early example. John Arnold included a **helical spring** design in his patent of 1775 and fitted it to all his chronometers, discovering, in time, that he could form the terminals so as to make the spring vibrate isochronally. Most chronometers have helical springs and most, but not all, watches with early lever escapements.

There are two methods of compensating for the effects of temperature on the elasticity of the balance spring – with a bimetallic device consisting, generally, of brass and steel laminae which, as the temperature changes, either alters the position of the curb pins, thus the operating length of a spiral spring, or, as part of the balance, changes its effective radius. The earliest extant **compensation curb** is in a watch of 1753 apparently to the design of John Harrison and signed by John Jefferys. Jefferys' apprentice, Larcum Kendall's watch (Plate 143), the case hallmarked 1771-2, has a spiral form of compensation; the tools for making this were purchased from Larcum Kendall's estate in 1790 and used quite frequently by Justin Vulliamy (Plate 201). Vulliamy had previously employed a U-shaped curb (Plate 186) and used it subsequently. It was fitted by other makers but it was more popular on the Continent. The compensation curbs seen with spiral springs on watches by Thomas Earnshaw are often called 'sugar tongs' (Plate 212).

John Arnold took out his first patent for a **compensated balance** (together with his second idea, a helical spring) in 1775. No watch, as opposed to a marine timepiece, with this balance is extant, if indeed he ever made one. Less than a handful of movements survive with original examples of his second, the so called 'double T' which appeared in 1778 (the best known, watch number 1/36, is in the Maritime Museum), and almost as few of his third, the 'double S' (Plate 168) which after 1782 gave way to the 'OZ' (Plate 179). Josiah Emery used a form of the double 'S' in his lever watches. A good example of Arnold's final balance – the 'Z' – is on a watch by his son (Plate 208).

Thomas Earnshaw's first form of balance is fitted to the watch in Plate 174. He seems to have moved quite rapidly to his second and final form (Plate 205). Robert Pennington made four types of balance, variations of one another – examples of three of them can be seen in Plates 206, 213 and 224. These would seem to have led to the 'modern' two-arm screw balance as, for instance, that shown in Plate 241.

TIMEKEEPING

Although the late eighteenth century contemporary evidence is slight, it is clear from more recent tests that a well-made watch with a verge or cylinder escapement was a very adequate performer when it was new and well maintained. A daily variation of rate of as little as a half a minute to probably not much more than a minute could be expected. A good duplex would have had a better rate, but of course this too would have been affected by such things as extremes in temperature – although a well-made compensation would have helped.

Eighteenth century levers, those from the early period, performed better still. In a short chapter on the subject in *Watches*, referred to above, Cecil Clutton reports on a test carried out on an Emery lever. Over a month the daily rate varied somewhat but with seven seconds a day in May and five seconds in August.

The best performance, of course, was achieved with pocket chronometers, watches with detent escapements. An early and well-known watch, number 1/36 by John Arnold, was tested at Greenwich between 1779 and 1780 and over thirteen months its total error was only two minutes thirty-three seconds, the daily rate never varying by more than three seconds on two consecutive days. Above all it was the fact that, assuming it was of high quality and well maintained, a watch with a detent escapement could be relied upon to perform at a good, constant and known rate which set it apart from the other escapements.

Plate 159. Walter Stacey Ward, London, no. 5.

Gold cases 22mm: both M.R in cameo (Mary Reasey), no hallmarks

There are a few extremely small English watch movements made during the 1760-80 period to fit rings, fans and such-like. However, there are very few, if any, surviving pair-cased watches such as this, which was made probably around 1775, measuring as little as 22mm. Ward, the son of the silversmith Michael, was apprenticed in the Clockmakers' Company to Thomas Griffing for seven years in 1760. He may well have been active in the trade but signed little of his own work.

The **cases** are perfect miniatures of their larger brethren. Working wives were common, but women rarely registered their own mark. Mary Reasey, who registered her mark in March 1773, is thought to be the widow of James.

Apart from its size, the **movement**, which is signed 'W S Ward London No. 5', has some unusual features. The balance, which appears to be original, is made in gold which, being heavier than brass or steel, the maker presumably considered would help the performance of the verge escapement. The contrate wheel is in effect rimless with the teeth cut vertically and the fusee has just three turns. There is a grotesque mask at the neck of the cock and the table symmetric decoration has 'C' scrolls in each quarter.

The design of the enamel **dial** is typical of the period, while the gold hands are very similar in style to those in steel used by James Cox (Plate 149).   PRIVATE COLLECTION

Actual size.

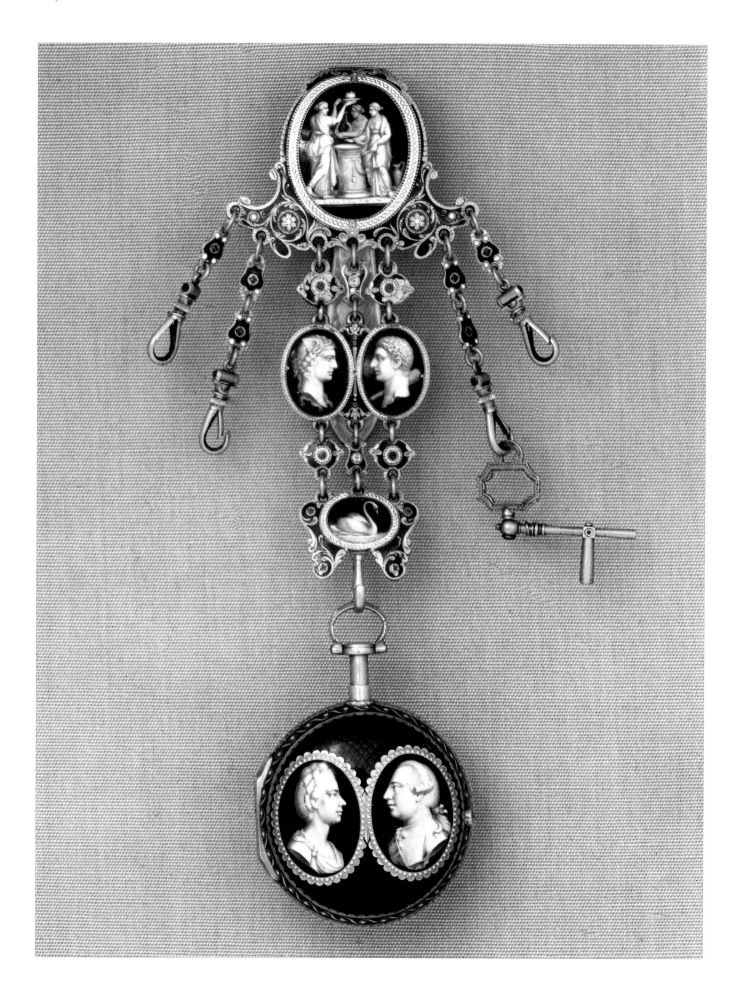

Opposite: Plate 160. John Leroux, London, no. 2979.

Gold cases and chatelaine 175mm long: inner I.M incuse (probably John Morecock), hallmarked 1778-9; outer MR in cameo (without pellet between, but probably Mary Reasey)
Enamels signed by William Craft (1730?-1810)

The two facing *en grisaille* portraits on the **case** are of George III and Queen Charlotte. Hugh Tait (*Antique Collector*, December 1983) notes that the strongly neo-classical images are closely related to medallions by William Tasse and a 1773 medal by Thomas Kirk. 'W' is below the truncation of the bust in the King's portrait and 'Craft' below the Queen's. The enamel is also signed and dated on the inside of the case: 'Wm. Craft 1777'. The head of Hercules is signed 'W.C.' while the opposing head, which Tait regards as Mercury, but which bears a striking resemblance to the image of Medusa on the hook plate of the watch by Strigel (Plate 156), is unsigned. The altar scene on the hook plate is signed 'W. Craft'.

The **dial** is signed 'Leroux, Charing Cross'. It has Roman numerals, no five minute figures and a gold 'late' beetle hour hand with a poker minute. The signed and numbered quarter repeating **movement** has a cylinder escapement.

This must surely be the watch purchased by Sir James Napier (knighted 13 March 1778) when he settled a bill from Leroux of £63.10.0 in February 1779.   THE TRUSTEES OF THE BRITISH MUSEUM

Plate 161. Benjamin Ward, London, no. 1052.
Silver cases 90mm: both cases TG incuse (probably Thomas Gosling's first mark), hallmarked 1778-79

A very large watch of high quality with a centre seconds hand and a stop/start lever on the edge of the inner **case,** clearly intended to be a timer. As is quite often found with watches of this size, the hinge of the outer case is significantly less than ninety degrees to the pendant. This is possibly to ensure that the front bezel will tend to remain closed even if the catch is inadvertently sprung when the watch is vertical.

The **dial** has the seconds divided into quarters. The seconds hand is counterpoised and the late beetle hour hand and poker minute are also of blued steel. The signature and number are on the dust cap as well as the **movement**. This has a pierced and engraved cock with a diamond endstone and square baluster pillars. The stop/start whip acts on the escape wheel of the verge escapement.

PRIVATE COLLECTION

Plate 162. Normand Macpherson, Edinburgh, no. 347.

Silver cases 68mm: both IA rectangular cameo (Joseph Allanson), hallmarked 1778-79

The arms on the back of the outer **case** are those of Johnstone of Annandale quartering those of Fairholm. The Earldom of Annandale and Hartfell, which went into abeyance at the end of the eighteenth century, was reclaimed in 1985.

The handsome **dial**, with a well-marked continuous seconds ring intersecting the lower hour divisions, is the more impressive because of the size of the watch. The blued steel seconds hand is counterpoised and there is a late beetle hour hand and poker minute. The **movement**, which is signed 'Norm.d Macpherson Edinburgh 347' has square baluster pillars and a verge escapement.

Macpherson, who is recorded as both Normand and Norman, was apprenticed to Andrew Dickie senior in 1749 and became a freeman of the Edinburgh Hammermen in 1764. He died in 1784. PRIVATE COLLECTION

Plate 163. George Goodman, London, no. 21619.
Gold single case 43mm: RP incuse (Richard Palmer), hallmarked 1779-80

The profile portrait *en camaïeu* upon a blue ground bordered with jargons on the back of the **case** is of Alexander Pope. His image was a popular subject and there would have been many sources: William Kutz Winsatt's *Portraits of Alexander Pope* published by Yale shows many of them.

   The **dial**, which has handsome elaborate gold hands, and the signed **movement**, with verge escapement and square baluster pillars through which it is wound, are typical of the period. This watch was in the Belin Collection sold by Sotheby's in November 1979.

   In his *Essay on Criticism* published in 1711 Pope observed: "Tis with our judgements as our watches, none/Go just alike, yet each believes his own'. Although watches have become far more reliable, the argument would seem to remain relevant!

Opposite: Plate 164. George Margetts, no. 128.
Paper volvelle (307 x 345mm) astronomical rotula, published 1779

Maybe only one or two of Margetts' astronomical rotulas survive. Another incomplete example, number 110, belongs to the Royal Scottish Museum. Printed at the lower edge of the zodiac ring is 'Published according to Act of Parliament 15th June 1779 – By Geo: Margetts No. 12 Ludgate Street' while below, and immediately above the dedication, is the engraver's name T. Blake and his address. The dedication is 'To his Grace the Duke of Marlborough'.

Margetts, in a petition to the Board of Longitude in 1789, fairly describes himself as 'a maker of astronomical Clocks and Watches with other Apparatus used in the Science of Astronomy and the Art of Navigation'. He was as much a mathematician as an horologist. In 1789, 1790 and 1793 he published two volumes of tables '…Containing the True Hoary Angle with the Altitudes of the Sun, Moon and Stars…' and a logarithmic rotula to accompany them. *New light on George Margetts* (A.J. Turner, *Antiquarian Horology,* September 1971) gives a good background to his career.
PRIVATE COLLECTION

Plate 165. John Scott, London, no. 1163.
Gold cases 49mm: inner IM incuse (James Marson or James Macklin), hallmarked 1780-1, outer HT incuse (probably Henry Cleaver Taylor); length with chatelaine 195mm

The basket of roses, pansies, peonies and forget-me-nots beautifully painted in polychrome enamel on the back of the **case** are on an *en grisaille* neo-classical stand. The floriate decoration extends beyond the translucent blue enamel on the case body and front bezel and, of course, the matching chatelaine. All the paintings are on grey backgrounds shaded left to right and can be compared to those on a watch by William Allam illustrated by Cedric Jagger in *The Artistry of the English Watch*. Although there is no clue as to the artist, it would be good to think that it was Mary Moser, daughter of Michael, who exhibited very similar paintings. According to Richard Edgcumbe, however, there has been no evidence found so far that she painted in enamel.

The dust cover and **movement**, which has a verge escapement, are signed and numbered with the address Gloucester Street, London. The white enamel **dial** has Roman numerals, five minute Arabic figures and gold late beetle and poker hands.

This watch was part of the important collection formed by Sir Chester Beatty sold by Sotheby's, London, in June 1963.
PRIVATE COLLECTION

Plate 166. Recordon Spencer & Perkins, London, no. 145.
Later silver-gilt case 52mm (2in.): WL incuse (probably William
Lewis, possibly William Laithwait), hallmarked 1807-8

Almost certainly the earliest surviving pedometer wound watch
movement according to patent number 1249 applied for by
Louis Recordon on 18 March and enrolled on 17 July 1780.
An indistinct signature on the mainspring – this appears to be
original – is accompanied by the date '27th May 1780'. There
has always been a considerable amount of discussion concerning
the history of the self-winding watch, the exact contribution to
the development by those involved and where the watches were
constructed (see below). The practice has always been to date a
spring when it is fitted which suggests the movement was
constructed in England, or at least in part.

The signature and number is on the silver oscillating weight
mounted on the back of the full plate movement which has a
going barrel, cylinder escapement and a balance mounted on
the bottom plate below the dial. The regulator is on the front

plate with the fast/slow notations in abbreviated Spanish.

The enamel **dial**, which has Roman numerals and gold
heart-shaped hands, is of the same period as the case which
has a Regency pendant and a spring-loaded front bezel.

Chapter five of *The History of the Self-winding Watch* by
Chapuis and Jaquet is devoted to Louis Recordon and his
patent. This book also considers the work of A-L. Perrelet,
Hubert Sarton and A-L. Breguet. Of these Continental makers,
either Perrelet or Sarton, it is not known which, developed a
somewhat different system from Recordon in the 1770s (Joseph
Flores, *Antiquarian Horology*, Autumn 1995). Breguet is said to
have developed his system, which is very similar to Recordon's,
in about 1780 – i.e. at the same time but not before Recordon
and his patent. The earliest known self-winding Breguet is
numbered 1 and dated AD 1781.

Plate 167. John Arnold, London, no. 45.
Later silver consular case 59mm: DW incuse (Daniel Walker),
hallmarked 1799-1800

Number 45, made about 1778, is among the first twenty pocket
chronometers by Arnold to survive. He and his son were in the
habit of updating the early machines and indeed only one with a
lower number – 1/36 now in the Maritime Museum – survives
unrestored and totally in its original condition. Number 45 was
apparently first in service with a member of the East India
Company and was on board the *Providence* commanded by Sir
Henry Addington in Monterey on 11 December 1796. In all
probability the updating was carried out subsequently to this and
when the consular case, hallmarked for 1799-1800, was supplied.

The **dial**, the style of signature and hands are characteristic of
the period around 1800. The basic **movement** is original,

together with its cock and
signature, but when, probably, John
Roger Arnold (Arnold senior died
in 1799) replaced the dial and case,
he changed the pivoted detent
escapement and what was almost
certainly a 'double T' balance for a
spring detent and a 'Z' balance.

Owned at one time by Sir John
Prestige, this watch was sold by
Percy Webster to the 5th Baron
Harris, Belmont Park, in 1945.

Vaudrey Mercer's *John Arnold &
Son* (AHS, 1972) is excellent and
includes an analysis and
explanation of their series of
numbers. A book written and
published by Hans Staeger in 1997
augments on this work.

PRIVATE COLLECTION

Actual size.

Plate 168. John Arnold, London, no. 23/78.
Silver consular case 70mm: ITP incuse (John Terrill Pain), hallmarked 1781-2

Arnold used the pivoted detent escapement for his watch **movements** from about 1772 and the spring detent from 1781-2. He took out a patent for a helical balance spring in December 1775 and employed this with his 'double T' and then his 'double S' balance between 1778 and 1782. About a dozen or so watches survive with one or other of these two balances, arguably the most elegant compensated balances ever produced. Only two survive complete with their original cases, dials and pivoted detents having a 'double T' balance (number 1/36 and 2/43 – although the balance of the latter has been restored) – and only this watch, number 23/78, survives without restoration with its original case, dial, pivoted detent and 'double S' balance.

Arnold has kept the **dial** divisions to a minimum and used the simplest of hands. The signature is followed by the denominator. The watch is wound via the back of the 'double bottomed' consular **case**.

This watch appears in the records of Joseph Bond, who had a servicing business in Boston, on 30 July 1834 (*Bond papers, M.M.G.* Vol. 1 F. 26). It was shown at the Antiquarian Horological Society tenth anniversary exhibition at the Science Museum in 1964.

PRIVATE COLLECTION

Plate 169. John Arnold, London, no. 39/88.
Gold consular case 74mm: ITP incuse (John Terrill Pain), hallmarked 1782-83

A large very handsome half-quarter repeating pocket chronometer of the type which Arnold called 'Of The Best Kind'. Only a handful of these have **movements** with their original short spring detents – the very earliest form of spring detent – because, whereas Arnold fitted a pivoted detent in the series up to 1781-82, he introduced a new movement calibre in which he employed a long detent (M.E. Cattermole, *Antiquarian Horology*, March 2001) very soon afterwards. This is the only example in its original case. It has an 'OZ' balance, a type Arnold used from 1782 until 1791: it may well have had a 'double S' balance to start with.

The **dial** has a more traditional layout compared with number 23/78 (Plate 168) but, while the second hand revolves once per minute in the normal way, the seconds ring is divided into 75. As the escapement unlocks every other beat of the balance the hand falls consistently on each division, thus allowing for more accurate reading.

The **case**, which has a good long pendant for repeating, is engraved with flowers and foliage, and these, with musical instruments, are on the back within an ovoid reserve.

Illustrated and described by Vaudrey Mercer (*John Arnold and Son,* AHS, 1972), this watch was in the Hornby Collection, Sotheby's, December 1978.   PRIVATE COLLECTION

Plate 170. Windmills, London, no. 9327.

Gold cases 50mm: inner marks rubbed, guild mark from 1776-95, outer no marks

Enamel signed and dated W. Craft fec.t 1782 for William Hopkins Craft (1730?-1810)

Craft's signature is on the reverse of the oval plaque which is held by gold tags in the outer **case**. A very well respected and accomplished enameller, Craft used antique gems, classical and contemporary sources for his work. His portraits of George III and his queen can be seen on the watch by Leroux (Plate 160). This miniature is of Erminia writing the name 'Tancred' on a tree (see Tasso, *Jerusalem Delivered*). Erminia, daughter of the Saracen king of Antioch, was in love with the Christian knight Tancred. The sheep in the foreground belong to the old shepherd who extolled to her the joys of his secluded, peaceful existence in contrast to the war raging not far away. There is a translucent dark blue surround and the back and front bezels have translucent dark red and, alternately, green enamel and gold rondels on an opaque white enamel ground.

The **movement** can be dated circa 1735 using published information on the firm's sequence of numbers (*Joseph and Thomas Windmills*, J.A. Neale, AHS, 1999). The plain inner case bears the number but the London guild mark is clearly from 1776-95. The white enamel **dial**, gold arrow hands and D-shaped bow are difficult to date precisely, but they could have been made a little after the plaque.

PRIVATE COLLECTION

Plate 171. Ellicott, London, no. 5211.
Gold cases 50mm: inner HT incuse (probably Henry Cleaver Taylor, possibly Henry Teague), hallmarked 1764; outer no marks

The unsigned high quality oval polychrome enamel of about 1780-85 on the back of the outer **case**, of a putto playing a lyre, was no doubt taken from a source inspired by an antique gem. Outside the frame of white enamel pearls is a deep border of translucent amber – an unusual colour – enamel over an engine-turned ground. The bezels are decorated with opaque white ovals within royal blue borders.

The enamel **dial**, with Roman numerals and Arabic five minute figures and gold late beetle and poker hands, is contemporary with the outer case. The dust cap and top plate of the dumb quarter repeating **movement**, typical Ellicott's work, are signed and numbered. There are cylindrical pillars and the escapement has been converted from a cylinder to a lever in the nineteenth century. PRIVATE COLLECTION

Actual size.

279

Plate 172. George Margetts, London, no. 312.
Later silver consular case 66mm: FC incuse (Frederick Comtesse) over, possibly, FHB
(rubbed), hallmarked 1813-14; pendant M.A in cameo, Michael Atkins

An astronomical register watch by Margetts with the preceding number, 311, sadly stolen from
the Royal Institution some years ago, had a gold case hallmarked for 1783-4: approximately the
same date can be assumed for number 312, the **case** being especially made later. Four or five
astronomical watches of this type completed by Margetts over a number of years are known –
number 1317 of 1802-3 is also illustrated (Plate 211) – together with two large tripod-
mounted timepieces numbers 341 and 342 measuring 160mm.

   The numerous indications on the **dials** are achieved with a special train of just sixteen gears.

Except for the fixed mean time dial in the centre, the gold north indicator and the two gold parallel parabolas, everything rotates clockwise, including the main dial and the twenty-four hour tidal dial. The tides at eight English ports marked on the mean time dial can be read off the tidal dial to which the moon hand is fixed. Not only does this hand indicate on the gold rim with four spokes the latitude of the planet, but also its position in the Zodiac and declination in degrees on the nearest calibration of the main dial. One of the spokes of the rim is engraved with a dragon whose extended tail points to the sign and degree of the Zodiac marked on the middle calibration. Furthest from the centre is an annual calendar which can be read against the sun hand which also indicates the sun's declination and position in the Zodiac.

The observer's horizon is indicated by the tangential parabola, while the space between it and the inner parabola is the astronomical twilight zone. In the area of the dial enclosed by them can be seen the rise, southing and fall of the constellations. The age of the moon can be seen engraved on gold through a circular aperture in the tidal dial. When there is an eclipse a black spot will appear, a

Actual size.

large one for an eclipse of the moon, a small one for the sun.

The full plate **movement** is signed and numbered and the dust cap is signed. Both are decorated in a manner typical of much of Margetts' work: a classical bust at the neck of the cock, the cap with an elephant and a pagoda within an Oriental landscape. There is a ruby endstone, a cylinder escapement with steel wheel and balance and Harrison's maintaining power. George Daniels describes and illustrates the under-dial work of 311 in his comprehensive article for *Antiquarian Horology* in March 1970.

This watch was owned by Lord Harris of Belmont and subsequently Lord Sandberg. PRIVATE COLLECTION

Plate 173. George Margetts, London, no. 316.
Gilt brass case 115mm without gimbals: no marks

A timepiece indicating both mean and sidereal time that, particularly as Margetts has employed an Arnold-type pivoted detent escapement, cannot be dated much later than 1782. Apparently intended as a marine timepiece, the original case and gimbals are mounted on a nineteenth century stand made in the manner of Thomas Cole.

The signed enamel **dial** has three subsidiary fixed dials and three rotating dials each showing hours, minutes and seconds. As the hands advance, mean time is read against the fixed dials while sidereal time is read against the inner dials which contra rotate. Sidereal (star) day is the time interval which elapses between two successive transits of a fixed star across a meridian, the sidereal day being 3 minutes 56.555 seconds shorter than the mean time day. Margetts' gearing produces a difference of 3 minutes 56.55, very acceptable for all practical purposes.

The signed and numbered **movement** is decorated with swags, foliage and trophies of war and the cock; fixed with two screws, is beautifully chased and engraved. The gilt-brass three-arm balance, which has a flat steel spring, is also engraved, and there is an adjustable bimetallic compensation curb. Importantly, there are friction rollers to the top and bottom balance pivots. These were used by John Harrison, occasionally by Mudge and Henry Scully, and in France by the Berthouds and Le Roy. The fusee has Harrison's maintaining power.

This is the only recorded piece by Margetts with a pivoted detent escapement. It is likely that this escapement was supplied by John Arnold prior to 1782-3 when he and Thomas Earnshaw introduced their spring detents. Margetts used the Earnshaw type of detent from then on. PRIVATE COLLECTION

Plate 174. Thomas Wright, In the Poultry, London, no. 2228.
Gold cases 64mm: IW incuse (John Wright), hallmarked 1784-5

Wright applied for a patent to Thomas Earnshaw's spring detent design on 1 February 1783: Earnshaw was unable to pay the one hundred guinea fee himself and paid Wright a guinea commission on each watch with the escapement he sold and did so until, it seems, the agreement was satisfied.

No expense has been spared on the **movement**, the quality and finish being phenomenal. There is no doubt it was made by Earnshaw for the patentee. It is the only one recorded with the spring detent and according to the patent signed by Wright. The false plate is signed and numbered and the cock, which has a particularly large diamond endstone, is engraved with a royal coronet at the neck and 'Wright Watch Maker to the King' on two ribbons. The wheel train is fully jewelled to and including the fusee, one of the earliest movements, maybe the earliest, so made. Earnshaw claimed that he invented a compensated balance in 1784, a claim which seems to be substantiated by the balance: it has three arms with cut, apparently bimetallic, rims each with interior semi-circular steel weights. The small size impulse roller is original – most, if not all, the other early rollers were changed for a larger, safer one by Earnshaw. There is a dust cap through which a stop/start lever operates a whip on the balance.

The fully signed **dial** has simple, legible markings and gold 'diamond' hands – an early example of the style; the diamond is invariably cusped and most often skeletonised.

For a fully illustrated article on this watch, which was at one time in the David Landes Collection, see Andrew Crisford, *Antiquarian Horology,* June 1976.

THE DJANOGLY COLLECTION

Plate 175. Justin Vulliamy, London, no. ouo.
Gold cases 59mm: both WQ incuse (William Quinton), hallmarked 1784-5

The cipher and coronet of Frederick Duke of York, second son of George III, is on the back of the outer **case** within an oval reserve surrounded by chased and engraved radial and foliate decoration.

The **dial** and the gold beetle and poker hands are classic examples of those found on watches by Vulliamy at this date, but note the single dots within the minute 'track' to mark each half-quarter. The polished steel counter-poised second hand, mounted between the hour and minute, is turned and of 'poker' form.

The dumb half-quarter repeating **movement**, which is signed and numbered with Vulliamy's code, has a splendid grotesque mask at the neck of the cock. A serpent points to the regulator scale, a typical Vulliamy feature, and the quality of the engraving is exemplary. There is a diamond endstone and a cylinder escapement, on the brass wheel of which a stop/start mechanism acts. The hammers strike on blocks fitted to the plain inner case.

History. The hallmark is for the year the Duke was twenty-one. Vulliamy's day books (held in the Public Record Office, Kew) record this watch's number, together with the correct description, showing it was returned for cleaning on two occasions – these entries noted by Roger Smith – although there may have been others. In November 1798 and

again in February 1809 the 'owner' was shown as Major General (de) Bude, a
Swiss soldier/courtier who, after a period as Governor to Frederick's
younger brothers, joined the Duke's household at least by the early 1790s.
Bude was officially Frederick's Secretary of Foreign Affairs but undoubtedly had
a wider remit. His address was in St. James's Palace and he died at Windsor
Castle in 1818. The association with Bude is consistent with the watch
being the property of Frederick Duke of York, but it is also possible
that the Duke might have given the watch to Bude at some
juncture.

The Duke of York was nominal Commander-in-Chief
of the British Army and an active administrative head
from 1795-1809 and 1811-1827. Somewhat maligned by
the famous nursery rhyme – unfairly, bearing in mind the
financial constraints the Army was under at the time – he
did much for the welfare of the men under his command,
and established the Duke of York's School for the Sons of
Soldiers in Chelsea. He was a handsome and popular man
who, in 1789, fought a duel on Wimbledon Common with
Colonel Lennox, later Duke of Richmond, when he coolly received
the Colonel's fire and then fired in the air.

PRIVATE COLLECTION   *Actual size.*

287

Plate 176. Markwick Markham Perigal, London, no. 2088.
Silver-gilt cases 51mm: no marks

A handful of minute repeating watches survive made by Thomas Mudge in the 1760s, but very few by other makers are extant until the early nineteenth century. This example was made for the Turkish market around the early or mid-1780s.

The body of the inner **case** is pierced and engraved around the band, while the wavy-edged outer is covered with green-stained tortoiseshell (turtle shell) with pierced gilt copper panels and pin-work. Note the long stirrup bow; the trend soon was for this to become D-shaped and the joints with the pendants more substantial. The fully signed **dial** has the generic form of true Arabic figures used on watches of this kind and blued steel late beetle and poker hands.

The very small minute repeating **movement**, 31.2mm in diameter and fully signed and numbered, has a chased and engraved cock foot and figure plate, the index with generic Arabic figures. The cock table is pierced out and has a diamond endstone. There is a cylinder escapement with a brass escape wheel. The Stogden-type repeating mechanism has a reversed hour snail and a four-armed minute snail. The repeating spring is signed Ansell and the bell Dury. PRIVATE COLLECTION

Plate 177. James Ryland(s), Ormskirk, no. 216.

Gilt-metal cases 48mm: inner marked V incuse

Although the dead-beat verge, sometimes known as the Debaufre escapement, was introduced at the beginning of the century, it was really only first taken up in any determined way by some of the makers in and around Ormskirk during the third quarter. Here James Rylands – the family generally omitted the last letter of their name when signing their work – has produced, circa 1785, an interesting and unusual variant of what is also called the 'Ormskirk' verge.

The pretty **movement** has a large fixed going barrel, square baluster pillars, a normal single verge wheel and a balance staff with two pallets shaped as pyramids. Each pallet is cut through and has an impulse face. There is a flat banking piece running between them parallel to the balance staff. The top plate is extended over the barrel and, outside an engraved semi-circular regulator scale between the cock foot and the contrate wheel, it has been extensively pierced, chased and engraved with a flower and scrolling foliage. There is a bird, possibly a pheasant, at the neck of the matching cock.

The **dial** has Roman numerals, Arabic five minute figures and single dots between an arcaded band. There is a counterpoised seconds hand and a stop/start lever at IX operates a whip to the escape wheel.

Plate 178. Josiah Emery, Charing Cross, London, no. 947.

Gold consular case 62mm: VW incuse (Valentine Walker), hallmarked 1785-6

Encouraged by Count von Bruhl, Ambassador to Great Britain for the Court of Saxony and a long-time patron of Thomas Mudge, Emery began to complete watches with lever escapements based on Mudge's plane but to his own design. This was towards the end of 1782. He made them in two sizes and a total of twenty-three are now known to have survived in various states. Ten are more or less complete and in their original condition; 947 is the third earliest of these in number sequence.

The signed and numbered **movement** has a two-plane lever escapement (see Glossary) with jewelled pallets and impulse, and slotted teeth to the steel escape wheel. As with all Emery's lever escapements, there is no draw. The balance is along the lines of the 'double S' type developed by John Arnold and patented by him in 1782. It has two brass arms, a helical blued steel spring, two gold timing screws, and two bimetallic compensation affixes each with a gold adjusting screw. The bridge cock, jewelling, fusee with Harrison's maintaining power are typical of these watches. The signed dust cap, which is numbered 946 rather than 947, is 'peg-fixed': a push inside the front bezel, adjacent to the pendant, releases a secret catch so allowing the cap to be removed.

The signed 'regulator' **dial** and hands with heart-shaped tips are typical of Emery's lever watches.

This watch was sold at Sotheby's in April 1963 by Lady Prestige, widow of the collector Sir John Prestige and sister-in-law of S.E. Prestige. It is included in the comprehensive and informative series of four articles on Emery and his lever watches by Jonathan Betts published in *Antiquarian Horology* (Spring-Winter 1996).

PRIVATE COLLECTION

Plate 179. John Arnold & Son, London, no. 99.

Silver consular case 62mm: IL in cameo (apparently John Laithwait – identical mark registered for him March 1778), hallmarked 1786-7

Arnold began signing his work in conjunction with his son in 1784. This is one of just a handful of their large size pocket chronometers to survive; it is in exemplary condition.

The **movement** is fully signed and the number is followed by Arnold's habitual 'Inv.t et Fecit'. It has a spring detent escapement, the slot and shaped foot finishing adjacent to the winding square shroud, and an early 'OZ' compensated balance. The helical spring is of gold. Arnold began fitting these some time before March 1784 when he informed the Board of Longitude that he found that they were not 'liable to be affected by moisture or taking up fresh phlogiston from the human body…'. It fitted to the typical Arnold cock with a blued steel stud arm.

The signed and numbered **dial** is typical of those used initially by the partnership: the Roman numerals with an inner ring and dots for the minutes within an outer track.

This watch is included in Hans Staeger's 1997 privately printed *100 Years of Precision Timekeepers from Arnold to Arnold & Frodsham.*

PRIVATE COLLECTION

Plate 180. Timothy Williamson, London, no. 2780.
Gilt-metal cases 139mm: outer W.C incuse (William Carpenter)

A large and impressive quarter striking coach watch, of a type intended primarily for export, dating from about 1785, possibly shortly before.

The decoration and piercing of the **cases**, the outer with a paste-set bezel, is a classic example of the genre. The **dial** is fully marked with Roman numerals, five minute Arabic figures and the minute ring with fifth second divisions. There is an interior ring for the age and phase of the moon. The hands are gold: late beetle and poker hour and minute, the moon and

seconds hand both cross-ribbed, the moon with a heart head and, as the seconds, with half-moon tail.

The dust cap and **movement** are both signed and numbered. The cock foot and figure plate are chased and engraved with foliate scrolls, the similarly decorated cock table has a grotesque mask at the neck and a diamond endstone. There is a plain brass balance, cylinder escapement, cylindrical pillars, and two trains, the going with a fusee. A lever for adjusting the age of the moon is through the bezel at three and for strike/silent at eleven.

Plate 181. William Carpenter, London, no. 4643.
Gilt-metal cases 74mm: inner marks rubbed, FM or PM coronet above incuse, outer no marks

Carpenter, who was active between 1770 and 1817 and had an address in St. Martin's Court, concentrated on the Far Eastern market. This was made around 1785, maybe a little after.

The **dial** has six subsidiaries around a central aperture having a five-arm balance set with red and green paste over a gilt ground. The hours are shown at the top and, clockwise, the minutes, seconds, jump quarter seconds, regulator, moon age and phase. Jumping quarter and fifth second indications are rare, but are seen mostly at this period on watches made for the eastern markets; certainly, when combined with a visible balance, they add to the watch's overall attraction. The heart-shaped hour and minute hands are typical of the period.

The outer **case** bezels are decorated with foliate sprays and rosettes, the back with a polychrome enamel of three maidens.

The one in the centre, her white dress suggesting purity, is seen resisting the temptations offered: on her right a garland of grapes, for wine, on her left a mirror, for vanity. Symbols associated with Bacchus, including a thyrsus and possibly a snake, are on the ground.

The profusely engraved **movement** is signed and numbered and has a verge escapement.

PRIVATE COLLECTION

Plate 182. John Grant, London, no. 1408.
Gold consular case 55mm: RP in cameo (Richard Palmer), hallmarked 1788-9

There are eight watches by Grant surviving with early lever escapements of which this is the earliest and the most important. The first owner was a Dr. John Ridout, who qualified in 1779, worked at Blackfriars and died in Sherborne, Dorset, in 1823. It was sold by his family at Sotheby's, London, on 31 October 1966.

The screwed-in **movement** is, along with the watch by Wright (Plate 174), one of the first to be jewelled up to and including the fusee. Like the Wright it has a three-arm bimetallic compensated balance with interior weights, but these are in gold and adjustable on the rim. Exceptionally, it is counter-sprung, one spiral spring above the balance (the arms are at the middle of the vertical rim), the other below. This is to keep the balance and its staff upright so as to ensure a constant engagement – as well as impulse – between the rollers and lever. It was later discovered the effect was better achieved by raising and incurving the outer coil of the (spiral) balance spring – see Glossary. It has been suggested that, rather than use a helical spring as Emery and others were doing, Grant was intent on keeping his watches slim, but it is just as likely that he was reluctant to use the helical spring because there had been problems arriving at the best configuration for it.

The balance assembly, lever with jewelled pallets, two-plain fork with jewelled horns acting on separate rollers – in much the same way as in Mudge's first lever watch – and brass ratchet-tooth escape wheel, are illustrated on page 144 of *The Camerer Cuss Book of Antique Watches* (Antique Collectors' Club, 1976). The escape wheel is shown with the dots to mark the arm crossings on the underside of the rim, very much in the eighteenth century manner, clearly visible. There is no draw. This watch belonged, for a while, to the Time Museum, Illinois, until the collection's dispersal and it is included in Anthony Randall's excellent catalogue of its chronometers.

The signed 'regulator' **dial**, with central minutes and subsidiary hours and seconds, has gold late beetle and poker hands.　PRIVATE COLLECTION

Plate 183. Justin Vulliamy, London, no. oso.
Gold cases 53mm: both WQ incuse (William Quinton), hallmarked 1788-9

The arms and motto in the oval reserve on the engine-turned back of the outer **case** belong to Frederick Irby, the third Baron Boston, for fifty years Lord of the Bedchamber to George III. Dumb – as opposed to bell – repeating watches were fashionable and the hammers strike blocks screwed to the inside of the plain inner case.

Vulliamy has used the long-established design for the **dial**, with five minute figures, minute 'track' – within which, however, is a single dot to mark each of the half-quarters – and an annular ring inside the Roman chapters. There are blued steel late beetle and poker hands.

The Stogden-type dumb half-quarter repeating **movement** has a cylinder escapement. The design and high quality finish of the cock, with its grotesque mask at the neck, and the regulator plate, with its serpent indicator, are typical of the maker's work leading up to 1790. The plate is signed in script, Just. Vulliamy, London with the number code, the dust cap unsigned.

PRIVATE COLLECTION

Plate 184. Brockbank, London, no. 1809.

Gold cases 63mm: JC incuse (probably Joseph Carpenter), hallmarked 1789-90

The partnership between John Brockbank and his younger brother Myles developed into a very successful and long-lasting business. The movement and dust cap are signed Brockbank, the dial Brockbanks. Although there are a few gilt-metal coach watches from the 1770s and 1780s bearing their name, they soon concentrated on pocket and marine chronometers.

The 'regulator' lay-out of the **dial** is reminiscent of those used by Josiah Emery and others on their lever watches (Plate 178 and 182) with the addition of a third calendar subsidiary. The hands, with fully defined arrow heads, are well in fashion by 1790, and so too are the dial markings, the minutes on just a single annular ring and the hour chapters without margin lines.

The long pendant remains in vogue, but the bow is D-shaped. The outer **case** has an interior hinge: it is flush on the outside.

The high quality **movement** follows a pattern that the Brockbanks employed in small numbers for some years. In addition to having Harrison's maintaining power, however, it is especially good because it has a ruby – rather than steel – cylinder escapement. The top plate is beautifully decorated in the neo-classical manner with, at the neck of the cock, a classical bust in profile wearing a laurel crown.

PRIVATE COLLECTION

Plate 185. D. Rutland, London, no 3965.
Gilt-metal cases 49mm: inner J.J rectangular cameo (possibly James Jackson)

The under-painted horn on the outer **case** on this watch from about 1790 has a scene of a huntsman in marshland holding up his trophy with his dog beside him. A brownish cloud within the horn seems to add to the atmosphere. It has a somewhat naive charm and is typical of the genre. Hunting scenes are common, but also sailors with ships in the background, sentries and forts and maidens waiting for their loved ones. Horn was also stained and under-painted to simulate tortoiseshell (this, in fact, coming from the hawksbill turtle). Cedric Jagger in *The Artistry of the English Watch* (David and Charles, 1988) goes into the methods of working horn in some detail.

The enamel **dial** and late beetle and poker hands, as well as the **movement,** which has a verge escapement, are of good ordinary quality.

PRIVATE COLLECTION

The second hand, mounted between the gold late beetle and poker, is steel polished flat, and compares to the earlier 'poker' variety seen in Plate 175.

In the nineteenth century the duplex escapement (and the variant, the 'Chinese' duplex) became popular for watches with centre seconds. It had a distinct advantage over the cylinder or verge in so far as the hand appears to travel in a 'dead-beat' fashion (in reality there is one long and one short movement).

PRIVATE COLLECTION

Plate 186. Justin Vulliamy, London, no. sis.
Gold single case 55mm:VW incuse (Valentine Walker), hallmarked 1790-1

The **movement**, signed in script, has an early duplex escapement and a bimetallic compensation curb in the form of an elongated U. The curb, which is to be seen between the spokes of the cock table – no doubt cut to show it to advantage – is similar in design to that adopted by the Parisian watchmaker A-L. Breguet. The figure plate has the maker's usual serpent indicator for regulation. It is quite usual for Vulliamy not to sign the dust cap.

Vulliamy continues to use the traditional **dial** layout, but it is noticeable that, compared with Plate 183, the figures are somewhat closer to the dial edge.

Plate 187. John Arnold & Son, London, no. 689/390.

Gold consular case 51mm: TH incuse (Thomas Hardy), hallmarked 1790-1

One of the three watches recorded by Vaudrey Mercer (*John Arnold & Son*) in the series the maker termed the 'second kind' in which he made an error in his sequence of fractional numbers and, abnormally, the movement is engraved with an improper fraction. This series has the numerator on the dial, but here it is the denominator. Also, the difference between the numbers is generally 301: it is probable that this watch was intended to be 390/691.

The signed and numbered **movement** (the partnership name, John Arnold & Son, was used from about 1787) is an excellent example of the series, being jewelled to the centre and having undercuts to the escape wheel and balance pivots for oil retention. The 'OZ' type compensated balance, gold helical spring (see Arnold 99, Plate 179) and the long detent, with a shaped foot, are good and original. Arnold used his 'OZ', which consisted of a plain steel three-arm balance with two bimetallic affixes having moveable weights on their free ends, from around 1781-2 until 1791.

The **dial**, markings and gold hands are typical of the series. The **case** pendant, a rosette on the top, and bow are typical.   PRIVATE COLLECTION

Actual size.

Plate 188. Francis Perigal, Bond Street, London, no. 1053.

Later silver case 55mm: PW incuse (Philip Woodman), hallmarked 1867-8

The majority of watches with early lever escapements were signed by Josiah Emery: this is the only known survivor by Perigal. The movement and dial can be dated to about 1790. Cecil Clutton had the later case, hallmarked 1867-8, altered to fit in 1957.

The rare and exceptionally early subsidiary **dial** is dependant on a bimetallic spiral similar to that first used by Larcum Kendall as a compensation device and purchased by Vulliamy when Kendall's workshop was sold by auction in 1790. A watch by Emery, number 939, having an identical dial and gold heart-shaped hands, is illustrated and described by Jonathan Betts (*Antiquarian Horology*, Winter 1996).

While the **movement** is numbered 1053, the dust cap is numbered 1079, together with 'Watch Maker to his Majesty'. One can speculate on the reason for this, but the

Actual size.

design of the cap follows that employed on lever watches and gives room for the compensation device.

Although the movement *ébauche* is much the same as that used for Emery's small size watches and to the same high order of finish – and like these too, by the look of it, Richard Pendleton was probably employed to make the escapement – there are some significant differences. Unlike Emery, Perigal has employed a plain balance with four arms and eight poising and timing screws. There is a straight bimetallic strip for regulating the spiral spring, the foot of which is fitted to a rack served by a square in the centre of the regulation index. Again, unlike Emery, Perigal has a conventional cock – the neck with a bald, raked and clearly insane mask – and the lever set at right angles like Thomas Mudge; the fork, however, is mounted on the end of one of the lever arms. The roller is cranked but the jewel fixed. There is no draw.

This watch is included, and the escapement separately illustrated, in *Watches* by Clutton and Daniels (Batsford, Sotheby's – all editions) as well as Clutton's own *Collector's Collection* (AHS, 1974). PRIVATE COLLECTION

Plate 189. George Prior, London, no. 26120.

Gold cases 52mm: no marks

George Prior exported a large number of watches to Turkey and Middle Eastern markets. Made probably in the early 1790s, this quarter repeating watch has both cases painted in enamel.

A diamond is set in the top of the pendant which is enamelled along with the bow. The back of the outer **case** is painted *en grisaille* with flowers and trophies of war on a pink ground. Beyond a cusped circular border there is a continuous white enamel scroll interspersed with gold foliage on a mauve ground. The front bezel is decorated in a similar manner and the push is diamond-set. There is a scalloped band and bezels close on enamelled wavy edges. The inner case has a similar principal painting, and the body has four pierced and engraved panels between pale green, mauve and white champlevé enamel decoration. The enamel designs are common to Continental work of the period but, generally, the painterly way they have been executed is not, and is more in the English tradition.

There is a dust ring for the signed and numbered **movement** which has a verge escapement. The pierced and engraved cock has an urn at the neck and a large diamond endstone. Whether the quarter repeating mechanism, which is of Continental design, was imported 'in the grey' is a moot point, but some of the workmanship is very English: not only the style of the plunge-piece bracket, but the overall shaping and finish of the parts. The bell is signed by Dury, the English bell maker.

The signed **dial** is typically 'Turkish market' with the generic form of true Arabic figures. The gold skeletonised hands have cusped diamond-shaped heads.

Actual size.

PRIVATE COLLECTION

304

Plate 190. Henry Borrell, London, no. 11848.
Silver triple cases 130mm: middle case IR incuse (James Richards), hallmarked 1791-2

Unusually, in addition to two trains for going and hour and quarter striking, the **movement** of this large coach watch has a separate third quarter repeating train operated by depressing the pendant. There are two hammers for striking, a further two for repeating, a fusee and verge escapement, pierced and engraved cock with an urn at the neck and diamond endstone. The top plate and dust cap are numbered and signed 'Henry Borrell, Marco, London'.

The **dial**, similarly signed, has numerals for the Turkish and Middle East markets and pierced and cusped diamond hands. The bands of the inner and middle **cases** are pierced and decorated with foliage and rondels, the backs engraved with trophies of war. The outer case is covered with horn, under-painted to simulate rayskin, decorated with pin-work and open panels of silver foliate cage-work.

Plate 191. James Tregent, London, no 3137.

Gold case 48mm: no marks

Tregent frequently signed himself 'Maker to the Prince of Wales' but he did not hold the Royal Warrant. There is a similar Tregent watch and chatelaine to this, which was made about 1790 or soon after, in the Royal Collection.

The diamond-set royal coronet and cipher on the back of the **case** is over translucent blue enamel on an engine-turned ground. Back and front bezels are set with split pearls and pearls and translucent blue enamel decorate the matching chatelaine. The links, key and seal have opaque white enamel borders, while the seal is set with chalcedony engraved with a forget-me-not and the legend 'a vous'. These are suspended from a rectangular locket containing plaited hair. A push in the top of the pendant releases the spring-loaded front bezel so that the watch can be wound and set.

The white enamel **dial** has radial Arabic hour and five-minute numerals. There are gold beetle and poker hands and a gold collar around the winding aperture. The signed and numbered full plate **movement** has a pierced and engraved cock table and figure plate. There is a diamond endstone, fusee and verge escapement.

PRIVATE COLLECTION

Plate 192. P. Litherland & Co., Liverpool, no. 69.
Silver pair-cases 54mm: both JW incuse (Joseph Wickes), London hallmark for 1795-6

Peter Litherland took out his first patent for his rack lever escapement in 1791. The introduction to his second of 1792 tells us that it is '… an entire escapement to be applied to watches…for use on sea or land…producing greater certainty of time than any hitherto invented being more simple and less likely to be out of repair…especially for ascertaining longitude at sea at much less expense than those now used'. He was aware that, in the mind of the public, marine timepieces with detent escapements were good, but expensive and delicate, and that those with cylinder escapements – which were frequently carried by first officers and captains of small ships – were less reliable and were inclined to be delicate.

Litherland died in 1804. Although he failed to achieve his primary ambition, his idea was taken up by many Liverpool makers, especially Roskell, and rack lever watches continued to be made for another thirty years or so. Vaudrey Mercer (*Antiquarian Horology*, June 1962), Dr. R. Kemp (June 1985) and G.C. Crabtree (March 1986), combine to give much information on Litherland and the rack lever watch.

This is a very early example. The **movement** has a typical bell shape cock engraved 'Patent', a diamond endstone, a three-arm steel balance with flat spring, a Bosley regulator, fusee and an escape wheel with thirty teeth. There is a slide adjustment for the lever, an arrangement common to most watches with rack levers, but unique to them (and those where the escapement has been subsequently changed).

The **dial** has radial Arabic numerals – a style becoming popular at this date – and good gold arrow hands. As with some other early watches by Litherland, the **cases** have a London maker's mark and hallmarks. The long pendant and broad D-shaped bow with substantial joints are typical of the 1790s.

PRIVATE COLLECTION

Plate 193. Sleightholm & Co., London, no. 1134.

Gilt-metal cases 63mm: inner IR incuse (possibly dot between) star above (possibly James Richards)

An English watch **movement** with a pivoted detent escapement is rare from any period; this is from about 1795. Of course, John Arnold made it very early on, but employed the spring detent from 1782 onwards. The English used the spring detent almost invariably; the Continentals, by contrast, favoured the pivoted detent. Although there is a J. Sleightholm recorded (late eighteenth century, no dates), the firm is not. The movement, which has a dust cap, has strong Prescot/Liverpudlian overtones – most obviously in the cock design. An interesting attempt has been made, no doubt for reasons of cost and simplicity, to combine an accurate and expensive escapement with a plain three-arm steel balance and a flat spring without any compensation. The form of the escapement is unusual, the pivot being at the extremity of the detent; indeed in the place where the foot would have been if a spring detent had been employed.

The **dial** and skeletonised arrow hands are typical of the period. So too are the **cases**, in particular the long pendant and D-shaped bow with large joints and a flat top.

PRIVATE COLLECTION

Plate 194. James Brickles, London, no. 7547.
Gilt metal cases 54mm: inner WH incuse (probably William Howard II)

The under-painted scene on the horn outer **case** is not uncommon. Quite often there are butterflies and other insects among the ferns and small ponds – moorland scenes which suggest the harmony of nature and so on. Some horn cases depict country pursuits (Plate 185) or couples in romantic settings, while others are plainly patriotic, with soldiers, sailors, ships and the like.

From about the mid-1790s, the cases, pendant, bow, enamel **dial** (Roman numerals, Arabic five minute figures, and gold beetle and poker hands) and signed **movement** – this has a verge escapement – are all of good ordinary quality.   PRIVATE COLLECTION

Actual size.

Plate 195. John Russell, Falkirk, no. 1.
Silver consular case 122mm: WL incuse (either William Laithwait or William Lewis), hallmarked 1796-7

Russell, who was responsible for some unusual watches, clocks and barometers, was patronised by both George III and the Prince Regent, later George IV. There is a fine barometer by him in the Victoria & Albert Museum and another in Buckingham Palace. The legend 'Invt. et Fecit' follows the signature on this remarkably large watch which was at one time in the Time Museum, Illinois, and sold at Sotheby's, New York, in December 1999.

Second hands normally travel forward in small increments but here the second hand moves in satisfying steps from one division to another. This is achieved by the **movement** having a pin wheel escapement, *pirouette* and a seconds beating balance. The brass escape wheel has a single row of upright pins and the anchor-like pallet arms are mounted separately on the same arbor, one being stepped so that the pallets are on the same plane. The fusee has Harrison's maintaining power.

The enamel **dial** has radial Arabic numerals, simple dot divisions and gold arrow hands and counterpoised seconds. The **case** has an early Regency pendant.

Plate 196. George Margetts, London, no. 201.
Gilt-metal consular case 81mm: WH incuse (probably William Howard II)

A large eight day nautical chronometer – as it says on the movement – made, probably, three or four years before 1800. Numbers 202 to 204, each with small differences, are also known, but quite possibly no others are extant. Number 203 is signed Margetts on the movement and Margetts and Hatton on the dial. Margetts was losing his eyesight towards the end of his life; he died on 27 December 1804 (Anthony Turner, *Antiquarian Horology*, September 1971) and not, as variously recorded, in 1806 or 1808. His apprentice and successor, James Hatton, continued the business.

Actual size.

The **movement** has an Earnshaw-type spring detent escapement, a compensated balance with two arms, brass wedge-shaped weights with screw adjustment and timing screws and a helical spring. Above the signature, which is followed by 'Inv. et Fecit' and the number, is engraved 'Eight Days Nautical Chronometer'.

The enamel **dial**, which has subsidiary seconds and all divisions fully marked, is signed and numbered together with 'Eight Days' and 'Timekeeper'. There are simple gold spade hands. The **case** is deep and the 'Regency' pendant very short: no doubt the watch was made to be boxed in some way.

PRIVATE COLLECTION

313

Plate 197. Richard Pendleton, Pentonville, London, no. 180.

Later three-part silver case 56mm: rubbed marks

It is certain Pendleton was involved, probably to a considerable extent, in the making of watches with lever escapements signed by Josiah Emery. Two other levers signed by Pendleton are known: number 172 (a movement only) and 175 which has its original case hallmarked for 1797-8 with Emery's name erased, but still discernible, on the dial (Emery died in 1796). Paul Chamberlain recounts on page 38 of his *It's About Time* (Richard R. Smith, New York, 1941) how he examined number 172 and 180 – the present watch – in 1935 when owned by Courtenay Ilbert (172 was purchased by the British Museum in 1959 along with much of Ilbert's famous collection).

The **movement** has a bridge cock and double 'S' balance much the same as those signed by Emery, but the escapement design is different (Plate 23, *Watches*, Clutton and Daniels). The escape wheel and straight-line lever are lighter than in Emery watches and the teeth and wheel are forked to hold oil. At the end of the lever is a loop which encircles the balance staff. It has two vertical pins mounted

Actual size.

on its extremity and these give impulse from the far side; the safety action is on the near side. There is no draw.

It is possible that Pendleton completed this watch as early as 1798 but also that he did so over time – the style of the **dial**, which is very different from Emery's, with radial Arabic chapters and a pierced spade hour hand, suggests any time from the late 1790s up to, say, 1810. Round **case** pendants were beginning to be fitted on the Continent and very occasionally in England, but there is something about this – the rib on the short stem, perhaps, and the case generally (although it bears the movement number 180 struck in an authentic way) – that suggests a still later date.

Plate 198. George Margetts, London, no. 1128.
Gilt-metal case 69mm: IH incuse – not I.H (John Hadley)

This watch, of about 1798, is significant for two reasons: first, very few watches have ever been made to show both mean and sidereal time, fewer to include the seconds but, secondly, it possesses an escapement which goes a long way towards the final development of the lever. A diagram of the complex but elegant motion work, together with another of a slightly less advanced version of the escapement, is shown, with full descriptions, in *Rees's Cyclopaedia* (first published in 1819-20). No other lever watch by Margetts is known and it is thought that this watch was first owned by the author of the horological section of the *Cyclopaedia*, Reverend Pearson.

In the Time Museum *Catalogue of Chronometers* (1992), written before the collection was dispersed, Anthony Randall describes this watch and includes photographs of the under-dial work and a close-up of the escapement.

The configuration of the **dial**, through which the watch is wound, is the same as the much larger timepiece by Margetts, numbered 316 on Plate 173. It has three subsidiary fixed dials and three rotating dials each showing hours, minutes and seconds. As the hands advance, mean time is read against the fixed dials while sidereal time is read against the inner dials which contra rotate. Sidereal (star) day is the time interval which elapses between two successive transits of a fixed star across a meridian, the sidereal day being approximately 3 minutes 56.555 seconds shorter than the mean time day. Margetts' gearing produces an approximate difference of 3 minutes 56.55, very acceptable for all practical purposes. In the Science Museum, London, there is a watch by James

Green, the case hallmarked for 1776-7, which also indicates solar/sidereal hours, minutes and seconds, but it is of different construction and not as accurate.

The **movement**, signed and numbered with neo-classical decoration, has a recess in the top plate for a three-arm bimetallic compensated balance and a sub-frame for the escapement. The balance has screwed wedge-shaped weights and a flat spring without an overcoil. Randall describes the escapement in detail, but principally it has a light, poised, straight-line lever with curved pallet faces and an escape wheel with ratchet-like teeth. Of course, the lighter the lever the less drag on impulse. The separate safety roller has been made very small so that, when the watch is jolted and the guard pin touches the roller, the effect on the oscillating balance is kept to a minimum.

The maker would have been well aware of 'draw' – John Leroux used this method of keeping the lever from moving during its supplementary arc as early as 1785 – but it would appear that, like his contemporaries, he believed its benefits were outweighed by its disadvantages: that is the need for greater impulse and the increase in friction. To employ draw would have exacerbated the problems with the only oil available at the time – this very soon thickened on the acting surfaces of the pallets. It has been suggested that the escapement was probably made by Richard Pendleton, but Pendleton seems to have favoured a more substantial lever, and one which has a loop encircling the balance staff to give impulse on the far side (Plate 197). PRIVATE COLLECTION

Plate 199. George Johnson, London, no. 7584.
Silver triple cases 69mm: WL stag above incuse (William Linsley),
hallmarked
1798-9

The majority of Turkish market watches, so called, have
tortoiseshell covered third outer cases, but this has one of green-
dyed rayskin attractively decorated with silver pins. The inner
cases are plain with just the bow having some modest
elaboration.

The **dial**, as usual signed in English, has the normal generic
form of true Arabic hour and five minute numerals with minute
ring, a further ring inside the chapters and gold beetle and poker
hands. The **movement**, which is signed and numbered, has a
pierced cock with foliate decoration, an urn at the neck and a
diamond endstone. The crested Egyptian pillars are much the
same as those popular at the beginning of the century, only very
much smaller! The silver regulator disc has generic Arabic
numerals and there is a verge escapement.   PRIVATE COLLECTION

Plate 200. Benjamin Webb, London, no. 99.

Silver cases 60mm: inner NTW in cameo (Nicholas Thomas Wood), hallmarked 1799-1800; outer no mark (bezel mark rubbed)

John Peckham stated in his patent number 2280 of 1798 that his was 'A new and improved method of constructing a watch so as to unite it with a mariner's compass…'. His idea was to '…substitute for those works which are usually made of steel, which are near enough to effect in the smallest degree the free action of the magnetic needle, works made of gold, silver, or any other metal or admixture of metals which have no influence on the magnetic needle…'. One or two makers other than Benjamin Webb may have taken up this patent, but certainly probably fewer than a dozen of these watches survive.

The **dial** is signed by the maker with 'By the King's Patent'. Subsidiary hours and minutes with gold arrow hands are at twelve, the compass at six and the locking slide for this is below in the bezel of the outer **case**. The slide is of the same design as those on similar watches by Webb. The pendant and the bow knuckle joints would seem to be a little later.

The signed and numbered **movement** has a verge escapement. Some of the components which one would normally expect to be of steel are of brass – in particular the screws – but, of course, the balance spring, fusee chain and arbors have to be steel.

PRIVATE COLLECTION

compensation. This is mounted on a revolving plate, the position of which can be altered with a micrometer screw fixed near the edge of the top plate; regulation is by means of an arm and scale opposite. The tool for making the compensation – sometimes called the 'Chelsea Bun' – is thought to be the one which Benjamin Vulliamy purchased in the sale of Larcum Kendall's workshop at Christie's in December 1790. As usual for Vulliamy the dust cap is unsigned.

The design of the **dial** and gold beetle and poker hands probably reflects the conservative tastes of Vulliamy's clients, but he adopted a new style for hands soon after the turn of the century (Plate 214).   PRIVATE COLLECTION

Plate 201. Vulliamy, London, no. nsu.

Gold case 60mm: GR incuse (Gaspard Richard), hallmarked 1799–1800; mahogany box

Justin Vulliamy signed his watches simply Vulliamy after about 1792: his son Benjamin had been in the business for some years. Justin died in 1797.

The arms in the central reserve on the engine-turned back of the **case** are those of Edward Lascelles, for several Parliaments the M.P. for North Allerton and who was created Baron Harewood in 1796 and Earl Harewood in 1812. Both front and back bezels are spring loaded to ease access for winding and hand setting. A start/stop lever between two and three in the front inner bezel operates on the balance.

The **movement**, dumb repeating to the nearest half-quarter, has a duplex escapement and maintaining power. The original repeating spring is signed and dated 'Bell …July 1799'. The firm used a bridge cock when they fitted bimetallic spiral

Plate 202. George Flote, London, no.1790.

Gilt-metal cases 52mm: inner IM incuse (possibly James Marson or James Macklin)

The under-painted horn outer **case** has the arms and motto of the Clockmakers' Company. It is well executed and has a charm often associated with this type of case. Generally a 'circa 1800' date is given; the bow is probably later. The simple verge **movement** is signed by an obscure maker who, curiously, was not a member of the Company: for this reason it is thought that the movement may not be original.

Actual size.

Plate 203. Ralph Gout, London, no. 38 and 197.

Gilt-metal case 56mm: IN incuse (James Nevill), outer saddle case 225mm: no marks

Presumably Gout, the maker of this watch cum horse pedometer, had a shared optimism with his main clients, the horse racing fraternity. His short series had small differences, but all were according to patent number 2351 which he took out in November 1799, this example being made fairly soon after.

The saddle case, double-numbered 38 and 197, has strap fittings. The watch is set in a cage mounted on a spring-loaded vertical runner and a cord is attached to the saddle case at one end and a lever which passes through the watch pendant to the pedometer mechanism at the other.

The **dial** has a subsidiary for hours and minutes with gold skeletonised diamond hands, two further subsidiaries with similar hands to record up to ten and one hundred paces and a gold centre hand, kinked to pass over the hand-set square, to record up to ten thousand paces (100 x 100).

The **movement** and dust cap are signed and numbered 197 and the movement is engraved 'By the Kings Letter Patent'. The cock, which is decorated with military trophies, has a diamond endstone. No special effort has been made to help the verge escapement withstand a particularly hard and uncertain life! PRIVATE COLLECTION

Plate 204. Grant, Fleet Street, London, no. 2315.
Silver consular case 53mm: no marks

The case does not belong to the movement which, together with its dust cap and dial, was made around 1800. John Grant was apprenticed to his uncle Alexander Cumming and, after he died in 1810, he was succeeded by his son, also John. This is one of about half a dozen known watches, including the one shown in Plate 182, signed by Grant with lever escapements. It is illustrated with a view of the escapement in *Watches* (Sotheby Parke Bernet, 1979) by Clutton and Daniels.

The **dial** lay-out is typical of those used by Grant, Emery, Pendleton and others for their lever escapement watches. In general appearance the **movement** is typical of Grant's work, the narrow cock (with a ruby endstone which he seems to have favoured) and barrel plate having neo-classical engraving. There is an early YCC balance, one, and it would seem the first, of four types accredited to Robert Pennington (see Plate 206 for further explanation). Grant seems to have always understood the advantage of using light components. He continued to employ a straight line lever, but by this date his pallet arms embraced four rather than five teeth of the escape wheel. With shorter arms inertia was reduced and the lift was more efficient; moreover the shorter impulse faces had less friction. The fork and safety action are conventional. There is no draw.

PRIVATE COLLECTION

Plate 205. Thomas Earnshaw, London, no. 626/3069.

Gold cases 59mm: both TC axe above incuse (Thomas Carpenter), hallmarked 1801-2

A classic Earnshaw pocket chronometer of the period in exquisite condition. It has strong aesthetic appeal and the movement is of the highest quality. At one time in the Knowles-Brown Collection, it is illustrated in *The Camerer Cuss Book of Antique Watches* (Antique Collectors' Club, 1976).

The **dial**, signed in block capitals 'Thomas Earnshaw, Inv.t et Fecit No. 626', has a full minute ring, Roman numerals with a traditional inner ring but no five minute Arabic figures. There are flat polished gold hands, the hour heart-shaped.

The inner **case** has a traditional long pendant and D-shaped bow with bold joints, and the **movement** swings out. It is signed and numbered as the dial and has the maker's secondary number 3069 on the barrel bridge (Earnshaw's double numbering system is curious and little sense has been made of it). The cock, steel helical spring and two-arm bimetallic balance with wedge-shaped weights, limiting bars and timing screws are characteristic of the maker's work. So too is the detent and block mounting, this having adjustments for depth and locking.

PRIVATE COLLECTION

Plate 206. Robert Pennington, London, no. 1/430.
Brass drum 95mm, mahogany box 135mm

While certainly not a watch, this small chronometer made, it can be assumed, in 1801, nevertheless in some senses is a watch writ large. It can be related to other precision timepieces made in the later part of the eighteenth century and the first few years of the nineteenth which contain much watch-work but which were never intended for pocket use. It was almost certainly made for the purposes of land survey and may well have belonged to the Royal Board of Ordnance, the coronet and GR cipher engraved on the dial denoting the Board's ownership. The first ordnance survey map (of Kent) was published on 1 January 1801 and about a third of England and Wales was mapped at the one inch scale over the next twenty years.

    The silvered **dial** is engraved with the maker's name, an outer minute zone, and two subsidiaries, one for twenty-four hours, the other seconds. The signed and numbered **movement** has an early

example of the 'YCC' balance, one, and it would seem the first, of four types of balance accredited to Pennington (Vaudrey Mercer, *Antiquarian Horology*, Spring 1981). These led directly to the 'modern' bimetallic balance, used almost universally for the rest of the nineteenth and much of the twentieth century. The three-arm brass balance has two semicircular bimetallic affixes and a helical spring.

There is a double mainspring barrel assembly similar to that employed by Thomas Mudge in his No. 1 timekeeper. Christie's catalogue of 12 June 1996 (lot 404) has 'Both springs dated *K Clark 1801*'. This scratched marking almost certainly also includes the day and month. The K is no doubt an R for Robert Clark who is known to have worked for John Roger Arnold, and almost certainly others. Pennington was an important member of the team which made, in the later part of the 1790s, some thirty or so timekeepers for Mudge junior to his father's design. Anthony Randall (*Watches in the British Museum V1*, 1990, pages 181-2) gives details of the system, calculations and a diagrammatic drawing by David Penney. The two advantages of the system are a) there is less frictional loss of power at the fusee and barrel pivots and b), because the combined lengths of the two springs allow for a lower reduction in the gear train, again there are lower frictional losses in the train. These advantages are partially offset by the reduction in available height and barrel diameter.

The escapement is Arnold-type but upside down in so far as the small discharge roller is beneath the impulse roller. The escape wheel is gold. Both the skeletonised detent and the passing spring have depth adjustments. The movement is wound with a Margetts-type external winding mechanism which is accessible in a recess of the hexagonal mahogany two-tier outer **case** (the hinged key is illustrated open). The hinged brass observation cover is signed in a manner typical of the maker, and the brass base has six cylindrical feet. Private Collection

Plate 207. Recordon late Emery, London, 7223.
Gold consular case 53mm: LC scroll (? fish) above incuse (Louis Comtesse), hall-marked 1802-3

A watch with several unusual and significant features: a half-ten-minute dumb repeating mechanism, a lever escapement made by Richard Pendleton, a half-plate lay-out and a spiral spring with overcoil to the Arnold-type balance.

The **movement** is signed on the barrel bridge within an engraved border; the cock – which is screwed directly on to the plate – the repeat spring cover and the fusee winding square dust sleeve are also engraved. The two-arm balance has platinum or white alloy weights, each arm having a gold poising and steel timing screw. The escapement is Pendleton's normal form and has looped impulse (see Plate 197), but the lever is set at right angles to the wheel – an arrangement

Actual size.

which was to become standard English practice. There is no draw. The lever and escape wheel share a cock; the fourth wheel has its own. This half-plate lay-out may be the earliest recorded on an English watch as, indeed, may be also the overcoil for the spiral spring. The stud is so formed as to enable the outer coil, raised and turned towards the centre, to pass directly below the cock (the underside of which is partly reduced for clearance).

Recordon acted as the London agent for Abraham-Louis Breguet and would have been familiar with his use of an overcoil, and he would have known as well, no doubt, that he had made a half-ten-minute repeating mechanism. After striking the hours, a double blow sounds the ten minutes, these followed by a further single blow if more than five minutes have passed.

The signed simple but effective **dial** has skeletonised spade hands. The plain **case,** which has a signed and numbered gold hinged inner cover, has a long cylindrical repeating pendant and D-shaped bow.

Plate 208. J.R. Arnold, London, no. 1869.

Silver case 63mm: TH rectangular cameo (Thomas Hardy), hallmarked 1802-3

There must have been a good deal of commercial competition between the Arnolds and Earnshaw, but a private diary and account book written by John Roger came to light in 2002 (it is now in the possession of the Clockmakers' Company) which demonstrates that, contrary to a general belief which has somehow grown up, they were far from being at daggers drawn. In January 1800 the Arnolds entertained Miss Earnshaw and several others to candle-lit supper and eighteen months later, shortly before this watch was made, Arnold bought a wedding present for her. It is possible, of course, that some strain was put on the relationship by Earnshaw's submissions to the Board of Longitude in 1805 and his Appeal of 1808.

This is one of three or four watches recorded where Arnold has fitted an Earnshaw type of spring detent escapement to one of his **movements**. It is otherwise typical, with a 'Z' balance, gold helical spring, standard signature and a griffin displayed on the cock. The four-arm escape wheel follows Earnshaw's early tooth profile but made in the Arnold manner where much more of the wheel has been cut away for lightness. The detent, in detail typically Arnold (only the reverse of normal), has a side-fitting jewel. The detent mounting is similar to Earnshaw's, consisting of a brass arm and block for depth adjustment,

but half of the block pivots on a rivet with two pairs of opposing screws for the left/right adjustment. Of course some Arnold watches have had their escapements altered to Earnshaw form by third parties.

It was probably good for Arnold to use Earnshaw's version occasionally, if only from a commercial point of view, in order to reaffirm his claim that the basic concept was his father's. But, also, he could well have had a natural desire to make some improvements on the escapement and test it in one of his own watches. Further, although he continued to retain the confidence of his customers, Arnold would have been well aware that his escapements suffered a greater degree of wear: he may well have considered it a wise precaution to investigate the competitor's system, even if he could not be seen to be taking it up universally.

When the off-white enamel **dial** is viewed from edge on, the strong glaze becomes iridescent, this over the slightly granular surface – lovely. John Roger Arnold fitted these very distinctive dials more or less continuously during this period. The substantial **case** has a long Regency pendant and D-shaped bow.

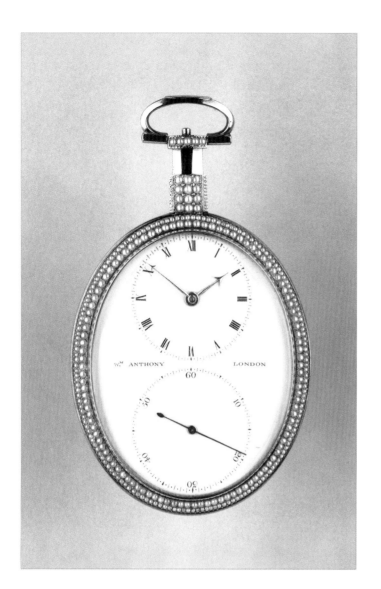

Plate 209. William Anthony, London, no. 1931.
Gold case width 58mm length excluding pendant 70mm: no marks

A large oval gold, enamel and diamond-set eight day going watch of about 1800, or shortly after, probably made for the Chinese market and probably made to be worn suspended from the neck or waistband. Formerly in the Marryat Collection, it is one of a small group of less than ten similar oval watches by Anthony known. It seems that most run for eight days and the enamel and stone-set backs of all the cases are slightly raised towards the centre.

Three were in the Sandberg Collection (Antiquorum, Geneva, March 2001), a matched pair, numbers 1913 and 1914, and 1935 which has the maker's address, St. Johns Square, on the dial. All three had the casemaker's mark IR incuse with W separately, possibly that belonging to the somewhat shadowy maker James Richards who registered several marks in London and perhaps also two in Chester (Priestley, *Watch Case Makers of England*, page 187). A matching pair was in the collection of King Farouk, sold as the property of the Republic of Egypt by Sotheby's in March 1954, and a slightly different watch, number 1705, with the hands expanding and contracting within the long and short axis of the dial, was sold as part of the Belin Collection at Sotheby's, London, in November 1979.

The **case** is unmarked but bears the number. Translucent and opaque polychrome enamel and split pearls decorate the back, the pearls towards the central group of diamonds linked with gold wire-work. A push in the pendant allows access to the signed and numbered inner cover, this engraved, rather charmingly, with a horse pulling a line indicating the direction to wind.

The **movement** design, with a large hanging barrel and four separate for the wheel train, has strong Continental overtones, but the style of the engraving and quality of the gilding suggest these were carried out in England. Significantly, there is no engraving below the English diamond settings for the six-arm steel balance and duplex escape wheel: they were fitted before the engraving.

The white enamel **dial** is signed across the centre with balanced subsidiaries, hours and minutes with gold arrow hands above, seconds with a steel counterpoised hand below.

PRIVATE COLLECTION

Plate 210. Rundell & Bridge, London, no. 3454.
Gold consular case 53mm: IM incuse (possibly James
Marson or James Macklin), hallmarked 1802-3

The arms are those of the Duc de Chartres (1773-1850)
who became King Louis Philippe of France in 1830.
When his father, the Duke of Orléans, was executed in
1793 he succeeded to the title, but came out in favour
of the Revolution calling himself 'Citroyen Chartres'.
He was in exile in England between 1801 and 1807,
returning to France after the Restoration. Rundell &
Bridge were very well connected goldsmiths and
jewellers. The firm began supplying the royal household
in 1797 and was appointed the principal royal goldsmith
and jeweller in 1804.

The **movement** is simple but of very good quality
and is similar in style to the watches sold by the firm of
Vulliamy. It is signed and numbered on the barrel
bridge while the figure plate and cock are engraved
with foliate decoration and there is a grotesque mask
on the cock table. There is a polished steel three-arm
balance, compensation curb, duplex escapement and
maintaining power. A push-piece in the head of the
Regency pendant flies the cover of the hunting **case**.
The glazed bezel is hinged at twelve so that the hands
can be set and, when necessary, the movement lifted
out. The enamel **dial** has Roman numerals, quarter-
hour Arabic figures and gold spade hands.

PRIVATE COLLECTION

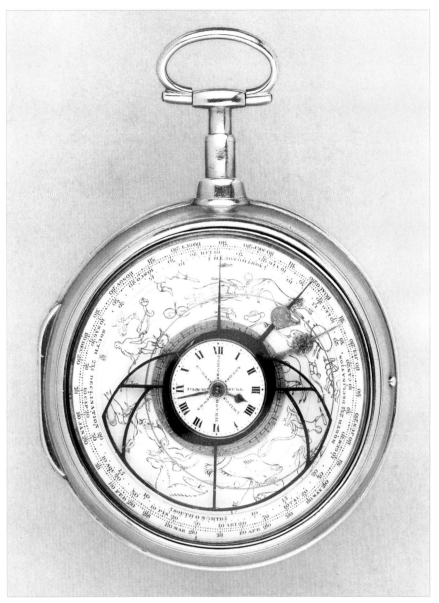

Plate 211. George Margetts, London, no. 1317.

Silver cases 56mm: both IR incuse (James Richards), hallmarked 1802-3

This astronomical register is not dissimilar to Margetts number 312 (Plate 172), but it is a very much smaller watch and with slightly fewer indications. It is a remarkable exercise in miniaturisation and must have presented a formidable challenge, not only to those involved in making the movement, but also the dial. Four or five watches of this type by Margetts are known, including number 312. One other of about this size is in the British Museum.

The **dial** functions are quite similar to those explained for Plate 172. The fully signed and numbered **movement**, which is typical of the period with foliate decoration and a grotesque mask at the neck, has a diamond endstone and verge escapement. The gearing for the astronomical indications below the dial is similar to that of Margetts 311, illustrated and described by George Daniels in *Antiquarian Horology*, March 1970.

PRIVATE COLLECTION

Actual size.

Plate 212. Thomas Earnshaw, London, no. 662/3114.

Gilt-metal cases 58mm: inner TC axe above incuse (Thomas Carpenter), outer no marks; three tier mahogany box

Earnshaw fitted his chronometers with plain steel balances, spiral springs and 'sugar tong' bimetallic compensation curbs from about the mid-1790s (he continued to use also the combination of compensation balance and helical spring). This example can be dated more or less exactly to 1803 (see Anthony Randall's Earnshaw number sequence, *The Time Museum Chronometers*, Illinois, 1992).

Shortly before 1800 he ceased gilding the plates and blueing the steel parts of many, although by no means all, of his **movements.** It is said he did this following criticism to the effect that his watches only worked well because of their high finish. Whatever the case, he began to finish some of his watches with all the important parts to the same high standard while cutting his costs. His detent escapement used, as here, in conjunction with a 'sugar tong' bimetallic compensation, steel balance and spiral spring, was probably also cheaper to make than a bimetallic balance and helical spring. The arms embracing the outer coil of the spring alter in length and shape, the curved ends moving closer together or further apart with changes in temperature, thus compensating for the effect caused by these changes on the balance and spring. Probably the timekeeping was not so constant, but not only is the balance lighter and so its pivots less susceptible to damage, but the watch would have been easier to bring to time, important for those watchmakers not fully conversant with timing screws.

The primary number 662 is on the signed plate – also engraved 'Inv.t et Fecit', the secondary number on the barrel bridge. The enamel **dial** has the primary number and is fully signed. The hands are gold, the hour with a heart-shaped head. The **cases** are not in precious metal: Earnshaw was intent on making an instrument for maritime or similar use to the highest standard but at the best possible price.

PRIVATE COLLECTION

Plate 213. Ellicott & Company, London, no. 9001.

Gold cases 56mm: both cases IM incuse (James Marson or Macklin), both hallmarked 1803-04

Shortly before 1803 Edward Ellicott the younger sought to bring in fresh blood to his business and the name style changed to Ellicott & Company. By about 1806 the firm became Ellicott & Taylor (David Thompson, *Antiquarian Horology*, Summer 1997).

The very high quality **movement**, unusually slim for chronometers of the period, is numbered and signed with the Royal Exchange address. It has a 'double T' compensating balance, a type generally accredited to Robert Pennington. This, and the fact that the Earnshaw-type detent escapement has Pennington's unusual gold escape wheel and depth adjustment, strongly suggests he was Ellicott's supplier. The 'double T' balance has two brass arms and two bimetallic rims, each arm carrying a curved brass piece, forming a 'T' shape, with limiting screws at each end. The 'double T' is thought to be the second balance of the four Pennington-types – see Plate 206. The cock is well engraved in the neo-classical manner.

The **dial**, with an arcaded signature, has a good pair of flat-polished gold hands and a blued steel second hand with a gold boss. The plain **cases** are of a good weight and the pendant has a D-shaped bow.

PRIVATE COLLECTION

Actual size.

Plate 214. Vulliamy, London, no. zxu.

Gold cases 53mm: no marks

Both cases are from around 1780, the movement from 1804. The back of the outer has the crest of George Spencer (1738-1817), fourth Duke of Marlborough, and the Order of the Garter and motto in relief. A surviving Vulliamy day book records that the movement, dial and hands were sold to the Duke on 31 January 1804 and fitted, according to his request, to previously supplied cases. At the same time the old movement was fitted to a new case for a total of 120 guineas. Roger Smith kindly searched Vulliamy's records held at the Public Record Office, Kew – the extant day books start in the early 1790s – and investigated the entry (C104/58/1, Day Book 31).

The entry describes the **movement** as being a small centre seconds repeater, with duplex escapement, hard pendulum spring, the four scape holes and the 3rd and 4th wheel holes all jewelled, a going fusee and cap, and 'one of the best coiled thermometers'. The function of the latter, the bimetallic spiral compensation, is the same as that outlined in Plate 201. The dust cap is cut away to show the symmetric scroll decoration and diamond endstone of the bridge cock.

Whereas the Duke would have enjoyed having a watch with this advanced mechanism, particularly as he had a strong interest in science – indeed he was made a fellow of the Royal Society in 1786 – it is fair to assume that he had a sentimental attachment to the old case. Vulliamy abandoned the spiral system of compensation soon after this watch was made and continued to use a U-shaped curb (Plate 186).

The **dial** design is broadly the same as that used by the firm for a good three decades and includes the two dots within the minute track at each quarter. However, the new style skeletonised heart-shaped hands have been fitted. Private Collection

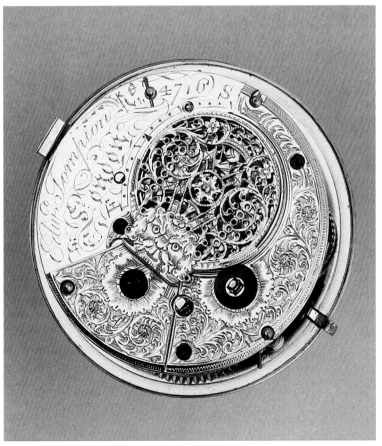

Plate 215. Edward Tompion, London, no. 4716.
Silver case 54mm: WH rectangular cameo (William Howard, Coventry), hallmarked Birmingham 1804-5

An early hunting cased watch, not without quality, having a variation of Joseph Bosley's form of regulation.

The **case** was made with no bezel or glass, the cover raised by a spring-loaded push in the Regency pendant. The simple but effective **dial** has Arabic numerals and single dot minute markings with stars at the quarters and a gold collet for the winding square. The gold skeletonised hands, which have unusual and attractive detail, have done well to survive.

The **movement**, which has a verge escapement, has an excellent signature with 'London' in fine Gothic script. The cock, with a grotesque mask at the neck, and false plate are also well engraved in a neo-classical manner. Regulation is adjusted via a square with a blued steel boss in the false plate and a small triangular pointer moves across the scale on the other side of the cock (see Plate 231 for the same arrangement).

PRIVATE COLLECTION

Plate 216. Joseph Godfrey, Sudbury, no. 5968.
Silver cases 60mm: both TB incuse (Thomas Bligh), both hallmarked London 1807-8

The polychrome enamel **dial**, painted in the manner of the picturesque, is an excellent and quite early example of the type. The scene, so redolent of Suffolk is, very suitably, signed by a Sudbury maker. The four gold sails of the windmill indicate the seconds. A driver leads his horse towards the mill in the foreground, a fisherman hopes, and a sailing barge passes by a farm with cart shed and haystack on the far bank. There are Arabic numerals and gold spade hands.

The signed and numbered **movement** is typical of the period and has a verge escapement. The inner **case**, which has a stop/start lever at three, is engraved 'LB, March 19th 1808'. The earlier style of long pendant, cylindrical in section, has been preferred to the ovoid Regency style now in vogue. PRIVATE COLLECTION

Plate 217. Brockbanks, London, no. 641.
Silver consular case 64mm: TC axe above incuse (Thomas
Carpenter), hallmarked 1807-8

The brothers John and Myles Brockbank were responsible
for some high quality watches and pocket chronometers.
Myles continued the business after John died in 1805 or
1806 together with other members of the family.

The **movement** has a cross-detent escapement, an unusual
escapement devised by one of the Brockbanks' employees,
James Petto. It was an attempt to combine Arnold's in-tension
detent and Earnshaw's impulse, but the detent has high inertia
causing considerable friction between it and the passing spring,
and oil was found to be necessary. However, the cross-detent
has a remarkable action, and it is a pleasure to watch it perform
together with the spectacular balance. It was thought at one

time to have been introduced in the early 1780s, now the late
1780s. A diagram of it, together with illustrations of
Brockbanks' distinctive balances, is included in a two-part article
about the firm by F. von Osterhausen (*Antiquarian Horology*,
September and December 2001). The three-arm balance, with
helical spring, has three bimetallic rims each with travel limit
screws, highly polished steel weights with lateral screws and
timing screws. The cock, well engraved with trophies of war,
has a ruby endstone and the wheel train is also jewelled.

The handsome **dial** has gold spade hands and is discreetly
signed. A push in the **case** pendant is split, the bezel and spring
loaded back cover being released independently.

PRIVATE COLLECTION

Opposite: Plate 218. John Roger Arnold, no. 211.
Cylindrical silver case 83 x 40mm deep, probably TH in
cameo (partly obliterated by winding shutter rivet),
hallmarked 1807-8

No other marine timepiece by John Roger Arnold with this
configuration is known and, in all probability, it was the only
one made. The back is engraved with the crest of a family of

Devon baronets named Acland and the monogram CDA (see
below). The combination of a silver case, pendant and bow
and enamel dial sets it apart from Arnold's series of marine

timepieces. These, probably numbered from 200 were, up to about 223, fitted in octagonal wooden boxes (Vaudrey Mercer, *John Arnold & Son*, AHS, 1972). George Margetts made a few 'Nautical Chronometers' which have gilt-metal cases and short pendants and these are of about the same dimensions (Plate 196).

The signed and numbered **movement** has an Arnold spring detent escapement. The balance is a Z+O type, a very unusual variant of the simpler Z. There is a diagram of it by J.R. Arnold dated 1804. In addition to the bimetallic rims of the standard Z balance there is an interior ring of steel screwed to the two arms with three movable weights. The cock carries a steel adjustable arm for the helical spring stud. This is, of course, an entirely different arrangement from that of the earlier OZ balance.

The fine **dial** is signed and numbered in Arnold's style of the period. There is a continuous seconds ring, Roman numerals, dot minute markings between 'tram lines', five minute Arabic figures and blued steel spade hands. Both the front bezel and back of the **case** are hinged, the back engraved with a crest and monogram on either side of a central flush fitted winding shutter. The top of the pendant is round and the bow has knuckle joints, an early example of this style.

Provenance. Hubert Chesshyre, as the Chester Herald at the College of Arms in 1991, investigated the crest and monogram and, having considered a number of families, the initials and the small changes to the Ackelan/Acklan crest from the sixteenth and eighteenth centuries, he established they are those of Charles Richard Dyke Acland. The second son of Sir Richard Dyke Acland, he was born 3 August 1793, married Charlotte Templer in 1819 and died without issue at the Cape of Good Hope in 1828 while in command of the ship *Helicon*. His family was well connected and prosperous (his mother and sister-in-law were both members of the Hoare banking family) and it would not be surprising to find them commissioning an expensive item such as this. Acland would have been fourteen in 1807 and entering Naval College.   PRIVATE COLLECTION

Plate 219. David Read, Glasgow (no.) 1807.
Gold cases 55mm: both JW incuse (Joseph Wickes), both hallmarked Chester 1806-7

David Read (or Reid, recorded Hutcheson St., Glasgow, 1805-1818) would have ordered this watch from the Lancashire trade, it having every appearance of having been made in that region.

It was normal for Liverpool case makers to have their work marked in Chester. The dedication on the back of the outer **case** to Allan Burns (1781-1813), anatomist and surgeon, is from his first class; it is dated 'Glasgow 29th April 1807'. This engraving is signed indistinctly 'Diarie (?) scupsit'. Burns had a short but distinguished career during which he published two books, one on the heart, the other on the head and neck, the second edition of the latter containing a brief but interesting biography. A stop/start lever on the edge of the inner case bezel allowed the doctor to set his watch to the second or use it as a timer.

The radial Arabic **dial**, gold moon hands (the stems with open rondels) and a steel second hand are characteristic of Prescot/Liverpool work. The barrel bridge, figure plate and cock mounted on the **movement** top plate are splendidly engraved, the signature in Gothic script with the number or date 1807, and the cock, which shows through the dust cap, has a bust (of Nelson?) at the neck. The mechanism, which has a cylinder escapement, is unusually shallow and allows for a relatively slim watch – in spite of the fact that the pair-cases are as substantial as one would expect.

PRIVATE COLLECTION

Plate 220. James Poynard, London.

Silver cases 57mm: both WH incuse (William Hodsall or Hammon I), hallmarked 1808-9

Very few clocks were made to have dials which followed Benjamin Franklin's design and this is a unique, or very rare, attempt to apply the general principle to a watch. It is thought that Franklin (1706-1790), multi-talented as he was, had the idea through his friendship with James Ferguson, the astronomer. This watch was formerly in the Time Museum, Illinois.

The twelve Roman hour numerals are grouped in threes at each quarter of the **dial** and are read in sequence off the spade hour hand. The short central hand indicates the cycle to be read, either 1, 2 or 3. The minutes are indicated as normal. There is a standard **movement** having a verge escapement and pierced and engraved cock and grotesque mask at the neck, which has the simple modification for hour cycle indication.

PRIVATE COLLECTION   *Actual size.*

Plate 221. John Roger Arnold, London, no. 2095.
Later purpose-made silver case 52mm: HWG in cameo (Henry William Griffin 3rd mark), hallmarked 1856-7

One of two very interesting watches by Arnold to survive from 1809-10, the **movements** having 21,600 trains and going barrels. The other, the following number 2096, also has a later case.

As early as 1767 John Harrison suggested in his 'Principles' – when discussing his timepiece H4 – that a fast 21,600 train could be used to advantage in smaller timepieces. Clearly, the heavier the balance, and the slower moving it is, the more it can be affected by any sharp rotational movement. And the detent escapement is especially susceptible, particularly if a twisting motion coincides with the speed and rotation of the balance. Here Arnold has employed an unusually strong balance spring and a powerful mainspring to drive it. The detent is of sufficient strength to avoid mis-locking, of sufficient strength in order that, after unlocking, it is fast enough to return to its position of rest before the next tooth of the fast moving escape wheel arrives.

A fusee and chain, man enough to transmit the necessary power for a 21,600 train, would increase the overall size of the movement to such an extent as to defeat much of the object of the exercise. Arnold used a going barrel in some of his marine chronometers with slower 14,400 trains from about 1807, but it was ten years before he used the going barrel for his watches with Prest's keyless work.

The typically off-white Arnold **dial** is signed in his normal cursive script and numbered. All three hands are unusually fine and light, the seconds with a gold boss.

PRIVATE COLLECTION

Plate 222. James Montague, London, no. 162.

Gold case 38mm: WJ incuse (William Jackson), hallmarked 1810–1

Comparatively few watches of small size, presumably intended exclusively for ladies, were made prior to the 1820s – and even then not so many.

The watch is wound through the enamel **dial** which is protected with a gold collet. There are two zones, the gold moon hour hand extending just to the central Arabic figures, the minute to the Roman numerals. The time can be viewed through a glazed lunette of the half-hunter cover of the **case** which is spring-loaded and can be raised for a fuller view with the push in the top of the Regency pendant. As is normal for the period, there is no glazed inner bezel. The bow has knuckle joints.

The **movement**, which has a verge escapement, diamond endstone and Joseph Bosley's form of regulation, is very well finished. The decoration can be compared to that on the watches by Edward Tompion and David Read (Plates 215 and 219).

PRIVATE COLLECTION

Actual size.

Plate 223. Robert Pennington, London, no. 224.

Silver consular case 57mm: IN incuse (John Nevill), hallmarked 1811-2

Pennington would seem to have supplied the trade with a fair number of escapements as well as complete watch movements during the period leading up to 1810-15, and continued to do so, but now sold a few more under his own name, particularly pocket chronometers. These last were probably all given rectangular mahogany deck boxes with signed and numbered brass observation covers, and at least the majority were no doubt primarily intended for marine use. The hexagonal box belonging to Pennington 1/430 (Plate 206) has a similar arrangement.

The **movement** has Pennington's so called 'double L' bimetallic balance which has a curved brass piece and a limiting screw at the end of each of the two brass arms. Number 1/430 referred to above has the 'YCC' balance, considered the earliest, and the watch by Ellicott & Company (Plate 213) has the second, the double T. There is a helical spring. The plate is cut away so that the engagement of the detent and escape wheel can be viewed.

The **dial** is signed and numbered. It has gold spade hands and a blued steel one for seconds. The substantial **case** has a Regency pendant and the bow has knuckle joints. PRIVATE COLLECTION

Plate 224. Robert Pennington, London, no. 671.
Gold cases 61mm: IN incuse (John Nevill), hallmarked 1812-3

Pennington employed John Nevill to make the **cases** of this handsome dumb quarter repeating watch as he did for the chronometer number 224 (Plate 223). The long cylindrical pendant is plunged to activate the repeating mechanism and the bow has knuckle joints. There is a commemorative engraving 'Francisco Salazar, Madrid, 1784' together with a crest on the inner case.

The **movement**, of very high quality, has a number of features characteristic of Pennington's work; in particular the bimetallic balance is his 'double L' type (see Plate 223) and the duplex escape wheel is made of gold. Early, especially for English work, is the cock-mounted regulator and index, and the maker, typically, has cut a sector in the cock table for the curb pins. The spiral spring has no overcoil.

The **dial**, signed very simply with the maker's name, is elegant and exceptionally clear. The fine line inside the short Roman numerals, just touched by the gold spade hour hand, relieves the space. PRIVATE COLLECTION

Plate 225. J. Freeman, London, no. 5143.

Gilt–metal cases 56mm: both J.P in rectangular cameo (probably John Palmer)

There are several makers to match the name and initial. Joseph, who began his apprenticeship in 1778, is a good candidate. The watch was made shortly after 1810 and probably before 1815.

A strong sense of timelessness pervades the patriotic naive polychrome enamel in the centre of the **dial**. As it makes its way seawards the British man-of-war is watched by a fellow seated on a beer barrel smoking his pipe outside, as the hanging sign suggests, the Anchor Inn. The style of the Arabic numerals is seen combined with fleur-de-lis quarter hour divisions on other dials of this genre and date. Written on the back counter-enamel are 'Ships...' and what may be the initials FH. The serpentine spade hands are gold.

The outer **case** is covered in tortoiseshell (which is, more accurately – or at least generally – the belly of a hawksbill turtle under-painted with colour). There is a Regency pendant and a bow with knuckle joints.

The signed and numbered **movement** has a pierced and engraved cock table with a grotesque mask and a verge escapement.

PRIVATE COLLECTION

351

Plate 226. Viner, New Bond Street, London, no. 317.
Gold case 56mm: LC scroll (? fish) above incuse (Louis Comtesse), hallmarked 1814-5

Not enough is known about Charles Viner. He was apprenticed to Thomas Savage in 1802 but, rather than serving for the normal seven years, he did not become free of the Clockmakers' Company until 1813. By about this date he was in business on his own account and was soon selling a range of good quality alarm watches. Some were repeaters, as this example; some had enamel dials, while others metal dials, invariably with bold Roman numerals, these dials matching the silver or gold cases.

The engine-turned single **case** has a hinged inner cover, a long repeating pendant, a ring bow and an alarm-set button in a ribbed band at six o'clock. The **dial** centre is also engine-turned, as are the alarm-set and minute zones which have polished markings. The chapter ring is matt and the numerals polished, as are the gold hands, the hour spade.

The **movement** quarter repeats on a gong – a quite early example of this. There is a fast/slow governor on the top plate for the separate alarm train which also sounds on the gong. Both this and the going train, which has a fusee and duplex escapement, have ratchet and click set-up. As with other repeating alarm watches by Viner, there is a simple screw-type two-arm bimetallic balance not unlike, but a little different from, Pennington's, probably last, form of screw-type, these without any amplitude limiting device.

PRIVATE COLLECTION

Plate 227. Prince & Cattles, York, no. 909.

Silver case 52mm: BM incuse, hallmarked Chester 1814-5

A half-hunting cased watch, indicating ship's watches or 'bells', signed by a business recorded in various guises at York between 1781 and 1827.

The **dial** inner zone, which can be seen through the lunette in the front cover, shows normal time. The outer ring has the ship's watches – an Arabic 8 at twelve o'clock, then 2, 4, 6 bells with 8 bells again at four and eight o'clock. The dog watches are placed neatly within the body of the second six and the third eight, 2 and 4 respectively; the minutes are marked on the edge of the dial up to thirty twice.

The **case**, which has a Regency pendant and bow with knuckle joints, is engraved with the letter W below one of the Willoughby de Broke family crests, a demi-bear. Above this, in good script, is the charming dedication 'Given to Roger Pierce for good conduct'. Did the young man leave his employer in order to go to sea? One can only imagine the background to this handsome gift.

The **movement**, typical of the period, has a verge escapement, diamond endstone and Bosley's form of regulation. The case was hallmarked in Chester, where cases for watches made in the Prescot/Liverpool area were generally marked.

Ship Watches or 'Bells'. On board ship the crew is divided into two portions, the starboard and port watches, taking duty alternately. In the British Navy the twelve hours of the night are divided into three watches of four hours – from eight to twelve the first watch, from twelve to four the middle watch, and from four to eight the morning watch. The twelve hours of the day have four watches, two of two hours, from four to six and six to eight. These are 'dog watches' and their purpose is to change the watches every twenty-four hours so that the men who watch from eight to midnight on one night shall watch from midnight to four a.m. on the next. Time was originally kept by an hour-glass every half-hour, the number of the half-hour shown by striking the watch-bell one blow for every half-hour; thus twelve-thirty a.m. is one bell in the middle watch and three a.m. is six bells.

Acatual size

Plate 228. William Waight, Birmingham, no. 440.
Gold case 49mm: LC scroll (? fish) above incuse (Louis Comtesse) hallmarked
London 1816-7

In November 1814 Edward Massey was granted patent number 3854
which covered both his first form of lever escapement and his pump
winding mechanism. This watch, signed by Waight, and engraved
'Massey's Patent' on the balance cock, has a ratchet toothed escape
wheel, short lever and pump winding. Much research was
carried out by Alan Treherne to confirm the importance of the
Massey family in the development of the lever escapement (The
Borough Museum, Newcastle-under-Lyme exhibition catalogue,
1977, and see Glossary). Originally from Newcastle-under-Lyme,
Edward (2) moved to Coventry, then Prescot and finally Clerkenwell,
while other members of the family settled in Liverpool as well as London.

Actual size.

The **movement**, which has a three-arm plain steel balance and Bosley's form of regulation, may well have been finished by the Masseys. The ratchet-toothed escape wheel has a short lever without draw and 'Type 1' of the five types of rollers used by the Masseys. A ratchet mounted on the going barrel arbor is wound by a spring-loaded rack operated when the pendant is depressed. The hands are set with a key in the normal way.

It is interesting that one of the best London makers has been employed to make the **case**. This is punch marked with the movement number. The type of **dial**, gold, with engine-turned centre and polished numerals on a matt ground, was becoming popular, also combined with gold hands. Each hand has a single tapering baluster from the centre, the hour terminating in a short, squat spade.

PRIVATE COLLECTION

Plate 229. Robert Roskell, Liverpool, no. 4825.
Gold case 52mm: TH incuse (Thomas Helsby, Liverpool), hallmarked Chester 1817-8

Robert Roskell and his family probably sold more watches than any other in the Liverpool trade during the first half of the nineteenth century.

The good, heavy **case** has an internal hinge for the glazed half-hunter cover, this released by a push in the Regency pendant. The fixed inner bezel is not glazed, the movement released by a catch at six and swinging out on a hinge at twelve. There is a gold collet around the winding square in the **dial**, this having two zones with Arabic figures. The gold minute hand is straight, while the spade hour has a well-shaped baluster to the centre so that the time can be read when the cover is closed.

The **movement** has a rack lever escapement with a wheel of thirty teeth. The cock, with cast decoration, has a bell-shaped table with 'Patent' on an indented foot. Roskell sold a good number of watches to Peter Litherland's rack lever patents (see Plate 192 and Glossary) from shortly before 1810 until a little while after 1830.

PRIVATE COLLECTION

The **dial**, signed Barrauds' with the address and number, has the seconds at twelve. The blued steel hands are typical of the series, half-round in section, the minute with a shallow taper and the hour, having a 'beetle' head, being a revival of this earlier style. The pendant of the numbered inner **case** has a cylindrical stem, oval top and a bow with knuckle joints.

It appears Robert Pennington supplied the signed and numbered **movement**. It has his 'double L' compensated balance (see Plate 223), his Earnshaw-type detent escapement, helical spring and, typically, an oval cut-out in the top plate for observing the engagement of the detent and escape wheel teeth. The cock is well engraved with symmetric foliate scrolls. PRIVATE COLLECTION

Plate 230. Barrauds', Cornhill, London, no. 865.
Silver cases 57mm: both JM incuse (James Melvill), and hallmarked 1817-8

Cedric Jagger in his book on Paul Philip Barraud and his successors (AHS, 1968, Supplement, 1979) indicates the business name and signatures changed to the plural (sometimes with an apostrophe either before or after the S) around 1810.

This is one of Barrauds' small series of 'upside down' pocket chronometers, where the inner case hinge is at six o'clock, the seconds dial is at twelve and the detent is 'hanging'. The small advantage in having the detent at rest in this position must largely be lost if the watch is kept flat and used in a deck box – here there is a good three tier mahogany **box**, the tray sprung from beneath so that it is always close against the underside of the observation lid.

Plate 231. S. Samuel, Louth, no. 215.
Silver cases 54mm: both HH incuse (probably Hannah Howard, Coventry) and hallmarked Birmingham 1817-8

A Samuel Samuel is listed as working in Louth, Lincolnshire during this period.

The naive enamel painting in the centre of the **dial** of a flautist serenading a young shepherdess is loosely after 'Evening' by William Hamilton (1751-1801). The hour chapters are made up of the ten letters of the name James Lymen and a radiant sun for twelve and a crescent moon for six. Both of the gold hands have skeletonised stems and spade ends.

The **movement**, which has a verge escapement, diamond endstone and Bosley type regulation with a blued steel setting square on the other side of the cock, is beautifully engraved and the cock table has remarkable pierced decoration. There are some strong similarities with the movement of the watch signed Edward Tompion, Plate 215. PRIVATE COLLECTION

Plate 232. William Goffe, Falmouth, no. 764.
Silver consular case 58mm: JD incuse (James Dow)
hallmarked 1818-9

Goffe was active as a watch and chronometer maker from
about 1800 to 1835 at Falmouth, Cornwall; this was, of
course a reasonably important port. Tony Mercer
(*Chronometer Makers of the World,* revised edition, N.A.G.
Press, 2004) lists some of his numbers with dates.

The **movement**, having spring detent escapement, two-
arm bimetallic balance with segmental weights, is very
much to Earnshaw's design. The helical spring has an
adjustable stud fixing on a separate cock.

The high quality **case** and **dial** have clearly been
made for marine use, the Regency pendant being broad
for strength, and numerals bold for clarity. The dial has
an unusual and attractive signature in script, somewhat
in the manner of J.R. Arnold. There are elegant
skeletonised spade hands. PRIVATE COLLECTION

Plate 233. David & William Morice, London, no. 5264.
Gold consular case 52mm: LC scroll (? fish) above incuse (Louis Comtesse), hallmarked
1818-9

Black **dials** were used, just occasionally, on English watches throughout the nineteenth
century. The heart-shaped hands with baluster stems are of flat polished silver.

The **movement** and dust cap are signed 'D. & W. Morice, London' and
numbered. It has a cylinder escapement and a three-arm flat brass balance
and has been made quite slim. This has allowed the **case**, which has a short
round pendant, ring bow and reeded band, to be relatively shallow
compared with most English cases made prior to 1820. The style of
pendant and bow, occasionally used from the beginning of the century and
already well established on the Continent, became increasingly popular. A
push in the pendant releases the numbered back while the bezel is hinged for
hand-setting and access to the movement. Long pendants continued to be used
for thicker watches and, of course, for repeaters. PRIVATE COLLECTION

Actual size.

Plate 234. John Roger Arnold, London, no. 3.
Gold case 42mm: TH in rectangular cameo (Thomas Hardy), hallmarked 1819-20

Numbered 3, and with the case hallmarked for the same year in which Thomas Prest took out his patient 4501, this must surely be the earliest watch surviving with his keyless (button) **winding** mechanism. Prest was Arnold's foreman. The system was an important step towards later more reliable arrangements which would also provide for keyless hand-setting (see below).

The **case**, with a reeded band, has a prototypical bow, stem and winding button fitted to a pinion on the inside. This meshes with the upright and slightly bevelled teeth of an exposed gear mounted on the bottom plate of the **movement**. This gear can only turn one way because the wheel it meshes directly with, which is mounted on the going barrel arbor, is held by a ratchet. There is a ruby cylinder escapement, broad polished steel balance, flat spring, regulator mounted on the underside of the cock and ruby endstone.

The gold **dial** has an engine-turned centre and polished numerals on a matt ground. The **hand-setting** arrangement is a little bit more than remarkable: while the gold hour hand is a good but standard flat polished spade, the minute has a small pin hole half way down its length. It was probably easier to move the hands with a finger!

PRIVATE COLLECTION

Actual size.

Plate 235. Barrauds' Cornhill, London, no. 2/1000.

Gold cases 55mm: both WW incuse (possibly William Wickes) hallmarked 1821-2

The single case was well established by 1820 but the demand for the pair-cased watch continued. The British preference for a substantial watch persisted, although some reduction in depth was achieved, particularly when the cylinder escapement was employed. By this date, of course, repeating watches had gongs rather than bells. For a short while the cylinder escapement had something of a renaissance, before the lever was fully accepted as the escapement of choice for watches made for everyday use. The duplex had become less popular, partly owing to its tendency to wear. The verge was robust and cheap and continued to be used, as did the detent for precision watches.

The outer **case** is fully engine-turned and the round plunge-repeat pendant has a bow with knuckle joints.

The **dial** has an engine-turned centre, polished numerals, subsidiary seconds and gold hands, the beetle hour being in the same revivalist style used by Barrauds' as that seen in Plate 230. The full plate gong repeating **movement** has a ruby cylinder escapement, plain three-arm brass balance and applied silver regulator scale. The mainspring set-up is on the barrel bridge. The pillars are screwed to the top plate: Barraud was one of those makers who, at about this time, ceased to pin them.

PRIVATE COLLECTION

Plate 236. Robert Roskell, Liverpool, no. 29076.

Gold hunter case 55mm: T.H over J.H incuse (Thomas and John Helsby, Liverpool) hallmarked Chester 1820–1

Gold dials were becoming fashionable and Liverpool makers began fitting them to watches with cast bands, pendants and bows. This is a large, early example of the best quality, the majority being made during the second quarter of the century when the trend was for watches to be quite small, often around 45 to 47mm in diameter.

The decoration on the matt ground around the edge of the **dial** is applied and in three colours of gold: green for the leaves, red and white for the flowers. The chapters are polished, the centre and seconds zone engine-turned, and the gold spade hour hand and minute have baluster stems.

The substantial, well made **case**, which has a very satisfying 'feel' in the hand, has engine-turned covers, and a body, pendant and bow with cast shell and floral decoration. The **movement** dust cap is cut around the balance cock which has cast decoration and is engraved 'patent' on the foot. Litherland's rack lever escapement is fitted. The top plate is signed and numbered, the escape wheel has fifteen teeth, and there is a diamond endstone, three-arm steel balance and a Bosley regulator.

PRIVATE COLLECTION

Plate 237. Barrauds', London, no. 2/1301.

Gold case 62mm: IM incuse (John Marsh), no hallmark

Sir Chester Beatty's important collection of watches was sold by Sotheby's, London, in December 1962 and June 1963. Catalogues in those days had very few colour plates, but this watch is illustrated in colour and, by coincidence, is on the same page as the watches by John Kentish (Plate 146) and John Scott (Plate 165). From the list of numbered watches with hallmarks which Cedric Jagger published in *Paul Philip Barraud* (AHS, 1968), number 2/1301 can be dated about 1821-2.

The oval portrait miniature of a young girl on the back of the **case** is within a glazed frame set with graduated diamonds. Sotheby's catalogue suggested that the portrait, which is executed in fine stipple-work on ivory, is probably painted by Simon Rochard (1788-1872). Champlevé enamel decorates the front and back bezels of the slim case and Regency pendant. The **dial**, with Arabic numerals and gold arrow hands, has a winding square at six o'clock.

The signed and numbered **movement**, which has a dust cap, is unusually slim. There are some strong similarities with Barrauds' 2/1000 (Plate 235). Both have cylinder escapements, the same style of plain brass three-arm balance, regulator with an applied silver scale, and plain balance cock with ruby endstone. Both watches have the top plate screwed to the pillars, rather than pinned, something Barrauds' were doing rather earlier than most.

PRIVATE COLLECTION

hand and ring have also been made with clarity in mind. This is set via a key square below the front bezel of the **case** at six o'clock. The case has a reeded band and engine-turned back, and the **movement** repeats the half-quarters through the pendant on gongs as the alarm mechanism. Both the alarm and going trains are wound through the signed inner dome, while the top plate is signed together with the Vulliamy coded number. There is a plain balance cock and brass two-arm balance with diamond endstone, spiral spring, duplex escapement and maintaining power on the fusee.

PRIVATE COLLECTION

Plate 238. Vulliamy, London, no. oxam.
Silver consular case 114mm: rubbed cameo mark (unidentified), hallmarked 1821-2

Undoubtedly, within the English watchmaking community the firm of Vulliamy had more wealthy clients than any other, and from these they had a limited call for high quality coach – or travellers' – watches. This is a particularly large and impressive example. It was at one time in the Sir John Prestige Collection.

Clearly it has been made to be set up within the box as a small clock. The **dial** and the blued steel heart-shaped hands have been made to be read at a distance. The central alarm

Plate 239. James Ferguson Cole, London, no. dl.

Silver case 56mm: HJ incuse (Henry Jackson), hallmarked 1821-2

Paul Chamberlain's *It's About Time* (Richard R. Smith, New York, 1941) remains one of the best written books on horology. It is an excellent source of late eighteenth and nineteenth century biographical and technical information, some of it not to be found elsewhere: Chamberlain's write-up of Cole (1798-1880), one of the most remarkable watchmakers of his day, is a case in point. Cole used a number code, yet to be deciphered, from the beginning of his career. This watch is one of the two earliest known by him; the British Museum has the other, number sx, also in a case hallmarked for 1821-2.

The **case** has a reeded band, round pendant and ring bow and a hinged signed and numbered inner dome. Simply signed, the handsome **dial** follows a traditional design, having a full minute track with five-minute figures and markings and Roman numerals with a fine interior ring. There are steel moon hands and subsidiary seconds.

The **movement** is highly individual. The pinned top plate is cut away to expose part of the fusee and barrel, the barrel bridge being fully signed (the number is on the far side of the balance cock). There are separate cocks for the train, two of which, together with the balance cock and the cock over the winding square, are foliate engraved. The duplex escapement has a plain steel balance, flat spring, diamond endstone, and a regulator arm over the cock. The foot of the cock has an indented edge, a form of decoration frequently seen on Liverpool watches during this period.

Plate 240. Frederick Fatton, London, no. 7 and 8.
Gold case 58mm: LC scroll (? fish) above incuse (Louis Comtesse), hallmarked 1823-4

For a while between 1801 and 1807 Fatton was acting for Breguet in Russia; by 1814 he was an independent agent and working in London (Emmanuel Breguet, *Breguet, Watchmakers Since 1775*, English edition 1997). He was one of a number of men who, having set up on their own, signed their work 'Elève de Breguet'. He took out two patents in 1822 (numbers 4645 and 4707) for an inking chronograph.

The **dial**, signed, marked 'Patent' and numbered 7, has two subsidiaries. The upper, calibrated for sixty seconds, has a hand, one part of which carries a nib, or drop pin, at its extremity immediately over an inkwell. A push-piece in the pendant thrusts the nib downwards through a hole in the well marking the dial with a small dot. The system is switched off by a short slide near the centre of the dial. The hand is started and stopped by a slide in the case band: it cannot be returned to zero, a function yet to be invented. The **case**, with a round pendant and ring bow, is signed, marked 'Patent' and numbered 8 on the hinged inner cover, the same as the **movement**. This has a three-quarter plate screwed to the pillars, a going barrel, gold three-arm balance, compensation curb, spiral spring and a cylinder escapement with a brass wheel.

Provenance. The engineer Isambard Kingdom Brunel F.R.S. (1806-1859) and also, possibly, his father, the inventor and engineer Sir Marc Isambard Brunel (1769-1849), through the family of Georgina, wife of the latter's eldest son, and by direct descent.

Marc married Sophia Kingdom, a niece of Thomas Mudge. His education of his son was remorseless. Isambard was sent to France when he was not yet twelve in September 1817 and, through one of his father's nephews, was introduced to A-L. Breguet. He attended university and, when he was fourteen, spent some time living with the Breguet family being given tuition in the workshops (see Adrian Vaughan's biography, *Isambard Kingdom Brunel*, John Murray, 1991). He returned to England in 1822.

Thus there was a connection through Breguet between Frederick Fatton and the Brunels.

PRIVATE COLLECTION   *Actual size.*

Plate 241. James Ferguson Cole, London, no. qz.
Gold case 58mm: FH incuse (Frederick Humbert), hallmarked 1824-5

Cole was responsible for a very limited number of watches which were, in most cases, technically highly individual. Like Thomas Cummins, he found a niche market where customers enjoyed technical innovation and were prepared to pay for individual pieces of high quality.

The skeletonised top plate of the quarter repeating **movement** is signed and numbered and engraved 'Inv.t et Fecit'. The lever escapement has curved arms and pointed jewelled pallets with all the lift on the teeth of the steel escape wheel, these being pierced out for lightness. The balance staff has a jewelled impulse roller for the forked lever and a steel safety roller. A micrometer regulation device for the spiral spring is mounted on the cock. The plate was skeletonised and the repeating train spring exposed to entertain the buyer. Repeating is through the pendant. The uncompromising **dial**, with its strong numerals, simple moon hands and a large seconds ring, reinforces the sense that this is a precision watch.

Paul Chamberlain's book, already referred to (see Plate 239), is an excellent source of reference for many of the variations to the lever escapement produced in the early nineteenth century; he covers a number made by Cole.

THE BURY ST. EDMUNDS MUSEUM

Edward John Dent (1790-1853). A drawing (or possibly a lithograph) by
Charles Baugniet.

Chapter Six

THE SIXTH PERIOD

1825-1970

THE SIXTH PERIOD

1825-1970

OUTLINE

Much has been written about the decline of the watchmaking industry in England during the nineteenth century. Production dropped from about 200,000 watches in 1800 to only 164,000 in 1862 (the latter figure according to *The Coventry Standard*, 15 April 1903). But the decline was far from inglorious, standards were maintained and watches of the very highest quality were made. There was an extreme and, in many ways, very efficient subdivision of labour within each small area of the manufacturing process. The industry was far from mechanized, however, and increasingly could not complete on price with those in France and Switzerland (and America – see below) which adapted more readily to new methods of production. It is estimated that the Swiss made about the same number of watches as the English in 1800: by 1862 the annual output by Continental makers had reached a total of 2,500,000 and 6 million by 1902. It was not long before the Americans, with no established industry, and thus no established divisions of skilled labour, realized the real potential of mechanized mass production. *The Coventry Standard* estimated they made 50,000 watches in 1862 and 2,750,000 in 1902.

Some attempts were made to meet the competition head-on using similar factory methods, and these account for the increase in the number of watches made in England during the years between 1872 (145,000) and 1902 (226,000). Rotherham & Sons and H. Williamson Ltd. in Coventry, William Ehrhardt and The English Manufacturing Watch Co. in Birmingham, The Lancashire Watch Co. in Prescot were all firms who met with varying degrees of success. J.W. Benson, in association with P. & A. Guye of Farringdon Road, London, offered a range of low priced watches. Initially the industry in Liverpool benefited greatly from being located in the seaport which handled much of the American trade. Marine and pocket chronometers, important during the early years, faded as the century progressed, the business being then dominated by London (mostly using rough movements – *ébauches* – purchased from Prescot). One or two businesses such as Roskell managed to evolve into brand names for a while (Roskell had successful agencies in both North and South America), and were joined by others, most notably by Thomas Russell & Sons.

Pocket Watches, 19th & 20th Century by Alan Shenton (Antique Collectors' Club, 1995) and *Watches* by M. Cutmore (David & Charles, 1989) are very informative on the less expensive and machine-made watch. D.H. Bacon's article 'Watch Production in English Factories 1870-1930' (*Antiquarian Horology,* Winter 1996) is an important contribution.

Perhaps it was unfortunate for the future prosperity of watchmaking in England that much of its production continued to be marketed along traditional lines, being sold especially signed with the retailer's name, sometimes using his serial numbers. Even in 1892, when the Coventry maker Bahne Bonniksen patented his very successful karrusel, the movement was supplied in the rough to watch finishers who then, in turn, generally sold individually to retailers.

London watchmakers, concentrated particularly around Clerkenwell, were fortunate to be established at the quality, less price-sensitive, end of the trade. The rough movements were bought, typically, in ones and twos and rarely more than half a dozen at a time. These were made into watches and supplied to the retail trade throughout Britain and indeed abroad. Although they too were affected by Swiss competition, the more so as the century progressed, they continued to make the best possible product, and were able to rely on the London made cases, dials and hands which were second to none. For repeating, calendar and chronograph mechanisms, they became steadily more reliant on Swiss suppliers. Some of the time they fitted these to English movements, at others, Swiss. How much of the finish they undertook varied greatly from watch to watch (see 'The Mechanism' later in this chapter).

The trade had a long Indian summer producing some fine watches in the period leading up to the 1914-18 war and equipped the British Navy very adequately during the conflict. Remnants of it remained for quite some years after 1918, finishing old *ébauches,* updating and modifying secondhand watches and so on. Small quantities of machine-made watches were produced. Marine chronometers were made into the 1970s. It was in the spirit of the pre-First World War period, when high grade pocket watches were produced with a view to quality, technical and aesthetic interest, as well as for usefulness, that George Daniels (Plate 295) made a limited number of mechanical watches during the later part of the twentieth century.

Most silver pair-cased watches were produced in Coventry and Birmingham but, after a while, largely Birmingham with verge and then, as late as 1875, with lever movements. They had a well-deserved reputation for sturdiness and dependability; maybe their continued popularity owed something to the fact they were known to be quintessentially English. Otherwise most watches were given a single case from around 1825. Slim, small and intermediate sizes (45-48mm) were fashionable for everyday use with the London and Liverpool trades up to about 1845; thereafter the trend was to larger sizes. Lady-sized watches (37-40mm) were not uncommon from 1870 onwards.

Early forms of keyless mechanisms had been invented (Plates 228, 234, 243 and 245), but it was not until Adolphe Nicole took out his patent in 1844 (Plate 253) that watches with both keyless winding and hand-setting began to be made in England, but even then in no great numbers. They were more expensive to make and could give problems without careful use, particularly initially, and when they were combined with a fusee. Some cheap watches were key-wound even after 1900.

The demand continued for high-grade chronometers, made either as deck watches or as pocket chronometers. Key-winding was preferred for precision deck watches until about the 1890s (Plates 266, 268, 269 and 273). Keyless chronometers for pocket use were made from the mid-1860s onwards (Plates 262 and 263, 272 and 278). A true chronograph watch must continue to run while the stopwatch facility is operated: the first English patent for such a watch having a three-pressure action chronograph with minute recording facility was granted to Adolphe Nicole in 1862 (Plate 258). Thereafter chronographs were reasonably common; some have split action (Plate 271), some minute repeating (Plate 264). Plate 281 is a split with minute repeating and a tourbillon. The karrusel, introduced in 1892, was much less expensive to make than the tourbillon and proved very successful (Plates 280 and 293).

Both annual (Plate 122) and perpetual calendar (Plate 129) watches were made – although the latter very, very rarely – in the eighteenth century. Still expensive to make, in the second half of the nineteenth century perpetual calendars could be had without repeating work (Plate 265), with it, and with, additionally, a chronograph mechanism (Plate 282).

SOME NOTABLE MAKERS

James Ferguson Cole continued to make a few highly individual watches of outstanding quality. Thomas Cummins, another London maker working at the beginning of the period, is known for about half a dozen very special watches (Plate 242). The Massey family name is famous in connection with the development of the lever escapement (Plates 228 and 246). Working out of Liverpool was Robert Roskell who sold many good quality watches (Plate 248). In Coventry J. Player & Son, a firm started by Joseph Player in 1858, assembled some excellent watches signing them for others, including Parkinson & Frodsham, London, but also with their own name. Bonniksen, who also worked in Coventry, is famous for his karrusels even though only a few of them are signed by him (Plate 280).

In London the Arnold business became Arnold & Dent and then Dent alone, although in several distinct parts and with a variety of titles (*Edward John Dent and his successors*, Vaudrey Mercer, Antiquarian Horological Society, 1977). The Frodsham family business devolved into two main parts – Parkinson & Frodsham and Charles

Frodsham & Co. The latter became the more important and it shared with E. Dent & Co., M.F. Dent, S. Smith & Son and J.W. Benson the premier position in the London retail trade. Watches signed by these firms are illustrated in this chapter. Vaudrey Mercer's book on the Frodshams was published by the Antiquarian Horological Society in 1981. Charles Allix organised a reprint of the 125 page catalogue produced by S. Smith & Son soon after it became a limited liability company in 1899, and this gives an excellent idea of the watches available at the time.

Watches signed by some other better-known names are also illustrated in this chapter. A few of these, and Kullberg (Plate 278) stands out, supplied many other firms including Frodsham and Benson. Plate 272 is a watch made by Victor Kullberg's company fully signed and numbered for Benson. Benson also bought from Usher & Cole (Plate 275), as did Barraud & Lunds. Both Frodsham and E. Dent purchased watches from Hector Golay (Plate 282) and Nicole, Nielsen & Co. (Plate 289) among others, which, for M.F. Dent, included John Hammersley (Plate 266). A.P. Walsh (Plate 263) sold to Parkinson & Frodsham.

THE CASE MAKERS AND THEIR MARKS

The best known maker by far from the beginning of the period is Louis Comtesse (Plate 242) who worked in London and used the Goldsmiths' Hall for assays. Thomas Helsby, who worked in Liverpool and had his cases hallmarked at the Chester assay office, made some excellent cases for the local watchmakers (Plate 248). Alfred Stram (Plates 259, 260 and 262), who registered his mark in 1850, produced some excellent cases from the beginning of what is considered by many to be the golden age of case making in England. George James Thickbroom (Plates 268 and 269), his mark registered in 1877, is recorded as active until 1889 when it is thought his business may have been taken over by Fred Thoms (Plates 273, 282 and 288). Thoms' name is synonymous with the best work of the later period. He may well have been responsible for some of the cases whose marks are those of retailers – Plates 271 and 285 for example – but not all. Edward Matthews and P. Woodman & Sons, both of whom were active into the twentieth century, no doubt also made some. And there are other possible candidates.

John Culme's *Directory of Goldsmiths & Silversmiths 1838-1914* (Antique Collectors' Club, 1987) has the London assay office makers' marks and biographies in two volumes. Philip Priestley's *Watch Case Makers of England 1720-1920* (NAWCC, 1994) is invaluable, and his *Chester Gold and Silver Marks* (Antique Collectors' Club, 2004), written jointly with Maurice Ridgway, covers not only the marks of the Liverpudlian makers, most of whom registered at Chester, but also makers working in Coventry, Birmingham and elsewhere in the Midlands who preferred to use the Chester assay office after an Act in 1854 relaxed boundary limitations.

THE CASE AND ITS DECORATION

The style of silver **pair-cases**, most of them made by Birmingham and Coventry makers, changed very little except that there was a tendency for the head of the Regency pendants to become circular as the century progressed. Some pair-cases were made as late as 1875. Single cased key-wound lever watches were generally given **dust caps**, but for the best London work screwed-in movements with hinged inner covers were preferred. Snap-on single backs were employed occasionally, for instance on early keyless watches supplied to E.J. Dent (Plate 253), but in London hinged covers were otherwise the norm.

Engine-turning was by far the most popular form of decoration but some, generally small sized, cases were foliate engraved (Plate 252). Engraved (Plates 265 and 271) and enamelled (Plates 268 and 277) **arms** and **crests** were executed by specialists. One of those meeting the demand in London was James Barnard, Holborn Viaduct, who advertised himself to the watch trade as 'Engraver, Enameller, Draughtsman & Goldsmith'. Key-wound watches invariably had simple round pendants and bows. Very early winding buttons were bun shaped and flat-topped. Some **pendant** makers continued to have their work separately assayed, but others worked for case makers in-house. One, J. Proctor, known to have worked for Alfred Stram, was employed from 1897 by Fred Thoms whose advertisements (*The Horological Journal*, August 1900) then offered 'The Trade supplied with Gold Pendants and Bows' and '**Revolving Pendants** a Speciality'. These pendants are to be found on some of the very best London cases. The bow is mounted on a collar which is able to revolve on a pipe fixed in the case body. These are frequently called 'thief-proof' pendants (or bows) as they make it impossible for a watch and chain to be separated by a twisting action. They also make it somewhat easier for the owner to handle and turn over a heavy watch.

The terminology used to describe nineteenth century case styles is confusing, not helped by the fact that original sources suggest that they have always been vague and used inconsistently.

The term **bassine** (bascine) has been used to describe the shape of a watch case since the seventeenth century. F.J. Britten (*Watch & Clockmakers' Handbook*, ninth edition, Spon, 1896) defines it as 'a form of watch case in which there is no bead or projection on the outside of the cover'. Taken literally, this would describe the case belonging to the watch by Nicole, Nielsen & Co. (Plate 289) and not, for instance, that belonging to the Hunt & Roskell (Plate 264); this last has what Britten refers to as a 'bead or projection'. So as to avoid 'bead', because it can be confused with a series of half-rounds or beads, I have employed 'single lip moulding' in the captions. His terminology is correct, but the bead needs to be visualized in section. No in-depth research has been done, but it is probable that, during the last quarter of the century when cases with double mouldings became popular, the term 'bassine' may well have been used by some in the trade, including Usher & Cole Ltd., to describe any smooth case, including those with single lip mouldings.

Kullberg has 'dome crystal hunter' in his workbook entry (Plate 278). This is a case style, with mouldings, and would have been entered by Usher & Cole in their books as a '½BH', in other words a partly bassine as opposed to a FBH (Full Bassine Hunter). In 2008 Martin Matthews had the recollection that his family, case makers for several generations, used a term '**double bassine**'. It is possible this may have been their way to describe a case with double mouldings (on each cover if it is a hunter). In point of fact in order to form two edge mouldings three 'basins' are required, one inside another! This is best seen on Plate 265. Perhaps bassine cases with simple lip mouldings should be described as '**half-bassine**' and those with more 'double bassine'!

Usher & Cole workbooks have '½B sight', sometimes '½BS', the 'sight' or 'S' denoting a **half-hunter**. It was only after about 1900 that '½B ½H' was used. Some entries for open face cases read '½B crystal' and '½BC'. '**Crystal**' refers to a type of case where the front bezel has a polished internal chamfer. This bezel was fitted, in general, with a totally flat glass which also has a chamfered edge – the two together reflecting light as a faceted crystal. A convex glass has a modest edge and is not so effective.

THE DIAL AND HANDS

From about 1825 and up to around 1840 there was a fashion in both London (the firm of Vulliamy followed it) and the provinces for slightly off-white enamel dials (Plate 246 and 249). Some provincial pair-cased watches were given painted enamel scenes as late as the 1860s (Plates 250 and 255-257). Gold and silver dials, some engraved, some with applied decoration, always had a following (Plates 242, 248, 253, 269 and 286).

The extraordinary high standard established by the London enamel dial makers during the last quarter of the century helped to ensure the survival of the trade. The complex dials for chronograph and calendar watches are very impressive, but the simpler dials are of equal quality. The proportions vary but they are always excellent. The name 'Willis' is found on the back of many fine dials. F.J. Britten in *Old Clocks and Watches & their Makers* (Antique Collectors' Club third edition reprint, 1977) has John Willis, 'enameller', from 1823 and his son, Thomas John, 'an excellent dial enameller', as dying in 1893 aged fifty-seven. The business continued after Thomas John's death and into the 1920s. *The Horological Journal* of August 1900 carries an advertisement: 'T.J. Willis, watch dial enameller, Established 1767' followed by the address and 'Specialities – Repeater, chronograph, perpetual calendar and Venetian enamel dials'. The off-white Venetian dials are found exclusively, more or less, on only the best watches shortly before and after 1900. Whether or not they were all made by Willis is unclear. The watch by Hector Golay (Plate 282) has a fine Venetian perpetual calendar dial with the Willis name on the reverse, while the H.L. Brown & Son (Plate 288) has a classic example of a simple Willis dial of late proportions: the Roman numerals are quite strong, condensed and close to the edge of the dial.

There were a wide variety of **hands** used with many variations. The spade style of hand was predominant, although the head was often so egg-shaped that in fact it bore little resemblance to a spade. The moon hand was probably at its most popular at the beginning but it was used throughout the period (Plates 243, 245, 252 and 291). The fleur-de-lis was used less frequently (Plates 251, 260 and 262). Serpentine hands, such as those belonging to the Robert Roskell in Plate 248, are generally found on Liverpool watches.

THE MECHANISM

The **cylinder** (Plate 243) and **duplex** escapements were little used after about 1830 although the duplex had something of a revival in the 1850s and 1860s. The **verge** continued to be the workhorse for cheaper watches into the 1860s (Plates 247 and 256).

Earnshaw's form of spring **detent** proved to be the most constant and accurate of escapements. There were subtle variations between one maker's work and another's; for instance, Kullberg (Plate 278) planted the detent on a north/south axis, the most favourable position when a watch is being worn. The escapement still had the tendency to set on occasions if the watch was given a sudden jolt, a problem which was not overcome successfully until about 1970 (George Daniels, Plate 295). It was given a bimetallic balance and a helical spring and fitted to full plate movements early on (Plate 251) and then half plate from about the mid-1860s (Plate 263). It appears that most deck watches with detent escapements were full plate until the 1890s (Plate 273).

Alan Treherne did much research during the 1970s into the Massey family's contribution to the development of the **lever** escapement and this was followed by an exhibition and catalogue at the Newcastle-under-Lyme Museum in 1977. Edward Massey's first form of lever is in a watch of 1816-7 by William Waight shown in Plate 228 in the previous chapter. Plate 246 has his rare form seconds beating type IV escapement with a type III roller signed by his youngest son, Edmund, the case hallmarked for 1828-9. By this date the Massey 'crank roller' ratchet-tooth lever escapement was being superseded by the 'single table roller' form of the ratchet–tooth (or 'English') lever escapement. Apart from the form of the roller, the principal difference is that, whereas Massey's safety action was between the end of the lever and the roller, the new escapement had an upright pin fixed behind the impulse slot which banked, when necessary, on the outer edge of the roller. Double rollers, one for impulse, the other – smaller – for the safety action, were sometimes employed on watches of the very best quality.

All escapements, however well made, suffer from some degree of positional error – the rate will be different between, most importantly, the horizontal and the vertical. The error can be mitigated when the escapement is mounted on a rotating carriage. Some remarkable results were achieved with the **tourbillon** (Plates 279, 281, 283, 294 and 295), but also with the **karrusel** (280, 290 and 293). The tourbillon, by far the most difficult to make, is found on some of the highest quality watches of the period. The karrusel was a simpler solution and more robust, and watches with this were produced in much greater numbers.

The **rough movement** or movement 'in the grey' is nowadays generally referred to as an *ébauche,* although *ébauche* can also be used for those much nearer completion. What constituted a rough movement varied, but it consisted of the plates and cocks with some holes drilled, unpolished screws, train wheels and fusee and keyless work where applicable. There were three standard forms of *ébauche:* **full, three-quarter** and **half plate** (Plates 242, 253 and 245). Two unusual layouts are shown in Plates 243 and 259. The full plate was used regularly for lever watches by provincial makers throughout the period, otherwise mostly three-quarter plate. Many provincial retailers bought a few high quality watches from specialist firms such as Joseph Player & Son, Coventry, and from the London trade.

London makers had largely abandoned the full plate by 1860 using it only for some cheaper pieces and a few high quality deck watches. Instead they favoured the three-quarter plate and, for some of their best watches, the half plate. These last had detent or, sometimes, a lever escapement; invariably they had a free-sprung balance and a **fusee**, and normally an up and down state of wind indicator (Plates 263 and 294). For most watches the fusee had given way to the **going barrel** during the last quarter of the nineteenth century. Three-quarter plate and half plate layouts were adopted also, of course, by makers outside London. The slow take-up of the keyless wind and hand-set mechanism, the cost and care required to use the early forms (Plate 253) were mentioned in the outline to this chapter. That the system's function is problematic when combined with a fusee has long been recognised, but so too has the quality of keyless fusee watches.

The London trade (indeed the entire English trade) became steadily more reliant on Swiss suppliers for **repeating**, calendar and chronograph mechanisms. It is probable that some of these were imported and finished locally, but it is certainly the case that on occasions English *ébauches* were sent to Switzerland for the complications to be fitted – the Usher & Cole archive demonstrates this. In other cases, although finished in England with English quality gilding and a ratchet-tooth lever escapement, the entire *ébauche* is of Swiss origin. There is a further group where, although the case is English and there is a ratchet-tooth lever escapement with a full English signature, the escapement is tightly packed into a three-quarter plate. And the gilding is often mean and weak. These are probably completely Swiss.

Aside from the importation of somewhat specialized *ébauches* mentioned above, some very ordinary *ébauches* were also imported, although not in vast numbers. Otherwise, makers of Prescot, but also to a small extent Coventry, were well able to supply the English trade and, when required, they produced the best quality product. In his fascinating article for *Antiquarian Horology* of September 1981, Dr. Robert Kemp gives an idea of the number of people involved and the degree of specialisation. He lists some forty initials he found stamped on a collection of 325 movements, making the point that these belong only to the final assemblers. The most famous of these was Joseph Preston & Sons (J.P) – see Plates 273 and 278 – and John Wycherley (J.W).

TIMEKEEPING

Wrist watches were, of course, no better timekeepers than the pocket watches they replaced, indeed often considerably worse. Even the average nineteenth century watch performed tolerably well. The challenge for an ambitious watchmaker was to submit his work to the forty-five day trials at Kew Observatory and obtain such a good mark as to gain a Class A certificate. If he wished to supply the Admiralty, the tests at Greenwich were equally stringent and rather more prolonged – twenty-nine weeks (sixteen weeks for ordinary deck watches) in the early twentieth century.

The Kew tests were divided into eight periods of five days each, and five intermediate and extra days in four of which the watch was not rated.

1st Period – Vertical position with the pendant up at the temperature of the chamber (60-65 degrees F)
2nd Period – Vertical position, pendant to the right at the same temperature
3rd Period – The same as the 2nd Period but pendant to the left
4th Period – Dial up in the Refrigerator at 40 degrees F
5th Period – Dial up at 60-65 degrees F
6th Period – Dial up in the Oven at 90 degrees F
7th Period – Dial down at 60-65 degrees F
8th Period – The same as the 1st Period

The intermediate and extra days, during which the rate was not recorded, were at the commencement of the 4th, 5th, 6th and 7th Periods, which extended one day each for that purpose.

To gain a Class A certificate the performance of the watch was such that:

1. The average of the daily departures from the mean daily rate, during the same stage of the trail, did not exceed two seconds in any one of the eight stages.
2. The mean daily rate while in the pendant up position differed from the mean daily rate in the dial up position by less than five seconds, and from that in any other position by less than ten seconds.
3. The mean daily rate was affected by change of temperature to an amount less than 0.3 seconds per 1 degree F.
4. The mean daily rate did not exceed 10 seconds while in any position.

The 100 marks awarded to an absolutely perfect watch would be made up as follows: 40 for a complete absence of variation in daily rate, 40 for absolute freedom from change of rate with change of position and 20 for perfect compensation for the effects of temperature. A score of 80 marks or more earned the endorsement on the certificate 'especially good'.

Plate 242. Thomas Cummins, London, no. 4=25.

Gold case 55mm: LC scroll (? fish) above incuse (Louis Comtesse), hallmarked 1824-5

About half a dozen watches are known signed by Thomas Cummins, all a little different from one another, but all made to a very high standard with regulator dials, full plate movements and lever escapements. They are all numbered in a similar manner, the number followed by the year of completion. The case of this example is engraved with the crest of Robert Smith, first Baron Carrington, and the balance cock with I.W. Smith, 8 Gray's Inn Square. It would seem Robert's crest was adopted by his brother or cousin; the first initial could be for John Smith, a member of the London banking family Smith Payne & Co. and M.P. for Nottingham (the J commuted, as was common, to I).

Actual size.

The **case**, made by Louis Comtesse – sometimes rendered Comptesse – the foremost London maker of his day, has fine engine-turning on the flat – 'collar' – band and a hinged inner cover with a winding aperture. The gold **dial**, also engine-turned, has engraved numerals on a matt annular ring for minutes and subsidiaries for seconds above and hours below. The steel hands are quite simple, the seconds counter-poised and the tip of the moon hour hand is pierced out.

The full plate **movement** is signed, numbered, with Invenit et Fecit abbreviated. The two-arm bimetallic screw balance has a free-sprung helical spring with steel adjustable stud and a beat scale engraved on the plate. The train is jewelled to the third wheel, the lever escapement is a sophisticated form of the Massey type IV with draw and resilient banking, there is maintaining power and Cummins' own form of fusee stop device. There is no motion work between the hands so that frictional loss and variations due to it are avoided.

This watch has been in a number of well-known collections including those belonging to P.W. Pegge (Christie's, London, February 1960), Cecil Rosedale and Thomas Engel.   PRIVATE COLLECTION

Actual size.

Plate 243. Sigismund Rentzsch, London.
Gold case 48mm: LC scroll (? fish) above incuse (Louis Comtesse)

The hallmarked case has no date letter. The case maker registered the first of his three cameo marks in December 1827; it is likely the watch was made very shortly before this date.

Little is known about Rentzsch, but from the small number of highly individual clocks and watches he signed he was clearly a very competent mechanic. Although no piece of his survives in the Royal Collections, he is recorded in the lists of royal tradesmen between 1821 and 1857. Accompanying this watch is a letter, dated 1937, stating that it was given by Princess Sophia to her lady-in-waiting, Miss Sophie Wynyard.

The initials on the back are almost certainly those of Jane Wynyard, mother of Sophie, whose husband was Lieutenant-General William Wynyard (1750-1819), equerry to George III.

The back of the engine-turned **case** rotates with an internal gear to **wind** the watch and a cap in the pendant lifts for hand-setting. The watch can be made to **repeat** the hours and quarters on a gong by rotating the front bezel, clockwise for the hours, anti-clockwise for the quarters. Fixed to the bezel is a small pawl extending a short distance over the edge of the dial (it can be seen between one and two o'clock in the illustration). An annular rack is carried by the bezel clockwise until the pawl comes in contact with the tip of the hour hand. A more detailed description of a similar watch can be found in an article my father wrote for *Antiquarian Horology* (December 1966). The **dial** is gold and engine-turned; the signature, numerals and minute markings are engraved and filled. There are steel moon hands.

Access to the **movement** is gained by rotating, and so undoing, the threaded circular reserve, monogrammed JW, on the back of the case. The collar of the internal gear rotates on a post, this on a steel strap screwed to the movement. The going barrel, which has 'Geneva' stop-work, is below the second winding gear and a steel bridge adjacent to the signature – there is no number. The brass escape wheel and the steel three-arm balance – which has a spiral spring and diamond endstone and ruby cylinder – have separate cocks. There is a short dampener on the repeating gong block. PRIVATE COLLECTION

Plate 244. Thomas Cummins, London, no. 17-27.
Gold case 52mm: probably ED incuse (probably Edward Delgrave), hallmarked 1826-7

One of half a dozen signed by Thomas Cummins, this appears to be the only small size watch – 52mm as opposed to 55mm – recorded. Otherwise it is all but identical in every respect to number 4=25 shown in Plate 242, with just small variations in the finishing.

The **case dial** and hands are of the same design. So too is the **movement** specification, with a bimetallic screw balance, helical spring, beat scale engraved on the top plate and a lever escapement similar to Massey type IV. Plate 242 has a fuller description. The signature is much the same. By this date the best quality watches generally had their plates screwed together, rather than pinned as previously.

This watch is illustrated in *Watches* by Clutton and Daniels (Sotheby Parke Bernet, third edition, 1979). PRIVATE COLLECTION

Plate 245. William Cribb, London, no. 553.

Gold case 50mm: JB in rectangular cameo (Josiah Barnett), hallmarked 1828-9

Patent number 5586 of December 1827 is one of the four patents taken out by the Clerkenwell maker Joseph Berrollas and concerns his remarkable keyless **winding** system. Probably not many watches were made with it, certainly not many survive. A cap in the top of the pendant (marked WC incuse by pendant maker William Collier) with a chain attached to it pulls outwards in quite an alarming fashion. The chain, constructed in the same way as a fusee, encircles a pulley mounted on the dial side of the barrel. When the cap is pulled out, a ratchet and click allows the spring to be wound from the centre and when the cap is released the spring rewinds the chain back on to the pulley. The process is repeated until the watch is wound. Unfortunately, the illustration showing the movement has the cap apparently attached to the bow; in reality it will come out two or three times as much again. This watch is illustrated in *The Camerer Cuss Book of Antique Watches* (Antique Collectors' Club 1976 edition, Plate 123) with the dial removed and showing the winding system.

The half plate **movement** is fully signed and numbered together with the address Southampton Row, Russell Square, London. It has a right-angled single table lever escapement, a plain gold three-arm balance, a spiral spring and a diamond endstone. The gold **dial** and its subsidiary seconds ring have engine-turned centres. There are gold moon hands.

Plate 246. Edmund Massey, 89 Strand, London, no. 303.

Silver cases 59mm: both TE over HF (Timothy Ellison and Henry Fishwick, Liverpool), hallmarked Chester 1828-9

The colour of the enamel **dial** – slightly off-white – became quite popular in the 1830s and 1840s. It is signed E. Massey with the address and number and has gold spade hands and a counter-poised steel centre seconds hand. The silver **cases** have a Regency style pendant.

The **movement** is engraved 'Patentee' next to Edmund Massey's name: Edmund was the youngest son of Edward, in fact the patentee. The two-arm bimetallic screw balance, of very large diameter, beats seconds, making use of a rare form of Edward Massey's escapement (type IV) included in his 1814 patent (see Alan Treherne, The Borough Museum, Newcastle-under-Lyme, Exhibition Catalogue, 1977) having a large escape wheel with vertical teeth. There is his type III roller. The cock is engraved to the London taste whereas a not dissimilar movement signed by Edward Massey, numbered 653, in an illustrated letter from Martyn Jones (*Antiquarian Horology*, June 2005) has one in the Liverpool style (and a plain gold balance, Bosley regulator and a roller similar to type V).

PRIVATE COLLECTION

Plate 247. Thomas Glase, Bridgnorth, no. 437.
Silver cases 56mm: JH incuse (James Heales, Coventry), hallmarked Birmingham 1830-1

Watch **dials** engraved with the admonition 'Keep me clean and use me well, And I to you the truth will tell' around the perimeter of the dial were popular around 1830. Beyond the fact that they are signed by a variety of names, there are only small differences between most of the surviving examples: the dials have the same layout but, for instance, there are different engraved designs in the centre. **Cases** made in Coventry were hallmarked generally in either Chester or, as on this occasion, Birmingham. It has a Regency style pendant.

The **movement** was probably made in Coventry or Birmingham for resale by the watchmaker in Bridgnorth, a town some distance west of Birmingham. It is typical of the period and type, with pinned plates, verge escapement and Bosley regulator. The cock is beautifully pierced and engraved, the table with scrolling foliage and flowers inhabited by a dolphin's head and a grotesque mask at the neck.

PRIVATE COLLECTION

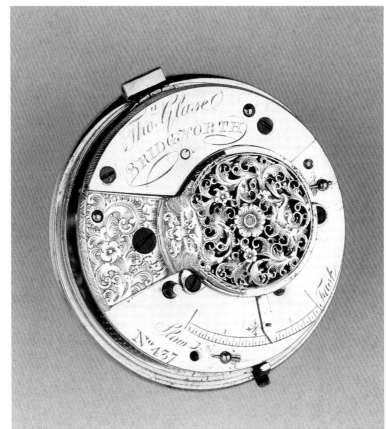

Plate 248. Robert Roskell, Liverpool, no. 10030.
Gold case 56mm: T.H incuse (Thomas Helsby), hallmarked Chester 1832-3

Joseph Berrollas took out patent number 3174 for a most unusual design of **repeating** mechanism in 1808. The cap in the pendant is on a worm: turned clockwise it will wind outwards striking the hours on a gong, anticlockwise it will return to the case striking the quarters. The system is hardly melodious but, not only is there no need for a repeating train and spring, it is ideal for the owner who prefers to count slowly, as slowly as he turns the cap. It was not widely taken up, however, and only a few watches with it are known, these signed by Roskell in the 1830s. This watch is illustrated with the dial removed and showing the repeating mechanism on Plate 132 of *The Camerer Cuss Book of Antique Watches* (Antique Collectors' Club, 1976).

   The **movement**, apart from the repeating mechanism (see above), is typical of good quality Liverpudlian work of the period. The plates are pinned together, it has a rack lever escapement and the cock is marked 'Patent'. Of course there are in fact two patents incorporated: the **case** inner cover is engraved 'Robt. Roskell's Patent Repeater'. The back is very well engine turned and the ribbing on the cap is matched by that on the band. The centre of the gold **dial** is also engine turned while the polished numerals are on a matt ground. The steel serpentine hands with spade ends are quite unusual but are typical of the period. PRIVATE COLLECTION

Plate 249. John Cohan, Liverpool, no. 301.
Silver case 105mm: RL in cameo (Richard Lucas), hallmarked Chester 1833-4

This is a giant and an extremely heavy watch, which might have been made to be a coach watch but, alternatively, perhaps, made as an exhibition piece.

The cream – slightly off-white – **dial** is signed 'John Cohan, Patent Lever Watch, Manufacturer, Liverpool'. A marine chronometer *ébauche* has been used for the **movement** and consequently the plates are very thick – and heavy (Cohan is recorded in 1834 as a watch and chronometer maker at 15 Cannon Place, Liverpool). The top plate is signed and numbered and the balance cock, which has a ruby endstone, is engraved 'Patent' within tight foliate decoration. The three-arm brass balance has peripheral timing screws and a spiral spring, and the escapement is made according to Massey's patented lever with a type II roller. The fusee has maintaining power. PRIVATE COLLECTION

Plate 250. Unsigned, numbered 343.
Silver cases 60mm: both WW in oval cameo (William Waterhouse, Coventry), hallmarked Birmingham 1840-1

The locations of the painted enamel scenes on **dials** of this type can rarely be identified, but this is of the first railway station in Nottingham. A train is crossing a bridge, in the foreground is a fisherman and a strolling couple and, in the background, Nottingham Castle.

The initials TD are elaborately engraved on the inner **case**. According to the 1922 entry to the accession register of the Nottingham City Museum, these initials may be for Thomas Edward Dicey, Chairman of the Railway until 1844. Case and pendant making were separate trades and at this period the pendant mark, although generally rubbed, can often be read – here the mark is TB incuse (Thomas Bickley, Coventry).

The **movement** is numbered but has been left unsigned. It has a solid foliate engraved cock, pierced table with radial foliate decoration and a diamond endstone. The plates are pinned, there is a Bosley regulator and a verge escapement.

NOTTINGHAM CITY MUSEUMS AND GALLERIES

Plate 251. Charles Cummins, London, no. 1210.

Gold case 48mm: GH within oval cameo (Gustavus Huguenin), hallmarked 1844-5

Charles Cummins was apprenticed to his father, Thomas, in 1832. Like his father he seems to have specialized in very high grade watches, but probably not many as very few survive. One, number 589 in the case hallmarked for 1837-8 and all but identical to his father's work, is illustrated by Cecil Clutton in his *Collector's Collection*; this is another and number 1275 (Plate 252) is a third. The sequence of numbers suggests that there should be many more watches by, or at least signed by, Charles Cummins than is the case.

The signed and numbered full plate **movement** has an Earnshaw-type spring detent escapement. The balance cock and train have ruby jewels and caps and the fusee has maintaining power. The bimetallic screw balance has a spiral spring with a double overcoil, this being preferred to a helical spring – normally used with a detent escapement – probably to produce a slimmer watch (small, slim watches were fashionable).

The double-bottomed **case** has a ribbed band and a foliate engraved back with a plain reserve in the centre. The gold **dial** has an engraved cartouche of flowers and foliage, slim roman numerals (currently in vogue for enamel dials as well), subsidiary seconds and steel fleur-de-lis hands.

PRIVATE COLLECTION

Actual size.

Plate 252. Charles Cummins, London, no. 1275.

Gold case 48mm: GH within oval cameo (Gustavus Huguenin) hallmarked 1845-6

Cummins has made the same size watch as that in Plate 251, employed the same case maker and used the same movement *ébauche*. The numbers are close and the hallmarks are one year apart.

However, he has chosen to fit the **movement** of this watch, which is signed and numbered in much the same way, with a Massey-type lever escapement according to his father's design (Plates 242 and 244). The balance is similar and so too is the spiral spring with a double overcoil. The signed plain gold **dial** has the same minute markings and the slim hour numerals and, again, there are subsidiary seconds. The back of the **case** is well engraved with a crest – an eagle's head above a cross moline – within a largely symmetric design of lush foliage and 'C' scrolls.

PRIVATE COLLECTION

Plate 253. E.J. Dent, London, no. 10523.

Gold case 49mm: AN in rectangular cameo (Adolphe Nicole), hallmarked 1848-9

Adolphe Nicole's patent number 10348 of October 1844 for **keyless winding** and hand-set was enrolled in April 1845. By 1846 E. Dent & Co had acquired the patent rights from Nicole and became sole licensee. Vaudrey Mercer (*Edward John Dent and his Successors*) devotes a short chapter to the patent and illustrates diagrams taken from the application.

The signed and numbered three-quarter plate **movement** is engraved 'Watchmaker to the Queen' and 'Patent'. The bottom – pillar – plate is stamped adjacent to the balance cock AN over JC (for Adolphe Nicole and Jules Capt, 80 Dean Street, Soho, London 1843-1868) and numbered 925. There is a going barrel. The winding mechanism on the top plate is the early form, the intermediate wheel being permanently engaged with the centre wheel and thus continuously turning with the hands. The nib-piece for engaging the hands is in the case band at one o'clock; they can be set only forwards. There is a duplex escapement. The patent also covers a safety device to overcome the escapement's tendency to set; too great an oscillation will make a kink in the outermost turn of the spiral spring engage with an upright pin in one arm of the balance.

The slim engine-turned half-hunting **case** has a single snap-on back and a good early winding button. The lunette or 'sight' in the cover has Roman numerals filled with blue enamel. The gold **dial** has subsidiary seconds, characteristically, at nine o'clock. Unusual is the silvered date ring aperture below twelve and the moon hands, the hour having the extra 'spade' portion to show through the half hunter cover normally found on spade hands.

PRIVATE COLLECTION

Actual size.

Plate 254. Viner & Co., 233 Regent Street & Royal Exchange, London, no. 3967.
Gold case 50mm: PC rectangular cameo (Peter Clerc), hallmarked 1850-1

Of a wide variety of keyless mechanisms not employing a rotating button in the **case** pendant, the pull-wind system employed by Viner is the most common. The cap in the pendant is fixed to a long stem which, via a crank and a ratchet system, winds the **movement**. The cap is required to be returned to the pendant for further strokes. The hands are on a square and set with a key in the normal way. Robert Leslie suggested a form of pendant winding in 1793 (number 1970, item 12): '…On the square where the key should go a ratch; the pendant, being alternately moved in and out turns this ratch by means of two clicks…'. See Plate 228 for pump winding.

It is fully signed and numbered (and engraved 'Inventors' after the name), has a hanging barrel, 'Geneva' stop-work (see Glossary), normal right-angled ratchet-toothed lever escapement and a bimetallic compensated balance. The signed gold **dial**, engine-turned in the centre, has subsidiary seconds and fine blued steel spade hands.

PRIVATE COLLECTION

Actual size.

Plate 255. Frederick Lawrence, Louth.
Silver cases 58mm: IW incuse (John Williams or John
Weston), hallmarked 1855-6

The painted enamel **dial** has a cartload of yokels with
rakes and a scythe hurrying along a country road, the
witty suggestion being that they would not be in such a
hurry if they had not finished their haymaking for the
day, and that the lazy hounds were probably off to the
pub. In truth, of course, for townsfolk the idea is also a
romantic one, many of whom had their origins in the
countryside and had affection for it. The removal of
grain import controls and duties during the period had
made country life much more difficult.

The signed **movement**, which has a verge
escapement, is typical of those found in watches of this
type; it was probably made in Coventry or Birmingham
and is not dissimilar to that shown in Plate 256.

PRIVATE COLLECTION

Plate 256. John Roberts, Dudley, no. 8713.

Silver cases 58mm: both RN in oval cameo (possibly Richard Neale, Coventry) Birmingham 1856-7

The painted enamel **dial** has a fellow on a bridge watching a train go by while two others rest, their spades idle. Like the scene shown in Plate 255, the theme is a pithy, yet affectionate comment on rural life and the dichotomy between it and urban life's advances, this clearly demonstrated by the steam train rushing through the countryside.

The signed and numbered **movement** has a verge escapement and a Bosley-type regulator which has been well used judging by the condition of the gilding on the plate around the index. One can imagine the owner moving the regulator arm back and forth in frustration: perhaps he would have done well to consider the admonition engraved on the dial of Plate 247: 'Keep me clean and use me well, and I to you the truth will tell'!

Plate 257. J. Telford, Bellingham, no. 7066.

Silver cases 58mm: R.S incuse (possibly Richard Swann, Birmingham), hallmarked 1861-2

Dials with 'Speed the Plough' above painted enamel ploughing scenes had been popular since the 1830s at least. 'Speed the Plough', which has medieval, or indeed earlier, origins in prayer – 'God spede the plow' – and song, for ploughmen and the farming community, also suggests a wish for success in any undertaking. It was the title given to a melody written in 1799 (originally 'The Naval Pillar') which was extremely popular during the nineteenth century.

These watches invariably seem to have been sold by watchmakers working in small towns in rural areas. The signed and numbered full plate **movement** has a dust cap, an engraved cock with diamond endstone, plain steel three-arm screw balance and lever escapement.

PRIVATE COLLECTION

Actual size.

Plate 258. Dent, 33 Cockspur Street, London, no. 25347.

Gold case 51mm: AN in cameo (Adolphe Nicole) hallmarked 1866-7

In May 1862 Adolphe Nicole was granted patent number 1461 for the first English chronograph mechanism where the hands for seconds and minute recording could be reset to zero: they could be started, stopped and reset consecutively by a single button.

M.F. Dent number 25347 is an excellent and early example which has, most unusually, a spring detent escapement.

The signed and numbered **dial** has a 'regulator' lay-out with subsidiaries for hours and continuous seconds and a central minute hand (in the photograph near 34 minutes and partly obscured by the tail of the chronograph minute recording hand). The chronograph second hand indicates 55 seconds, the minute recorder 5 minutes.

The signed and numbered **movement** is engraved with the address, 'Watchmakers to the Queen' and 'Patent'. Part of Nicole's winding (Plate 253) and chronograph mechanisms can be seen on the top plate. The Earnshaw type detent escapement has a bimetallic screw balance, spiral spring with double overcoil and a finely engraved cock.

PRIVATE COLLECTION

Actual size.

Opposite: Plate 259. Barraud & Lunds, 41 Cornhill, London, no. 3/127.

Gold case 52mm: AS rectangular cameo (Alfred Stram), hallmarked 1869-70

Less than a handful of pocket chronometers by the firm of this type are known. Cedric Jagger, in the supplement (AHS, 1979) to his book *Paul Philip Barraud* (AHS, 1968), illustrates one other example and discusses this highly unusual half plate calibre (see Glossary).

The partly skeletonised signed and numbered **movement**, of very high quality, has the *ébauche* mark J.P (Joseph Preston & Sons of Prescot, Lancashire, founded in 1829). The finish is perhaps a little reminiscent of the work of J.F. Cole (Plate 241). There is a spring detent escapement with bimetallic balance and helical spring (the long steel detent has a separate cock and wedge adjustment), a separate cock for the escape wheel and another for the third and fourth. The main plate, to which the balance cock is screwed, is cut away to expose part of the barrel, fusee and fusee chain.

The inner cover of the beautifully engine-turned **case** is glazed, possibly for exhibition purposes, and pierced for winding. The signed, well-proportioned **dial** has a large seconds ring and gold spade hands.

PRIVATE COLLECTION

Opposite: Plate 260. Barraud & Lunds, 41 Cornhill, London, no. 2/9743.

Gold case 51mm: AS rectangular cameo (Alfred Stram), hallmarked 1870-1

By 1870 the demand for watches which could be wound and set with a button was well established. There were problems to making a keyless watch which incorporated a fusee – a going barrel was far more practical – but the English were very reluctant to abandon the fusee with its timekeeping qualities. J.A. Lund's solution was simple: to have the head of the key as a winding button, the shaft snapping into the head of the pendant. This enabled his customers to appear as if they were in fashion while retaining the benefits of the fusee. He took out his patent (number 914) in March 1870. John Alexander Lund probably became a partner of the firm Barraud(s) and Lund in about 1864 – his father had become a partner in the late 1830s – and watches are signed Barraud and Lunds from about this date.

So that it can be seen, the high quality **movement** is illustrated with its inner cover open but with the button cum key in position on the fusee square. Access to the female set-hand square is also through the inner cover. The top plate is signed and numbered and the raised barrel and balance cock have tight foliate engraving. The ratchet-tooth lever escapement has a free-sprung bimetallic balance, the spring with a terminal curve. The **dial** is signed and numbered and there are gold fleur-de-lis hands.

PRIVATE COLLECTION

Actual size.

Plate 261. Barraud & Lunds, 41 Cornhill, London, no. 3/1075.

Silver case 85mm: P:W incuse, colon between (Philip Woodman's first mark), hallmarked 1872-3

Frederick Fatton took out his patent for an inking chronograph in 1822 (Plate 240), this having a nib or drop-pin at the end of the second hand. This watch is made on the same principle, but it has also a minute recording facility and in this respect it would seem to be the only one recorded. It is illustrated by Cedric Jagger in his supplement (AHS, 1979) to his book *Paul Philip Barraud* (AHS, 1968).

The signed and numbered **dial** has a sweep seconds minute hand and subsidiary seconds, both with inking nibs, and subsidiary hours. A slide in the case at eleven o'clock operates the start/stop mechanism, and a push in the keyless winding button brings the inking nibs into action simultaneously.

The **movement**, which is signed and numbered, has spotted plates, a decorative finish normally applied to marine chronometers. The complex set-hand mechanism, mounted on the top plate, is engaged by a nib-piece adjacent to the pendant in the case band, and the keyless work for the going barrel, also on the top plate, has two intermediate wheels. The ratchet-tooth lever escapement has a bimetallic balance and spiral spring.

PRIVATE COLLECTION

Plate 262. James McCabe, Royal Exchange, London, no. 08325.

Gold case 52mm: AS in cameo (Alfred Stram), hallmarked 1875-6

James McCabe moved from Belfast to London in 1775, establishing a very successful family business which flourished up until Robert McCabe closed it, retiring as 'a man of independent means' in 1880. A short history of it was published by Paul Hackamack (*Antiquarian Horology*, Summer 1977).

Most marine chronometers, of which the firm sold many, have silvered dials, and these would seem to be the inspiration for the design of the **dial** of this fusee keyless pocket chronometer. It is of silver, horizontally grained, with the subsidiary seconds, up and down state of wind indicator, numerals and signature all engraved. The fleur-de-lis hands are gold.

The half plate **movement**, similarly signed and numbered, has a spring detent escapement, helical spring, compensated balance and fusee. Note that there are key squares for both winding and hand-setting which can be used when the movement is out of its case, and also if a problem develops with the keyless mechanism. These can often be accessible on watches of this type through the hinged inner cover of the **case**.

PRIVATE COLLECTION

Plate 263. A.P. Walsh, 5 George St., Euston Rd., London, no. 2017.
Gold hunter case 54mm: HW incuse (Henry Webb), hallmarked 1875-6

The **case** is engraved with three crests of the Chandos-Poll-Gell family and the inner cover with Henry and his son Harry Anthony's initials. Care is required in winding fusee chronometers if the chain is not to break and the detent damaged. A clever safety winding and hand-set mechanism has been incorporated which will operate only after the button is pushed and the cover is open. The winding mechanism will be activated automatically, while a steel push by the inner bezel at four o'clock disengages the winding and engages the hand-set. The action of closing the cover will de-activate both, and the button will again be free to turn.

The **dial** has an up and down state of wind indicator which, importantly, helps the user in judging how far to wind. The half plate **movement**, which is fully signed and numbered, has a fusee, spring detent escapement and bimetallic balance. This has a duo-in-uno spring, a spring which has both spiral and helical coils, which both Walsh and John Hammersley (Plate 266) employed quite extensively, a few others just occasionally. Walsh's obituary in the September 1893 issue of the *Horological Journal* was followed by a letter the next April from W.B. Crisp concerning the duo-in-uno spring and its invention by John McLennon.

According to Paul Chamberlain (*It's About Time*, pages 456-9, Richard R. Smith, New York, 1941),

Robert Gardner (1851-1931), '…the person who, above all others, could tell me the history of watch and chronometer making in London…' admired Arthur Paul Walsh and called him 'the prince of pocket chronometer making'. Chamberlain goes on: 'After Gardner's death I tried to get the one by Walsh Gardner carried but not soon enough…'.

PRIVATE COLLECTION

411

Plate 264. Hunt & Roskell, 156 New Bond Street, London, no. 13123.

Gold hunting case 56mm: HW incuse (Henry Webb), hallmarked 1877-8

Hunt and Roskell were important retailers at this time (John Culme, *Directory of Goldsmiths and Silversmiths*, Vol. 2, Antique Collectors' Club, 1987).

The fully signed and numbered minute repeating **movement** has the unusual combination of a lever escapement and a helical free-sprung balance spring. Helical springs are generally found, of course, on watches with detent escapements. The ratchet-tooth lever escapement is at right angles in the normal manner, but it is beautifully finished, and the lever is with a particularly long arm and counterpoised, reminiscent of the work of John Poole. Much of the chronograph mechanism is on the top plate.

The **dial** has the subsidiaries for continuous seconds and minute recording at nine and three o'clock – a more visually satisfying layout than at six and twelve. The centre sweep seconds hand is started, stopped and returned to zero via the push in the **case** band at twelve. Each of the covers has a single lip moulding (see pages 380-381). The hand-set olivette is by the pendant and the repeating slide is at six.

PRIVATE COLLECTION

Plate 265. Charles Frodsham, 84 Strand, London, no. 05521, AD Fmsz.

Gold hunting case 57mm: AS in rectangular cameo (Alfred Stram), hallmarked 1877-8

Perpetual calendar watches always command attention, not only for their practicality, but for their attractive dials which bear witness to the complicated and necessarily well-made mechanism beneath.

The **dial** has the normal layout – a four year monthly calendar which takes into account the leap year at twelve, days of the week at nine, date at three and moon phase and continuous seconds at six. The three-quarter plate **movement**, with a ratchet-tooth lever escapement, is fully signed and numbered. Vaudrey Mercer in his book *The Frodshams* (AHS, 1981) suggests the AD Fmsz is probably a simple code for AD 1850 using the company's name, F being for 1, m for 8, s for 5 and z for 0. This was the year it 'commenced' to make high quality watches.

The **case** is of high quality with well-defined mouldings to the covers (see page 381). The inner cover is engraved J. Court, Staveley, while his crest, a unicorn's head out of a ducal coronet, is engraved at the top of the arms on the front cover.

PRIVATE COLLECTION

Plate 266. John Hammersley, 14 Barclay Road, Fulham, London, no. 3682.
Silver case 54.6mm: JTW in oval cameo (James Thomas White), hallmarked 1881–2

Hammersley worked mainly for the trade, M.F. Dent and others. He is well known, justifiably, as a successful springer and adjuster. He supplied a number of deck watches to the Admiralty and signed a small number of pocket watches with his own name.

The half plate **movement** *ébauche* has the maker's mark J.P (Joseph Preston & Sons, Prescot). The layout is somewhat unusual; in particular the balance cock is raised and undercut for clearance. The finish to the train and detent escapement is quite superb, even the underside of the detent is 'black' polished. There is an excellent duo-in-uno balance spring (Plate 263), a close-up of which is included in Anthony Randall's entry for this watch in *Time Museum Catalogue of Chronometers*. Published in 1992, the catalogue was written before this part of the contents of the Illinois museum was dispersed in a series of auctions between 1999 and 2004.

Watches of this period are generally keyless. The fact that this is key wound suggests that it was intended to be a deck watch (or similar), made the more probable by the unusual 13 to 24 hour zone engraved and filled with blue enamel on the reflector inside the front bezel of the **case**. The signed enamel **dial** has an up and down state of wind indicator below twelve and subsidiary seconds above six.

Actual size.

PRIVATE COLLECTION

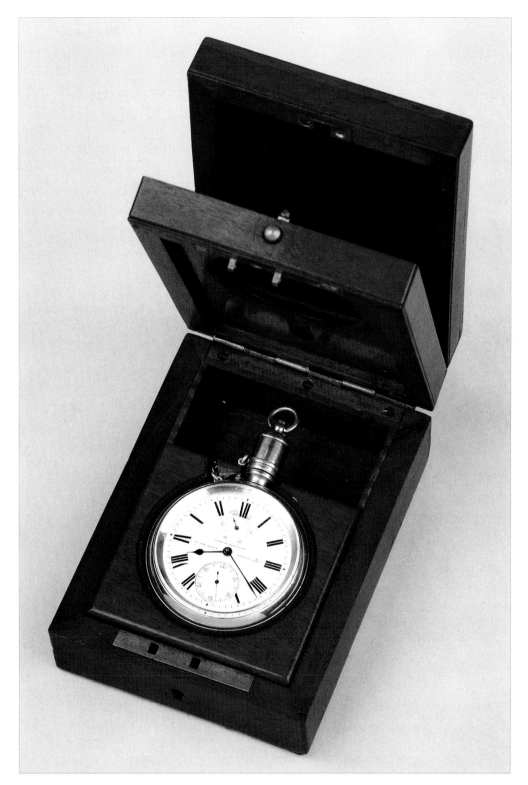

Plate 267. Lund & Blockley, 42 Pall Mall, London, no. 2/1089.
Silver 'watertight' case 59mm: PW oval cameo (Philip Woodman), hallmarked 1884-5, three tier mahogany box.

Lund & Blockley and their successor Herbert Blockley sold these 'travellers" type deck watches, the majority made for them by Usher & Cole of Clerkenwell, from the late 1870s right up until about 1925. A watch by this firm (Plate 275) shows the 'watertight' (so described in the supplier's extant workbooks) characteristics of the **case**, a leather-lined screw back and cap over the pendant. By far the largest single buyer was the Royal Geographical Society to whom Lund & Blockley and their successor sold some twenty-eight or so. The Society, who purchased a total of about forty of these watches, lent them to their members for Polar expeditions and journeys to the African sub-continent including some of the most famous ones. A number of extant Usher & Cole catalogues, printed before 1910, used the term 'travellers' watch while, in the same period, S. Smith & Son described it as an 'RGS explorers' and 'travellers' watertight' watch. A few were also sold by firms such as Brockbank & Atkins, Frodsham and Dent.

The fully signed and numbered **movement** *ébauche* was supplied by the Lancashire Watch Company. It was then 'made up' for Lund & Blockley, probably by Usher & Cole. It is an 18 size half plate fusee with ratchet-tooth lever escapement. A table giving inch equivalents of the Lancashire movement size is to be found in F.J. Britten's *Watch and Clock Makers' Dictionary and Guide* (Spon, 1896). The **dial** is also signed and has a large subsidiary seconds ring and an up and down state of wind indicator.

PRIVATE COLLECTION

415

Plate 268. Charles Frodsham, 84 Strand, London, no. 06836 AD Fmsz.
Silver case 68mm: GJT incuse (George James Thickbroom), hallmarked 1884-5

A large silver cased two day chronometer of quite exceptional quality, this is one of a series of twenty-two Frodsham put through their workshops over a period of some forty years of which eleven are known to be extant. The first two, rather different from the rest, were sold around 1856-7. These were followed some twenty-five years later by the present watch and a group of four of which number 07324 (Plate 269) is a part. The remainder were finished in three small groups in the late 1880s and 1890s.

Research in the 1980s by T. Woodcock at The College of Arms established the arms beautifully executed in enamel on the back of the **case** – which has gold

Actual size.

hinges – as belonging to the Weare family of Devonshire. More specifically, bearing in mind the hallmark date, they belong to Lieutenant General Sir Henry Edwin Weare (subsequent research has discounted his nephew).

The silvered **dial**, with blued spade hands, is signed below the up and down state of wind indicator, numbered above the subsidiary seconds and engraved with medallions announcing awards and appointments at nine and three.

The entry in Frodsham's manufacturing records held at the Guildhall Library gives the names of the various specialists who completed the 32 size **movement** *ébauche* purchased from Joseph Preston & Sons, Prescot. The top plate is signed, numbered and engraved much as the dial and in a similar manner to the watch in Plate 269. The spring detent escapement with a helical spring and bimetallic screw balance is of the same outstanding quality. PRIVATE COLLECTION

417

Plate 269. Charles Frodsham, 84 Strand, London, no. 07324 AD Fmsz.

Silver case 68mm: GJT (George James Thickbroom), hallmarked 1885-6, three tier mahogany box

To exactly the same specification as the watch shown in Plate 268, Frodsham number 07324 is complete with a three tier mahogany deck box. The company's sales books – as opposed to the workbooks – are missing, but it was almost certainly purchased for use on a private yacht. There was at the time, of course, a great enthusiasm for competitive yacht racing on a grand scale. Another watch in this very special series of deck watches, number 07622, has RYS *Valhalla* on the box lid escutcheon; her owner, the Edinburgh astronomer John Lindsay, 26th Earl of Crawford, was a member of the prestigious Royal Yacht Squadron.

The **case** has gold hinges to the back and bezel. The engraved and silvered **dial** is signed and numbered, has a 54 hour up and down winding indicator, subsidiary seconds with 'By appointment to the Queen' in a semicircle above and medallions showing appointments and awards. The **movement**, wound and set through an inner cover, is similarly engraved and has a fusee, spring detent escapement, bimetallic screw balance and helical spring.

PRIVATE COLLECTION

Plate 270. John Hammersley, 14 Barclay Road, Fulham, London, no. 1/3097.

Gold case 49mm: HG in oval cameo (Henry Green), hallmarked 1885-6

The famous Parisian watchmaker A-L. Breguet introduced the *montre à tact* right at the end of the eighteenth century; Hammersley has used the same basic idea. The hand mounted on the back of the **case** is free to be turned until it arrives at a stop, a point governed by the movement, and the time can be read, or rather assessed, against the touch pieces on the case band. Clearly the system would be invaluable to someone who is blind or someone who wishes to find out the time with the utmost discretion. The cover, which has a cut-out to allow for the linkage between the hand and the movement, records the election of W.G. Ainsie as a Member of Parliament for Lancashire in December 1885. Heaven forbid that, in wanting to know the time, he should put another Member off his speech!

The mechanism for the *à tact* hand, mounted on the **movement** top plate, incorporates a ratchet system and is linked to the motion work of the standard hands and their setting. There is a going barrel and free-sprung ratchet-tooth lever escapement. The full signature and number is engraved together with 'Highest Award Diploma of Honour Inventions 1885' – a reference to the maker's success at the Inventions Exhibition of that year. The **dial** and hands are very typical of the period.

Breguet used his invention quite frequently but few others took it up. It is difficult to recall any English maker other than J.F. Cole to do so – that is apart from Hammersley with this example. PRIVATE COLLECTION

Plate 271. Charles Frodsham, 84 Strand, London, no. 07468 AD Fmsz.

Gold case 54mm: HMF in cameo (Harrison Mill Frodsham), hallmarked 1886-7

The crest and motto on the back of the **case** are those of Sir Andrew Noble (1831-1915), world authority on explosives and chairman of Armstrong Whitworth & Company 1900-1915.

The back of the **dial** has the name Willis, the foremost dial maker of his day, and is slightly off-white, a colour he advertised as 'Venetian'. Frodsham's signature is within a sixty minute chronograph recording subsidiary below twelve and there is a continuous seconds ring at six. The split chronograph hands, one blued steel the other gold, may be started together, stopped and returned to zero via the winding button, the gold hand being split and returned by a push at two o'clock in the case band. The nib-piece at eleven is for engaging the hand-set.

The signed and numbered **movement** was supplied to Frodsham by Nicole Nielsen of Soho Square, London. The winding and chronograph mechanism, much of which is mounted on the top plate, is typical of their work (see Vaudrey Mercer, *The Frodshams*, AHS, 1981 for the Nicole's single chronograph patent). The balance of the ratchet-tooth lever escapement has a wishbone micrometer regulator, the small cock by the centre being engraved with a slow/fast indication for the micrometer screw.   PRIVATE COLLECTION

Plate 272. J. W. Benson, 25 Old Bond Street, London, no. 52110.

Gold case 52mm: E.W rectangular cameo (Edgar Wilkins), hallmarked 1890-1

James W. Benson, successful retailers, acquired the business of Hunt & Roskell in 1889. They purchased some of their best watches from the manufacturer Victor Kullberg: this is an excellent example of the best quality English half plate fusee pocket chronometer with the up and down and subsidiary seconds in the most popular positions. Kullberg signed them for Benson in the normal way with, in any event on most occasions, a zero added to their own number sequence.

Kullberg's workbooks, owned by the Clockmakers' Company and held at the Guildhall Library, record some details of the manufacturing process and the suppliers. The white enamel **dial** with subsidiary seconds at nine and up and down state of wind indicator at three was supplied by Willis. He and the hand maker, Hood, are regarded as the best of their day.

The half plate **movement** has a reverse fusee, spring detent escapement and a 'standing' detent (north/south when the watch is being worn, the favoured position) and helical spring. The 'examining' – an all important part of the process – was carried out by Peter Wennerstom, Kullberg's nephew and, after 1890 when he died, his successor in the business. My father's excellent and lucid – dare I say – summary of the manufacturing process and the responsibility of the examiner are given on pages 291-293 of *The Camerer Cuss Book of Antique Watches* (Antique Collectors' Club 1976 and subsequent editions).

The recorded weight of the 18 carat gold hunting **case**, the covers with well-defined mouldings (see pages 380-381), is 2 troy ounces, 16 pennyweight 13 grains (87.93 grams). The winding mechanism is disengaged when the cover closes upon a nib by the bezel at four: the hands can be set when this nib is fully depressed.

PRIVATE COLLECTION

Plate 273. A. Ericsson, St. Petersburg, no. 61.

Silver case 62mm: F.T oval cameo (Fred Thoms), hallmarked 1891-2

Victor Kullberg supplied over 130 deck chronometers (and many more marine chronometers) to Ericsson, the vast majority having 24 size full plate movements. Number 61 is no exception, but it is an early and, having a twenty-four hour dial, an unusual example. As the watch signed J.W. Benson 52110 (Plate 272), it appears in Kullberg's workbooks (with the number 5347).

The **dial** is made by Willis. The state of wind indicator is small enough to avoid the twenty-four hour Arabic chapters; marking the large seconds ring through them would have been quite an exercise! The **movement**, with a reverse fusee, is much like a marine chronometer's, only miniaturized. The superb two-arm bimetallic balance, set across the top plate, has gold screws and helical spring, and the spring detent escapement is between the plates. The other side of the pillar plate, below the dial, is stamped with the *ébauche* maker's mark J.P (Joseph Preston & Sons) beneath 24x7 (the Lancashire size) and 5347 (Kullberg's number). The back of the **case**, which has gold hinges, is engraved B. T. O. N. together with the fractional number 125/18058.

PRIVATE COLLECTION

Plate 274. John Taylor, Rochdale, no. 2093.

Silver case 59mm: C.H in rectangular cameo (Charles Harris, Coventry), hallmarked Chester 1892-3

The centre sweep hand rotates every two seconds, the **dial** being marked for each second in sixteenths, each with quarter divisions. 'Williams Patent No. 4762' is in a semicircle, 'Sole Maker, John Taylor Rochdale' below. There is a normal subsidiary seconds ring and gold spade hands. The patent (with a diagram) was dated March 1890. The patentee took out two previous patents – the first provisional – in 1881 (323) and 1883 (4496).

The **movement** is signed in the same manner as the dial and numbered. It has been suggested that the engraved mark consisting of two facing arrows in the centre of the top plate can be associated with Coventry work. The straight-line ratchet-tooth lever escapement beats sixteen times a second. A start/stop whip acts on a roller mounted on the staff of the plain three-arm balance, the whip being operated by a slide in the case band. The pendant has the same maker's mark as the **case**.   PRIVATE COLLECTION

Plate 275. Usher & Cole Ltd., London, no. 28968.

Silver 'watertight' case 59mm: no marks (Philip Woodman, modified Fred Thoms)

The extant workbook record shows that this was originally sold as a keyless going barrel deck watch to the Admiralty in March 1893 for £16.0.0, repurchased in May 1929 for £6.0.0, and converted to a 'travellers" watch to be resold a month later in a new box for £18.10.0 to R. Ogle Esq. Another watch, 28613, was repurchased in 1925 and modified to the same specification and then sold to the retailers J.W. Benson.

The workbook records the various costs involved and the men employed. Of course, Philip Woodman's mark would have been in the original back of the **case** together with the hallmark which was changed, as the records indicate, by Thoms (1862-1930) in May 1929. It is unclear whether or not some of the original was used. Certainly the gold hinge joints would have had to have been removed and a new back and bezel with screw threads fitted to the existing body, this also with screw threads and leather seals, together with a new pendant with screw cap.

The 18 size (see Plate 267, Lund & Blockley) three-quarter plate going barrel **movement** *ébauche* was supplied by the Lancashire Watch Company. It has a ratchet-tooth lever escapement with a free-sprung bimetallic balance. The signed top plate retains the Admiralty's engraved broad arrow mark. This mark is also to be found within the **dial's** subsidiary seconds ring. Unlike the Lund and Blockley which has a fusee, this watch has a going barrel and there is no state of wind indicator. PRIVATE COLLECTION

Plate 276. Charles Frodsham, 115 New Bond Street, London, no. 07659.
Gold case 58mm: HMF in cameo (Harrison Mill Frodsham), hallmarked 1897–8

Of generous proportions, this watch has a very pleasing 'feel' in the hand. The signed and numbered **dial** has all the quality, sober proportions and clarity associated with the work of the firm T.J. Willis during the last few years of the nineteenth and the beginning of the twentieth centuries. The blued spade hands are also in excellent proportion with the dial. The **case** has all the qualities of the very best of this period: a flat 'crystal' glass, well-defined mouldings to the front bezel and back, and a tapered olivette (see Glossary).

   The three-quarter plate going barrel **movement** – in the company's records the *ébauche* supplied by Haswell - has a ratchet-tooth lever escapement. It is numbered and signed with the address and also with 'Late of 84 Strand' and 'By appointment to the Queen'. Charles Frodsham moved addresses 1896-7.

PRIVATE COLLECTION

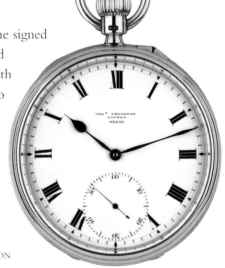

Actual size.

427

Plate 277. Charles Frodsham, 115 New Bond St, London, no. 08759 AD Fmsz.
Gold case 53mm: HMF in cameo (Harrison Mill Frodsham), hallmarked 1899–1900

The beautifully painted enamel arms on the back of the **case** belong to the Sandford family.
There is a minute repeating slide in the band at three, chronograph button at eleven and
set-hand olivette at one.

The signed **dial**, by Willis, has continuous seconds at three and 60 minute
chronograph recording at nine. The centre sweep seconds hand is started, stopped and
returned to zero via the three-pressure action chronograph button on the case band.

The three-quarter plate **movement** is signed and numbered in the same manner as
number 07659 (Plate 276), making reference to the company's previous address. It was
supplied by Nicole, Nielsen & Co. who have used a Swiss *ébauche*, fitted the ratchet-tooth
lever escapement, balance and cock, and carried out some of the finishing. Much of the
chronograph mechanism is on the top plate, the minute repeating beneath the dial and between
the plates. One hammer can be seen next to the balance cock.

PRIVATE COLLECTION   *Actual size.*

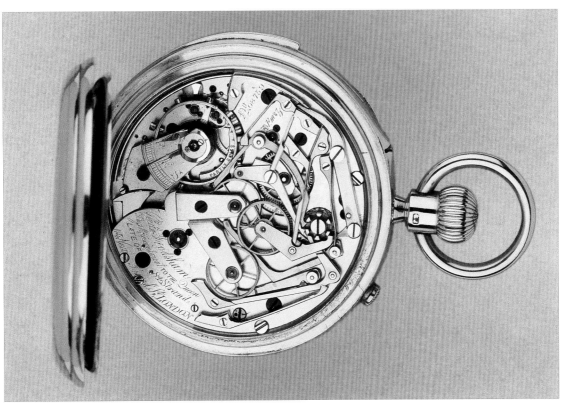

January 9th 1900 £31 16 5
1901 £26

The owner of this watch. G. Aborland
46 Avenue de Bretenil Paris
Alfred Clark. Feb. 20th 1901
Sent to Exhibition Paris

Order B., Page No.

Fol. in L., No.

Fol. in L., No.

	DATE OF ORDER.	18 : WHEN WANTED.	WHEN DELIVERED,		
	MANF. NO. 6261	DESCRIPTION.	TO WHOM SENT.	L.	
Movement	Movement	P.K.t Chron: fusee 18 size	Preston Dec. 18th 96	1	
	Fusee depth		Foster March 21 96		1 6
Esc. Jewelling	Escapement		Wilde July 14th 96	4 5	
Main Spring	Esc. Jewelling		Milligan June 96		10 6
Esc. W. & Stns.	Balance				16
Balance Aux.	Automatic stop		Lundquist Feb. 17th 99 materials		18
Balance Ord.	Keyless on Plate		Lundquist March 3	1	15 10
Escapement Pivoting	Case Work		" Oct 10th 98	1	10
Planting	Dial	N.K.	Willis April 7th 97		11
Stud	Case	Dome crystal hunter loose circle weight 3 . 14 . 16 fach. £2.	Thoms.	— — —	8 6.
Brass box	H. Circle		Wilde & Roberts	14	9 9.
Finishing	Eng. Turning				
Chain	Monogram				1
Jewelling	Spr. Case				
Cutting, &c.	Pinning up		Guimebert 21st 98		5
Balance Spring	spotting barrel & fusee wheel		Dean Nov. 12th 98		2 3.
Springing	Polishing off				
Timing	Motion				2 8
Examining	Index				
Hands	Finishing		Lawrence Oct. 22 98	2	10.
Box	M. Spring		Colton Oct: 7th 98		1
Cymbling	Chain		Harwell Oct 24th 98		1 3
Eng. Dial	Jewelling	3 d 4 centro & fusee	Milligan Oct: 7th 98	1	6
„ Name	Engraving »	N.K.	Clare. Jan. 16th 1901		7 9.
„ Tablets	Gilding		Johnson Oct 99 Ripodown Nov. 18th 98		1
„ Badges	Hands	double spades .	Hood. Oct. 25th 98.		2 6
Winder	Glass	Lundquist Jan. 25th 1901 10/			6
Outside Box	Examining	Tyler gilding top plate Jan. 21st 1901 4/- Lundquist gilt top & C. Colton 5/4 6/20	Lundquist	3	14
	Morocco Case	Tyler gilt top plate March 1900 4/ Balance spring dec. 98 . Ramberg	Robinson Feb 14th 90		16
Sundries	Sundries	Sills hooking on spring Feb 14th 97			1

Plate 278. Victor Kullberg, 105 Liverpool Road, London, no. 6261.
Gold case 57mm: F.T in oval cameo (Fred Thoms), hallmarked 1899–1900

Kullberg's workbooks, now owned by the Trustees of Clockmakers' Company Museum (the page opposite illustrated with their courtesy), indicate that this watch was shown at the Paris Exhibition of 1900, that immediately afterwards the top plate was engraved with the new awards and re-gilded, and that it was then delivered to a Frenchman, G. Aborlard, in February 1901. The workbook details the watch's progress, starting as a movement 'P.K.t chron: fusee 18 size' *ébauche* being delivered in 1896 by Joseph Preston & Sons, then the suppliers and outworkers – with the dates, costs and so forth. The half hunter **case** weighing 3 troy ounces, 14 pennyweight and 15 grains (116.05 grams), made by Thoms, was delivered as a 'dome crystal hunter lose circle'. He charged £2 for fashioning. The charge of 3/6 from Wilde and Roberts was presumably for engraving and enamelling the circle with a half-hunter chapter ring, this then screwed, as now, to the case.

The half plate reverse fusee keyless **movement** has a spring detent escapement with a 'standing' detent and helical spring. Kullberg had his firm plant the detents so that they were in the most favourable position when the watch is being worn (and the pendant vertical) – that is on the north/south axis. The detent is largely hidden behind an arm of the balance in the photograph – see Plate 272. A narrow steel cock running parallel to the balance cock holds the detent banking stud. The signed and numbered top plate records various diplomas and medals and is engraved 'Grand Prix Paris 1900'. The **dial** supplied by Willis has the seconds at nine and the up and down state of wind subsidiary at three. The winding mechanism is disengaged when the cover is closed upon a nib by the bezel at four: the hands can be set when this nib is fully depressed.

PRIVATE COLLECTION

Plate 279. S. Smith & Son, 9 Strand, London, no. 302-14.
Gold case 58mm: SS rectangular cameo (Samuel Smith) m below incuse, hallmarked 1901-2

Smith & Son were important, largely retail, jewellers, silversmiths, watch and clockmakers. They sold some fine watches and are especially well known for their tourbillon watches, watches where the escapement is mounted on a revolving carriage in order to even out its positional errors. The most normal period of rotation for the carriage is one minute – as in this example which was at one time in the Plaut Collection (number 102).

The signed and numbered **movement**, also engraved with 'Makers to the Admiralty and the Indian Government', has a fusee and ratchet-tooth lever escapement. The escape wheel pinion turns about the fixed fourth wheel whose arbor is free to turn the carriage once in a minute. Reinhard Meis in his comprehensive book *Das Tourbillon* (Richter, 1986) – also translated as *Le Tourbillon* (Editions de l'Amateur, 1990) – identifies Nicole, Nielsen & Co. of Soho Square as being, almost certainly, the movement supplier. He has a diagram of the movement on page 57, of the carriage (Nielsen type 1) on page 47 and illustrates a watch by S. Smith & Son, number 302-41 on pages 208 and 209. He has concluded that Smiths sold about twenty–five tourbillons.

The off-white 'Venetian' **dial** certainly looks to have been made by T.J. Willis. It is fully signed below a small state of wind indicator. The **case**, with well-defined mouldings to the bezel and back (see pages 380-381), has a flat 'crystal' glass and a long tapered olivette. There is a revolving pendant (see page 380).

PRIVATE COLLECTION

Plate 280. Richard Thorneloe, 13 Stanton St. Coventry, no. 57075.

Silver case 57mm: W.B in rectangular cameo (William Bullock, Coventry), London hallmark for 1902-3, two tier mahogany box

This watch 'headed the list' at the Greenwich Observatory trial for the period 18 June 1904 and 7 January 1905. The twenty-nine week trials were undertaken on behalf of the Admiralty who paid considerably more for those watches which were well placed. Many watches failed the test. To 'head the list' was a great feather in the cap for the craftsman concerned as well as being of significant financial benefit. These trials were equally stringent and rather more prolonged than the tests at the Kew Observatory summarised on pages 384 and 385.

The signed and numbered **movement** has a 34 minute karrusel carriage for, most unusually, a spring detent escapement with bimetallic balance and free-sprung spiral spring with overcoil. Of course, the Admiralty broad arrow mark on the movement was engraved after the watch was acquired, hence the poor gilding. Bahne Bonniksen, a Dane, who spent most of his life in Coventry, took out his karrusel patent (number 21421) in 1892. On most karrusels the carriage, mounted on a wheel driven off the third wheel pinion, revolves every 52½ minutes (the escape wheel is separately driven) but, so that the centre second hand could be fitted, Bonniksen also produced a modified design where the carriage revolves every 34 minutes. This was preferred by navigators. The advantage of detent escapement is that, in showing dead-beat half seconds, the hand will land on the main division on every other movement: the subsidiary fifth-second markings on the **dial** are only applicable if a lever escapement is fitted. The book by Reinhard Meis referred to in Plate 279 has two explanatory diagrams (page 62-3, figure 94) of a 34 minute karrusel with a lever escapement.

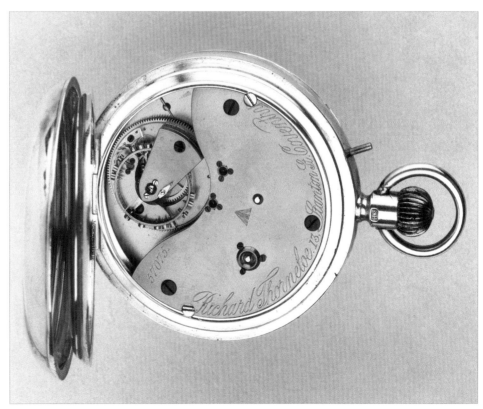

The **case** pendant and hand-set nib are longer than the norm so that they can fit in the cut-outs provided for them in the open brass drum of the mahogany deck box.

PRIVATE COLLECTION

433

Plate 281. Charles Frodsham, 115 New Bond Street, London, no. 08920 AD Fmsz.
Gold case 62mm: HMF in cameo (Harrison Mill Frodsham), hallmarked 1902–3, original
presentation box

One of a very special group of watches which J. Pierpont Morgan, banker – and collector of
watches – purchased over a number of years and gave to close friends: a minute repeating keyless
lever tourbillon with a split second chronograph, the inner cover simply engraved 'W.G.H. from
J.P.M. 1903'. William Gould Harding became Governor of the Federal Reserve Board in 1916.

The superb **case** is the ultimate in English case making of the period. It has a flat 'crystal' glass,
a very slightly half-round band and well-defined mouldings to the front bezel and back. There is a
long tapered olivette for the hand-set, the hinges have five knuckle joints and there is a revolving
pendant. The signed and numbered off-white 'Venetian' enamel **dial**, supplied by T.J. Willis, has
generous subsidiaries for 60 minute chronograph recording at nine and continuous seconds at
three. The centre second hand is started, stopped and returned to zero via the winding button, the

split hand with a push in the case at eleven.

The **movement** was supplied by Nicole, Nielsen & Co. who used a Swiss *ébauche*. It is fully signed and numbered and engraved 'By appointment to the King'. Much of the chronograph mechanism is visible on the top plate. The minute repeating is operated by a slide in the case band. The ratchet-tooth lever escapement has a spiral spring with terminal curve and bimetallic balance and the tourbillon carriage and cock are steel. Reinhard Meis, in his comprehensive book on tourbillons referred to in Plate 279, calls the carriage Nielsen type 2.

THE DJANOGLY COLLECTION

Actual size.

Plate 282. Hector Golay, London, no. 2546.

Gold case 58mm: FT in oval cameo, London below incuse (Fred Thoms) A
above incuse, hallmarked 1902-3

Golay did not sign many of his watches, the majority of which he made for other
members of the trade, including Frodsham.

The **movement** of this minute repeating perpetual calendar chronograph is built
on a Swiss *ébauche*, but some components, such as the ratchet-tooth lever escapement,
balance and balance spring (this has a micrometer regulator) would have been made
in England. The quality of the gilding suggests this is certainly English and some at
least of the final finishing would have been done in London. The top plate is simply
numbered, the chronograph mechanism leaving little room for the signature.

The fine off-white 'Venetian' **dial**, signed below the moon phase, was made by
Willis. The four year monthly calendar, which takes leap years into account, is at
twelve, the days of the week at nine and date at three. These are adjusted via a steel
piece in the glazed bezel at eleven. At seven another moves the moon phase within
the continuous seconds ring. The three-pressure action (start, stop and return to
zero) chronograph is operated by a push in the case band when the front cover is
open. The sixty minute recording hand is within the perpetual calendar subsidiary.

The excellent **case** is by Thoms and typical of his work. He registered two
new marks to include London within the cameo in November and December
1902; for this case he seems to have added an incuse London to his previous
mark. The A above it, seen quite frequently on Thoms' cases, is thought to have
belonged to his foreman, Bamford. PRIVATE COLLECTION

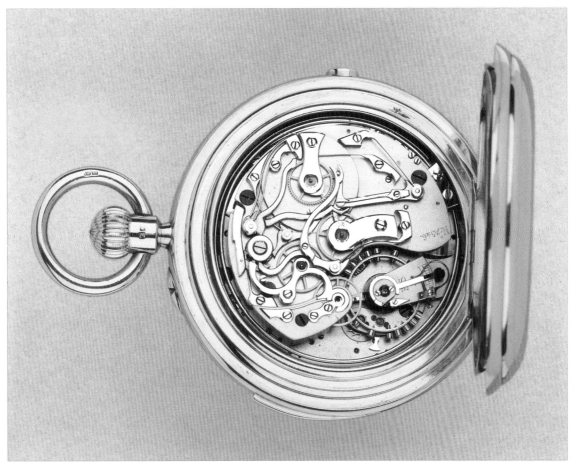

Plate 283. Carley & Clemence, 30 Ely Place, London, no. 51613.

Silver case 59mm: C&Co in oval cameo (Carley & Clemence Ltd) hallmarked 1903–4

Andrew Taylor took out patent number 16623 for his 'annular' tourbillon in September 1895. The name 'annular is derived from the patentee's description in which he refers to the ring of interior cut teeth fitted to the pillar plate as an 'annular wheel'. More expensive to make than the karrusel – effectively its rival in England – the annular tourbillon was not a commercial success. Probably less than a dozen were completed. The majority seem to have been sold to the Admiralty which suggests their performance was up to scratch.

The **movement**, which is jewelled to the centre, has the *ébauche* mark AT for Andrew Taylor on the dial side of the pillar plate. The top plate is signed over the raised barrel and numbered together with the Admiralty mark. The bridge and carriage are of brass and the ratchet-tooth lever escapement has a bimetallic balance and free-sprung spiral spring with a double overcoil. The **dial** is signed by the vendors. It has the Admiralty broad arrow mark, as does the back of the **case**.

Number 51619 is illustrated with the carriage disassembled in *Catalogue of Watches in the British Museum VI* (Anthony Randall and Richard Good, The Trustees of the British Museum, 1990). PRIVATE COLLECTION

Plate 284. Dent, 34 Cockspur Street, London, no. 32675.

Gold case 57mm: RN in rectangular cameo (Robert Benson North), hallmarked 1903-4

M.F. Dent sold a series of watches around this time which revived, or rather interpreted, an early nineteenth century combination case and dial design made popular by the Parisian watchmaker A-L. Breguet and occasionally employed in England at the time by such makers as Recordon and Vulliamy. Although these makers rarely set their numerals radially, others did (Plates 195 and 219), and others used cases made in a comparable style (Plates 226 and 242) but not in combination – or certainly not with the same overall effect. The inspiration for the revival may well have come from a renewed interest in Breguet's work.

The **dial**, which has a gold engine-turned centre, is fully signed below twelve on the radial Arabic chapter ring. There is a good pair of blued steel hands, of a style which probably falls into the collective 'spade' description, although the shape of the hour hand head is clearly ovoid. The **case** bezel and snap-on single back – plain but engraved with a monogram AN – have half-round lip mouldings over a plain flat or 'collar' band. The minute repeating three-quarter plate **movement**, supplied by Nicole, Nielsen & Co., has a ratchet-tooth lever escapement and is fully signed, numbered and engraved 'Watchmaker to her Late Majesty'.

PRIVATE COLLECTION   *Actual size.*

Plate 285. S. Smith & Son, 9 Strand, London, no. 309-2.
Gold case 77 x 25mm thick: SS in rectangular cameo (Samuel Smith), hallmarked 1903-4

Part and parcel of the efforts by the trade in England, and that in London in particular, to resist foreign competition and the effects of mass production was a flight towards exclusivity.

The Indian summer of watchmaking in England resulted in some quite remarkable watches of quality and complexity of which this is a fine and indeed exceptional example. For the

complexity the trade was assisted in no small part by small Swiss establishments whose survival also depended on quality.

The three-quarter plate **movement** of this *grande* and *petite sonnerie* striking two-train clock-watch repeats the minutes and has perpetual calendar and split-seconds chronograph. Swiss components are employed, but the ratchet-tooth lever escapement, bimetallic balance, diamond endstone (with double-overcoil spring and micrometer regulator), together with the finish and gilding and engraving of the plates at least would appear to have been done in England. The fact remains, not only did English makers import both finished and partly finished Swiss *ébauche*s at this time, quite frequently they also sent partly finished movements to Switzerland for repeating, striking and chronograph mechanisms to be fitted (to support this I have a letter-book containing copies of letters written in French by Usher & Cole, makers of Clerkenwell, to Montandon-Robert and Goy Baud, both of Geneva).

The quite remarkable and beautifully made **dial** is by the London dial maker Willis, his name being on the reverse. It is made up of ten separate pieces of gold and enamel. The gold hand indicates the date on the blue enamel annular ring, this between gold margins. The day and month are engraved on the gold subsidiaries at nine and three, these within the chronograph sixty minute and continuous seconds zones. Below twelve a gold dial indicates the four year cycle – including the leap year – within a state of wind sector. The split chronograph hands, one polished steel, the other blued, are counter-poised.

The high quality **case**, with a revolving pendant, has S. Smith & Son's registered mark and was made in London on

their behalf, possibly by Thoms. The chronograph hand is operated through the pendant with the split-hand push at eleven. Slides for strike/silent and strike selection are in the band together with a release slide for the repeating train.

The third edition of Smiths' very early nineteenth century fascinating 125 page catalogue was reprinted by Charles Allix, courtesy of Smiths Industries, in 1969 and again in 1978. This contains a technical description of the chronograph mechanism with illustrations.

PRIVATE COLLECTION

Actual size.

Plate 286. Jump, 93 Mount Street, London, no. m.x.e.j.

Platinum and gold case 49mm: no marks

Huyton Richard Jump was working for the firm of Vulliamy when Benjamin Lewis Vulliamy died in 1854 and its goodwill was acquired by Charles Frodsham. Jump joined two of his sons in business establishing Jump & Sons at 1a Old Bond Street in 1855. Although the ownership passed to the next generation, and the business moved premises over time – arriving at Mount Street in 1898 – it is not surprising the designs and styles it adopted continued the Vulliamy tradition, these broadly relating at times to those of the Parisian watchmaker A-L. Breguet. In his article for *Antiquarian Horology* (December 1983), in which he gives a well-researched history, Vaudrey Mercer suggests the coded numbering was introduced soon after the move to Mount Street. He has tabulated the code against known hallmarks in sequence; the preceding number to the present watch, m.x.e.i., has a case hallmarked for 1904.

Breguet's watches have always been highly prized, not least at the end of the nineteenth century when David Solomons formed his remarkable collection, and a few very high quality reproductions were made, this being an outstanding example. It is key-wound and, in the manner of Breguet, has a short chain and ratchet key with a female square for hand-set opposite a male winding square.

The **case** is very slim but it is remarkably heavy because the body, which has an engine-turned band, is of platinum. The pendant, bow, bezel and back are made of a slightly redder gold than is normal for an English watch, but is the same, or much the same, colour of gold that was used to make Breguet's cases. The back is bayonet fitted and rotates as a shutter to reveal the female winding square. The engine turning is very fine and, although the case is unmarked, it puts one in mind of those by James Ayres. This maker is known to have worked for Jump; indeed the case for the watch in Plate 291 is by him.

The silver engine-turned **dial** has engraved numerals and a signature on a polished offset ring. Above this is a moon phase while below a sector shows the date in gold; the adjustments for these are via gold push-pieces recessed in the case band. The half plate **movement** is signed together with the address, the coded number and, unusually, a further number – 4311. There is a ratchet-tooth lever escapement and bimetallic balance.

PRIVATE COLLECTION

Plate 287. J.W. Benson, 62 & 64 Ludgate Hill, London, no. 155.
Gold case 48mm: JWB in oval cameo (James William Benson), B below incuse, numbered 1250, hallmarked 1904-5

The fully signed and numbered **movement** is also engraved with 'By warrant to H.M. the late Queen Victoria' and 'Best London Make'. Benson, like many of his contemporary retailers, not only sold English watches, but also offered Swiss watches of similar exterior appearance at a lower price. Some sold American movements in English cases as well, again at a lower price. The customer had a choice but, if he could afford it, would have been encouraged to buy English when he was shown the movement. He

would have been reassured too, as no doubt he had heard that foreign watches were being passed off as English. The quality of the movement is certainly good. It is three-quarter plate with going barrel, has a ratchet-tooth lever escapement, bimetallic balance, spiral spring with overcoil, diamond endstone and is jewelled in settings to the third wheel. It is thought that, generally speaking, the star between the F and the S on the balance cock indicates Coventry movement manufacture.

The Arabic **dial** is of an attractive off-white colour which at the time was sometimes called 'Venetian'. The hour hand is a double-spade so that the time can be read through the lunette in the half-hunter cover of the **case**, this with dark blue enamel Arabic numerals. Both covers have a single lip moulding (see pages 380-381). The inner cover is engraved 'W. Perry W. Woodward', the back with his crest – a wolf's head between two rosettes. Private Collection

443

Plate 288. H. L. Brown & Son, London & Sheffield, no. 37918.

Gold case 52mm: F.T London in shaped cameo (Fred Thoms), A incuse above, hallmarked 1905-6

Exceptional, especially for an English watch, is that the fusee half plate **movement** is made of nickel silver and the wheel train of a gold alloy. It is jewelled to the centre, these with gold settings. The lever is also gold, the ratchet-tooth escape wheel brass. There is a bimetallic balance with micrometer regulator, spiral spring and diamond endstone. The top plate is signed and numbered and engraved 'Maker to the Admiralty'. Nickel silver is an alloy less liable to tarnish than brass; it generally consists of 50% copper, 30% zinc and 20% nickel.

The high quality **dial**, signed and with a state of wind indicator, is a classic example of the type at this period. It is 'Venetian' white with the hour numerals quite strong, condensed and closer to the edge of the dial than hitherto.

The **case** mark has an A above, a mark which is thought to belong to Thoms' foreman, Bamford. The olivette for the set-hand is at four, while a push-piece at two engages the winding mechanism. Both covers have well-defined mouldings and there is a revolving pendant.

Brian Loomes (*Watchmakers and Clockmakers of the World*, vol. 2, N.A.G. Press, 1976) records Harris Leon Brown, Sheffield, for 1871. This appears to have been a successful retailing business. The Clerkenwell makers Usher & Cole supplied them with a repeating chronograph (their number 28180) in October 1894, especially signed and numbered 26515.

PRIVATE COLLECTION

Plate 289. Nicole, Nielsen & Co. 14 Soho Square, London, no. 12184.

Gold case 56mm: RN in rectangular cameo (Robert Benson North), hallmarked 1905-6

Although they were an important part of the London trade, and supplied well-known firms such as Frodsham, M.F. Dent, E. Dent & Co. and others, Nicole, Nielsen & Co. signed relatively few watches for themselves. Much of their output, and this two-train full and quarter striking clock-watch is an example, was based on *ébauches* imported from Switzerland but, for the Frodsham in Plate 292, for instance, they used a Prescot *ébauche*.

The fully signed and numbered three-quarter plate **movement** is jewelled to the centre and has a ratchet-tooth lever escapement with a bimetallic balance. A further number, 9533, is on the dial side of the pillar plate. The two trains, one for going and one for gong striking, are wound in opposite directions. A lever beneath the front bezel at four selects either full strike (the hours and, at the quarters, both the hours and quarters) or quarter strike (the hours and quarters only). These are often termed *grande* and *petite* striking (or *sonnerie*) respectively. A strike/silent lever is at nine.

Apart from nib-pieces for lifting front bezel and back, to give access to the strike levers and movement and, of course, the olivette for the hand-set, the **case** is perfectly smooth. This is a true bassine (bascine) style of case (see pages 380-381). The layout of the 'Venetian' white **dial**, which has the name Willis on the reverse, is typical of the best of the period. There is a good arcaded signature.

PRIVATE COLLECTION

Actual size.

Plate 290. William Douglas, Stourbridge, no. 19076.
Silver case 56mm: inner cover T.C in cameo (Thomas Cleaver or Thomas Cobb), hallmark rubbed
(probably London 1906-7), pendant CH in cameo (Charles Hill) hallmarked 1900-1, back ATO
(Albert Thomas Oliver) hallmarked 1937-8

William Henry Douglas (1837-1913), a working watchmaker of Stourbridge, Worcestershire,
registered eleven patents of which no less than seven are relevant to this watch. The first is a
chronograph patent dated June 1880 (number 2500), and the last for a karrusel – or, as he termed
it, 'a tourbillion' – the application dated March 1906, this accepted January 1907 (number 6858).
He claimed '…The object of this invention is to provide for the arrangement of a tourbillion with
an ordinary watch… without any material modification… and for the convenient combination
with the same as a chronograph…'.

The Admiralty purchased the watch for £25 in October 1909. Records held at the Maritime
Museum, Greenwich, show that number 19076 spent much of the First War going back and forth
between the Admiralty and Usher & Cole Ltd., watchmakers in Clerkenwell (Douglas retired in

1911). It was issued to H.M.S. *Cyclops* in May 1918 which, together with H.M.S. *Victorious*, was based at Scapa Flow to assist in the fitting of the Dreyer firing system to all Dreadnought battleships. A chronograph was essential when testing the behaviour of shells in flight at long range in all weather conditions at different speeds.

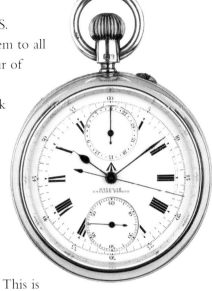

The **dial**, signed 'Douglas, English Patent', has the Admiralty broad arrow mark and is calibrated to the nearest fifth of a second for the centre seconds chronograph hand. Up to thirty minutes are recorded anti-clockwise on the subsidiary below twelve and continuous seconds are shown above six. The three-pressure action chronograph mechanism, operated through the pendant, is mounted on the **movement** backplate. This is numbered below the Admiralty mark but is unsigned. The carriage for the ratchet-tooth lever and free-sprung bimetallic balance rotates every 34 minutes. The patent of 1906 provides for a one hour rotation on watches without chronograph.

Actual size.

Only one other watch of this type, also signed by Douglas, is known to exist. This is numbered 1909 and was also supplied to the Admiralty. A number of chronographs by him without the karrusel are recorded. One, based on an 18 size *ébauche* purchased from the Lancashire Watch Company in 1906, is signed by Usher & Cole and numbered 30459. It was given a gold case made by Philip Woodman and sold in January 1912.   PRIVATE COLLECTION

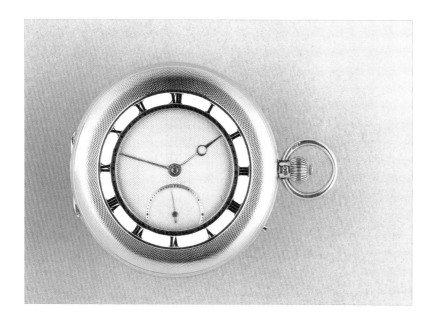

Plate 291. Jump, 93 Mount Street, London, no. m.x.g.v.

Gold case 45mm: J.A in oval cameo (James Ayres) hallmarked 1909-10

A brief outline of this firm is given with another watch by Jump in Plate 286. Although to quite different specifications, these watches share similar characteristics. The **dials**, especially the narrow Roman figured chapter rings, both signed 'Jump, London', and the engine-turned centres are very similar. So too are the gold moon hands, although for this watch the hour has two moons, one for showing through the large half-hunter cover.

The slim **cases** are of the same, slightly reddish gold and have the same fine engine-turning. Jump was fond of especially large lunettes or 'sights' for his half-hunter covers, these with a narrow enamel ring of numerals on an opaque ground. The edges of the keyless three-quarter plate going barrel signed and numbered **movement** are made to follow the shape of the case. The tail of the right-angled lever is slotted to make for resilient banking within a counter-sink. The teeth of the gold escape wheel are made for divided lift and the bimetallic balance has a spring with a terminal curve and there is a ruby endstone. PRIVATE COLLECTION

Plate 292. Charles Frodsham, 115 New Bond Street, no. 09299 AD Fmsz.

Gold case 57mm: HMF in oval cameo (Harrison Mill Frodsham), hallmarked 1909-10

An example of the outstanding quality English horologists were still producing just before the First War showing that, as the dial demonstrates, they were still alive to attractive and unusual designs.

The remarkably heavy high quality **case** has a five joint hinge, revolving pendant and an attractively tapered olivette. The silvered **dial**, with engraved numerals and signature, has a recessed up and down state of wind sector. Nicole Nielsen is recorded as supplying the **movement** which is based on an *ébauche* supplied by Joseph Preston & Sons, Prescot, Lancashire. It is half plate with a reverse fusee and the full signature includes engraved medallions on the raised barrel. There is a ratchet-tooth lever, bimetallic balance with diamond endstone, and the spring, with a double overcoil, is free-sprung. Squares on the fusee arbor and over the centre wheel allow the watch to be key-set (for setting-up and testing prior to casing and also if the keyless mechanism were to fail). The centre wheel is jewelled below the square.

PRIVATE COLLECTION

Plate 293. Dent, 61 Strand & 4 Royal Exchange, London, no. 57347.

Silver case 57mm: Dent within a triangle incuse (E. Dent & Co. Ltd. trademark), hallmarked 1909-10

A thirty-four minute centre seconds karrusel which scored 86.6 marks and gained a 'Class A Especially Good' test certificate (number 14580) at the National Physical Laboratory, Kew

Observatory, in July 1911. At one time it belonged to Cecil Clutton and is illustrated in his *Collector's Collection* (AHS, 1974).

The **case**, with a gold hinge, button and bow, has the trademark first used by E. Dent & Co in 1876. This mark is used as part of the signature on the slightly recessed centre of the **dial**, this calibrated in fifths for the sweep seconds hand. The trademark is used for the signature on the **movement** which is engraved with the address, number and 'Watchmaker to the King'. It is a Bahne Bonniksen *ébauche*, his punch mark – this includes his patent number – being on the inside of the pillar plate. Further information on this type of movement is given with the watch by Thorneloe, Plate 280.

The tests at Kew were made over forty-five days, divided into eight periods of five days each and five intermediate and extra days in four of which the watch was not rated. Watches were assessed first in vertical and then horizontal position at a range of temperatures. A summary of the conditions can be found on pages 384-385).

PRIVATE COLLECTION

Plate 294. Northern Goldsmiths, Newcastle-upon-Tyne, no. 2097.
Gold case 56mm: NGCo in cameo (Northern Goldsmiths Co), hallmarked 1918-9

Sidney Better, a Clerkenwell maker, made a small series of high quality one minute tourbillons for the Northern Goldsmiths Company. The original certificate for this watch shows that it was tested at the National Physical Laboratory, Kew, between 2 December 1919 and January 1920, and that it achieved the remarkable score of 92.2 marks with a 'Class A Especially Good' certificate.

The **movement** is fully signed and numbered for the retailer. It has a going barrel, Better's first style of steel cage, a club-tooth lever escapement, spiral spring and bimetallic balance. The pillar plate is stamped NG above Co in a rectangle and numbered 2097. The escapement is of Swiss origin.

The signed 'Venetian' white enamel **dial** is of the best quality, as is the hunter **case**. This has a glazed inner dome.

PRIVATE COLLECTION

Plate 295. George Daniels, London e.m.h.
Gold case 62mm: G.D in oval cameo (George Daniels),
hallmarked 1970

A retrospective exhibition of pocket and wrist watches made by George Daniels was held at Sotheby's, London, in July 2006. Their excellent catalogue, written by Andrew Crisford, illustrates and describes twenty-three superb pocket watches made by Daniels between 1968 and 1994. The movement signatures of the first eight are followed by the initials of the original owner, in the manner of a coded number. This, the fourth, was made for Edward Hornby whose well-known collection of antique watches was sold at Sotheby's, London in December 1978. Three watches from this collection are illustrated, that signed CWP Invt., possibly by Charles Goode (Plate 60), Fromanteel & Clarke (Plate 68) and John Arnold (Plate 168).

The engine-turned **case** has a single back and a Daniels bow. There are male squares for winding and hand-set at each end of the blued steel key, this attached to the watch with a short double-link chain. The silver engine-turned **dial** has a polished ring for minutes and sector for hours, the hour hand being retrograde. The signature is below the minute ring

and either side of the seconds subsidiary.

The **movement** has two going barrels, both engaging a common offset centre pinion. The Earnshaw-type spring detent escapement is on a steel one minute tourbillon carriage which has a steel bridge. There is a steel four-arm balance with gold adjusting weights, an overcoil spring and a screw for isochronal adjustment. In his introduction to the catalogue, Crisford notes that Daniels has altered the geometry of the chronometer escapement to overcome the tendency for the balance to stop, on occasions, when the wearer makes a sudden movement. Daniels' chronometer will always self-start because the escape wheel is always unlocked when the balance is in the quiescent position. Private Collection

Actual size.

GLOSSARY

This glossary includes some terms not used in the main text, but which are likely to be met with by those interested in the technical aspect of watches

ADJUSTED. A watch is said to be 'adjusted in 5 positions' if it has been rated in the two horizontal and three of the possible vertical positions – i.e. dial up, dial down, pendant up, pendant left, pendant right and pendant down. 'Adjusted for temperature' means that the compensation has been observed in at least three temperatures.

AFFIX. A small bimetallic blade, one end of which is fixed to the rim on the balance: used to correct the temperature compensating properties of the main compensating arrangement.

'ALL-OR-NOTHING' PIECE. In a repeating watch, a device which ensures that the striking is released only if the lever or push-piece for the repeating action is fully depressed. Without this mechanism, if the actuating lever or push-piece is insufficiently depressed an incorrect number of hours is sounded. With this improvement the watch has to strike *all* or *nothing.* Both Tompion and Quare incorporated it.

AMPLITUDE. The maximum angle by which a balance swings from its position of rest. By observing the arms of a balance it is possible to estimate this angle. See **ARC**.

ANTI-MAGNETIC. Unaffected by magnetism. If those parts of a watch most affected by a magnetic field (balance, balance spring and escapement) are made of non-magnetic materials the watch is termed 'anti-magnetic', although more strictly 'anti-magnetic' up to a specified strength of field. The earliest non-magnetic balance springs were gold as used by John Arnold.

ARBOR. The spindle, shaft or axle upon which the wheels of a watch train are mounted.

ARC. The arc of a balance is twice the amplitude (q.v.). A balance with an amplitude of 270 degrees has an arc of 540 degrees (1½ turns of the balance).

ATTACHMENT. The 'point of attachment' or 'pinning-point' is the point at which the balance spring is pinned to the collet on the balance staff.

AUXILIARY COMPENSATION. An additional and subsidiary compensation sometimes fitted to a bimetallic balance to eliminate the middle temperature error (q.v.).

BACK PLATE. See **TOP PLATE.**

BALANCE. A plain wheel with two or three spokes known as 'arms'. Coupled to its spring, the balance of a watch is the controlling device; its oscillation, its to and fro swinging properties, regularise the movement of the train powered by the mainspring, and hence the timekeeping ability of the watch.

A plain balance, or a monometallic balance, is an uncut ring, with or without timing screws. It may be made of brass, steel, gold, nickel or palladium. A modern alloyed metal such as 'Invar' or glucydur produces a balance which for all practical purposes is unaffected by temperature changes.

A 'compensated', cut bimetallic balance has its rim made of two metals of different coefficient of expansion (normally brass and steel) fused together. The rim is cut near each arm of the two-arm balance and is in two parts, each part with a fixed end and a free end. The free end moves inward or outward on a rise or fall (respectively) in temperature, thus altering the moment of inertia of the balance by shifting the mass of the rim closer to or away from the centre. This counteracts the effect of temperature changes upon the elasticity of the balance spring. Brass has a higher coefficient of expansion than steel and is on the outer side of the rim. Screws or weights on the balance rim enable the compensating property to be adjusted.

An 'unsprung balance' is a balance without a spring – i.e. before the introduction of the balance spring in 1675.

BALANCE COCK. See **COCK.**

BALANCE SPRING. A spiral or helical spring attached at its inner end to the balance staff and at its outer end to the balance cock or movement plate. The sprung balance regulates the timekeeping, the period of each swing depending upon the ratio of the moment of inertia of the balance to the stiffness or elasticity of the spring. The elasticity of any given spring depends basically upon the material from which it is made and upon its effective length.

Most springs were made of steel although other materials including gold were used. A steel spring will lose its elasticity in heat and become more 'springy' in cold. Methods for compensating for this were introduced in the later part of the 18th century using either bimetallic curbs or balances.

A helical spring, one formed into a helix, is normally found in conjunction with a detent escapement. John Arnold took out a patent for this in 1775. He discovered by empirical methods that isochronism could be achieved by a helical spring with the two terminal coils or ends incurved.

In 1796 A-L. Breguet introduced the equivalent arrangement, the overcoil, for spiral springs. The outermost – terminal – coil is raised over and incurved across the rest of the spring. See **ISOCHRONOUS, BALANCE** and **COMPENSATION CURB.**

BALANCE STAFF. The spindle or arbor upon which the balance is mounted.

BANKING PIN. With the verge escapement, a pin protruding from the outer edge of the balance. The extreme arc of balance swing is limited by stops on the balance cock, against which the pin would 'bank' if the arc were excessive.

In later escapements an equivalent provision is included and in the lever escapement the device of two banking pins is used to limit the angular movement of the lever. Occasionally, instead of two pins, banking takes place against walls forming part of the movement plate or of the pallet cock.

BAR. Bridge as distinct from a cock which has a foot by which it is secured to the movement plate.

BARREL (GOING). A cylindrical box (barrel) with a toothed disc (a wheel) on the outer edge. The disc is the 'great wheel' and the box contains the mainspring. The barrel (box) turns freely on its arbor, the mainspring being hooked to the barrel at its outer end and to the arbor at its inner end. The great wheel meshes with the first pinion of the watch train. In a watch movement with going barrel, the fusee (q.v.) is dispensed with. The barrel in fusee watches is a plain barrel without teeth.

In winding a going barrel, the barrel arbor is turned round, drawing the spring away from the rim of the box and coiling it round the arbor. A click and ratchet prevent the arbor from recoiling while the mainspring is being wound and when it is fully wound. The tensioned spring, in striving to 'unwind', expends its force in turning the barrel, this same force being utilised to drive the watch train via the great wheel. The barrel makes as many turns in unwinding, of course, as were given to the arbor in winding. See also **STOP-WORK** and **SET-UP.**

BARROW REGULATOR. An early form of regulator of balance spring watches. Two pins (curb pins), held upright in a slide, embrace the end section of the balance spring which is straight, not coiled. The slide moves along a worm (endless screw) which has a squared end to take a key. An index engraved on the movement plate indicates the amount the slide may be moved with the aid of a key, as the effective length of the spring is altered for regulation.

BASSE-TAILLE ENAMEL. Translucent enamel laid over a ground engraved to enhance the pictorial effect.

BASSINE. A type of watch case that is rounded on the edge and smooth.

BEETLE HAND. The type of hour hand of foliate design which faintly resembles a stag beetle.

BEZEL. In general terms the rim holding the glass.

BIMETALLIC. Formed of two metals, generally brass and steel, whose different coefficients of expansion are utilised for compensating the effects of temperature changes on a balance spring. See **BALANCE.** Mostly in the early 18th century, alternatively, a bimetallic strip, formed by riveting or fusing, was utilised, which bent under the influence of temperature changes. This strip was known as a compensation curb (q.v.).

BOTTOM PLATE. See **TOP PLATE.**

BOW. The metal ring hinged, pivoted or looped to the pendant (q.v.) of the watch case, by which the watch may be attached to a chain or fob.

BULL'S EYE GLASS. A flattened dome glass in shape, but with a small circular flat ground in the centre.

CALIBRE. The size and type of design of a watch movement. The term was used by Henry Sully in about 1715 to denote the dimensions and layout of a movement.

CAM. A part shaped with an irregular contour so as to give the requisite reciprocal irregular movement to a lever in contact with it.

CANNON PINION. A pinion, part of the motion work carrying the minute hand. Its hollow arbor, or pipe, is merely a friction fit on the centre wheel arbor, thus allowing the hand to be set.

CAP JEWEL. See **ENDSTONE.**

CENTRE WHEEL. The wheel, normally centrally planted, the arbor of which carries the cannon pinion and minute hand. See **TRAIN.**

CHAMPLEVE. An area of metal which has been hollowed out with a graver to take enamelling: *champlevé* enamel. A *'champlevé'* dial is a metal dial with portions removed to leave others standing proud of the main surface – i.e. the hour numerals and minute markings. The hollowed-out numerals are then filled with black or coloured wax, or pitch.

CHAPTER RING. The ring upon which the hours and minute graduations or half- and quarter-hour divisions are engraved. An alternative name is 'the hour ring'.

CHASING. Unlike engraving, metal is not removed but is pushed from one place to another and left in relief.

CHATELAINE. A chain for suspending a watch or piece of jewellery. In addition to the watch, the winding key, seals or other trinkets were often attached. Normally the decoration on the watch case is en suite with the decoration on the chatelaine. See also **FOB CHAIN.**

CHRONOGRAPH. A watch which, in addition to the time-of-day hands, has a centrally mounted seconds hand which can be started, stopped and returned to zero by means of a push-piece or slide. A subsidiary dial is provided which records the number of revolutions (each normally of a minute) made by the centre seconds or chronograph hand. See also **SPLIT-SECONDS.**

CHRONOMETER. Among English watchmakers and collectors, a chronometer is understood to be a watch or portable clock (hence a ship's, marine or box chronometer) which has a detent escapement (q.v.) although the use of the word preceded the detent escapement. Of recent years there has been a tendency – regretted by many – to use the word in the French or Swiss sense to indicate a watch which has obtained an official rating certificate issued by the observatories at Geneva or Neuchâtel. Etymologically, any instrument for measuring time.

CHRONOSCOPE. See **WANDERING HOUR DIAL.**

CLICK. A pawl or lever with a 'beak' which engages in the ratchet-shaped teeth of a wheel, it being under the tension of a spring, and pivoted. The usual purpose of a click, its spring and the ratchet wheel is to allow the wheel to turn in one direction only. On watches the ratchet wheel is fixed to the arbor of the mainspring barrel, thus enabling the mainspring to be wound; the tension of the mainspring is held up against the tensioned click. See **SET-UP.**

CLOCKMAKERS' COMPANY. The Worshipful Company of Clockmakers was granted its Royal Charter in 1631, with David Ramsay as its first Master. Prior to its incorporation, the craft of clock and watchmaking was controlled by the Blacksmiths' Company. In the City of London apprentices were admitted through the Guilds, and after they had served their term they were granted the freedom of the craft. The Clockmakers' Company had the right to regulate the manner, order and form in which the craft should be conducted within the realm of England. It had powers to make laws and ordinances for all persons using the 'Art' within a ten-mile radius of the City of London and had wide powers touching the 'Trade, Art or Mystery'. The Company had the right to make a general search and view all productions made in this country or brought in from abroad: it had powers to seize and to destroy unworthy work or cause it to be amended. None but admitted members might sell their wares within the City or ten miles thereof. An apprentice was bound for seven years and, after admittance as a Freeman, served a further two years as journeyman and then produced his masterpiece before being admitted as a workmaster. A Brother was allowed to engage only one apprentice, a Warden or Assistant Warden two only.

CLOCK-WATCH. A watch which strikes the hours at the hours. Not to be confused with a repeating watch. Clock-watches were made from the earliest period.

CLOISONNE. Divided into 'cloisons' or compartments by means of flat metal wires, forming a design in outline on a flat or curved surface. In *cloisonné* enamel the partitions are filled with coloured enamels, and then fired. After polishing, the metal strips show off the design inlaid in the enamel. The metal used is mostly gold.

CLUB-FOOT VERGE. A frictional rest dead-beat escapement, derivative of that invented by Debaufre *circa* 1704. Sometimes referred to as the 'dead-beat verge', or 'Ormskirk escapement' after the town in Lancashire where watches with this escapement were made.

CLUB-TOOTHED LEVER. A lever escapement with the form of escape wheel usually found in Continental lever watches, as opposed to the English form of ratchet-tooth escape wheel. In the club-tooth escape wheel the 'lift' is divided between the pallet stones and the impulse faces of the teeth. In the English form the impulse is taken entirely by the pallet stones.

COCK. A bracket for supporting the pivot of a wheel. In English watches the balance cock which supports the top pivot of the balance staff normally has a single foot to secure it to the top plate. There is a short narrow neck between the foot and the table. The bridge-type balance cock, with two screw fixings, was used just occasionally in England and then generally only on watches of the highest quality. Bridge-type balance cocks, the normal form used by 18th century Continental makers, appear on poor imitations and fakes of English work.

COLLET. A cylindrical collar. An example is the small ring of metal which is fitted friction tight to the balance staff to secure the inner end of the balance spring. A 'hand collet' is a dome-shaped washer to render secure the fitting of the hands.

COLOURED GOLD. See **TINTED GOLD**.

COMPENSATED BALANCE. See **BALANCE**.

COMPENSATION CURB. A laminated bar (or bimetallic strip) composed of brass and steel fixed at one end and free at the other, the latter end carrying the curb pins (q.v.). The earliest known is in a watch made for John Harrison by John Jefferys in 1753. The effect of a rise or fall in temperature causes the strip to bend, thus moving the curb pins in relation to the balance spring. The more usual form of the strip is an elongated U with one curb pin fixed to the free end of the strip, which is caused to move away from (in cold) or closer to (in heat) the other pin, thus varying the play of the spring between the pins and roughly compensating the effects of temperature on the steel balance spring and the balance itself. The U form of compensation curb was used by Justin Vulliamy from about 1790 onwards. It was fixed to the index (q.v.). See also **'SUGAR TONGS'**.

CONSULAR CASE. A single double-bottom watch case. The style was introduced in the late 18th century before Napoleon became Consul of France but named after him. The back of the case is hinged and, when opened, a second back (or 'bottom') is revealed in which are the two holes for winding and hand-setting. The movement itself swings out from the front when the bezel is opened.

CONTRATE WHEEL. A wheel the teeth of which are at right angles to the plane of the wheel. In a watch with a verge escapement, it is the wheel which drives the escape wheel pinion.

CONVERSION. A watch is said to have been 'converted' if, for instance, an escapement of one kind has been substituted for another. Thus a verge escapement may have been converted to a lever, and the escapement is a conversion. See also **ESCAPEMENT CONVERSION**.

COUNT WHEEL. A wheel in the striking train that controls the number of hours struck. It consists of a series of eleven notches cut on the periphery of the wheel at increasing distances between each corresponding to the hours struck. A detent or L-shaped lever rides over the raised portions and drops into the slots as the count wheel revolves, which it is allowed to do at each hour when the detent is raised. The striking train is free to run when the detent is lifted, and the watch strikes for as long as the detent is held raised by the projections. There is no projection for 1 o'clock since the detent is merely lifted for a sufficient interval for one blow to be struck, and dropped again. Similarly, if half-hours are struck, the notches are sufficiently long to allow the detent to lift once and drop again before the next projection is reached. The system, though simple, has the disadvantage that the hours are struck in regular progression without reference to the positions of the hour hand. The alternative name for the count wheel is 'locking plate'. 'Rack-striking' superseded it.

CRESCENT. The crescent-shaped hollow cut out of the roller in a lever escapement to permit the guard pin to pass.

CROWN-WHEEL ESCAPEMENT. Another name for the verge escapement (q.v.). The name derives from the form of the escape wheel which somewhat resembles a medieval crown.

CURB COMPENSATION. See **COMPENSATION CURB.**

CURB PINS. Two pins which embrace the balance spring at its outer end near to its attachment. The pins are fixed to the regulator or index; 'index pins' is an alternative term. The time of vibration of a balance is adjusted by altering the position of the pins. If the pins are moved towards the outer attachment point, the effective length of the spring is increased and the watch is made to lose; if the regulator (and therefore the curb pins) is moved the opposite way, the reverse takes place. See Figure 10.

CUT BIMETALLIC BALANCE. See **BALANCE.**

CYLINDER ESCAPEMENT. See Figures 1 and 2. The escape wheel teeth in this escapement, unlike the verge, lie in a horizontal plane. The escape wheel usually has fifteen wedge-shaped teeth, standing above the rim of the wheel, the pointed end of the 'wedge' leading. Mounted on the balance staff is a polished steel tube or hollow cylinder – which gives the escapement its name – nearly one half of which is cut away allowing the teeth to enter as the balance swings back and forth and the wheel rotates. As each tooth enters the cylinder it impulses the balance on the entry lip of the cylinder wall. The tooth rests within the cylinder while the balance completes its oscillation (the 'supplementary arc') and begins its return journey. In due course the tooth escapes from within the cylinder, again giving impulse as it leaves. The succeeding tooth drops against the outside wall of the cylinder and the balance makes its excursion and return, after which the tooth enters the cylinder, and the process is repeated.

The diagram (Figure 1) shows the cycle of operation. Position 1 shows a tooth the instant before it enters the cylinder. 2 shows a tooth entering and giving impulse by sliding motion. At 3, the tooth has dropped on to the inner wall and the escape wheel is locked while the balance completes its excursion and begins its return journey, as seen in 4.5 shows the position reached when the tooth escapes from the cylinder giving impulse as it does so to the balance in its back swing. Immediately it does escape, the next tooth following drops on to the outer wall of the cylinder, as seen in 6. See also **RUBY CYLINDER ESCAPEMENT.**

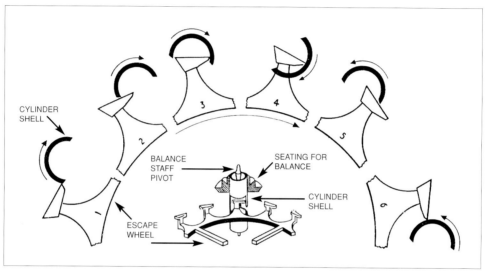

Figure 1. Cylinder escapement.

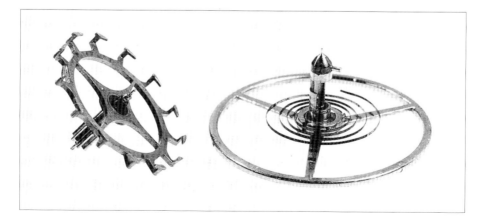

Figure 2. Cylinder escape wheel, arbor and pinion. Balance, balance spring and cylinder. Also showing cylinder plug, banking pin and lower pivot. These parts are from a movement by George Graham. Hallmarked 1739.

DEAD-BEAT ESCAPEMENT. An escapement in which the escape wheel does not 'recoil' (q.v.).

DEAF-PIECE. See **PULSE-PIECE.**

DEBAUFRE ESCAPEMENT. A dead-beat frictional rest escapement invented by the London maker Peter Debaufre in about 1704. Makers in and around Ormskirk, Lancashire, revived it during the later part of the century and also used a variation of it which had been tried by Henry Sully in about 1721-2. Watches with these are called 'Ormskirk verges'.

There are two escape wheels, on the same axis, the teeth being saw-cut, and each set alternately in relation to each other, or 'staggered'. The balance staff is equidistant between them and at right angles to their axis. Fixed to the balance staff is a pallet, a semi-circular disc with an inclined plane cut on its edge. One tooth of the escape wheel alternately rests on the flat surface of the pallet while the balance oscillates, until the slope of the inclined plane is presented to it when it escapes, giving impulse as it slips down the inclined plane. Thus a succession of teeth, first one wheel and then its fellow, rest upon the pallet and then give impulse to the balance.

DECK WATCH. A large-sized and accurate watch used on board ship when making observations to find the ship's position, and to check the marine chronometer with an alternative time source.

DEPTH. If the meshing of two gears is excessive, the depth is said to be too great; if it is insufficient, the depth is too shallow. Bad gearing can have very adverse effects on timekeeping. In general, depth is a term used by watchmakers for the degree of intersection or penetration between two parts. See also **END SHAKE.**

DETACHED ESCAPEMENT. An escapement in which the controller is free (or nearly so) from interference by the train. The lever escapement was often called specifically the 'detached escapement' or the 'detached lever' in its early history to distinguish it from the rack lever.

DETENT ESCAPEMENT. See Figures 3, 4 and 5.
Often called the 'chronometer escapement', it is the escapement with the greatest degree of detachment. It requires no oil on the acting surfaces. The escape wheel is unlocked by a jewel mounted on a detent and impulse given to a pallet on the balance staff every other oscillation of the balance.

The detent is a pivoted lever or alternatively a blade spring. The pivoted detent escapement was introduced by John Arnold in the 1770s and used by him up to 1781-2. Few English makers employed it thereafter, preferring the spring detent escapement. Arnold and Earnshaw each developed their own form of spring detent escapement, the principal difference being that in Arnold's the detent was in tension while Earnshaw's version was in compression. Arnold's escape wheel teeth suffered greater wear and it was Earnshaw's final design which in the end proved superior.

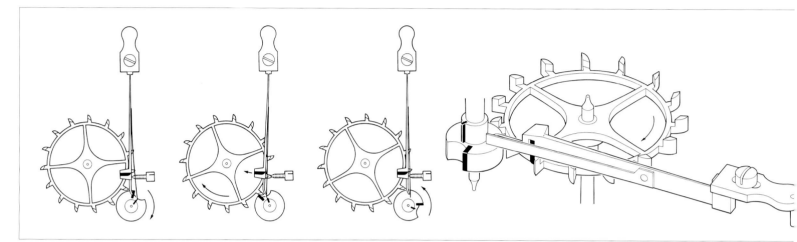

Figure 3. Arnold spring detent.

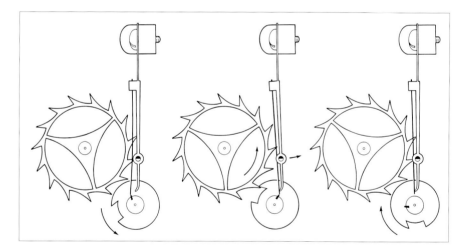

Figure 4. Earnshaw spring detent.

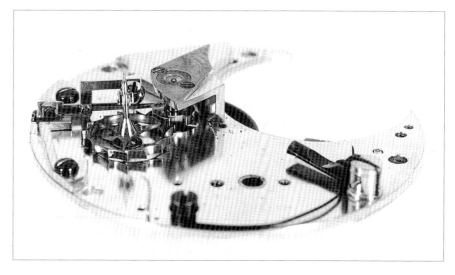

Figure 5. Spring detent from the Earnshaw pocket chronometer in Plate 205. The underside of the front plate showing detent, wheel and roller.

DIFFERENTIAL DIAL. The centre of the dial is a revolving disc, with the hour numerals I to XII. This disc revolves $\frac{1}{12}$ of a full circle in an hour. An ordinary minute hand, centrally placed, revolves once an hour, and is thus always passing over the current hour. A few were made *circa* 1700, but later examples are known.

DIVIDED LIFT. If the impulse angle is divided between the impulse faces of the pallets and the teeth of the escape wheel, the lift is said to be divided.

DOUBLE-BOTTOM CASE. A form of case in which the inner section is in one piece with the band on the case, the movement being attached to the case by joint and bolt. With the bezel opened, and the bolt pushed back, the movement hinges out of the case. The double bottom has a hole in which the key is inserted to wind the watch when the back is opened. See **CONSULAR CASE.**

DOUBLE ROLLER. A lever escapement in which the upper roller carries the impulse pin and the lower smaller roller is notched for guard action.

DRAW. In the lever escapement, by inclining the pallet faces, so that there is a tendency for the locked pallet to be drawn towards the centre of the escape wheel. It is a safety action which counteracts the tendency of the lever to leave the banking before being impelled to do so by the impulse pin. In an escapement without draw, a jolt may cause the fork of the lever to move away from the banking pin during the supplementary arc so that the guard pin comes into contact with the roller's edge, thus creating friction.

Draw is achieved by the relative angles between the escape wheel teeth and the locking faces of the pallet stones. These are so formed that the pressure of a tooth on the locking face of the pallet produces a drawing-in motion of the pallet towards the wheel.

DROP. The free travel of the escape wheel after impulse and before locking.

DUMB-REPEATER. A repeating watch, the hammers for the hours and quarters striking upon a block in the case, or the case itself, instead of upon a bell or gongs.

DUPLEX ESCAPEMENT. An escapement with two wheels on the same arbor or – what is found on English watches – an escape wheel with two sets of teeth: one set for locking and one for giving impulse. It is a single-beat, frictional rest escapement. See Figures 6 and 7.

Long pointed teeth on the periphery of the escape wheel lock or rest against a hollow ruby cylinder fitted to the balance staff, and planted so that it arrests the teeth in their path. Cut in this cylinder or roller is a notch through which a tooth may pass (escape) when the balance is travelling in the opposite direction to that in which the escape wheel rotates. As a tooth is unlocked and escapes, a long finger (the impulse pallet) mounted on a balance staff above the roller receives an impulse from one of the shorter teeth which stand up from the face of the wheel and which are in the same plane as the impulse pallet. Impulse completed, the next pointed tooth drops on to the roller where it rides while the balance completes its swing – the supplementary arc. On the return swing, the roller notch slips past the tooth at rest on the roller without allowing it to escape. Hence there is impulse in one direction only – when escape wheel and balance are travelling in opposite directions.

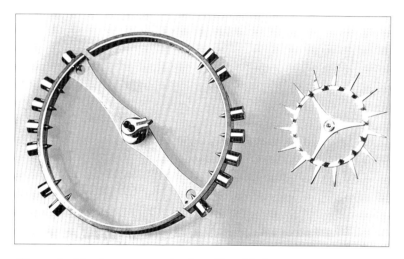

Figure 6. Duplex escape wheel, staff and balance.

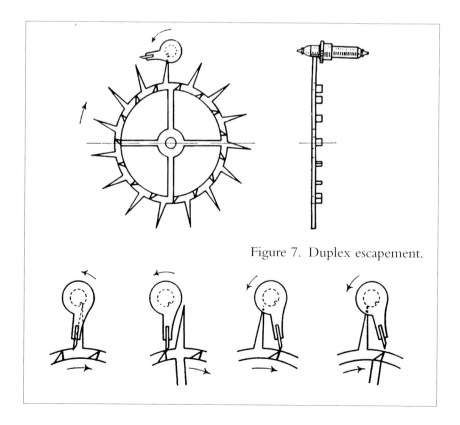

Figure 7. Duplex escapement.

DUST CAP. A cap to exclude dust fitted over the movement from about 1705-10 onwards.

DUST RING. Similar to a dust cap but covering the edge of the movement only.

EBAUCHE. A term which is used in a rather broad sense, but a movement in an early, incomplete stage. In the 19th century the *ébauche* was made up of two plates with pillars and bars, barrel, fusee, index, click and ratchet wheel and assembly screws. The parts were roughly filed and milled. In England during the 19th century Lancashire became the centre of the movement trade. One of the best known makers was Joseph Preston & Sons of Prescot, founded in 1829. Their movements were stamped 'J.P'. The work was much sub-divided.

EMERY LEVER. See also **LEVER ESCAPEMENT.**
Josiah Emery began making watches with lever escapements based on Thomas Mudge's plan but to his own design towards the end of 1782. Figure 8 shows the action of the escapement in three stages. A pivoted roller on the balance staff acts within a simple fork and in (a) it is about to unlock the escapement. In (b) it is receiving impulse from the lever at the same time as the escape wheel, which has slotted teeth for oil retention, is giving impulse to the entry pallet. In (c) the wheel has been locked by the exit pallet. All the lift is on the pallets which are jewelled. Safety is provided by a gold guard pin acting on a steel roller with a passing slot. There is no draw.

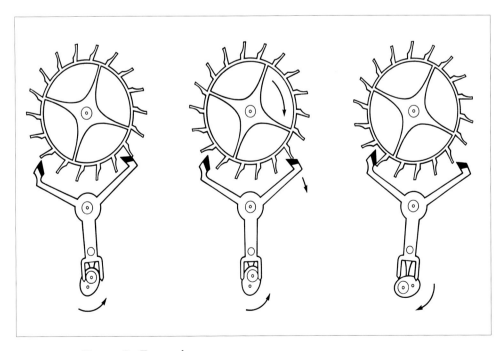

Figure 8. Emery lever escapement.

END SHAKE. Axial play, or necessary clearance between the ends or shoulders of an arbor and the bearing surfaces.

ENDLESS SCREW. Also called a 'worm' or tangent screw.

ENDSTONE. An end-plate made of a jewel. A jewel set in a ring upon which a watch pivot rests, particularly for the balance staff pivot. It is generally fixed to the balance cock by means of screws.

ENGINE TURNING. Decoration performed by an engine-turning lathe, producing a variety of patterns on a metal surface. It is also known as guilloche. It was a very popular method of decorating watch cases from about 1770, often being overlaid with transparent or translucent enamel.

ENGLISH LEVER ESCAPEMENT. A lever escapement in which the escape wheel teeth are pointed – ratchet toothed – and the lift is entirely on the pallets. See also **LEVER ESCAPEMENT.**

ENTRY PALLET. The receiving pallet, which receives impulses from the escape wheel teeth as they enter. The exit pallet, or discharging pallet, receives impulse as the teeth leave.

EQUATION OF TIME. Adding to or subtracting from true solar (sun) time the amount necessary to obtain mean time, mean time being the average length of all the solar days in the year, which is therefore a mathematical division. The 'equation' was worked out by John Flamsteed in about 1670. He tabulated the difference between noon mean time and true solar noon. The tables were used to check a watch against a sun dial. A few watches have been made to show the equation. Watch papers were sometimes printed giving the equation.

ESCAPE WHEEL. The last wheel in the going train, which permits 'escape' of the motive power, giving impulse to the balance. It is alternately locked and released.

ESCAPEMENT. That part of the movement which controls the release of the motive power. The escapement both controls the release of the driving force and also imparts energy (impulses) to the balance to maintain it in oscillation. The regularity with which this dual action takes place is controlled by the balance and its spring. The *timekeeping* properties of an escapement, therefore, depend essentially upon the balance and spring.

Escapements may be classified as:

(1) Frictional rest, in which the balance is constantly in contact with a part of the escapement – e.g. (a) recoil escapements in which the locking faces are eccentric, causing a recoil of the escape wheel; (b) dead-beat escapements, with concentric locking faces, which give no recoil.

(2) Detached escapement, in which the balance is detached from the escapement except at the time of locking and receiving impulse.

The verge escapement is an example of 1(a). The cylinder is an example of 1(b) and the lever an example of 2.

A single beat escapement gives a single impulse for each double swing of the balance. The chronometer detent escapement is an example. A constant-force escapement employs an intermediate spring, a 'remontoire', wound periodically by the train, which spring impulses the balance.

ESCAPEMENT CONVERSION. Watches that typically have verge, cylinder and duplex escapements converted to another more modern. Very often there is an extra cock between the movement plates – see Figure 9. At the same time the balance together with its spring is normally replaced and occasionally the cock. The new escapement required fresh pivot holes in the plates, leaving the original ones empty and these were often filled and the plates regilded. Modifications from early to later forms of the same escapement are also found.

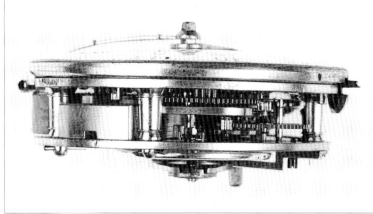

Figure 9. Escapement conversion. Late 18th century movement with escapement converted in the 19th century to lever. A new cock, balance, balance spring and an extra cock between the plates have been fitted as well as an escapement.

EXIT PALLET. See **ENTRY PALLET.**

FALSE PENDULUM. Also called a 'mock pendulum'. A small disc on one arm of a balance, visible through a slot or aperture in the dial or balance cock. The motion of the arm with disc attached gives the appearance of a pendulum, the second arm and the rim of the balance not being visible. The type was popular around 1700.

FIGURE PLATE. See **REGULATION.**

FIVE-MINUTE REPEATER. A repeating watch which gives the hours and a blow for each five minutes past the hour. In some cases the quarters are given in addition.

FLAGS. The pallets of the verge escapement are so called.

FLIRT. A lever or other device for causing a sudden movement of mechanism.

FLY-BACK HAND. In split-seconds chronographs (q.v.) a centre seconds-hand that can move while remaining superimposed on the first hand, but which can be stopped independently and then made to fly back (or forward) to join the first hand as it moves round the dial.

FOB CHAIN. A short chain (or ribbon with metal attachments) fixed by swivel or bolt ring to the bow of a watch, and hanging outside the pocket.

FORK. The fork-shaped end of the lever in the lever escapement within which is the notch.

FOUR-COLOURED GOLD. See **TINTED GOLD.**

FOURTH WHEEL. The wheel in a watch that drives the escape wheel pinion, to the arbor of which the seconds hand is often attached.

FRAME. The movement plates.

FREE-SPRUNG. A balance spring unfettered by curb pins. Used in marine chronometers, pocket chronometers and very high grade watches. The rate of a watch so sprung can be adjusted by the timing screws on the balance.

FRICTIONAL REST ESCAPEMENT. An escapement in which the balance is never free, or only momentarily so, from the escapement – e.g. the verge, cylinder and duplex escapements. It is therefore inferior to a detached escapement – e.g. the detent and the lever escapements.

FULL PLATE. A watch calibre in which the top plate (that furthest from the dial), as well as the pillar plate, is a circular plate, with the balance mounted above the top plate.

A three-quarter plate movement has a section of the upper (top) plate cut away to allow the balance to be mounted in the same plane as the plate, the balance and the escape wheel having separate cocks. In a half plate movement, the fourth wheel, escape wheel and balance have separate cocks.

FUSEE. A mainspring-equaliser. A spirally grooved, truncated cone with the great wheel mounted upon it. A length of gut – after about 1670 a chain – connects the fusee to the mainspring barrel, one end being attached to the barrel and the other to the fusee. The winding key fits over the squared end of the fusee arbor, and the act of winding draws the chain from the barrel on to the fusee, starting at the wide end of the 'cone' and taking it up the spiral groove. As the chain is taken off the barrel, the mainspring is wound. The mainspring when fully wound exerts a greater torque than when it is only partially so. In unwinding, the chain is, of course, drawn off the narrow end of the fusee first, where it is acting with less leverage and this compensates the greater pull of the mainspring. Greater leverage comes into play as the chain is drawn towards the thicker end of the fusee; thus the tapering fusee matches the diminishing strength of the spring. This ensures a relatively constant motive force. The early long, tapering fusees were only moderately effective, but as time went on, and by empirical methods, a form with correct hyperbola curves was evolved.

A stop is fitted to the upper end of the fusee. As the chain coils round the last groove of the fusee, it lifts a lever which comes up against a cam on the fusee and stops the mechanism. The mounting for the fusee stop lever or arm was given decoration after about 1650. The fusee was known – it appears in early manuscripts – in about 1450-70.

A fusee with maintaining power is known as a 'going fusee'.

FUSEE CHAIN. A steel linked chain as a substitute for a gut cord was introduced in about 1635, but it was some years before it was made small enough for watch movements. One should not expect to find them on English watches before about 1670. Some early watches have had the profile of the fusee groove altered and a chain fitted.

From the early 19th century Christchurch in Hampshire specialised in fusee chain making. For the first quarter century the work was done by young women and children in the Christchurch workhouse, but it later developed into a cottage industry.

GADROONING. Ornamentation found on the edges of late 18th and early 19th century watches. The decoration consists of either hammered or cast radiating lobes of curved or straight form.

GATE. The name sometimes given to the decorative piece covering the fusee stop finger. More correctly, the piece over the locking detent of the striking chain.

GATHERING PALLET. Part of the rack-striking mechanism; a finger which makes one revolution for each stroke of the hour and gathers one tooth of the rack.

GOING BARREL. See **BARREL (GOING)**.

GOING FUSEE. A fusee with maintaining power (q.v.).

GOING TRAIN. See **TRAIN**.

GONGS. Coiled wire used for striking or repeating watches in place of a bell.

GRANDE SONNERIE. A watch which strikes both the hours and quarters at each quarter.

GREAT WHEEL. The first wheel in the train. In a going barrel watch it is on the going barrel. See **BARREL (GOING)**.

GUARD PIN, safety pin or dart. In the lever escapement, a pin at the end of the lever which will act against a roller on the balance staff so preventing a shock unlocking the escape wheel during the supplementary arc.

GUILLOCHE. See **ENGINE TURNING**.

HAIRSPRING. A common name for the balance spring (q.v.).

HALF PLATE. See **FULL PLATE**.

HALF-QUARTER. A repeater which, in addition to repeating the hours and quarters, also gives an additional single stroke if 7½ minutes or more have elapsed since the last quarter.

HALLMARK. The mark made by punches on gold or silver, consisting of the standard mark, the mark of the Hall (e.g. the Goldsmiths' Hall, London, the Birmingham mark, etc.), the quality of the metal, the date letter and the maker's mark.

HEART PIECE. A heart-shaped cam used in chronograph work to cause the chronograph hand to fly back to zero. Patented by A. Nicole in 1844, no. 10348.

HELICAL SPRING. See **BALANCE SPRING.**

HORIZONTAL ESCAPEMENT. See **CYLINDER ESCAPEMENT,** which is the alternative and now more usual name.

HOUR RACK. Part of the striking mechanism that is moved one tooth for each hour. The rack – which is a pivoted toothed sector – has a tail which drops on to the snail (q.v.) and its position in relation to this determines how many teeth are to be gathered by the gathering pallet (q.v.) which in turn determines how many hours are struck. A quarter rack acts similarly for the quarter-hours. Rack striking was invented by Edward Barlow in 1676.

HOUR WHEEL. The wheel which carries the hour hand.

HUNTER. A watch the case of which has a front as well as a back cover, thus affording protection to the glass. The front is opened by means of a push-piece. A half-hunter has a small thick glass (a 'pebble glass', 'sight' or 'lunette') fitted into the front cover allowing a portion of the dial and hands to be seen.

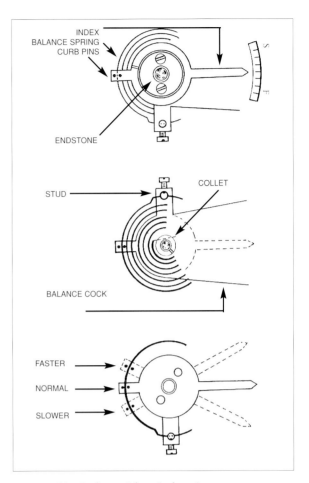

Figure 10. Index with spiral spring without overcoil.

IMPULSE. The energy or 'push' derived from the mainspring via the train and the escapement and imparted to the balance to maintain its oscillations.

IMPULSE PIN. Alternatively called the 'ruby pin'. In the lever escapement it is generally fixed into the roller and works in the notch of the fork. On entering the notch it unlocks the escape wheel, receives impulse from the lever and passes out of the notch on the opposite side of the fork. The impulse pin is made of ruby or sapphire and may be elliptical, semi-circular or half-moon, or triangular in shape.

INDEPENDENT SECONDS. A watch having a seconds hand driven by a separate train.

INDEX. Regulator. A small lever, the shorter end of which carries the curb pins (q.v.). The longer end passes over a scale to serve as an indicator of any alteration made in the position of the curb pins when regulating the watch by moving the index forwards 'S' (slow') or 'F' ('fast'). See Figure 10.

ISOCHRONOUS. Occurring in equal periods of time. A balance would be truly isochronous if the duration of the oscillations was the same whether the arcs were long or short, if the duration of the arcs was independent of the amplitude of swing. The arcs are affected by – among other factors – the position of the balance (e.g. whether vertical or horizontal) and by the impulses delivered by the escapement. The technique of timing consists in achieving the isochronism of the oscillations of the balance. The chief factors that impair isochronism are: the escapement, the play of the balance spring between the curb pins, faulty poising of the balance and its spring. A Parisian, Pierre Le Roy, was the first watchmaker to investigate the supposed isochronal properties of the watch balance and spring in 1760. John Arnold found by experiment that a helical spring can be made isochronous, or very nearly so, by 'incurving' the terminal coils. See **BALANCE SPRING.**

JEWELS. Bearings in a watch movement made of ruby, sapphire, or garnet. Their purpose is to reduce friction and to 'trap' the oil. See Figure 11. A 'jewel hole' is a stone pierced to take a pivot of a wheel. The chief types of watch jewels are: a flat jewel hole, the hole being cylindrical for a shouldered pivot; a domed jewel with endstone for a conical pivot, the tip of the pivot resting on the endstone; the pallet stones; the impulse pin. In the cylinder escapement the cylinder shell is sometimes a jewel, and is then referred to as a 'ruby cylinder'.

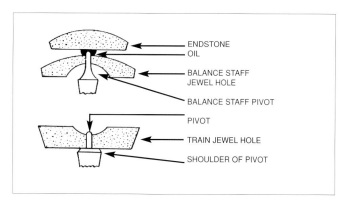

Figure 11. Jewels.

KARRUSEL. A type of watch incorporating a device to eliminate errors of rate in the vertical positions. The escapement is mounted on a carriage or cage, the carriage being driven by the third wheel pinion. Also see **TOURBILLON.**

KEYLESS WATCH. A watch which can be wound and the hands set without the aid of a key.

KEYLESS WINDING. A watch which can be wound without a key. A variety of systems were evolved during the 19th century, among the first that of Thomas Prest, who took out patent no. 4501 in 1820. See also **PUMP-WIND.**

LEVER ESCAPEMENT. An escapement with a pivoted lever between the balance and escape wheel. As the balance oscillates a projection mounted on its staff engages a fork in the lever and moves the lever between two positions. As this projection, normally a single pin, exits the fork it receives an impulse, this maintaining the oscillations of the balance. Two pallets at the other end of the lever engage with the escape wheel, alternately locking and unlocking and receiving impulse. Some form of safety device to prevent a shock disengaging the pallets from the escape wheel during the supplementary arc is always present between the lever and the balance. Figure 12 shows the standard form of ratchet-tooth right-angled English lever escapement employed from about 1830 onwards. It is at the point of unlocking. The safety device, consisting of a guard pin and a roller on the balance staff, can be seen in the diagram. See **EMERY LEVER, MASSEY LEVER** and **SAVAGE TWO-PIN.**

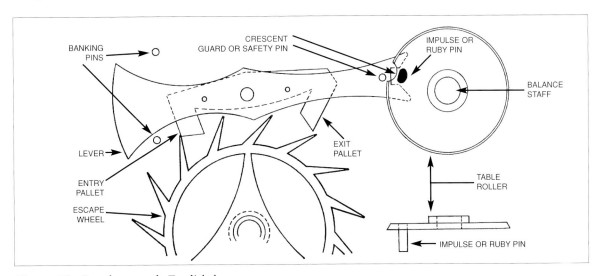

Figure 12. Ratchet-tooth English lever.

LEVER NOTCH. In the lever escapement, the opening in the fork into which the impulse pin penetrates.

LIFT. The angle through which the lever travels (in the lever escapement) during the impulse and escaping action. Lift may be divided between the pallets and the escape wheel teeth (the club-tooth) or be all on the pallets (pointed wheel teeth) or all on the teeth (with pointed pallets).

'LIVERPOOL' JEWELS. Inordinately large but impressive movement jewels, popular with Liverpool makers in the second half of the 19th century.

LOCK(ING). The period between impulse when the train is locked and the balance is completing its oscillation, in either direction – i.e. during its supplementary arc (q.v.).

LOCKING PLATE. See **COUNT WHEEL.**

LUNETTE. A rounded watch glass, only slightly domed. Also a term used to describe the small opening or 'sight' in a half-hunter cover.

MAINSPRING. The spring which provides the driving power for the going or striking sides of a watch movement.

MAINTAINING POWER. A device for driving a fusee movement by means of a ratchet and click or occasionally a 'sun and planet' during the action of winding when the power is otherwise taken off.

MALTESE CROSS. A wheel of that shape forming part of a stop-work (q.v.). It is associated with the 'Geneva' stop-work.

MASSEY LEVER. See also **LEVER ESCAPEMENT.** Edward Massey (1768-1852) took out his first patent for a detached lever escapement in 1812 (no. 3559) and his second in 1814 (no. 3854). From 1814 onwards he set his lever at right-angles to a ratchet-tooth escape wheel and over time employed five different types of roller. Unlocking and impulse is achieved with a projection, later a pin, on a cylindrical roller, this made so that the fork will only pass when the projection or pin is within the lever slot. When the projection or pin is not within the slot any movement of the lever is stopped by its banking on the curved surface of the roller. Massey employed draw from about 1820, or shortly before, but at first not in every case.

MIDDLE TEMPERATURE ERROR. The elasticity of a balance spring does not vary with temperature changes in the same proportion as the compensating effects of the bimetallic balance (q.v.). A watch with such a balance will only be accurate in its rate for two given temperatures. The inaccuracy between the two extreme temperatures (the M.T.E.) may be corrected by auxiliary compensation.

MINUTE REPEATER. A watch which not only repeats the hours and quarters, but also the minutes which have elapsed since the last quarter.

MOCK PENDULUM. See **FALSE PENDULUM.**

MOTION WORK. The gearing under the dial which causes the hour hand to travel twelve times slower than the minute hand. It consists of the cannon pinion, minute wheel and pinion and hour wheel.

MOVEMENT. The main assembly of a watch comprising the power, transmission, escapement, regulating, winding and handsetting mechanisms. In short, the 'works' without the case, hands or dial. Also see **EBAUCHE.**

NIB-PIECE. Pin projecting through a case band which may be depressed with the thumb nail so as to engage, generally a set-hand mechanism.

NOTCH. See **LEVER NOTCH.**

OLIVETTE. Guard for a nib-piece (q.v.) mounted on a case band.

OPEN FACE. An 'open face' watch is one without a front cover – i.e. neither a hunter nor a half-hunter.

ORMSKIRK. A town in Lancashire. In the late 18th and early 19th century a number of watches with a type of Debaufre escapement were made there, and these are known as 'Ormskirk verge' watches. See **DEBAUFRE ESCAPEMENT.**

OUTER CASE. The outside case in a pair-case watch. Such cases were often embellished.

OVERCOIL. See **BALANCE SPRING.**

PAIR-CASE. Until the beginning of the 19th century most English watches had two cases. In the 17th century the inner was called the 'box' and the outer the 'case'.

PALLET. In particular, the part or parts through which the escape wheel teeth give impulse to the balance.

PASSING CRESCENT. See **CRESCENT.**

PASSING SPRING. Also known as the 'gold spring', out of which metal it is usually made. It is mounted on a detent in the chronometer escapement. The discharging pallet on the staff unlocks a tooth in one direction. On the return swing it passes the detent without disturbance due to the flexibility of the passing spring.

PEDOMETER WATCH. Sometimes understood to mean a watch and pedometer combined. Ralph Gout took out patent no. 2351 for such a watch in 1799. Otherwise, a watch which is wound by an oscillating weight.

PENDANT. A neck, fitted to the case of a watch, to which the bow (q.v.) is fitted. In a keyless watch, the winding button is at the top of the pendant, the winding button stem passing through the pendant.

PENDULUM WATCH (DIAL). A watch in which a 'mock' or 'false' pendulum appears through an aperture in the dial or is visible through a slot cut in the balance cock or bridge. See also **FALSE PENDULUM.**

PERPETUAL CALENDAR. A calendar watch which takes into account not only the short months, but leap years, without manual adjustment.

PILLARS. The pillars of a watch movement are the 'distance pieces' which serve to keep the two plates in their relative positions.

PILLAR PLATE. The plate nearest the dial, to which the pillars are fixed.

PIN WORK. See **PIQUE.**

PINCHBECK. An alloy of zinc and copper – named after its inventor, Christopher Pinchbeck, about 1730 – which resembles gold in colour. The term is used rather indiscriminately for gilded brass.

PINION. A small toothed wheel. The 'teeth' are spoken of as 'leaves'. In watch work the wheel is the driver and the pinion is the follower, except in the motion work.

PIQUE. Or 'pin work'. Pins of gold, silver or brass, the purpose of which is to secure the leather, shagreen or tortoiseshell covering to the outer cases of watches. The practical purpose also served decorative ends in that the heads of the pins were arranged in a decorative pattern. Indeed, more pins were inserted than was strictly necessary in order to form a decoration.

PIVOT. The extremity of a rotating arbor on which it is supported.

PIVOTED DETENT. The pivoted detent performs the same function as the blade spring. See **SPRING DETENT.** John Arnold used this form of detent on his early chronometers.

PLATES. The flat discs between which the wheels and pinions are pivoted. They form the foundation of the movement.

POISE. A balance is in poise if it has no heavy point, if its equilibrium is unaffected by change of position.

POSITIONAL ERROR. Changes in the rate of a watch arising from the different positions – e.g. the horizontal and the vertical.

POTENCE. Also spelled 'potance'. A hang-down bracket supporting a pivot; in particular (in watch work) the underslung bracket supporting the lower pivot of the balance staff in full plate watches.

POTENCE PLATE. An alternative name for the top plate to which the potence is fixed.

PULL-WIND. See **PUMP-WIND.**

PULSE-PIECE. A pin projecting from the edge of a repeating movement and through to a hole in the bottom edge of the case. The finger, held against the pin, receives the blows of the hammer when the watch is striking instead of the bell. Also called a 'deaf-piece'.

PUMP-WIND. An early form of keyless winding. The watch is wound by moving a shaft, located in the pendant, in and out: a pushing or pulling action.

PURITAN WATCH. A simple form of English watch, oval in shape, without decoration and usually in silver. They were made between about 1635 and 1660.

QUARTER RACK. See **HOUR RACK.**

QUARTER REPEATER. A watch which repeats the hours and quarters when a push-piece is depressed or a slide-piece moved.

RACK. A toothed segment. See **HOUR RACK.**

RACK LEVER ESCAPEMENT. See Figure 13. A form of lever escapement patented by Peter Litherland in 1791, patent no. 1830, but an earlier escapement embodying the same principle was invented by the Abbé de Hautefeuille in 1722. The lever terminates in a rack which meshes with a pinion on the balance staff. The balance is never detached. It was made in large numbers in Lancashire in the early 19th century.

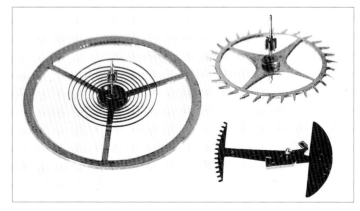

Figure 13. Rack lever. Balance staff with pinion. Lever with rack, jewelled pallets and counterpoise. Brass escape wheel. Thirty inclined teeth.

RACK STRIKING. See **HOUR RACK.**

RATCHET WHEEL. Saw-toothed wheel. The fronts of the teeth of a ratchet wheel are radial and the backs straight lines. Used in conjunction with a click (pawl) and spring and fixed by a square hole to the barrel arbor. The click prevents the wheel turning in the unwinding direction. Ratchet wheel set-up was the first form of regulation of the fusee watch.

RATE. The timekeeping performance of a watch. Thus 'daily rate' is the term used to denote the difference between two states of a timekeeper separated by an interval of twenty-four hours.

RECOIL. Backward movement of the escape wheel during the unlocking process.

RECOIL ESCAPEMENT. An escapement in which recoil takes place, as opposed to a dead-beat or frictional rest escapement.

REGULATION. In pre-balance spring watches regulation depended primarily upon altering the set-up of the mainspring but also the depthing of the escapement.

The earliest form of adjustable set-up is the ratchet and click, found on fusee watches up to about 1640, when it gave place to the tangent screw and wheel, although the two forms overlap in period. After the introduction of the balance spring, the set-up was transferred from the top plate (where it was readily accessible for regulation) to between the plates, regulation now being possible by altering the effective length of the balance spring.

Tompion's form of regulator was universally adopted. It consists of a segmental rack, which follows the outer coil of the spring, and is geared to a small wheel carrying a key square and an index dial. Using a key, the position of the curb pins where they embrace the balance spring can be altered, either by shortening or increasing the effective length, thus causing the watch to gain or lose on its previous rate. The index dial known as the 'figure plate' or 'rosette' gives a guide to the alteration made, although the numbers engraved on it are arbitrary.

The only other form of regulation dating from this period has been accredited to Nathaniel Barrow, although with no good reason. This consists of a worm with squared end to take a key. This worm carries a slide on which are mounted two curb pins embracing the straightened outer end of the balance spring. The slide has a pointer which moves across an index engraved on the movement plate, thus indicating the amount the slide has moved when regulating. Very few watches with this form of regulation have survived.

In 1755 Joseph Bosley patented 'A new-invented slide, which slide has no wheel attached to it'; that is, he dispensed with the Tompion segmental rack. Bosley's consisted of a small lever, the shorter end of which carries the curb pins which embrace the balance spring, the longer end (by which it is moved) travels across a scale which served to indicate the alteration to 'fast' or 'slow' in the position of the curb pins. A 'free-sprung' watch can only be regulated by altering the timing screws on the balance.

REGULATOR. See **INDEX.**

REMONTOIRE. A spring (or other device) which is wound by the train and discharged at regular intervals.

REPEATER. A repeating watch in which mechanism can be set in motion to denote the approximate time by hammers striking bells, gongs or a block within the watch case. This last is known as a 'dumb repeater'.

REPOUSSE. A term used to describe an embossed and chased case.

ROLLER. In the lever escapement, the disc fitted on the balance staff and carrying the impulse pin, the latter receiving impulse via the pallets. The roller may also work in conjunction with a guard pin. In later lever escapements, with double rollers, a smaller, safety roller was introduced which has a crescent or passing-hollow cut in it for the guard pin. In the duplex escapement (q.v.) the roller is a hollow ruby cylinder against which the teeth of the escape wheel are locked.

RUBY CYLINDER ESCAPEMENT. A cylinder escapement in which the cylinder shell is made out of ruby. It was probably introduced by John Arnold in 1764. Though not used to any extent for some years, it was employed by some of the best London makers in the late 18th and early 19th century and widely by makers on the Continent.

RUN-TO-BANKING. In the lever escapement, the movement of the lever towards the banking pins after a tooth has given impulse to the pallet. This is a safety factor to ensure the passage of the escape wheel teeth. See **DRAW.**

SAFETY PIN. See **GUARD PIN.**

SAFETY ROLLER. See **ROLLER.**

SAVAGE TWO-PIN. A form of lever escapement named after George Savage in which the roller carries two pins which unlock the escapement via the fork. A third pin, mounted upright at the end of the lever, acts as the impulse pin, passing into a narrow notch cut in the roller, when the escape wheel has been unlocked. This third pin also serves as the guard pin for the safety action during the supplementary arc. Savage introduced his escapement about 1814, certainly before 1818 when he emigrated to Canada. There he founded the firm of Savage & Lyman. Very few watches signed by Savage have survived. He made for Edward Bracebridge of Red Lion Street, 1805-15.

SECONDS PINION. The extension of the fourth wheel arbor to which the seconds hand is attached.

SECRET SPRING. The fly and lock springs of a hunter watch case.

SET-UP. The degree of tension to which a mainspring is set when the watch is fully run down. The use of stop-work enables a going barrel watch to be 'set up' so that only the middle turns of the mainspring are in use, thus providing more even torque. By altering the set-up, a degree of regulation was effected in the fusee, pre-balance spring watch.

SIX-HOUR DIAL. A watch dial of the late 17th century period in which the chapter ring is marked in Roman numerals I to VI and superimposed on these are arabic numerals 7 to 12. The single hand revolved once in six hours. Due to the larger spacing between the numerals (only six instead of twelve), the divisions between them can be legibly calibrated into two-minute divisions, and the time read to two minutes from the one hand.

SNAIL. A cam shaped like the profile of a snail; part of the striking mechanism in the rack-striking layout. The snail determines – owing to the steps cut thereon – how far the rack may fall when it is released, and hence how many blows are struck, each step corresponding to an hour.

SPLIT-SECONDS. A form of chronograph in which there are two centre seconds hands, one over the other. When the chronograph is started, the hands travel together, but with a secondary push-piece the under one is halted while the other continues. The stationary hand can be made to rejoin its fellow, which can also be stopped independently. Once together and stationary, both can be returned to zero.

SPRING BARREL. The barrel containing the mainspring.

SPRING DETENT. In the chronometer escapement a blade spring carrying the locking jewel. A detent mounted on a spring. It is sometimes called a 'footed detent'. Patented by John Arnold in 1782.

STOP-WORK. A device to prevent over-winding of a mainspring and to enable the spring to be set up. (See **SET-UP.**)

STRAIGHT LINE LEVER. A lever escapement in which the escape wheel arbor, the pallet staff and the balance staff are planted in a straight line.

STUD. A small piece of metal pierced to receive the end of the outer coil of a balance spring.

'SUGAR TONGS'. The name given to the compensation curb used by Thomas Earnshaw, its shape roughly resembling a pair of tongs.

SUN AND MOON DIAL. A popular dial in the late 17th and early 18th century. A sun is depicted on one half and a moon on the other of a disc revolving once in twenty-four hours. Each is visible in turn through a semi-circular hole cut in the dial plate. Above the hole a segment of the dial is marked from VII to XII and from I to VI. The sun indicates 6 a.m. to 6 p.m. and the moon 6 p.m. to 6 a.m. The minutes are indicated in the normal way.

SUPPLEMENTARY ARC. The arc described by an oscillating balance outside the function of escapement, after the impulse and before unlocking.

SURPRISE PIECE. A device fitted to the quarter-snail of a repeater to prevent incorrect striking just prior to the next hour.

TANGENT SCREW. An endless screw, or worm gear. Tangent screw and wheel were used rather before the mid–17th century, replacing the ratchet wheel method, as a means of setting up the mainspring and as a means of regulation. A small dial mounted on the top plate served as an index. Soon after 1675 the worm and wheel were mounted between the plates.

TEMPERATURE COMPENSATION. Any device to counteract the effects of temperature changes on the rate of a watch; in particular, the effect on the steel balance spring which loses some of its elasticity for a rise in temperature with the contrary effect for a fall. See also **BALANCE** and **COMPENSATION CURB.** 18th century watchmakers usually referred to the 'thermometer'.

TERMINAL CURVES. See **BALANCE SPRING.**

THIRD WHEEL. The wheel between the centre wheel and fourth wheel.

THREE-QUARTER PLATE. See **FULL PLATE.**

TIMING SCREWS. Properly, only those screws at the ends of the arms of a cut, compensated balance which are used to bring the watch to time; hence 'mean time screws'. In a chronometer balance there are two timing screws or nuts, one at each end of the arm. Timing screws should not be confused with those balance screws used for adjusting the compensation.

TINTED GOLD. Also called 'coloured gold'. A form of decoration applied to watch cases and dials. The gold is coloured by alloys to produce a reddish, greenish, silvery or yellowish hue.

TOMPION REGULATOR. See **REGULATION.**

TOP PLATE. That furthest from the dial. Also known as the 'potence plate'. The movement plate seen from the back, the other plate being the 'bottom' or 'pillar plate'. 'Back plate' is the equivalent plate in a clock movement and is so called.

TOUCH PINS. Pins were usually inserted at the hour positions in 16th century watch dials to enable the time to be read with the aid of a finger during darkness.

TOURBILLON. A-L. Breguet's invention (patented in 1801) for neutralising the positional (vertical) errors inherent in a watch. The escapement is mounted in a revolving carriage or cage with the result that the positional errors are repeated (with a cancelling-out effect) in every revolution of the carriage. The speed of revolution of the carriage depended on the layout. In some instances the escape wheel pinion turns about the fixed fourth wheel, but whose arbor is free to turn the carriage mounted on it once in a minute. In others the revolution is made in two, four or six minutes. A 'tourbillon watch' is not a watch with a special kind of escapement.

TRAIN. The wheels and pinions which connect the going barrel or fusee with the escapement. In watch work, the wheel is the driver and the pinion the follower, except in the motion work. The 'going train' concerns the timekeeping part of the mechanism, the 'striking train' that side concerned with the striking. In the case of a fusee watch the great wheel, and in a going barrel watch the teeth round the barrel, drive the centre pinion, to the arbor of which is attached the centre wheel. This drives the third wheel pinion, the third wheel driving the fourth wheel pinion, the fourth wheel driving the escape wheel pinion. The number of teeth in the various wheels and pinions in general is determined by the following considerations (among others): the minute hand, being fixed to the centre wheel and pinion arbor, must make one revolution in an hour; the fourth wheel, to the arbor of which the seconds hand is fixed, must make one revolution in a minute.

TRIAL NUMBER. A symbol used to express the relative excellence of chronometers and watches in competitive trials. The Greenwich Observatory method was to multiply the difference between the greatest and the least variation by twice the difference between one week and the next.

TRIPLE-CASED. A watch, usually made for the Turkish market, which has an additional case to the outer case of pair-case watch.

TRIPPING. The accidental passing of two or more teeth of the escape wheel instead of one.

TWO-PIN ESCAPEMENT. See **SAVAGE TWO-PIN.**

UNDER-DIAL WORK. Complications such as calendar, lunar or repeating mechanism in addition to motion work, situated on the dial plate under the dial.

UP-AND-DOWN DIAL. A subsidiary dial indicating the state-of-wind of the mainspring.

VERGE. In the limited sense the verge is the rod or spindle upon which the balance or foliot is mounted. It carries two 'flags' or pallets. In the wider sense the word implies a watch with the verge or crown-wheel escapement.

VERGE ESCAPEMENT. See Figures 14 and 15. Sometimes called the crown-wheel escapement, it was used in the earliest watches; its inventor is unknown. It consists of a crown wheel (the escape wheel), the arbor of which carries a pinion driven by the train. A vertical arbor (the verge) is at right angles to the crown wheel and has two pallets or 'flags' separated by a distance approximating to the diameter of the crown wheel and at an angle of approximately 100 degrees to each other. The verge carries at its upper end a balance and is pivoted at its two extremities. The teeth of the crown wheel act upon the pallets alternately and cause the balance to oscillate.

The eleven or thirteen teeth of the crown wheel are very approximately a sloping triangle in shape and the wheel itself somewhat resembles a medieval crown. A tooth of the crown wheel comes into contact with one pallet, thrusts upon it (gives it impulse) and imparts circular motion to the balance, which motion moves the pallet away from the tooth until this is free to slip past the pallet which has been pressing upon it. The crown wheel is momentarily free to advance, but almost immediately a tooth on the opposite side of the wheel comes into contact with the other pallet, the circular motion of the balance having brought it down into the path of the wheel. In order to free itself (escape) this tooth thrusts the second pallet out of its path, thus giving the balance an impulse in the opposite direction. The continued process results in the oscillatory movement of the balance and a tooth by tooth advancement of the crown escape wheel.

The verge is a recoil escapement. There is a supplementary arc of balance swing – i.e. the balance continues its gyration after it has been impulsed, and the teeth of the crown wheel are undercut to free the face of the pallet during the resulting recoil. The inclination of the teeth is about 30 degrees. Figures 14 and 15 show a verge escapement with balance spring.

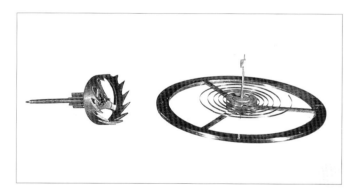

Figure 14. Crown (escape) wheel, arbor and pinion. Balance, balance spring and verge. One flag (pallet) can be clearly seen on the verge.

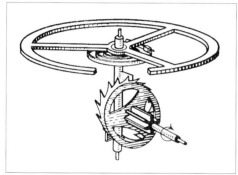

Figure 15. Verge escapement.

WANDERING HOUR DIAL. Sometimes called a 'Floating Hour Dial'. A semi-circular slit opening in the upper half of the dial reveals Roman hour numerals, appearing one at a time and in ordinary succession. On the outer edge and beyond the slit are the minute graduations occupying the corresponding half-circle to the inner slit for the hour numerals, and marked 0-60 minutes. The hour numeral travels from left to right, indicating the minutes in its passage. On reaching the 60 minute mark, it disappears beyond the slit and is succeeded by the next hour numeral following in its wake. A third, and innermost semi-circle, is marked off in quarter-hours.

Wandering hour watches were quite popular at the end of the 17th century and during the earlier years of the 18th. They are also called 'chronoscopes'.

WARNING. The preparatory operation of the striking mechanism occurring a few minutes before the striking is released on the hour. A wheel in the striking train (the 'warning wheel') carries a pin which is arrested and then released by the 'warning' piece'.

WATCH PAPER. Embroidered cambric or muslin or printed papers that were placed in the backs of the outer case of pair-case watches. These served to prevent the back of the inner case becoming scratched and also took up any slackness between the two cases. Towards the end of the 18th century they also served as advertisements of the watchmaker or repairer. Many have sentimental rhymes or admonishing proverbs, and some gave the equation of time.

WINDING SQUARE. The squared end of the barrel or fusee arbor on which the key is fitted in order to wind the watch. A similar squared end is on the arbor carrying the hands, by which the hands may be set in key-winding watches; this is called the 'set-hand square'.

WORM WHEEL. See **TANGENT SCREW.**

INDEX OF MAKERS AND RETAILERS

INDEX OF CASE MAKERS

INDEX OF ENGRAVERS, CHASERS AND ENAMELLERS

GENERAL INDEX

movements – *see* mechanisms
   rough – *see ébauches*
Mudge, Thomas, 178, 179, 182,
   201, **Plate 118**, 213, **Plate 129**,
   Plate 137, **Plate 140**, 256, 262,
   282, 288, 290, 296, 303, 371
   portrait of, 176
   (junior), 258, 327
   and Dutton, 183, 227
museums
   Ashmolean, 15, 22, 29, 108, 218
   British, 15, 16, 20, 25, 58, 86, 104,
      114, 201, 213, 219, 249, 262,
      267, 314, 335, 369
   Bury St. Edmunds, 372
   Clockmakers' Company, 36, 233,
      262, 431
   Dole, 214
   Hartlebury, 170
   La-Chaux de-Fonds, 125
   Merseyside National, 27
   Metropolitan, 214
   National Maritime, 236, 264, 273,
      446
   National Museum of Scotland, 35
   Newcastle-under-Lyme Borough,
      356, 382, 392
   Nottingham City, 397
   Patek Philippe, 58, 107, 113, 201
   Royal Scottish, 271
   Science, 106, 316
   Time, Rockford, Illinois, 29, 75,
      78, 158, 296, 310, 316, 346, 414
   Victoria & Albert, 23, 32, 34, 52,
      80, 158, 165, 202, 310

Nantes, Revocation of the Edict of,
   100, 108, 148
Napier, Ballikinrain,
   Dumbartonshire, 252
Napier, Sir James, 267
Nash, William, **Plate 9**
Nau, George, **Plate 66**
Naukratis, 49
Navy, British, 355, 377

Nawe, Francis, 16, 18, **Plate 2**
Neale, Richard, **Plate 256**
Nemmich, P.A., 259
Nevill, James, **Plate 203**
Nevill, John, **Plates 223-224**
Newcastle-under-Lyme, 356
Newcastle-upon-Tyne, 258
Newsam, Bartholomew, 15
Nicholls, Roger, 149
nickel silver, 444
Nicole, Adolphe, 378, **Plate 253**,
   Plate 258
Nicole, Nielsen & Co., 379, 380,
   421, 428, 432, 434-435, 439,
   Plate 289, 449
Noble, Sir Andrew, 421
North Allerton, 321
North, Robert Benson, **Plate 284**,
   Plate 289
Northern Goldsmiths Company,
   Plate 294
Nottingham, 103, 140, 386, 397
   Castle, 397
Nottinghamshire, Lord Lieutenant
   of, 239

Ogle, R., 425
Oldenburg, Henry, 107
Oliver, Albert Thomas, **Plate 290**
Ordnance, Royal Board of, 326
Orléans, Duke of, 334
Oriental market, 247
Ormskirk, 289
Orpheus, 128, 214
Ovid, 17, 34, 128
Oxford, 62, 117
   and Mortimer, Earls of, 167

Pain, John Terrill, **Plates 168-169**
pair-cases, 16, 46, 380
Palmer, John, **Plate 225**
Palmer, Richard, **Plate 146**, **Plate
   163**, **Plate 182**
Parbury, Ishmael, 105
Paris, 203

Parkinson & Frodsham, 378, 379
Parsons, William, **Plate 60**
Partridge, William, **Plate 24**
Passe, Simon de, 34
patents, 108, 174, 261, 263, 264,
   272, 284, 290, 307, 319, 323, 356,
   358, 363, 365, 370, 394, 396, 400,
   405, 408, 421, 424, 433, 438, 446,
   447
Pattinson, Ann, 160
Payne, Richard, **Plate 132**
Pearson, Reverend, 316
Peckham, John, 319
pedometer wound watches, 272
pendants, 47, 104, 181, 259-260,
   380
   revolving, 380, 432
Pendleton, Richard, 258, 262, 303,
   Plate 197, 317, 324, 328
Pennington, Robert, 258, 261, 264,
   324, **Plate 206**, 327, 337, **Plates
   223-224**, 352, 359
Perigal, Francis, **Plate 127**, 262,
   Plate 188
Perigal, Markwick Markham, **Plate
   176**
perpetual calendars, 179, 219, 413,
   436
Perrelet, A-L., 272
Petto, James, 262, 342
Picart, Bernard, 202, 250
Pierce, Roger, 354
Pierrepont, Evelyn, Duke of
   Richmond-upon-Hull, 239
pillars
   1585-1630, 19
   1630-1675, 51
   1675-1725, 109
   1725-1775, 182
Pitcairn, 236
plague, bubonic, 15, 22, 25, 27, 44,
   68
   Great, 45
platinum, 442
Player & Son, J., 378, 383